FUTURE VALUE

The Battle for Baseball's Soul and How Teams Will Find the Next Superstar

Eric Longenhagen
and Kiley McDaniel

TRIUMPH
BOOKS

Copyright © 2020 and 2021 by Eric Longenhagen and Kiley McDaniel

First Triumph Books paperback edition 2021

No part of this publication may be reproduced, stored in a retrieval system, or transmitted in any form by any means, electronic, mechanical, photocopying, or otherwise, without the prior written permission of the publisher, Triumph Books LLC, 814 North Franklin Street, Chicago, Illinois 60610.

Library of Congress Cataloging-in-Publication Data available upon request.

This book is available in quantity at special discounts for your group or organization. For further information, contact:

Triumph Books LLC
814 North Franklin Street
Chicago, Illinois 60610
(312) 337-0747
www.triumphbooks.com

Printed in U.S.A.
ISBN: 978-1-62937-880-0
Design by Patricia Frey

For our parents, and other enablers

Contents

FOREWORD *by Keith Law* | vii

AUTHORS' NOTE | xi

INTRODUCTION | xiii

CHAPTER 1. *You Can't Know What You Don't Know* | 1

CHAPTER 2. *The Draft* | 19

CHAPTER 3. *The Mad World of J2* | 65

CHAPTER 4. *The Changing (But Still Mad) World of J2* | 99

CHAPTER 5. *Prose About Pros Scouting Pros* | 123

CHAPTER 6. *But I Wanna Be a Ballplayer* | 143

CHAPTER 7. *How to Scout* | 163

CHAPTER 8. *How to Scout Hitters* | 183

CHAPTER 9. *How to Scout Pitchers* | 207

CHAPTER 10. *The Tricky Job of Summarizing* | 233

CHAPTER 11. *Everybody Wants a Job in Baseball (But Nobody Wants to Die)* | 269

CHAPTER 12. *Is Data Swallowing Baseball?* | 295

CHAPTER 13. *Running a Modern Team* | 323

ACKNOWLEDGMENTS | 359

SOURCES | 361

Foreword

Baseball scouting is at a crossroads as we enter the 2020 season. Just as multiple teams have moved away from traditional scouting—the Houston Astros have almost completely eliminated their domestic scouting operations, and other clubs have trimmed their staffs as a form of mimicry—the need for the information scouts can provide would appear to be higher than ever, and the return on the investment in scouting can be positive with just one or two successful player acquisitions.

I first began working for the Toronto Blue Jays in 2002, at a point when scouting was the only game in town. I was the entire statistical analysis department, which rather overstates the extent of my capabilities. But compare my department of one to roughly 20 scouts covering amateur players for each year's draft, another dozen or so pro scouts, some unknown number of scouts in the international department (many of whom were part-time), and so-called "special assignment" scouts who existed outside of those three scouting departments and reported directly to the general manager. Teams had very little statistical information that wasn't publicly available; it was easier to get minor league data, especially split data (e.g., performance against left- or right-handed pitchers), in ready-to-use formats, but the numbers themselves weren't proprietary or confidential. The main way to differentiate your decision-making from that of other teams, short of hiring analysts, was to have better scouts.

In my 18 years in the business, the last 14 of them as a writer for ESPN and now The Athletic, however, the way the industry perceives and employs scouts has changed dramatically, and I don't think it has changed for the better. There are fewer scouting jobs in baseball than there have been in decades, likely the fewest since the expansions of the 1960s increased the number of scouting jobs by increasing the number of teams. Twenty years ago, only the Oakland A's had any significant statistical analysis capability in their front office; today, all 30 teams have entire departments, often called research & development, and you'll hear executives mocking the teams that haven't done enough to keep up on the analytics front.

If everyone has a sizable analytics department, however, that one big competitive advantage you could get by adding one is now off the table; you have to have the department just to be in the game at all. You might hire better analysts, or hire more of them, although they're expensive since those jobs tend to require PhDs and you compete to hire those folks with major tech companies.

Consider swing optimization, one of the most visible ways in which a team can help a player change his entire game in a short period of time. Teams like to look for players who make hard contact, but tend to do so with a "launch angle"—the angle between the ball's path as it leaves the bat and the ground—that is not conducive to power. The Dodgers have done this a few times recently, with other teams' castoffs like Max Muncy and Chris Taylor, as well as with their own prospects like Will Smith, with great success. They're not alone, and there are more things you can do to help players than just tweaking how they get their hands ready or get the bat head into the zone. Analysts can help teams identify which players have certain leading indicators in their data—such as hard contact with a suboptimal launch angle—that might make those players good candidates for overhauls.

But not every player can make those adjustments; if they could, the baseball world would be overrun with future stars. Whose job is it to identify which players might have that capacity to learn, to make adjustments, to execute something different physically from what they've been doing their whole baseball lives? Scouts do that. Scouts go to the games and talk to players and coaches and gather a different kind of data. Sure, scouts go and offer evaluations of whether a player can hit or whether a pitcher's curveball is average or plus or a slow roller or loopy or just a show-me pitch that he casts out of his hand—and that's still data, just data of another sort. But there's a role for scouts in helping teams figure out which players are more likely to be willing and able to make the adjustments their analysts and their player-development staffs will want them to make. You can lead a horse to water, but you can't make him change his launch angle if he doesn't want to. If I'm running a team, and I'm looking for that next Max Muncy, I'm asking my

R&D folks and my scouts, and when they agree, *that's* the player I'm going to go out and get. There's still a place for scouts in this brave new world.

Eric Longenhagen and Kiley McDaniel are your guides, pulling back the veil on my favorite part of the baseball industry and one of its most fascinating areas, the world of scouting. Both worked for me while I was at ESPN and I couldn't be prouder of how much they've gone on to achieve since then. In *Future Value*—a nod to one of the more important evaluations a scout can give, the Future Value (FV) grade, saying just how good he thinks the player in question will eventually become—they give you the grand tour of scouting without asking you to leave your couch. They'll walk you through the draft, the most important three days in the entire year for amateur scouting; the Wild West of international free agency (where players can sign at age 16, and often strike verbal deals with teams before they're teenagers); and professional scouting, where scouts evaluate players already in the minor leagues. They'll walk through some of the basics of scouting. And they wrap it all up by talking about the intersection of scouting and data, and that very crossroads I mentioned at the start of this foreword. You couldn't ask for a better pair of tour guides. Buckle up.

—Keith Law

Authors' Note

We don't think it's reasonable to expect everyone who picks up this book to have an opinion about our objectivity the way some might from reading our collective work for the last decade. Those who do not, especially those who refer to their favorite team as "we," are at risk of being pissed at us for presenting unflattering facts or opinions about their favorite club sometime during this book.

Inherent in baseball is an awful lot of failure, from all parties involved, and not even those atop their field are immune to it. Recognizing this about ourselves is part and parcel of thriving in baseball, and any attention called to successes and failures in this book is only to help illustrate a point, not with the intent of bolstering nor denigrating those involved. Taking unwarranted shots at people would destroy our credibility in the game that we're lucky to work in. We fuck up too, after all. And we'll continue to, in perpetuity. Trying not to is part of what makes this so much fun.

Everyone working in baseball is grinding, exhausted to the point where many emotions are just wrung out of them. This may seem far-fetched to passionate baseball nerds apt to pick up this book, but a lot of those making a living from the game are nodding to themselves right now. Our opinions in this book are strong, but unemotional, not because we choose to feel this way, but because it just happened as an ironic, arguably tragic byproduct of our passion and pursuit. We look at baseball differently than those who wear a jersey to the ballpark. It's not better or worse. We're not belittling anyone. It's just different.

The last chapter of the book breaks down how each team goes about their business and you can see the more successful organizations (either by process or outcomes) tend to have more positive things written about them in the other chapters. In the interest of transparency, we're taking time to roll up our sleeves, show you our hands, and divulge details about where we've worked or come close to working. We have contacts with all 30 teams, some of which are the folks who chose not to hire us or have been publicly critical of our work or of the field of professional prospect analysis generally. And we're cool with that.

Kiley has worked for the Yankees (2005–07), the Orioles (2009–2010), the Pirates (2010–11), and the Braves (2015–17) in addition to writing for Baseball Prospectus (2009), ESPN (2012–13), Scout.com (2013–14), and FanGraphs (2014–15, 2017–2020). One person interviewed for the book, current Giants national crosschecker and former Braves scouting director Brian Bridges, was a former colleagues of Kiley's, but everyone else is just industry connections made independent of cowork. Particularly in the 2008–2013 period, Kiley had so many job interviews with teams that led to nothing that he lost count.

As this book was going to print, Kiley was hired by ESPN as a Baseball Insider. You'll notice throughout that we reference working together at FanGraphs and even how we might do things in the future. Instead of going back and updating all these moments to reflect Kiley's new position, we chose to leave the manuscript as a record of where we were in our lives when we wrote it.

Eric worked for the Phillies' Triple-A affiliate (2008–2011), many of the friends he made at Baseball Info Solutions (2012–13) are spread across baseball now, and he's written for ESPN (2014–16) and FanGraphs (2016–present), as well as several other online publications. During his years as an intern or freelancer he interviewed with Houston and Cleveland, who hired other candidates, and since 2014 he's had prospective employment discussions of varying depth and seriousness with at least a half-dozen teams.

We've put together some materials at futurevalue.fangraphs.com to supplement this book, with links to relevant articles and research along with videos to bring the things we're describing to life. It can stand alone as a guide to scouting principles and this book can also stand alone, but they're best used together. We'll keep the page updated as we find new things we think you should know about.

Introduction

There's a scene you'll hear certain baseball scouts quote if you spend enough time around them. It comes from the 2012 film *Skyfall*, in which an older, wiser James Bond prepares, once more, to head out into the field. This Bond has been slowed by injury and attrition, and, the "experts" in the film predict, is more than likely slipping into obsoletion.

He's sent to meet his new quartermaster (the weapons and gadgets guru) at an art museum and encounters a bookish-looking young man while sitting in front of a painting of a battleship.

The young man confidently states, "This makes me feel a little melancholy. Grand old warship being ignominiously hauled away for scrap. The inevitability of time, don't you think? What do you see?"

Bond defiantly answers, "Bloody big ship. Excuse me." He starts to get up to find an open bench, but then the young man identifies himself.

"Double-oh-seven. I'm your new quartermaster." They begin a rat-a-tat-tat dialogue.

"You must be joking."

"Why, because I'm not wearing a lab coat?"

"Because you still have spots."

"My complexion is hardly relevant."

"Your competence is."

"Age is no guarantee of efficiency."

"And youth is no guarantee of innovation."

"Hazard I can do more damage on my laptop sitting in my pajamas before my first cup of Earl Grey than you can do in a year in the field."

"Oh, so why do you need me?"

"Every now and then a trigger has to be pulled."

"Or not pulled. It's hard to know which in your pajamas."

Bond's glare softens a bit and he extends his hand as an olive branch, smirking while giving the young man a nickname: "Q."

Q accepts the handshake and smiles. "Double-oh-seven."

Bond is given instructions, travel accommodations, a tech-enabled gun, and a basic radio. He's not overwhelmed in light of what past meetings like this have yielded. "Gun and radio. Not exactly Christmas, is it?"

"Were you expecting an exploding pen? We don't really go in for that anymore. Good luck out there in the field. And please return the equipment in one piece."

Bond mutters, "Brave new world."

IT'S THIS SAME FOUND BALANCE between old-school scouts in the field and laptop-wielding, analytics-minded quants which defines baseball's current era of player development and the search for future stars. Kiley even represented both parties in the Atlanta Braves front office in 2017; he was tasked with heading up the analytics effort for that year's draft room, while also spending all his weekends on the road to scout players in person.

Organizational shifts in philosophy are often most evident in the weeks before the draft. Dozens of people, most of them remote workers, sit in a room and watch hundreds of decisions made at a deliberate pace. If a computer model is making the decisions over the rest of the year, only the decision-makers really know. During the draft process, everybody knows.

Draft rooms have become a ground zero for scouting opinions becoming marginalized in favor of data being fed into statistical models. We've heard of multiple draft rooms where the scouts set the draft board then leave the room for a meal and the general manager and the analytics staff stay behind to change the board to what the model says. At least one team's staff is pretty sure the model is actually *making* the picks, so no one executive is responsible for a bad pick, making the draft an objective collaboration rather than an exercise with a singular leader. Another GM, who has never been a scouting director or crosschecker, made all 40 picks for his team last year, leaving the scouting staff sitting powerless in stunned disbelief. Many teams are actively reducing their scouting staffs or replacing scouts with an entry-level video scout/analyst in the office. In most cases, the remaining scouts just get more work to do as a result.

It's the GM's prerogative to make these decisions, but none of these things had happened even a decade after the book *Moneyball* came out in 2003, as scouts feared. They're happening now, and more often each year. Baseball is becoming more corporatized by GMs with that background and point of view; teams are acting more similarly as big data helps them draw similar conclusions to each other, causing teams to have increasingly homogenous strategies. But a balance is still possible.

Kiley's first draft with the Braves in 2016 wasn't the most personally eventful affair. He was told to sit in the back of the draft room and to not say anything, just observe and learn how the room works. It wasn't a punishment or referendum on his ability, but the Braves were in their second draft under scouting director Brian Bridges and had just had what already looked like a great first draft, taking Kolby Allard, Mike Soroka, and Austin Riley with their top three picks.

The Braves were generally seen as one of the most successful organizations historically driven by traditional scouting, with centuries of collective experience in the room working under Bridges, a protégé of Roy Clark, who ran the drafts of the Braves' heyday and was also in the room as a senior advisor. Just watching felt right; Kiley didn't need to be told.

He had built a bond with the scouting department throughout the season and was seeing a lot of players, despite working in the front office, having turned in 62 draft-worthy players he saw that spring. He was mostly out seeing the best games that the core scouting staff wasn't able to see. He'd wait around for a particular reliever to throw during the weekend, or see a guy that the crosscheckers couldn't get to for a few weeks because their schedule was already full.

He was sent to sit on a player for two whole weeks to suss out his makeup (it was horrendous, the Braves passed, and the player hasn't met expectations) and then was sent to scramble around the Midwest late in the spring, ultimately lucking out and getting the org's last look at Joey Wentz before the Braves gave him $3.05 million in the compensation round of that year's draft.

Some of those 2016 reports were strong, some weak, but his overall report quality and bond with the amateur staff grew into a bigger role for the 2017 Draft. He'd made progress in the front office, so in addition to his growing analytics role, he saw about twice as many players.

To give you an idea of where he was in the pecking order of seeing top targets, the Braves only drafted one of those 116 players he wrote up. The

Braves were among the most careful teams about telegraphing their interest by sending every scout in to see targeted players, relying on their top handful of evaluators instead of the entire cavalry.

This created a dynamic in the draft room that was almost the exact opposite of Kiley's first draft. When a player would come up for discussion, the scout who was closest to the player, who had the most intimate knowledge of his skills, would start the discussion and give about a minute of overview, then all the other scouts who saw him that spring would chime in with their account, usually 15 to 30 seconds of how their views differed, or adding more detail.

Once every scout who had seen the player had spoken, Bridges would point to Kiley, who would then give the analytical view of the player. For college players at schools with TrackMan units, there was a lot of weighty information that needed to be communicated, still usually in under 30 seconds. For high school players who didn't have a robust summer performance to analyze, there wasn't much to offer, other than possibly TrackMan data from a pre-draft workout.

Because Kiley got out to see so many players that year, he was often speaking in the merry-go-round of scouts who had seen a particular player that spring, then jumping in again at the end. The rhythm of the room had been established and some scouts would come to Kiley during breaks to get clarification about the analytics of players they were interested in.

Bridges noticed this. "It really helped that the guy pushing the numbers stuff also saw as many players as a lot of people in the room. It buys you a lot of credibility in the room." It was stimulating to have that many different backgrounds exchanging ideas without ego. Guys that were against analytics in many situations were earnestly asking about fastball plane, spin rates, launch angle, and exit velos privately, just to learn.

Bridges continued, "It was a different vibe in the room that year. Nobody had an agenda, it was all for one. You were a new voice, hadn't really been a figure in the room before but you earned a spot, to be a part of it. Too often, people are old school vs. analytics and we didn't really have that issue. We had a unified front, scouting, analytics, medical, and psychological, everyone pulling in the same direction for the same thing."

Then came the discussion about University of Michigan catcher/first baseman Drew Lugbauer. He was a somewhat known player in high school, going to some major events and showing left-handed power, but struggling with contact and offering marginal defensive value behind the plate, in part due to his 6'3", 220-pound frame.

In his draft year, Lugbauer only caught a few games and the scouting staff explained that he should've been catching most of the games, were it not for a primary catcher that was the son of a program booster. In the handful of games that Lugbauer did catch, the Braves scouts got advance word and at least one of them was at each of these games to get a sense of how his defensive ability had progressed. They felt like he was good enough defensively to stay at catcher in pro ball.

Offensively, Lugbauer led the Wolverines in homers with 12 and his .288/.401/.518 triple-slash line was solid, but his 25 percent strikeout rate was a problem. Everyone in the room knew that anything over a 20 to 22 percent strikeout rate was almost disqualifying from a historical standpoint, with just a handful of useful big leaguers in that group. The scouts explained that they thought he had a correctable swing flaw, so there would be enough contact in pro ball to let most of his plus raw power play in games.

After the group of scouts that had been all over Lugbauer all year had shared their stories of everything they could do to get an edge on other clubs, things got pretty tense. "I was nervous when we turned it over to you," Bridges later recalled. "This guy is striking out a lot, there isn't enough there in the analytical profile to hang your hat on, but our guys worked hard on him. I was worried you were gonna kill him. If you're just looking at the numbers in a narrow sense, you had to kill him."

Kiley leaned back and, instead of announcing how problematic this strikeout rate was, started asking questions. "And we're talking about this guy where? After the top 10 rounds? $125,000 bonus?" The group agreed that's where he fit, maybe thought he was better on talent, but that was the reasonable amount of bonus space to use and spot in the draft to take him.

We won't act like we remember exactly what Kiley said in this moment, but he's compared notes with other people in the room to make sure the sentiments are accurate. "So we have a catcher with plus raw power, enough contact skills, and we think he can catch?" The room agrees. "And we can get him for $125,000?" The room agrees.

"Hell, he could strike out 50 percent of the time, you have to take that guy *there*. Where do those tools go if he's performing? Is that guy even in the draft? Don't we have to sign four catchers in this draft class anyway?"

The air returned to the room and the trajectory of the Lugbauer discussion continued how it would've gone if there was no analytics department, about the strategy of how to get the player.

You may be tempted to Google Drew Lugbauer or check our rankings at FanGraphs to see where he is now. Take a look when you're done reading this part, but you probably don't recognize his name because he wasn't a big prospect then and still isn't one now. He's hit a couple dozen homers and struck out a lot in pro ball, playing catcher mostly but more corner infield lately. He's probably not a big leaguer, but you never know.

In the 2017 11th round where the Braves selected Lugbauer, there are a couple guys who have a little more prospect value than Lugbauer, and Houston Astros RHP Brandon Bielak is the best one. He's likely a back-end starter or high-volume reliever who might be a big league average pitcher for a stretch. That's the "correct" pick, an excellent one that late in the draft.

Yet a tiny fraction of players drafted ever reach the big leagues, and the chances get slimmer the later you go in the draft. You can't let one selection of an 11th round organizational player weigh on your mind, even if someone else found a big leaguer in that round. There are at least 30 more picks just like that for every team, every year. Kiley isn't heroic in the Lugbauer story. He was just put in a position to speak his mind and answer questions honestly in a setting with some stakes, which isn't as common as it should be in a draft room.

Kiley's tasks during the prior draft had created a foundation of trust between him and others in the draft room and helped him act as a conduit between the scouts and the analytical aspects of player evaluation. The collective effort of the scouts to assess Lugbauer's talent and, even further, understand how his circumstances might be obscuring it, created enthusiasm in the room. Kiley had enough feel for the situation to know not to rain on the parade with the numbers, not because he was being intellectually dishonest, but because all the other stuff was enough to be excited about the player.

It is in the spirit of this sort of process that we'd like to embark on this several-hundred-page journey into a world that rarely has wholly right or wrong philosophies. From a 2017 Braves draft class that included big names like Drew Waters and Kyle Wright, the Lugbauer discussion is still what stood out in the minds of many people in the room.

Bridges summed up how he approaches the job: "You have to listen to people. It's a people business. No one person has all the answers. My goal was to keep people unified and engaged, going in the same direction for the same goal. If there's an agenda, it's gonna go haywire. The agenda could be selfish, or just to exclude scouting or analytics because of fear or ego."

Months after the draft, Kiley joined the amateur scouting staff as a crosschecker. Months after that, then-Braves GM John Coppolella was fired and banned from baseball for life for international scouting indiscretions. Months after that, Kiley left the team to go back to FanGraphs. Almost exactly one year after that, Bridges went to San Francisco after helming one more draft for the Braves. Just over a year after a happy medium was struck with the draft process, most of those involved have spread out around baseball, or out of it completely.

CHAPTER 1

You Can't Know
What You Don't Know

Before we get to the meat of the next couple hundred pages, we need to cover the rules and broad strategies of each market below the Major League level, a Scouting and Player Development 101 of sorts. This'll be a quick refresher for some, an introduction for others.

Player Development (the Farm System)

Player Development is the term MLB clubs use for the department that is focused on developing and managing their minor league players. All MLB organizations have four full-season minor league clubs (from top to bottom: Triple-A, Double-A, High-A, Low-A) and at least three short-season clubs that start playing games in June (top to bottom: Rookie-Advanced and/or Short Season, Rookie, and Dominican Summer League). The two Rookie-level leagues (the Gulf Coast League in Florida and the lazily-named Arizona League, disdainfully nicknamed the "Fire League" by those who sweat through their polo shirts at the games) often are referred to as the "Complex Leagues" since the games are played at the spring training complex back fields (and at times in the spring training stadiums), but always with little-to-no crowd at the games outside of scouts and players' family members.

Many teams will double up and deploy two ball clubs at one or several of these lower levels (for instance, in 2019 the Cubs, Indians, Giants, Dodgers, Padres, Brewers, and Athletics each had two AZL teams), and some organizations have two of *each* at times, giving them six short-season teams to go with four full-season teams for a total of 10 minor league affiliates, which means 10 rosters worth of minor league players. The Yankees, for example, have at times had two DSL teams; two GCL teams; an Advanced Rookie affiliate in Pulaski, Kentucky, part of the Appalachian League; a Short-Season club in Staten Island; plus their four full-season affiliates.

Complex leagues generate zero revenue from ticket sales, and the cost of running a team is in the six figures (equipment, staff, chartered buses, etc.), so these two leagues can expand and contract clubs on a yearly basis, based on the needs of the parent MLB organization or in response to a larger-than-usual wave of new players. Have a particularly large collection of talent coming up from Latin America? The autonomy created by playing games at your spring training facility enables teams to add a team when needed for developmental purposes. The same goes for the Dominican Summer League, which is played at the various Dominican academies (every team has one) and expands/contracts each year, with even fewer fans at games. Kiley has been to some of these and it's unusual to see anyone other than team staff, the official scorer, and, depending on the setting of the academy, a handful of kids from the local neighborhood.

Rookie-Advanced and Short Season leagues are typically located in the smallest viable markets in the country or in the recesses or outskirts of bigger ones. Those leagues are the Pioneer League (which includes teams in places like Boise, Grand Junction, Billings, and Ogden), Northwest League (Eugene, Salem, Spokane), Appalachian League (teams stretch from the eastern reaches of Tennessee up through Princeton, West Virginia), and New York–Penn League (teams scattered all over the Northeast), so adding a new team at that level means literally creating a team and logo and all the legal copyrighting associated with that stuff, as well as a stadium, staffing, etc., so this happens much less often, as it's a long-term commitment for several parties that runs into the seven figures.

With few exceptions, MLB franchises don't own their minor league affiliates. The ones who do tend to be the big brands with big payroll. They have conveniently located affiliates they don't want to lose, due to easy player movement and local fan loyalty (Braves in the Southeast, Yankees/Red Sox in the Northeast, Cubs in the Midwest). But the majority just provide the players and pay their salaries; that's it.

Minor league front office people make no player personnel decisions, though that doesn't stop some variation of uninformed or senile fans from calling front office people suggesting someone be benched. Instead, they're charged with marketing the franchise to get people through the gates of the ballpark, then putting on a good mid-inning show while making the concessions and merchandising operations run smoothly and lucratively. Flush with poorly paid interns, minor league front offices have short half-lives. It's a lot of late nights with early-morning turnarounds for young, transient people seeking promotions with other teams while a shrinking core sticks around. It's akin to running a small-to-mid-sized theme park where a corporate body supplies the rollercoasters.

The MLB team and the minor league clubs to which they send their players agree to a Player Development Contract that lasts for a few years as both parties assess each other. Some of these partnerships last for many decades (the Phillies and Tigers have had an ongoing PD contract with their Double- and High-A clubs, respectively, for over 50 years), while other minor league franchises have trouble retaining their current partner due to poor geographic location (either due to distance from the big league club or things that affect gameplay, like high altitudes or especially big/small outfield dimensions), stadium quality, or because there's friction of some kind between the two sides.

There's a yearly game of musical chairs when PDCs end and there's a shuffling of which minor league clubs are tied to which Major League organization. Inevitably, the last few teams remaining every year look at each other with 1:45 AM desperation. Dev contracts (as they're called) are typically one to five years in length.

There's also been some movement (more in recent years) where low-revenue minor league teams are targeted to relocate to a city that will build a new (often downtown) stadium as part of a revitalization plan, usually with some public money involved. Sometimes that has meant moving a team between leagues, like Bakersfield and High Desert (from the High-A California League) moving to Buies Creek and Kinston (the High-A Carolina League). This move made sense since both Cal League clubs were undesirable for a number of reasons, and moving two clubs at once keeps the numbers even for scheduling purposes.

These teams have roster and age limits that vary by league and level, but each can have something like 30 to 35 players on a roster when you factor in spots on the injured list, with 25 active spots, sometimes a few more. This means that complete farm systems range from about 200 players (seven teams of about 30 players each) to about 350 players (10 teams of about 35 players each), depending on how aggressive teams are at using every possible roster spot.

The injured lists for some affiliates are full year-round, as player/coaches, emergency catchers only needed in case of injury, and bullpen catchers are signed as players (with an understanding between the team and player of the actual arrangement), since clubs can save money paying them the minor league freight (usually $1,000 to $2,000 per month for the five months of the season) on a more temporary basis rather than the salary and benefits of a full, non-playing staff position. Yes, that's a comically low salary and it's what the vast majority of minor leaguers make. More on that later.

Various arrangements like this are referred to in the industry as the "phantom IL." It's second nature in player development meetings when there's a sudden surplus of players, someone will ask "Can we phantom player X?" meaning "Will he play along with this, or ask to be released for a chance to actually play with another club?"

Clubs also take a page from the Branch Rickey playbook and try to get as many lottery-ticket-type players as possible, so using every possible roster spot is prudent, often putting players on the injured list that aren't injured (if the player agrees) because there isn't an active roster spot, and he'd be released otherwise. This would be expected for a hitter transitioning to pitcher, when he'll need at least a few weeks not playing in games to work in practice settings.

It's very common at the upper levels of the minors. Clubs like knowing they'll have a 26-year-old veteran ready for emergency roster shortages or the inevitable future shortage when players will get promoted, and have an extra coach/mentor on staff at a discounted rate until then. Players do this since there isn't a minor league union and the general attitude of the vast majority of players is to play as long as a team will let you. These sorts of roles can often act as coaching auditions and sometimes transition into full coaching gigs; yet another way huge organizations use this massive supply of willing labor to save money.

Pro Scouting (Scouting Minor League Players)

We'll get into the structure and strategy behind pro scouting (along with international and amateur scouting) in future chapters, but will just focus on the core rules and broad outline of the department in this section. MLB clubs send scouts to minor league games to gather information about potential trades or free agent signings. Some teams do the same at the MLB level, but that's increasingly becoming automated and is generally referred to as

Major League scouting (picking MLB players to acquire) or advance scouting (looking for tendencies to exploit in an opponent, within a week) rather than pro scouting, since the jobs differ in key ways.

Clubs either organize their pro scouting department by region (leagues/teams that are near each scout's hometown) or by organization (seeing a whole farm system of one team top-to-bottom). We'll get into the pros and cons of each approach later, but the main factor is balancing travel cost vs. depth of knowledge about an organization from one singular scout.

The other important aspect to note, which we will also expand on later, is that clubs are moving toward doing less in-person scouting at the upper levels (MLB, Triple-A, and Double-A) and doing more of it at the lower levels. There are lots of reasons why this is the case, but the umbrella reason is that there are lots of things known about upper level players, thus there's little asymmetry between the information that dictates all 30 clubs' value of a particular player. On the other hand, there are lots of unknowns at the lower levels, thus increasing the odds of finding asymmetry in the 30 values of a player, and thus a match for a potential trade.

The two rules-based concepts to understand on the pro scouting side are something we recently added to our prospect rankings at FanGraphs: Rule 5 Draft status and options remaining, which both refer to 40-man roster status.

It's important to note that MLB teams have an active 26-man roster (i.e. the players that play in the big league games) and a 40-man roster (those 26 plus those on 10-day injured list and some minor leaguers that are usually inventory/depth type players). During the season, players that won't be playing for 60 days or more can go on the 60-day injured list and not count toward the 26-man or 40-man roster limits (teams get a free spot for a replacement), but in the off-season they do count.

The Rule 5 Draft exists so that high-payroll clubs can't 1) hoard veteran talent in the minor leagues at huge salaries, and 2) blocked or otherwise mishandled prospects have an automatic method to get a chance to play in MLB. It's a little confusing, but the simple version is that any player that's not on the 40-man roster and has been in pro baseball for three-to-five years (figuring out which length applies to each player is the complicated part) can be picked by any of the 29 other clubs.

Once picked, a player is a full-fledged member of the selecting club if they stay on the 26-man roster for a full season, which is usually tough to do on merit for a player not previously on a 40-man roster. The Rule 5 Draft has picks in reverse order of the standings like the MLB Draft (college and high school players, much more on that later) and teams can trade all picks freely, unlike the MLB Draft. A common practice is the "selling" of a Rule 5 pick. When that happens, one team, drafting lower, has a team drafting higher pick a player for them, and then "buys" the selection (and the attendant 26-man-roster responsibility) for a six-figure cash sum.

The Rule 5 Draft happens on the last day of the Winter Meetings in December, the yearly industry conference. Clubs have to submit their 40-man rosters before the event begins and rival clubs then have a few weeks to sort through available players before the draft occurs. There's often a couple dozen picks in the MLB portion (there are some way less relevant minor league portions as well) and there are usually no more than a half-dozen players that "stick" into year two with their new club. Johan Santana, Dan Uggla, Shane Victorino, Odubel Herrera, and Josh Hamilton are some of the exceptions where a Rule 5 pick became a solid everyday player.

Options are important, as there is a clock on a player once he's on a 40-man roster of how long he can be left in the minor leagues. The details of this can also be complicated but, generally, each player has three "options" which means there are three years where you can spend a non-trivial amount of time (more than a week or two) in the minors and be on a 40-man roster. Once those have all been used, the player is "out of options" and has to clear waivers to go to the minors.

"Clearing waivers" means that the other 29 teams can claim the player for $50,000 to put on their 40-man roster, which is a low-cost way for teams to add talent. Waiver order goes in reverse order of record, one league at a time, starting with the league the player is currently in. This order only comes into play when there are multiple claims; waivers is an electronic 48-hour system where clubs submit claims blindly. This is also one of the underrated advantages of being a rebuilding club: when a big league team is the weakest, they get first choice of the best castoffs in the leagues.

Said another way, waivers is the cheapest possible way to acquire a young MLB-caliber player, so it's seen as akin to giving the player away. Out-of-options players are almost always the best players on waivers, since they come with very limited roster flexibility, as they have to stay on the 26-man roster as well or else be put back through waivers.

The MLB Draft

The draft is the mechanism that allows MLB teams to add new domestic players to their farm system. High school seniors are all eligible, with some exceptions, such as players that systematically remove themselves from the draft pool (for instance, by being on MLB's list of top prospects and refusing to take a pre-draft drug test) or high school juniors who accelerated their classes to graduate in three years. Junior college players are all eligible, every year, without exception. Four-year college juniors and seniors are all eligible, along with redshirt sophomores and any four-year college player that turns 21 within 45 days of the start of the draft, no matter their class. These rules apply to the U.S., as well as any U.S. territories (such as Puerto Rico), and Canada.

There are now 40 rounds of the draft (it was 50 rounds for a while) and there is now a hard-capped bonus pool. But as recently as 2011, the draft had no spending limits, only MLB-suggested bonuses at each pick to anchor negotiations. There are compensation picks after each of the first three rounds, for having lower/medium local revenue, for losing high-level free agents, or for not signing a top-three-round pick in the previous draft.

There are six competitive balance picks after both the first and second rounds that are randomly selected to qualifying lower-revenue clubs. The free agent compensation rules are changing every few years and the current iteration is a bit complicated, based around how much the new contract is and the payroll of the club losing the player. With every pick in the top three rounds protected via compensation for two years (i.e. not signing the eighth pick this year means you get the ninth pick next year, fail again and you'd get the 10th pick the year after), it gives clubs increased leverage to negotiate without fear of getting nothing in return for a top pick.

The bonus pools are set using the concept of suggested bonuses from the uncapped era of the draft. There are still suggested bonuses for negotiating purposes, but those suggested amounts for every top-10-round pick are added up to form your pool figure. Clubs can also go over their pool number by up to 5 percent before the punishment includes the loss of future first-round picks. No club has done this yet. Clubs often spend up to the 5 percent threshold, with the punishment being a 75 percent tax on the overage. The other loophole to spend more money on your draft is that beyond the 10th round, the first $125,000 you give a player doesn't count toward your pool. This has many implications for strategy that we'll discuss later.

The CBA—and this is true in all sports, not just baseball—is what makes things like the draft—which is technically a violation of U.S. labor laws—legal. The MLB Players' Association, which only includes big leaguers but negotiates labor rules on behalf of minor leaguers and amateur players, has traditionally used amateur and minor league interests as a bargaining chip during negotiations. Want the seat next to you on the bus to be vacant during Major League spring training trips across Florida? Give owners hard-capped spending in international free agency. Big leaguers have already been drafted or signed, they're not incentivized to care what happens to teenage prospects coming out of Latin America, and so they don't. This is how the Red Sox spend $63 million on Yoán Moncada one year, and then the Angels pay $3 million for Shohei Ohtani a few years later, when both were generational young international talents subject to the same process, with a key rule change between their free agencies.

Because of how long they've been part of our American pro sports institutions or perhaps because some people view sports as frivolous, the notion that drafts are unfair to labor hasn't really taken hold in our culture, even though imagining a similar process for other jobs, like lawyers, teachers, firefighters, accountants, or strippers, would seem ludicrous to everyone.

International Signings (July 2)

The International Signing Period (or July 2/July 2nd/J2 for short) is the mechanism that allows MLB teams to add new international players to their farm system. The period starts each year on July 2 and runs until June 15, with a short closed period until the next period opens. Players from countries not subject to the draft (U.S., Canada, Puerto Rico, other U.S. territories) are eligible to sign as early as 16 years old, but they have to turn 16 by August 31 (the end of that year's minor league season), or they are eligible for the next signing period. Players turning 16 between July 2 and August 31 can't sign until they turn 16. Any players 17 or older are all eligible for the entire signing period.

The majority of players signed are from the Dominican Republic or Venezuela, with a number of other Latin countries contributing strongly like Mexico (mostly players from the Western part of the country, while the Eastern side prefers soccer), Colombia, Bahamas, Curaçao, Aruba, Panama, and Nicaragua, among others. There's a strong history of signing players from Australia, some history in Europe, and some, but not much, in Africa and China. Brazil, which has a sizeable population of people with Japanese heritage, is thought of as a potential area of growth for talent procurement.

Other notable baseball-playing countries have some barriers for player acquisition. Typically, Japanese high school players sign with Nippon Professional Baseball (NPB) clubs (the top Japanese pro league). There's an uneasy truce between MLB and NPB to continue this way, with MLB getting Japanese players only once they've reached their mid-twenties and played multiple years in the NPB as a way of preserving the quality and cultural core of Japanese baseball. Shohei Ohtani notably almost signed with the Dodgers out of high school, but still opted for the NPB. Taiwan and South Korea both allow top players to sign with MLB clubs as amateurs, but only after high school, typically at age 18.

Cuba is the other big exception. For the moment, players have to defect, establish residence in a third country (they would be draft-eligible if that country is subject to the draft), and be cleared by OFAC (a U.S. government agency) and MLB. Only then do they become a free agent. Based on their age and level of professional experience, the player is either subject to hard-capped international signing pools or is a free-and-clear free agent. That bar to clear is 25 years old and six years of experience in the top Cuban League, with the vast majority of good players defecting years before they reach that standard. There hasn't been a notable (multi-year MLB deal) Cuban defector with those qualifications in years and there aren't any clear candidates currently on the island, so the island is effectively subject to July 2 international bonus pools.

Like the draft, the international market used to have no spending limits and now has a hard cap with limited wiggle room, via trading for another club's pool space (only up to 50 percent of your starting pool space), usually with upper-level minor leaguers that act as MLB inventory. In the old market, clubs could spend whatever they wanted, so players and their trainers wouldn't strike verbal deals until at least January before they were eligible to sign.

These verbal deals are non-binding and technically illegal by MLB rules, but have never been enforced and MLB has been telling teams in recent years that they will not enforce it. The deals are somewhat binding socially and the top trainers tend to have the best players each year. In the current hard-capped pools, clubs are limited in what they can spend, so international departments look for value by locking players up earlier and earlier, often trying to project which 13-year-old will be the best 25-year-old so they can get enough of a discount by acting early to allow them to have the most pool remaining for later-peaking players. There are instances in almost every recent signing year of deals done two years in advance and some as much as three years in advance. Almost every seven-figure bonus (there's usually a couple dozen each year) is struck at least 12–18 months in advance.

Sixteen-year-old prospects always sign a contract for the next season, so the club gets an extra year of protection from the Rule 5 Draft instead of the player playing two months in the DSL. To make up for these two months of lost game situations, clubs have informally created what's known as the Tricky League. Teams have signees that can't play in DSL games, players working their way back from injury, or those not getting enough reps in DSL games, along with players trying out to be signed. Most MLB clubs have a team in this league and they set up games around the DSL matchups to get the needed reps after morning practices for every player in the academy.

Some Dominican team academies can house, feed, and train two full DSL teams and a Tricky League team along with some tryout players, often close to 100 players, along with some staff members. These complexes range in cost from about $1 million to $10 million, and conditions, while drastically improved in recent years, can still vary a good bit. The top academies look like resort hotels and have something like SEC-football-level amenities, nutrition, staffing, and training, while others are rented facilities with fine but not great conditions.

What this means is that top July 2 signees will sign in July, spend the summer at the team complex playing in unofficial Tricky League games, spend much of the fall at the Dominican complex, then usually either go to the U.S. for fall instructional league (a more formal version of the Tricky League for the top prospects in the organization) and/or stay in the Dominican for the lower-level-focused Dominican instructional league. They would then go to minor league spring training in March, stay in extended spring training until short-season leagues begin in June, and finally play their first official minor league game in a complex league 11 months after they signed. For second-tier or less-polished players that play their first games in the DSL, they only leave the complex to visit home, celebrate holidays, and take breaks from training for that first year.

This process is very different for foreign professional players, which basically applies to players in the top league in Japan (NPB) and South Korea (KBO). A handful of players go from these leagues to MLB teams each off-season. Some teams consider this part of the pro scouting department since those leagues are akin to the upper minor leagues, but most consider it an extension of the international department since the scouting context is more similar to that than scouting a Triple-A game.

Players from NPB are posted after qualifying via service time (usually five to seven years, but the club has discretion). It's rumored that Ohtani had a handshake deal with his club when signing out of high school to post him after a set amount of time in return for him choosing the NPB. Most amateur players in Japan aren't high profile enough to make this demand, so they just sign with an NPB club and wait until the club decides it's the right time to sell the player to MLB. The posting system, like the international and draft systems, used to have no spending limits in place, but the two sides negotiated a fee last year that's capped at $20 million and is tied to the value of the MLB contract the posted player receives.

Daisuke Matsuzaka's NPB club, the Seibu Lions, got a record $51.1 million posting fee in November of 2006 from the Boston Red Sox, which was subject to a blind bid process, with a six-year, $52 million contract on top of that for the player. On the other hand, Shohei Ohtani, arguably the most sought-after and valuable international free agent of all time (worth about $150 million as a free agent by most estimates), signed as part of the international bonus pool for a $2.3 million bonus, while his NPB club, the Hokkaido Nippon-Ham Fighters, got the maximum-allowed $20 million posting fee in December 2017 from the Los Angeles Angels. Before becoming a free agent, Ohtani will play two years at the league minimum, then four years through the arbitration process, where he will earn a fraction of his market value.

A Quick Statistical Aside

This is by no means a book about statistics, but there are a few that we will casually use as the industry standards for performance. For hitters, we'll lean on the triple-slash line, denoting batting average, on-base percentage, and slugging percentage. Batting average is the number of hits divided by at bats, on-base percentage is that same thing but with walks and hit by pitches added, and slugging is number of total bases (a single is one, double is two, triple is three, homer is four) per at-bat. Average measures contact, on-base measures how often an out is made, and slugging measures how much power you have when you hit it. It's pretty simple and is presented with three slashes. Here are the 2019 MLB averages: .252/.323/.435.

For hitters, offense is the main input to value and the triple slash summarizes that performance. Once you adjust for park effects and other environmental adjustments, you'd get a single rate stat, like wOBA or wRC+ and once you know the number of plate appearances, you can turn what's done in the batter's box into an amount of runs produced. The details aren't important, but go with us here. We can also do that with baserunning, based around the value-add of stolen bases, caught stealing, and expectations about what's been done in every situation by baserunners in every conceivable situation.

Once you also add in a run value for the position the player plays and whatever defensive statistic you prefer (they're all a little flawed compared to the precision of the hitting stats), you can add all these numbers together for WAR, or wins above replacement level. Runs are added and, depending on the year, a win is worth something around 10 runs. Replacement level also is a tough concept to understand, but the idea is however good the freely available guys that teams can call-up from Triple-A are. WAR is the lifeblood and framework of all meta analyses of baseball these days, even if you quibble with its limitation and some inputs, which we do in specific instances, but over a number of years it captures what's going on.

On the pitching side, we like ERA, but if we're looking for something that's predictive, there are things called ERA estimators, with FIP and xFIP the most known and referenced. The idea is that after studying what factors a pitcher can control (strikeouts, walks, how often contact is made, what general type of contact is made), we can then strip out the specifics of the outcome (instead of a triple, it's a line drive in the gap; we ignore the two slow outfielders) to then make something more predictive of the future than ERA is.

Much like wOBA and wRC+ for hitters, these are the advanced rate stats for pitching, so include innings pitched and you can convert performance into runs saved vs. a replacement pitcher. Replacement level is different for starters and relievers, so the calculation is a bit different depending on role. There's also a slight difference between pitching in the first inning and the ninth inning, all things being equal, so some adjustments are made, eventually ending with pitcher WAR. Like how defense is the weakest part of position-player WAR, which ERA estimator you use and what assumptions it makes can shift pitcher WAR a fair amount. This is most obvious when you're comparing the WAR of Cy Young candidates and seeing that most of them benefit from one approach or another depending on the type of luck they got that year.

We're Going Through Changes

For most people who consume baseball, it acts as an escape from real life. It's hooky from work with an $8 beer during an immaculate, 76 degree afternoon in May. It's a way to stick it to Seasonal Affective Disorder in February with the endless sunshine of spring training. It's something to take the edge off the news all throughout the summer. And while baseball fans come in different flavors—you have your autograph hounds, fantasy players, hecklers, tailgaters, scorekeepers, people who prefer to socialize without eye contact, card collectors, ice cream helmeteers, people who like how baseball pants fit Anthony Recker, adrenaline junkies, stadium-visiting completionists, etc.—they almost all seek baseball as a respite from their daily grind.

But for countless people around the world, baseball *is* their daily grind. It's work—a grueling vocation shaped by changes to the real world the same way online streaming has eroded cable viewership, taxi services are impacted by ride-sharing apps, or the healthcare industry is changed by governmental policy. There are countless, global external variables impacting baseball and, it follows, those who make their living off of it. And there are far too many to cover with the sort of comprehensive detail and perspective they deserve. But because this tome is so focused on a relatively small slice of the baseball industry, we can at least provide some important context for what you're about to read about player evaluation, which we think will be especially important for those of you who are picking up this book years from now, in whatever fallout shelter you happen to be reading it in as you hide from deadly heat and/or sentient machines.

When *Moneyball* came out in 2003, it was a strategic revelation for most who read it. Pore over its pages now and it reads more like a Biblical parable, its overarching themes all that remain as most of the specific, baseball-y, player (e)valuation aspects have either been improved upon or just become obsolete. Changes to how baseball players are evaluated and who is evaluating them seem inevitable to us as we sit and write this thing, so this semi-exhaustive dossier on where things stand in our world right now is as much about us covering our own asses in the eyes of smarter, future readers as it is to give you proper context before you dive into the meat of this publication.

We're going to talk a lot about the proliferation of technology and objective means of evaluation throughout the book, but we're writing it at a time when the development of radar and optical unit technology like TrackMan and Rapsodo is in its early adulthood—capable but not entirely reliable—while its use as a means of evaluation and tool in player development varies, team by team. A TrackMan radar unit—which measures all kinds of pitch and batted-ball data like spin rate, spin direction, exit velocities, and more—is currently at every Major League stadium, nearly every minor league ballpark, many minor league back fields at spring training facilities, and nearly 100 colleges, junior colleges, high schools, and multi-field independent facilities combined. MLB is moving away from TrackMan and to an optical tracking system called Hawk-Eye, at least at the big league level, starting in 2020. MLB thinks Hawk-Eye, which is used in and has been well-received by other sports, like tennis, is more accurate in measuring pitch location and movement. Its implementation is likely a precursor for an electronic strike zone, which will probably have scout-related ripple effects, such as in how we evaluate catchers.

Some of our discussion regarding the various talent markets and means of acquiring players may be rendered moot a few years after publication. We're writing this at a time when minor league pay is becoming a more central part of industry discourse. Players get a bonus when they sign, but only a small subset of players' bonuses are very lucrative, and many college seniors sign for as little as $1,000. Regardless of their bonus, minor leaguers then get paid based on their level and years of service, and most of their paychecks total around $1,000 per month during the season (three to five months), while they go unpaid during spring training and other pre/postseason developmental activities, like fall instructional league.

With enough time at the upper levels of the minors, the Mike Hessmans of the world make a very nice living even without years of big league per diem, but many of the younger players in the minors struggle to get by, while their ridiculously named affiliate makes its ownership group (which is typically not affiliated with the big league club in any way) a lot of money.

Again, most families at minor league games are there to watch some ball, eat funnel cake, giggle at the mascot, and forget about the rest of the world for a few hours, totally unaware that the young men on the field are exploited employees of a billion dollar Major League Baseball franchise, a microcosm of American labor issues.

And because this is so obvious to anyone who can form half a thought, it's likely to change during the next Collective Bargaining Agreement negotiations. The arbitration process, the default length of team control over a player before he hits free agency, and the amount he makes during those years of team control are all likely to be points of contention during the CBA negotiations that will follow this book.

Minor leaguer pay might change, too, though possibly due more to public outcry and activism than an incentive-driven request by the players' union. With that may come a drastic restructuring of the minor leagues that would render much of what we covered earlier in this chapter outdated. If individuals are going to make more money, then owners will seek to pay less individuals by eliminating a level or two of the minor leagues. Days before our manuscript deadline, *The New York Times* released a leaked list of the 42 affiliates MLB is considering scrubbing, many of which are Short Season clubs. This will ruffle the feathers of people within the game: less affiliates means fewer coaches and development personnel, less for scouts to see, perhaps no summer job for the teacher or retiree trying to make some extra money by ushering a section at the ballpark.

These changes will also change how baseball thinks about player development timelines for individuals. Less minor league roster spots means less room to try to teach intriguing athletes with little baseball acumen how to play. The low-and-slow barbecue of developmental projects may become less viable, which may then increase how the industry values polished players in various markets. The clubs also may just shift those roster spots to more complex-league teams to limit losses of lottery ticket–type talents. The two of us love the idea of trying to develop athletes from other sports, but this may soon be less frequent a pursuit in baseball than it already is. Maybe it gets outsourced to a more robust independent league that takes the place of eliminated affiliated minor league teams. Then again maybe not, when the indy teams have to pay their players (the parent MLB club pays all minor league salaries, not the minor league team), but those clubs may need to win to sell tickets and stay viable as a business, with little ability to keep good coaches.

Because a huge percentage of pro ball players come from foreign countries, baseball also rubs up against U.S. foreign policy and global politics. The United State's diplomatic relationship with Cuba began to thaw under the Obama administration and for a bit it appeared as though sanctioned avenues for talent to come from the island to MLB were coming, and the days of human trafficking elite talents like Yadier Alvarez and Yasiel Puig might be coming to an end. Then, an agreement between MLB and the Cuban Baseball Federation, which delineated that players could go to the U.S. without defecting, was blocked by the Trump administration, citing CBF's ties to the Cuban government as cause. So Cuban players still often have to sneak away from the island or away from the National Team while abroad and establish residency in a third country (usually one in Latin America but occasionally in a European one if there's a tournament happening there), then be cleared by the U.S. Office of Foreign Asset Control, before they're eligible to sign with an MLB franchise. But this could change quickly depending on 2020 U.S. election results.

Then there's Venezuela, which is in such socioeconomic ruin that teams have shut down their academies there, and domestic-based scouts were loath to travel there to see players for a while, until the current state where they aren't even allowed to go. This humanitarian crisis transcends baseball. It has so badly destabilized the infrastructure of the country that it's hard for Venezuelans to stay fed, let alone have operational baseball facilities. Folks in baseball have been mugged at gun- and knifepoint near baseball facilities in Venezuela because desperate people know they can target people making a living at those places. This situation is so severe that short-term change is less likely here than in other areas; this one's a long-term rebuild.

We also talk about Fall Instructional League throughout the book, and we anticipate "instructs" will look very different just a few years after publication, if it even still exists at all. We go into greater detail about instructs in the pro scouting chapter, as the inter-team scrimmages are a fertile and exciting, if sometimes frustrating venue in which to scout. But newer player development theories suggest it's more valuable to use this time for other instruction, and that there's diminished marginal utility for playing more games after a long season has already ended.

The Mariners, for instance, focus on weight training and nutrition, and talk about baseball concepts in a classroom setting. The Brewers recently began a pitch-design camp rather than having a typical instructs. The Angels and Cubs play some intrasquads against teammates, but Anaheim totaled maybe 10 weekly innings the Fall prior to publication. The Giants moved their instructs to January and most of the outdoor baseball activity consisted of infield drills and simulated games with hitters taking hacks off a high-speed pitching machine. In 2019, only six teams with Arizona facilities had a traditional instructional league. It seems to be going away.

The summer showcase season for prep prospects has begun to change, with MLB putting their thumb on the scale to have more control over the process in lieu of independent, for-profit companies with misaligned incentives. MLB's PDP (Player Development Pipeline) events are now alongside the major independent events and MLB-approved scout-run events to make up most of the well-attended events over the summer. Two All-American games (run by Perfect Game and Under Armour), a post-draft summer-kick-off showcase (Perfect Game National), an expanding West Coast–focused event (Area Code Games), and various travel team tournaments (mostly in Arizona, Florida, and Georgia, largely run by Perfect Game) still stand as non-MLB-or-scout-controlled tentpoles that could get marginalized further in the coming years.

There are also a few things that were happening as this book was being finalized in editing. In December 2019, there was an adjustment to the CBA where marijuana was taken off the banned substance list and opioid testing began after the tragic death of Angels pitcher Tyler Skaggs. Also in December 2019, after years of not cooperating, the NCAA and MLB agreed to have the MLB Draft be a live event in a theater in Omaha just before the College World Series begins. Lastly, again in December, we broke a story about how MLB owners voted to end exclusive TrackMan data collection, which directly changes the state of play as we describe it later in the book regarding junior college TrackMan data. Links to these stories are in the references at the back of the book.

Also, in the few days before this book went to press, results of MLB's investigation into Houston's electronic sign stealing altered a significant part of baseball's landscape. Not only did Houston owner Jim Crane find it necessary to fire manager A.J. Hinch and general manager Jeff Luhnow, but Red Sox manager Alex Cora and Mets manager Carlos Beltrán, who were named in commissioner Rob Manfred's report on the scandal, were also let go due to their roles in the sign stealing and, for Cora, perhaps a role in similar infractions during Boston's 2018 title run. Specifics surrounding Boston's infractions and potential punishment were not yet known at that time, and this entire book was written before the chaos unfolded.

CHAPTER 2

The Draft

"Every scout has missed. This is just one of mine."

Scouting is an endeavor that requires confidence, inherent or acquired. Watching a bunch of teenagers and believing that you can predict their futures better than anyone on Earth is an exercise in hubris. It's also, for every scout, eventually humbling. There isn't one of them who won't volunteer the guys they've missed on at the drop of a hat. They're almost proud to remind you how hard this is, so the big success stories seem that much more amazing when they happen. It's likely because the game itself is so famously married to failure.

Tim Wilken is a legendary scout. He's been at it for over 40 years. Here are some of the players he's drafted (while a national crosschecker, special assistant to the GM, or scouting director): Roy Halladay, Javier Báez, Kris Bryant, Josh Donaldson, D.J. LeMahieu, Michael Young, Orlando Hudson, Alex Rios, Vernon Wells, Jimmy Key, Jeff Samardzija, Kyle Schwarber, Wade Davis, Josh Harrison, Jake McGee, Andrew Cashner, and Jeremy Hellickson, along with a couple of current top-100 prospects in the Diamondbacks system.

Wilken spent 1979 through 2003 with the Toronto Blue Jays, an incredible stretch of baseball monogamy, especially at the start of one's career. He joined the Tampa Bay Rays as scouting director for the 2004 and 2005 Drafts, then went to the Chicago Cubs as scouting director for the 2006 Draft. "Some people described our 2006 Draft approach as 'drunken sailors' because of how much we gave Chris Huseby and Jeff Samardzija," Wilken recalls.

In 2007, the Cubs were picking third. They knew David Price was going first to the Rays and Mike Moustakas was going second to the Royals a good bit in advance of the draft, so the Cubs draft room was able to narrow down their choice without having "ifs" as part of the process.

Price has accumulated the most WAR in that draft class (41.7 WAR through 2019) and was seen as a slam-dunk first pick a whole year before the draft, holding the top spot in that class wire-to-wire for not only his junior season but, because of his big league production, for over a dozen years. Moustakas ranks 15th (16.1 WAR), due to a slow start to his eventually excellent MLB career, only eclipsing 3 WAR twice, and never topping 4 WAR. He's clearly better than the average second overall pick, but ultimately wasn't the second-best player in the draft class.

	2007 MLB Draft Career WAR (through 2019)		
	Player	Pick	WAR
1	David Price	1	41.7
2	Josh Donaldson	48	41.4
3	Giancarlo Stanton	76	39.3
4	Jonathan Lucroy	101	37.0
5	Freddie Freeman	78	34.6
5	Corey Kluber	134	34.6
7	Madison Bumgarner	10	31.3
8	Jason Heyward	14	31.1
9	Anthony Rizzo	204	29.2
10	Rick Porcello	27	27.9
11	Jordan Zimmermann	67	25.4
12	Todd Frazier	34	24.2
13	Jake Arrieta	159	23.8
14	Matt Wieters	5	17.4
15	Mike Moustakas	2	16.1
16	Danny Duffy	96	14.0
17	Zack Cozart	79	13.0
18	Greg Holland	306	11.6
19	Sean Doolittle	41	11.1
20	Derek Norris	130	9.6

Source: FanGraphs

The other top players in the class largely weren't seen as premier prospects on draft day, which is unusual and made the Cubs' position much more difficult. Donaldson, Stanton, Lucroy, Freeman, Kluber, and Rizzo are all legitimate stars who lasted beyond the first round.

The Cubs draft room was unanimous in their support of one player for the pick. Usually there's some dissension when there are only two players off the board. At least a few people in the room think this or that other player should be the pick or, at least, in the mix. But in this case there was only one dissenter in the room: Wilken.

He wanted high school right-hander Jarrod Parker, and the room wanted high school third baseman Josh Vitters. "The room was extremely strong on Vitters. Literally everyone in the room would pick him over Parker. I had Parker."

"Vitters was a fairly accomplished hitter for a high school draft, he had power, marginal third baseman. I like Josh as a person, but there were concerns. He didn't present himself like he liked the game. I got the sense he was getting pushed, there wasn't a lot of life to him. Not that you have to have that. John Olerud had a low heartbeat like Vitters, too. Some can play with it, but you can't have too many of them on one team."

Wilken describes himself as the arguer in the room, so he'd ask questions to try to figure out what his staff was seeing that he wasn't. He'd say that Vitters' energy level was low as an open-ended statement and the room would answer that he's a steady-minded player. "We didn't have a blowout argument. I had to sit with myself and think. 'Everyone is really on this guy. Maybe I'm totally missing something.'"

Other players went in the dozen picks after the Cubs' pick that could've been a realistic and superior option. "We did a horrific job on Bumgarner. I got a bad look and he didn't have a chance to get in our mix. We couldn't have covered [Matt] Wieters financially after all the money we spent in 2006. We were just okay on [Jason] Heyward."

Ultimately, the room won out and the Cubs took Vitters third overall. "Looking at all the years of experience in the room, I told myself to step back. That wasn't my M.O., so I still give myself a slight pat on the back for doing the tough thing. You have to listen to the room, or else why have a staff?"

Vitters posted a -1.4 WAR in 36 MLB games. Parker posted 5.2 WAR in 62 MLB starts by age 24, but eventually retired in 2018 after four arm surgeries. "From a traditionalists' viewpoint, there's something to be said for gut feel. My gut feel kept telling me 'no.' The room was thankful and appreciative, to a man, that I took the guy the room wanted."

He felt a bit better about the Cubs' second pick that year.

"He wanted to catch, he was a third baseman, converted to catcher on the Cape, I think just to be more valuable. His competitiveness was a 12 on the 1–10 scale. I thought he could hit 20 homers, 15 consistently. I had a pretty good conviction on him, but not like MVP-level conviction. He was such a gamer, had baseball savvy, a little bit of redneck, but really knew the game. An intense competitor with some flair. It was an easy pick—I was kinda surprised he was there, to be honest. Chris Buckley with Cincinnati told me they were gonna take him five picks behind us if we didn't take him. They took Todd Frazier like a dozen picks ahead of us. Imagine that draft if the Reds got Frazier and this guy, both in the comp round."

The Cubs second pick was 48th overall. You may remember from earlier that the 48th overall pick is also the player with the second-most WAR in the 2007 Draft: Josh Donaldson.

WHEN TALKING ABOUT THE DRAFT, fans and general media tend to give accolades or allocate blame toward the general manager and the scouting director. While those two almost always have the decision-making power (in several cases the director makes the picks while the GM works the agents), the myriad of information they analyze to make those decisions comes almost exclusively from other employees.

Scouting directors picking outside the top few picks will sometimes complain to us that they were only able to see a high-profile selection a few times, sometimes just two or three, before sticking their neck out to pick him. Whether or not an important pick pans out can have a real impact on a director's job security, and if things go awry for the player because of visible and severe character/makeup issues, the director's judgment can look especially poor. Many scouting directors have done exceptional work in lesser roles in pursuit of that job, only to find once they arrive that their performance suddenly depends on the work and life habits of teenage boys who have just been handed a couple million dollars. You need to be right or you need to update your résumé, so you'd better have a quality group of people helping you decide.

Here, we'll show you how teams run a domestic amateur scouting department, often called the "amateur department," colloquially. We don't understand why there aren't more jokes about this.

Hiring a Staff

The top level of the amateur scouting staff is the scouting director. Every team has one, although the function of this role has evolved throughout the last five or so years, as we'll cover in later chapters. They typically have autonomy over department staffing, budgeting, and organization, and answer directly to the general manager.

The bottom level of the amateur scouting staff is the area scout. Most teams have anywhere from 12 to 15 of these, and they're responsible for knowing about every draftable player in their area. In areas that typically have lower talent density, like the upper Midwest, an "area" will encompass about a half dozen states. Covering the Mid-Atlantic? You'll likely have the Eastern half of Pennsylvania, Delaware, Maryland, and Virginia. If you have some experience that demands a bigger area, it could expand north/east to include New Jersey and New York or south/west to include western Pennsylvania and West Virginia. Scouts in lighter areas may also be asked to fold in relevant coverage in cities on the outskirts of their area. Four Corners (Arizona, Utah, Colorado, New Mexico) scouts, for instance, are often also responsible for scouting Las Vegas and El Paso, which aren't really near any other area.

For talent hotbeds, a state gets split up into multiple areas: Southern California is so packed with good baseball schools around Los Angeles and San Diego that it's divided into two or three chunks (sometimes one of these scouts also gets stuck with Vegas) and so is Florida (with Puerto Rico included in someone's coverage).

The basic responsibilities of an area scout are to know something about every draftable player in their area, even if the only thing they know is "this kid isn't good at baseball." The ones whom they consider to be viable pro ball players get "turned in," meaning the scout is alerting his club of all the player's pertinent information: full biographical and medical history, signability (more on this later), makeup (vague, semi-problematic shorthand for any number of potential mental attributes), a long history of scouting looks, projection of their future outlook, etc. Scouts will know about a lot of high school players that they like but don't end up turning in, since they want more than teams are willing to pay for them to pass up college. Scouts rank all the players in their area in a preference list, universally called a "pref list," or just "my/the list," the core deliverable for an area scout and what they measure themselves by. It's common for area scouts to bemoan bad judgment or preen when a big leaguer comes up in conversation, based on where they were on "my list."

To get promoted to the next level of amateur scouting, an eye for talent is most important, but good communication and organizational skills, as well as attention to detail, are the easier-to-evaluate abilities. In the role of area scout, higher-level evaluators tell us the most important qualities are being able to broadly bucket players on ability for the higher-ups to sort through, and staying on top of your paperwork/general administration skills.

Some scouts have the short-term, immediate skill set for being an area scout but lack the standout evaluation ability and/or communication skills to progress. Other scouts stay in the area role for a long time because they like the temperature of the water. They like the flexibility of being in their own bed almost every night (common for the smaller-sized, better-paying, hotbed-state areas) more than the prestige, tough travel, and higher pay of the next role up on the ladder.

The position above the area scout is that of crosschecker (often just "checker"), and there are two tiers of crosschecker: regional and national. A regional crosschecker manages a region, as defined by stitching together four to five area scouts' areas. Often regions are West Coast (typically California, Nevada, Montana, Washington, Oregon, Idaho, British Columbia, often the Four Corners), Southwest (Arkansas, Texas, Oklahoma, occasionally Four Corners states, and Wyoming), Midwest (Iowa, Kansas, Tennessee, Michigan, Illinois, Ohio, Nebraska), Southeast (Louisiana, Alabama, Mississippi, Florida, Georgia, South Carolina), and Northeast (every state between Maine and North Carolina, plus Eastern Canada, which is often Toronto-area high schoolers), but there are some variations on this boilerplate set up. Another common setup is West, Midwest, Southeast, and Northeast, with those exact states varying depending on where one area ends and another begins.

Teams take advantage of natural tidal shifts in the spring schedule and move crosscheckers around pretty creatively. For example, it's common for a Northeast regional crosschecker to spend February and some of March in the Carolinas or Florida. It's too cold for baseball in the Northeast at that time, so teams in that region typically begin their season south of the Mason-Dixon line, playing round-robin tournaments at big colleges, and sometimes spring training sites. The crosschecker is either following their teams down there, or they're helping sift through players from those warmer places early in the year. Hotbed states like the Carolinas and Georgia have more players to check early in the spring, which can help inform your bosses' priorities later in the year. All scouts like getting out of their area to see what players other scouts on staff will be pushing for, in direct competition with the players they like.

A scouting director told us recently that regional crosschecker is the hardest position to hire, because he wants someone who hasn't done it before (i.e. hasn't been fired from this role in the past), it's a very different job than area scout (the pool he's hiring from), and if he doesn't have a clear, internal candidate amongst his top few area scouts, he likely has no personal experience with this scout, nor a chance to do a month-long crosschecker test run after a scout "finished" their area for the year. An external, first-time regional crosschecker hire is one where a scouting director would rely on industry friends, and a more extensive interview process, to ensure they are making a good hire.

The level above the regional crosschecker is, typically, national crosschecker. It's easier to think about that job as serving as a sort of vice scouting director, while the regional crosscheckers serve as a filter for the information initially provided by the area scouts, sorting through their lists and reports and refining them for the higher-ups. The national checker crisscrosses the country, comparing players across regions the same way the scouting director does, as another layer of sanity checks and balances.

This may seem redundant, but remember the scope of each scout's job means their perspective on a given player is very different. An area scout knows where a player's talent fits in the context of their area, crosscheckers see them within the context of the region, while national-level eyeballs have seen all of the top 75 or so draft-eligible players during the spring (and any easily scheduled players below that level). The best player an area scout sees all year might be a second-round talent.

Clubs usually have about four national checkers spread around the country, typically near the hotbeds which act as their base, although they're flying all over the place regularly. Given the need for something that approaches work-life balance, even during the busiest draft season, high-level evaluators often get a "home weekend" once a month or so, where they will sleep in their own bed for an extended period, be able to drive the kids to school in the morning, etc.

These jobs vary in pay, contract length, and responsibility by club, but some general ranges for salaries of these jobs are:
- $40,000 to $70,000 for an area scout
- $70,000 to $90,000 for a regional crosschecker

- $90,000 to $125,000 for a national crosschecker
- $150,000 to $350,000 for a scouting director.

For the sake of context, the top of a baseball operations staff looks like this:
- $150,000 to $750,000 for an assistant general manager
- $1 million to $4 million for a general manager on the first or second contract (usually three to five years per deal)
- $1 million to $4 million for a president who functions as head of business operations, no baseball responsibilities
- $500,000 to $5 million for a president who functions as a head of baseball operations or a GM with a decade of tenure (but doesn't get the president title due to a powerful head of business operations).

Most of these employees are on one- or two-year deals, with the director and top national guys sometimes getting more when the GM has history with them, or because the team wants to lock up someone who they think might otherwise be pursued for jobs with other teams.

Deploying a Staff

The same way good football coaches can tailor their schemes to suit the talent on their roster, good amateur departments let a staff's strength dictate how they are deployed. Lots of former players can both scout and coach. They may get a smaller area, then run a summer scout team for showcase season, or act as a coach at the GCL/AZL complex-level affiliate after the draft.

Another option is for a top area scout to become a junior crosschecker, where they may scout a mini-region or a state that has so many players as to constitute a region, such as Florida. At the same time, another full-time scout takes an area under their supervision, and/or a part-time, entry-level scout (think $20,000 to $30,000 per year, often classified as an hourly employee without benefits) will be a junior area scout, on one coast of Florida in a developmental role under the tutelage of the senior scout.

There's also flexibility amongst typical area lines. Georgia is often a full area, but some of the more experienced scouts will pick up Alabama or South Carolina or the eastern third of Tennessee. Another way to reward a top area scout when you don't have a crosschecker role to promote them into is with a long-term deal with a high-end salary for their position. And when a scout invariably "finishes" their area and has turned in reports on the top 20-ish-round talents in their coverage kingdom, they might be asked to do some targeted crosschecking, often in the next area over, or in the scout's specialty (hitter/pitcher, prep/college, etc.).

When is a scout "finished" with their area? Depends on the area. The average is sometime in April, but the Northeast typically finishes very close to the draft. Florida area scouts that have the benefit of extra eyeballs in March can be rolling their eyes at games by the end of March because they've seen this high school player five times before some Northern prep squads have even played a game. Florida uniquely also has varied start times for junior colleges and high schools, some fields without lights that only play day games, and lots of early season tournaments played at non-peak times, so it's typical to get three games in a day. On the other hand, Southern California and Atlanta both have tons of traffic and more uniform start times without random spring training facilities to host events, so scouts are often limited to one game per day once the season is in full swing.

To lure top talent, some clubs are making hybrid roles (rather than letting conventional roles evolve into hybrid roles) where a scout will be an international crosschecker in the busiest three to four months of that season, then be an area scout (and be home most nights) the rest of the year, then spend the month or so before the draft as a hitting or pitching crosschecker.

Instead of working regionally, some clubs just make custom crosschecking regions where a certain crosschecker will supervise the same four or five area scouts as the role demands, but they'll be spread all over a time zone or two. We've spoken with crosscheckers who, for example, live in Florida and their crosschecking region is Florida, Georgia, East Tennessee, Virginia, Maryland, Delaware, Ohio, and Indiana, as well as one who works New England and Michigan, Illinois, and Tennessee.

Decades ago, clubs less frequently separated Southeast and Northeast regions, and just had East, Midwest, and West regions, with two regional and two national crosscheckers per region. More experienced Northeast area scouts (often the east half of Pennsylvania to Maine) will have a part-time scout (usually stipend-based, either very young/starting out or very old/retired) do some day-to-day work that the area scout will crosscheck in some way.

We're often asked if certain scouts are much better at evaluating hitters or pitchers, or if certain teams have a hitting or pitching crosschecker. Many scouts are clearly better at one, often due to their coaching or playing background, and clubs often have crosscheckers with a clear core competency who are asked to focus more on hitters than pitchers, or vice versa. There are also members of the player development department called coordinators (catching, infield, outfield, hitting, baserunning, pitching) who will often see top players that fit into their specialty, specifically when there's disagreement in the amateur department about the evaluation. The vast majority of teams have at least one scout in the amateur department who is known to be a standout with hitters or pitchers, but still sees all types of players. A minority of teams have a literal pitching crosschecker, but all of those teams usually have a player development member or two acting as a scout for a couple months, because that person is arguably in a better position to project what is fixable in pro ball since they're the one doing the fixing.

It's most common for catching coordinators to see many of the top catchers, since that position has many of its own intricacies. The technical aspect of catching and the increased importance of makeup, mental skills, constitution, game awareness, swing-reading, and an overall understanding of the game makes catching such a significant on-field role relative to other positions. This minutiae can be tough to evaluate, especially at the college level where scouts' attention is divided among more players than is typical at a high school game. It's also now rare for catchers to call a game (the pitcher's pitches) at top programs, as the coaches are now making so much money that they want to call every pitch.

Particularly, scouts who never played the position are often uneasy about pounding the table for a catcher without the blessing of the club's catching coordinator, or at least a top scout who used to be a pro catcher. It's also common for a pitching coordinator who is biomechanically inclined to watch video of all the top pitchers and write short reports on each, both because the team gets another opinion, but also to ease the transition when the player goes into the minor league system because the staff feels some ownership over the pick.

Having an ace area scout is a real asset for a scouting director, particularly when there are multiple defensible selections at every pick and many more for later-round selections. When Kiley worked for the Braves, the whole draft room knew that Carolinas area scout Billy Best was the guy that scouting director Brian Bridges leaned on when the choice wasn't clear: "I call them 'bullet scouts.' Not every team has 15 60-grade area scouts. Every staff has some. I can lay my head on the pillow and know that, if I took five of Billy's guys, that he knew them inside out and know what we're getting."

This level of certainty is a coveted feeling for scouting directors. Yankees international scouting director Donny Rowland was Bridges' domestic scouting director when Bridges started his scouting career as an area scout with the Angels. "We have a saying we use: CAA. Come as advertised. The player needs to show up to pro ball like the report says. If those don't match up after a while, the scout has an issue."

One of the things that these directors point to with bullet scouts is nailing the background, the makeup, the mentality of the player. We have almost an entire chapter about scouting makeup later in the book, including some of our favorite stories to help explain why scouts are so focused on this concept, while progressive clubs see it as less and less useful.

Makeup can be a separator amongst similar players, giving you margin for error because a player's background shows you how he handles tough or stressful situations. Stan Meek is currently the Marlins special assistant to the president of baseball operations, but he ran the drafts as amateur scouting director for the Fish from 2002 to 2017, landing Giancarlo Stanton, Christian Yelich, and José Fernández, among others.

Fernández is a great example of how a background can make you feel at ease about projecting a future. Meek recalls when Fernández told him about his third, ultimately successful attempt to defect: "He got on a boat three times. He was caught twice, went to jail at 13. The water is rough and it's night, he tells me it's so dark he can't even see the face of the person sitting next to him. Someone flips out of the boat, he didn't know who it was, but he instinctively dove in to save them. He put himself at huge risk, he may have never got back in that boat. Turned out it was his mother."

You can see how that one action in his past informed Fernández's mindset and ultimately his performance: "Before his first big league start at age 20 against the Mets, our scout that signed him, Brian Kraft, asked him if he was nervous. That's when Fernández put things in perspective for us all: 'When I left Cuba on the boat, I was scared. When they shot at me trying to get out of the boat, I was scared. In prison, I was scared. I ain't scared of David Wright.'" Fernández gave similar quotes to reporters after his first outing.

Every first-round pick has the ability to make the big leagues and perform well. Injuries are a significant, unpredictable variable, but if you can pair the ability with that mentality and you feel good about both on draft day, it's potent. Scouts love drafting multi-sport athletes, particularly football players. Playing multiple sports at a high level means both that there's elite athleticism and some measure of discipline and mental strength, as well as potential helium when the player's focus is eventually on just one sport.

Jeff Samardzija's father, Sam Sr., played semipro hockey, while Jeff was a first-round baseball and football talent at Notre Dame and Jeff's brother, Sam Jr., was an all-state football and baseball player, and is now Jeff's agent, as a VP for Wasserman Baseball. Hockey, football, and wrestling are the sports that scouts tend to point to that have the best makeup and general mental discipline that they like to see in baseball players.

A scout who declined to be named told us a story about seeing Jeff play in a high-profile USC–Notre Dame matchup where Samardzija caught 6 passes for 79 yards and a touchdown against the third-ranked team in the country, full of NFL players on the defense. After Samardzija had caught a few passes in a row, he started chirping at the defensive back covering him: "How is my ass showing you up on TV in front of 5 million people? What's your buddy's name on the other side [of the defense]? Go grab him and see if both of you can cover me." Sam Jr. concedes that sounds like his brother.

Some scouts will worry that a prospect can't handle The Moment, due either to nature or nurture. The lights are as bright as the player perceives them to be. Unless a player is competing in an intense state playoff game or in the College World Series, you can't truly know how an amateur prospect handles The Moment. Seeing Samardzija face the best that college football has to offer, on the biggest stage, having success, and asking for more would make a scout feel at ease with this aspect of his makeup. We've heard stories about Jeff being the first out of the dugout in the big leagues when there's a brawl. Sam Jr. explained to us that this is in their family's DNA.

We've also heard stories about baseball players with football or hockey backgrounds being the enforcer to their own teammates, when necessary. Positive anecdotes of this ilk (being prone to fighting on its own is a bad thing) were noted in the Braves draft room while Kiley worked there. Each scout got to pick one player of the hundreds on the board as the person they'd want on their side in a fight in a dark alley, akin to the old "you want him in a fox hole with you" designation. It was called the "All Fight Team."

There are two notable stories we've had confirmed along these lines, but we'll omit the players' names. One includes a rookie showing up a veteran on the field during his September call-up, after a final warning. It ended with a coach finding the rookie (whose career never matched his prospect pedigree) in the elevator at the team hotel, unconscious, missing a few teeth, with a broken nose. The other story is something similar, a standout underclassman (and eventual high pick) on a college team showing up a role-playing senior. A future top-10 pick took the offending sophomore (listed at 6'3"/210, hasn't met draft expectations in pro ball yet) and literally tossed him into his own locker.

Both of the enforcers have outperformed their draft position and prospect pedigree thus so far. The principal from the second story made the All Fight Team for a draft Kiley worked on. It's a small sample to be sure, and totally subjective, arguably regressive and problematic, but there's a reason scouts gravitate to these stories. Without context, this reads like run-of-the-mill, male-athlete bravado. But in both situations the player was sticking up for a teammate, an elder, enacting vigilante justice, and that is a force that can galvanize a ball club.

This is another reason why some clubs, as a strategy, take accomplished football players who have demonstrated baseball ability, but have limited baseball experience. In recent years, the Red Sox have drafted and signed Florida Gators quarterbacks Jeff Driskel (currently an NFL backup, but they own his MLB rights) and Feleipe Franks (hit 95 in a pre-draft bullpen after not playing in college) and Montana QB Caleb Hill. When Kiley interviewed for an entry-level, smaller-than-normal area scout job at the beginning of his career, he said he'd aggressively look for top football and basketball recruits with grade issues keeping them from enrolling at top programs. Calvin Johnson is a classic example of an elite athlete that has a surprisingly good swing (look up video of his BP with the Tigers when he was in the NFL) that could've played minor league baseball whenever he wanted and been a real prospect. (Tim Tebow is not.)

It can also manifest in a subtle adjustment to their training regimen, something that gives you a peek into their psyche. Tim Wilken was visiting the Cubs Double-A affiliate in Knoxville, Tennessee, and was chatting with D.J. LeMahieu, the 79th overall pick from two years prior out of LSU, who'd gone to a high school outside Detroit. "D.J., you really stay inside the ball. You're from Michigan. Did you like Jeter? Did you emulate him with your swing?"

LeMahieu gave an unexpected and surprisingly mature answer: "No. I mean, I like [Jeter], we're both from Michigan. If I grew up in a Sun Belt state, I might let it out a little more. But I might only hit outside four or five times a year up north, so I just kept my swing the same." Very few players at that stage in their careers, when they're getting attention from top-tier schools, have the self-awareness to know why they keep things simple at the plate, especially when it's something the veteran scout hadn't considered.

The Support Staff

We're broadly using the term "support staff" to mean people who are in the draft room and contribute to how players are ranked on the draft board, but who aren't scouts as we've defined them above. Every club also has some version of a director of mental skills, video analysts, or some other high-level opinion from a sect that isn't analytics or scouting. Every team has their own version of a personality test of sorts, testing the mental type and strength as a way to drill down more objectively on "makeup" with scores on adaptability, coachability, how the player deals with failure, an interview score, etc. Most teams have a version of an eye test to determine how a hitter's vision may impact his hitting ability. The more progressive clubs will also have a sports science group which broadly tries to measure the movements of prospects, drilling deeper on physical projection and body composition, looking deeply at motion-captured mechanics and more, all in an effort to project future athleticism, predict injuries, etc.

Analytically focused teams know that these areas, along with makeup, could serve as an effective tiebreaker, so they try to put a number or rating on things which have traditionally been seen as intangibles. For instance, we were told one club's makeup scale was broken by Louisville second baseman Nick Solak (a 2016 second-round pick of the Yankees, who has since been traded to Tampa Bay, then Texas, and had a strong rookie season in the big leagues), meaning he scored higher than they thought was possible. Clubs without formal models for makeup also felt like Solak was one of the better bets for intangibles amongst top-round prospects, but in those cases it impacted his position on the draft board in more of a "do you like him more than this guy?" manual, eye-balled sort of way.

Some teams will have a more cluttered organizational chart at the top, with a number of vague titles of highly paid—and typically well-regarded—evaluators who float around departments, with titles like special assistant to the GM, vice president of scouting, director of player personnel, and so on. This varies greatly and sometimes it's a scouting director who has been promoted in title and salary, and essentially fills the scouting director role, with the scouting director title going to a protégé that's learning a leadership role on the fly.

The front office will also have a handful of other people who mostly work in the amateur department. The exact titles will vary, but the main roles are: operations manager, coordinator, assistant scouting director, and baseball operations assistant. The operations manager will handle the logistics and budgeting of supplies for scouts, summer travel teams that the club sponsors, private workouts, the draft room, and administrative or rules-based support.

The coordinator is mostly the scheduler, letting the staff of 20-ish scouts and the other 10 or so floating evaluators know which games to be at on which days, based on changing game times, weather, scouting preferences, updated medical information, and, particularly, putting together scouting runs.

"Runs" have a much different meaning in baseball than they do if you've just finished a buffet at Golden Corral. In baseball it means there's a particularly efficient way to see a number of top prospects in a short amount of time, usually around a major metropolitan area. We sometimes rely on these people to also help us put together our own runs, though our needs (often top-two-round players are the focus) don't always align with the clubs' needs on runs for their scouts (players they are targeting in any round).

The assistant scouting director role overlaps with these first two, but has a higher-level scouting focus. This role is often an additional national crosschecker that's based in the office and is on track to be the scouting director one day. Other times it's someone who is there to be a third person in the aforementioned administration, scheduling tasks while also getting to scout some. Or they may be the senior person of these three. Lastly, the baseball ops assistant is usually an entry-level employee that's just finished an internship or two and is available to any department, but usually has a specialty or track they'd like to be on, filling some or all of the functions of the other three support staff members. Increasingly, that's in support of modern techniques, like working with the analytics group on models, doing video scouting and analyzing TrackMan or Blast Motion data.

We'll hit this topic again later, but it's also important to note that, while it doesn't usually have a full-time employee dedicated to it, the best organizations have a link between amateur scouting and player development. Many teams still don't, or it's an inconsistent one handled at a high level (VP of scouting and development) that can sometimes only focus on top prospects. We've mentioned many times at FanGraphs that the New York Yankees are seen as leaders in this area, but the Los Angeles Dodgers and others also excel. The key is to have open communication and aligned goals between departments, which is more rare than it should be.

Who Is In the Draft Room?

Combined, crosscheckers and area scouts comprise a roughly 20-person staff, with the amateur support staff, executives/scouts/coaches from other departments and floating high-level evaluators adding another eight to 12 sets of eyeballs that are various levels of available during the spring to see targeted players.

Beyond those 30 or so evaluators, there are a number of other people in the room at various times who still haven't been mentioned. Team doctors and members of the medical staff will be in at times. The team president and/or owner is often in the room for the first pick or two, as is at least one member of the public relations staff, to coordinate press releases and post-pick interviews for the GM and scouting director.

Depending on the club, the analytics staff (more in the "Draft Model" section in a few pages) can range from just a couple people to five or more. Ambassador-type special assistants are also floating around: former or occasionally current players that take a stipend (or no salary) to work about 30 days per year, go to team events, see/speak with players similar to themselves, etc.

With in excess of 50 people making appearances in the draft room, there's a need for lots of space. Often the draft room is the home MLB clubhouse in the team's stadium, a giant all-purpose room in the offices, or a couple of normal-sized hotel ballrooms combined. Some teams also handle the draft at their spring training home since the offices are much quieter and holding pre-draft workouts at those stadiums is much easier than at the MLB stadium.

The area scout meetings start this process, about a month before the draft, where each area scout meets with a small- or medium-sized group of decision-makers and support staff to talk about every player they've "turned in," short-hand for recommended to sign them for some amount of money. After this week, some area scouts aren't around the draft room again, as some teams limit it to just crosscheckers and office staff in the room with the director, with the crosscheckers speaking for their area scouts and staying in close touch with them for updates.

Some clubs send the area scouts out after their meetings for a break or to see games (this is around the college postseason), keep a few around throughout the process on a rotating basis, then bring them all back for draft day so they feel more involved in the process than if they were at home. The draft room itself will break for days at a time for the sake of everyone's sanity, and when lots of games are happening.

The bottom line is every club agrees that it's unwieldy to have every evaluator in the room for the weeks leading up to the draft (it's much harder to reach consensus and it gets cramped) and it's impractical to not scout the late games, so clubs juggle these issues differently. One end of the spectrum is no area scouts present after their presentation of their area, and some try to keep the whole scouting staff as engaged as they can be, a treat of sorts for a job well done.

How to Out-Scout Your Competition

Scooter Gennett was a 16th-round draft pick out of high school in 2009, didn't sign for a huge bonus, was never a top prospect, and wasn't even a notable big leaguer until his breakout seasons in 2017 and 2018. This lower profile was due mostly to his stature: listed at 5'10"/185, in an era before shorter players like Mookie Betts and José Altuve were getting MVP consideration and teams were more biased against small players.

If you dug a little deeper, you could see that how Gennett talked about hitting indicated a deeper understanding and vision, rather than just being more physically talented than his competition. We spoke with an evaluator who has followed Gennett closely, but wanted to stay on background: "He had an uncanny ability to see the ball. If you talk to him, he's a hitting genius. He wouldn't know what anyone was talking about in today's hitting environment. Recognize pitch, get the bat on the ball, he was like Rain Man. He's not talking about exit velo and launch angle; he's old school, he's not that guy. He'll talk about mechanics and getting through the ball, contact points, swing plane. He sees early, recognizes early.

"There was a high school game that I spoke to him afterwards. He went 1-for-4 with two strikeouts. He complained to me that the umpire's zone was all over the place, pretty standard stuff from a kid that talented after a game like that. He said, 'That ball was 3.5 inches off the black. I will roll over every time to second base if I swing at it.' He broke down every at-bat instantly, not just complaining, but pointing out how much the umpire's zone, and what pitches he was miscalling, by how many inches, and in what direction. He wasn't even thinking about the pitcher."

Kiley still asks amateur and low-level pro hitters questions to see if one will answer a question with that kind of specificity; no others have. This seemed to be a window in Gennett's thinking and detail his superior vision in action, the kind elite big league hitters need, further underlining why his stature wouldn't hold him back. Even knowing this and having conviction about the player because of it couldn't have predicted Gennett's career trajectory, just that he was someone that would be worth drafting. "Why didn't he hit in Milwaukee and he did in Cincinnati?" the evaluator said. "I don't know."

Stan Meek has an example of head-on-a-swivel scouting landing the Marlins one of the best players in baseball. "[Marlins scout David] Crowson goes to see Tyler Skaggs in high school," Meek said, "and calls me after the game to say there was a pretty good lefty on the other team, a junior for next year for Westlake named Yelich. At that point, we got on him and stayed on him."

"We got kinda lucky. His throwing wasn't good, didn't like him much at third base or first base, but he could run so we thought maybe he could play the outfield. We thought he'd go ahead of us because of the bat, but the position and arm scared some teams so he slid to us at 23 [overall]."

The backup plan if Yelich didn't get there was another position player that's received a number of MVP votes over the years, though less than Yelich. "Had we not taken Yelich, we would've taken Andrelton Simmons. He went three picks ahead of us in the second round or we would've been thrilled to get him there. Lots of people had him in as a pitcher—over half the teams did—but we liked him as a shortstop. He wasn't a runner but he just kept making plays [at shortstop] and I saw him pitch—up to 96 with a plus hammer. It was real. He would've been a big money saver if we took him in the first round."

"Getting your pocket picked" is a common term in draft rooms, for when the player you target goes a pick or two ahead of you. When a number of targets go in succession, more than you were expecting, your draft board has "blown up." We can't say the team, but a club that picked just before the Marlins took Yelich were set to take Yelich, but a player they liked slightly more surprisingly got to their pick and they passed. That player didn't get to Double-A.

Scouts have told us stories about other high-profile near misses. The Astros were set to take Nolan Ryan in the 12th round in 1965, the first year of the MLB Draft, but the Mets took him 10 picks earlier. Wilken had two near misses he recalls. When with the Cubs, he had a private workout with Matt Moore and was set to take him in the eighth round in 2007. Two picks earlier, the Rays took him and Wilken still believes that the Rays' (his former employer a few years earlier) area scout Jack Spencer was closer to Moore and he tipped them off to the Cubs' interest after a pre-draft workout.

When with Toronto, Wilken recalls that his boss, baseball legend Pat Gillick, liked to take tough signability high school players. Once, they were set to take a high school pitcher from Tampa in the seventh round of the

1991 Draft, but Gillick instead decided to take Carlton Loewer, who ended up not signing, going to Mississippi State, and going in the first round in 1994 en route to a four-year MLB career. The initial target, the prep pitcher from Tampa, went off the board before the Jays' next pick, at the top of the eighth round to the Twins: Brad Radke.

One of the clubs Kiley worked for had their pocket picked in the third round and the room was crushed. The player they ended up with was a good bit lower on the board than the one they wanted; ultimately both are bench players in the big leagues, nice finds in the third round but the difference was hardly worth the angst.

Having a closer relationship with the player appeared to help the Rays land Matt Moore and also landed Brian Bridges a job with the Braves. After the area scout that covered Georgia and helped draft Jason Heyward, Al Goetz, left the Braves in 2007 just after the draft to become an agent, Bridges was uniquely positioned. "I got to know [Heyward] more than anybody. I saw him play 18 or 19 games that spring because he wouldn't swing the bat, getting pitched around. I knew the kid, knew the family, trusted the ability, you don't see that kind very often. He had the God-given ability to do whatever he wanted to in the game. I brought my own video camera to all the games so that I would have all of his swings on video."

Bridges was covering Georgia as an area scout for the Marlins at the time. They drafted Matt Dominguez at 12th overall, just before the Braves took Heyward 14th overall. Goetz left the Braves before they had signed Heyward, so hiring someone who knew Heyward to replace Goetz was a priority. "Roy [Clark, Braves scouting director] told [Braves general manager John Schuerholz] that there's only one guy that knew Heyward better than us. So Mr. Schuerholz told Roy to hire that guy. I had to go down and throw BP every day to Heyward. It was a terrible drive, but I had fun, it was a blast."

Heyward was misevaluated by some clubs that put too much weight on the spring high school season, because he didn't swing often and it left them feeling like they didn't have enough information to take him high in the draft, despite the tools and summer looks.

Working around that issue with a different player in the same 2007 draft, Meek successfully isolated the good qualities of a position player with historic tools and looked past the concerns that caused other teams to pass.

"He didn't make that much contact," Meek said, "wasn't scouted much at all that spring, even though he showed 70 raw power at Area Codes that summer at age 16. He was in Southern California, where 20 scouts will show up at a game between a ball being hit and it falling over the fence. There were one or two scouts at most of his games in the spring.

"He swung at everything. Ball out of the hand, he's swinging. I told our area guy to just chart his swings at pitches in the zone. [Tim McDonnell] lived in Fullerton and I was making him go twice a week to the Valley to see this guy and chart his at-bats. I killed him with those drives. But then he calls me and says that 'He's starting to make contact in the zone.'

"I sent in a pro scout to see him and Matt Dominguez on a double-up on the same day. He asks me, 'You're taking this guy at 12, right?' and I say, 'Don't know if we will,' then I start talking about him as a third baseman, thinking he's talking about Dominguez and he cuts me off. 'No, I mean the other guy, Mike Stanton.' I tell him we don't have to take him anywhere near that early, may be able to get him in the third round. He tells me there's no way you get that guy in the second round." Stanton changed his first name for professional purposes to Giancarlo in 2012.

The Marlins took Dominguez rather than Heyward (31.1 WAR through 2019) at twelve, then took Stanton in the second round, 76th overall (39.3). In retrospect, given Stanton's age on draft day, if all of this happened today exactly the same way Stanton would go at least a couple dozen picks higher just because of that (more on why later). "He was 17 on draft day, birthday in November, so he was really young for the class. [J.T.] Realmuto was 19, we always looked at age, another tool, like makeup. Friends with other teams told me they brought Stanton in for pre-draft workouts and he was hitting balls out of stadiums. I still don't know why they didn't take him."

Working around a bad scouting look (watching a player play poorly, not showing his full potential) is another art, an advanced skill that helps the best scouting groups to separate players better than others. Angels South Florida area scout Mike Silvestri (disclosure: he worked with Kiley with the Braves) was all over high school infielder Sean Rodriguez in the 2003 Draft.

His scouting director, Donny Rowland recounts the first time came he came in that spring to see Rodriguez: "He was playing a terrible team, he popped up, got pitched around. I could see the plus arm and actions at shortstop. We asked for BP after the game to get some sort of look and I saw explosive hands, some buggy whip. Mike is down in the dumps at dinner after the game and I ask him where he'd take Rodriguez. He's surprised; he didn't think I'd like him. He says second or third round."

On draft day, that request from Silvestri was still an option for Rowland. "In the second round, the board had completely disintegrated. We were down to Rodriguez or Anthony Whittington, a 6'5" lefty from West Virginia. I call timeout to poll the room, these two are back-to-back on the board. Whittington was a paramedic in the off-season, tough guy, hunter, fisher. The room says the lefty, so we take him. I only saw him twice but I was good with it. Then we shift to the next pick. Who are we taking? Rodriguez isn't getting there. The pick keeps getting closer and we're getting excited and nervous. He's all by himself on the board, no one else is even close to him. Somehow he made it." The Angels took Rodriguez 90th overall in 2003 and he produced the third-most WAR of anyone that signed in that round, just behind Shaun Marcum and Matt Harrison.

The Draft Model

The biggest aspect of the draft room that we haven't covered yet is analytics. Obviously back in the Moneyball draft of 2002, this didn't really exist in most draft rooms, or it was a solitary, mostly-ignored person, which was why Oakland was able to pick some low-hanging, mathematical fruit during that era, plucking Nick Swisher and Joe Blanton with this approach. With the addition of TrackMan at the college level in 2014, the amount and quality of data, particularly at the highest levels and generated by the best players, has exploded. With this new data, a bigger staff is needed to sort through it, and a much more complete, and often different picture of certain players emerges.

The short version is that as the corporatization and MBA-style or hedge fund–style analysis proliferated around the sport, the focus around baseball with "Big Data" was in minimizing risk and analyzing objective data for an edge. This is an extrapolation of what was done in *Moneyball* by Oakland. The fear amongst scouts after that book became popular is that scouts would be replaced by an army of analysts. In a way, the opposite happened. At least for a while, scouting actually became more important because many analysts concluded that their opinion was the most predictive piece of information about many players, amateur ones specifically. With TrackMan later available at the amateur level, it's become possible, in some cases, to better summate aspects of a player's ability with that data than with your best scouts seeing just a game or two of the player during the spring.

With this happening, we saw a data arms race begin in draft rooms just like it did at the big league level years earlier. After the market adjusted to Oakland using first-level stats (on-base percentage, walk rate) to target college players, the edge was in analyzing that data better, then it moved to analyzing the first wave of optical tracking and radar-based technology (PITCHf/x,

TrackMan), and now we're reaching the end of that wave now that every team is doing it and into a new wave of new sources of data that we'll detail in Chapter 12.

Astros GM Jeff Luhnow came from corporate America and top management consulting firm McKinsey and made his name running the Cardinals drafts from 2006 to 2009. His standout picks during that period allowed him to jump from having zero baseball background to being a GM in six years, right as radar-based technology was emerging. He and Houston staffers quickly sifted through the new data and better understood what components drove success (especially as far as pitching is concerned), who had those components, who could be taught them, and how. Houston used that new edge to make the Astros organization highly competitive, and Luhnow's eventual head of amateur, international, and pro scouting, Mike Elias, would later be hired as the GM of the Baltimore Orioles for the 2019 season. Elias is now installing Astros-style processes in Baltimore and is going through the same sort of rebuild that he helped Luhnow execute when they joined the Astros.

We mention all that to say that draft models have now become an inescapable, but sometimes reviled, part of the modern draft room. These models use TrackMan data from top colleges and a number of high school events, as well as standard statistics, scouting reports, publicly available rankings, medical information, historical draft trends, and just about anything else you can think of, like biomechanical data and various sports science or psychological profiles.

We'll get into more detail about models in a later chapter, but there are some broad takeaways from their impact on draft rooms. First, models vary a fair amount from team to team and will spit out results based on what you put into them and how you tell it to weigh them. The Yankees drafts run off a model, but it's thought to be a more scouting-focused amateur operation, and we've been told that scouting reports make up a large percentage of their overall evaluation. This makes it hard for us and teams to predict which players they're on, since we obviously don't see their reports. The most intellectually progressive clubs (Houston, Baltimore, Milwaukee, Cleveland) will empower their model even more, at the expense of scouting reports and scout input. These teams can be easier to predict, as the types of players they prefer (high exit velo, high spin curveball, young-for-the-class hitters, performs well at showcases, etc.) are based on information we have.

The actual impact of a model in these terms is either using all non-scouting data (historical trends, TrackMan, etc.) to add context to a scouting report (a more Dodgers or Yankees type approach) or taking scouting mostly out of the hands of your scouts and into the computers of your analysts (the progressive approach) with reports as one of many key inputs.

Looking back at past cases, either approach can be correct. Aaron Judge was performing just okay as a junior at Fresno State and most draft models/analysts didn't like him. Judge's power, body, and swing-and-miss profile were rightly compared to Giancarlo Stanton by scouts (both were California guys), but in a pre-exit-velo world, draft models didn't have them even close: Stanton had 56 HR in the big leagues through his age-21 season, while in 169 college games through his age-21 season, Judge hit 18 homers in the Mountain West/WAC conference. Four years after being the 32nd overall pick, Judge posted an 8.3 WAR rookie season, 1 WAR better than Stanton's best season.

On the flip side, Corbin Martin had a checkered three seasons at Texas A&M, never settling into a consistent weekend starter role that his talent suggested he should. Many scouts used this underperformance to question his aptitude or toughness, while Houston focused more on his strikeout rate and three nasty pitches that all graded as plus, based on TrackMan metrics measured when he pitched well in the Cape Cod League (henceforth referenced to as "the Cape"). He slid to the 56th overall pick in 2017, rose to become FanGraphs 50th-ranked prospect in baseball before the 2019 season, made his MLB debut that year, then became the centerpiece of the Zack Greinke trade, even though he had just blown out his elbow and required Tommy John surgery, shelving him until late 2020 at the earliest.

This is all to say that there essentially aren't any hard-and-fast, universal truisms when it comes to the draft, or draft models. We don't love the idea of ignoring makeup completely, or ignoring stats completely, but there are a couple teams that do those things and they've all had picks where they beat the industry with that approach. In the same way that we can guess what a draft model emphasizes after a couple years of picks using the same approach, after a few years of seeing who a club picks and hearing about their process via industry gossip or observing their scouts, we have a decent idea if they're a top-, middle-, or lower-tier operation even without watching the draft room firsthand.

It's also important to point out that scouts, who mostly don't like the corporatization of the draft or draft models in general, love data: 60-yard dash times, home-to-first times, pop times for catchers, velocity for pitchers, and so on. They collect numbers and analyze them to make lists of players just like everyone else in the game does. Rowland tells us about how he made a weighted OFP (Overall Future Potential) system in 1999 that weighted tools based on specific positional profiles; that's the earliest we'd heard of a system of that type. Former scout and current agent Hank Sargent tells us about how other scouts, decades ago, would tell him about what sort of triple-slash lines to look for when doing pro coverage of minor league teams. It gets touchy when a number is being used to replace the ones that a scout is collecting.

What We Can Get On and Off the Record

As you'll see from the rest of this book, we can get scouting directors to talk on the record about their picks and their background. It's basically impossible to get a director of analytics (the department is sometimes called "Research and Development") on the record. We could get their boss (general managers) on the record about analytics, but the quotes are often benign, evasive snoozers since they are wary of giving away a competitive advantage or even indicating where they are on the spectrum of trusting traditional data (scouting reports, makeup grades) vs. more progressive data (sports science, TrackMan, and other tech).

It's very common to hear executives from clubs in the traditional half of baseball vigorously defend their use of analytics with the media. Every specific detail they give about "having an analytics department" or having "proprietary metrics" is technically true. That said, it's a pretty good indicator your favorite team isn't using analytics as much as they could/should when they're vociferously defending their use of analytics to the public. These questions are usually asked of executives when things are going wrong, and front office folks don't want to openly admit to being behind. Some traditional teams take a more honest approach and privately acknowledge to us or other media people focused on the topic that they only use analytics in some sorts of decisions, not all of them. One team proudly calls their draft room process "anti-lytics." Another scout told us he wished FanGraphs and other publications that analyze the draft as part of their baseball coverage "never existed, so we could just go watch games like we used to."

We can triangulate where these teams stand based on whom they pick and, secondly, from what we hear from principals (scouts, analysts) who can only speak with us off the record or on background. There are plenty of stories we hear from one source that later get substantiated, for instance about how one GM won't enter the draft room until draft day and has barely any input on the process, while another makes literally every pick himself for all 40 rounds. We also hear from area scouts who know they can't get a player because he isn't "model friendly" and so it doesn't matter what their report says about the player, since there isn't enough weight on reports in the model, much less the scout's individual report.

Thirdly, we can usually get an idea of organizational priorities based on staffing. Those most progressive clubs are reducing the number of scouts they employ almost yearly, often with one or two large culling times that send panic through the scouting industry. Others, like the Yankees and Dodgers, seem to value scouting and analytics as essential and weigh them differently depending on the circumstance, using their financial muscle to staff and budget both approaches in the top five or ten clubs in the game by any measure.

From looking at picks, we can tell that the Pirates prioritize tall pitchers, but don't care as much about the age of high school prospects. It's an ongoing punchline in the industry that the Indians will draft any high school prospect that is 17 years old on draft day and that Houston will take any high-velocity pitcher with a high-spin-rate breaking ball, regardless of their other qualities, often disregarding makeup completely. Some of these things are shrewd uses of a model or of leveraging organizational strengths, while others are more over-fitting historical trends to the present, focusing on the trees but losing the forest.

The age-on-draft-day research can be read a few different ways and Kiley did the research when he worked for a club. It doesn't mean much for pitchers in college or high school; you'd rather the pitcher be younger all things being equal, but age alone doesn't move the needle in the first round. The logic is that a velo spike changes a pitcher's projection but it can come at any time, so being six months younger is good but not a big factor as it's only a physical consideration.

It's more meaningful for hitters. Pitchers dictate the action on the field, so being a hitter that's a year younger than the pitcher has value. There's the physical factor, that you could get stronger when you're the age of the pitcher, but there's also the natural selection–style consideration in your performance. If the younger hitter can still stand out as a supreme talent when older, more physical and varied-in-style pitchers are dictating the action, that's a very meaningful ability to adapt and survive. Comparing that hitter's overall posture to that of a pitcher just throwing a ball at the mitt seems pretty different.

The takeaway could be to significantly move old- or young-for-the-class hitters based on these historical findings (it could be up to a full round of adjustment), but we think that generic adjustment is overfitting the historical data and prefer to take the logic behind the adjustment and apply it as much as we think it applies to each individual hitter. Players with limited reps and gangly bodies that will mature are indicators of improvement relative to performance thus far, so young hitters like that may get a bigger boost, while those with tons of high-level reps and mature frames would get a smaller adjustment as they're more of a finished product, and so on. You can see how clubs would approach this specific age-adjustment issue in their models very differently.

We've heard one example of this general approach that we'll anonymize. A club in the middle of the progressive/traditional spectrum got a new group of top executives from a very progressive club. Therefore, they had a strong scouting department, but wanted to run their first draft off of a model, with limited scout input. They ranked every turned-in player, then a player expected to go at least a dozen picks ahead of them fell into their laps, unexpectedly.

They hadn't prepared for this to happen and hadn't been scouting the college pitcher down the stretch. The model said to take him, but the scouts didn't want to, as they weren't comfortable with the pick. The team picked the player the model dictated. This player will likely make the big leagues, but was a late first-round pick and appears to be a non-impact prospect. It's not a disaster, but there are limits when trying to overrule scouts and replace their intuition completely with a model. This binary, draft-or-don't-draft choice dynamic would change a good bit with the expected addition of trading picks in the next CBA, or almost certainly the one after that, as teams are making implicit decisions on every pick by not trading up for them.

After chatting about that instance, Bridges told us he has a different approach. "I don't do it that way, keeping who's popular in play no matter what the information is. You have to listen to people, the ones who are at the games. Your words mean something. If you don't like them, we aren't taking them. Can't get too far into either approach, or you'll make a bunch of mistakes. We valued the whole picture. Patton was like this; he could motivate anyone, he was a good leader, he didn't just plow his opinion through because he'd make a mistake."

In Kiley's first year in Bridges' room, he was amazed when Bridges would look at the picks the Braves had, where guys were ranked, where they'd probably be picked, and where they'd not be affordable, and take perfectly fine players off the board just because he couldn't see a scenario where they'd pick the player. Sometimes it was makeup that he wasn't comfortable with, a signability number that didn't match the club's value, a sort of player (high school righty with a head whack) that he didn't like to take with a high pick, etc. He just carved away at the board like a sculptor, until just the players he wanted were left. It would probably give an inclusive, progressive executive hives to see a first-round talent taken off the board because he wasn't the right flavor, but you could feel confident that if the player was on the board when the action started, Bridges felt really good about taking him, knew everything he needed to know about them.

We spoke with an agent who recounted a conversation he had with a scouting director of a club that's known to be model-reliant in their drafting. A couple weeks before the draft, the agent asked the director why they aren't showing interest in one of his clients, a high school pitcher. The agent rattled off three or four qualities that he knew fit this team's type, similar to other high school pitchers they'd taken recently. The scouting director shrugged and said they couldn't take the agent's player because his arm action was "inverted," an elbow that's higher than the shoulder at foot strike, something their model had essentially forbade them from drafting and is at least a yellow flag for almost every team. The agent immediately rattled off that this team's top four pitchers on their big league team were all inverted, too.

The scouting director simply replied, "Yeah, I know."

Other Considerations

An important issue for scouting directors to handle is budgeting their department. Directors would love to approve every budget decision that would incrementally improve their information in the draft room or staff morale, but every organization has owner-imposed limits.

This decision starts with how many scouts to have on staff, with exact roles, responsibilities, titles, contract lengths, and moving expenses as the variables to make the pieces fit. We know of one area scout who's a former regional crosschecker (let go from that role when his director was fired) but now covers both of the traditionally separate areas in Florida for his club, all but the panhandle of the state. As an area scout, it's a lower-stress job, he's home with his family most nights of the year, and his club pays him the salary for both area scout jobs that he's filling, so he's making low-end national crosschecker money without the ludicrous travel schedule that comes with it. Covering most of Florida means he gets players drafted every year and his club is paying a standard rate for what they're getting.

A handful of clubs—and the Dodgers are a well-known example in the industry—will get these crosschecker-level evaluators who don't currently have that title for whatever reason (blocked with their current/previous team or became a free agent when their department was subject to a new regime's house-cleaning) and pay them at the top of the area scout scale to ensure that they have a top-notch evaluator on staff who is happy with their role, working in talent-rich areas.

Traditionally, if a team hires a first-time scout to an area job and they quickly show potential for promotion, the scout will get antsy or get permission requested from rival clubs to interview for crosschecker jobs. So even a perfect hire becomes a problem for teams to solve within a few years. What the Dodgers do is a logical way to invest a little extra and potentially get a lot more in the way of quality information. Other clubs, the Yankees being an example, have seemingly limitless spots on staff for different sorts of crosscheckers and specialists who focus on hitting or pitching or biomechanics or the Cape, whereas other clubs won't have much of a headcount beyond the traditional titles we've listed above.

Some clubs on the intellectually progressive end of the ledger are notorious for nickel-and-diming their scouts on hotel prices and other expenses. This may seem small, but getting 100-plus nights in the same hotel chain (Marriott is the choice for about 99 percent of scouts) means status, upgrades, points, and free off-season vacations. It is not difficult to make $5,000 in hidden value in a calendar year just in hotel points if you have a regional or national focus, with national crosscheckers and directors possibly making thousands more than that on hotels, and again separately in airline points. Delta is the airline of choice, particularly for scouts East of the Mississippi, and National is the preference on rental cars.

Disclosure: Kiley may have played the travel points game competitively with coworkers during his time working for the Braves. He may also be spending his nest egg of points for the next decade. Eric dislikes big corporations and stays in weird bed and breakfasts and boutique hotels when possible. His experiences have varied.

Anyway, mandating that the after-tax hotel bill be under $100 to $110 (depending on the year or team) means the scout can't stay in their preferred chain in larger cities, forcing them to choose a lesser room last minute via Priceline or other hotel deal sites. Effectively, the team is making a scout be 10–20 percent less comfortable in nights away from home (many scouts have young children) while simultaneously taking a few thousand dollars in off-season vacation points off the table. This is a real consideration for many scouts, and it may eventually be a problem for analytically inclined teams to hire and retain good scouts because of seemingly stupid stuff like this.

Staffing considerations and travel expenses are the two big parts of a department budget, but there are all kinds of other, smaller decisions to be made. If a club wants to get to know prospects better by running a scout team in the summer or fall (where the coaches are your scouts and you pick the prospects for the team), that will get you better info for the draft room, but will set you back possibly tens of thousands of dollars. Do you want to spend $50,000 for a series of touchscreens to make a virtual draft board, or stick with the magnet system scouts have been using for decades?

Another method to get better information on the draft board and improve morale is when a whole staff meets throughout the year (dozens of hotel rooms, large ballroom, flights, four-figure dinner tabs, etc.) to review the draft board and build camaraderie. If you're an organization that lets the model make decisions, where area scouts are often first-time scouts who are paid at the bottom of the scale, then improving morale and communication a bit for $15,000 for three-day meetings a half dozen times a year may seem inefficient. If a club is already paying area scouts at the top of the scale to get slightly better information, that $100,000 to improve the outcome is less than the $125,000 bonus given to the lowest-grade prospect you sign in the draft, so it seems like a bargain.

The Basics of Finding Players

As an area scout, your job "begins" the day after the draft ends, but in reality, you've already done some work for the next draft class over a year in advance. It's standard for scouts with superlative attention to detail to pay attention to underclassmen in any game. A Florida vs. LSU game may feature over 30 draftable players of various draft classes, but many or even most scouts won't pay more than marginal attention to players not eligible for the draft a few months later. A common refrain is "I don't scout for drafts that I don't have a contract for." A way for us to identify which scouts tend to be correct more than their peers is to find the ones who preternaturally absorb this extra info.

With that in mind, most scouts are getting their first look at the draft class in the weeks after the previous draft, all in the month of June. The

Cape Cod League, over a dozen lesser collegiate summer leagues, and Collegiate Team USA all begin play in June, while the high school summer showcase season also gets underway. The college circuit is pretty simple. A bunch of teams play in a traditional league format, while USA Baseball has a large trials roster that scrimmages against itself for weeks before playing in international competition both in the US and abroad (usually Asia and/or Cuba). The specifics of the high school summer showcase circuit are a little more complicated, so we'll save that for the next section and a deep dive in Chapter 6.

Scouts get a representative sample of most of the top of the draft class by going to just a few events, or covering a summer league or two. At this point, every scout on staff files what is called a "follow report," or a slimmed-down version of the full report you file on players the following spring. Instead of grading every tool, noting performance, getting makeup information, signability, medical history, and a long multi-look scouting history over months like they'll be able to do in the spring, the scout just writes a skeletal paragraph on every player they see who they think worthy of going back to see in the spring. It's often as simple as one sentence about the event and length of the look; another about performance; another about physical appearance and athleticism; another one or two about tools, projection, and areas for improvement; then a handful of words about the group or round the player fits in, often with a qualifier if it was a particularly short look. They also bucket players into groups or tiers based on past experience. Something like "Group A" might be a first-round talent, while "Group B" is Round 2–3, and so on. Scouts may also put a projected bonus on the player, especially ones near the top of the draft, as a more specific way of indicating how much they like the player.

This is a relatively low-stress time for amateur scouts, with sometimes weeks between assignments. Even when they're grinding it out at, say, a weeklong event with games all day, there's downtime at the field once it's clear most of the players involved aren't really prospects. This is when you get a lot of scouts (and we can be guilty of this, too) half paying attention and just waiting to be impressed by someone—anyone—on the field full of players they know little about beyond their college commitment.

As these events pile up, scouts put together their list of follows for the summer. Crosscheckers and directors prioritize a chunk of the high-profile regional and national events to see the cream of the rising senior crop across the whole country, while area scouts see one or two of those big events and all the local action in their area, often events that are attended by only area scouts.

As school begins in September, the summer events wind down and the focus shifts to college players now back on campus and their scrimmages and scout days (colleges have a showcase of just their draft-eligible players) while there's a few windows for high school players to play in travel tournaments around holidays, or notable weekend events, like the Florida Diamond Club (a scout-run showcase and games for prep players in Florida and Puerto Rico) or the WWBA World Championships in Jupiter, Florida (where more than a hundred travel teams play on the tens of fields at the Cardinals and Marlins joint spring training facility, all day, for five days in front of 250-plus scouts).

This winds down in November and there's little to scout until late January when junior colleges start playing and the major, Southern-based colleges start playing preseason scrimmages. For a couple weeks, junior colleges get lots of attention from all scouts as they're the only game in town until mid-February when the college season begins, roughly when the warmest-climate high school seasons begin.

This is when the spring has started in earnest, and decisions have to be made about prioritizing coverage. If a team is picking 30th and there's a player that looks like he'll go in the top five, but even with an injury would go 15th, the team will shift top evaluators to more reasonable targets. A 10th look on a player you might draft is more valuable than the second look on a player you almost certainly won't be able to.

On any given day, every scout has multiple options for which games to go to. Scouts are scrambling to get early looks at every player of interest in their area and chasing down rumors of "pop-up" guys, a term for late-rising, previously unknown players. The earlier an area scout can wrap their arms around their area, put each player in the right evaluative bucket for their bosses, the earlier the scout can get key players crosschecked and the area scout can focus on doing the little things that make key players easy to draft, like assessing signability, makeup, etc.

It might seem silly for area scouts to stress out about getting a player crosschecked in early March vs. early April as both dates are well clear of draft day, but there are a handful of examples every year where it matters. If a player gets hurt, or isn't well-known and has a short season, there are teams every year that like these players but can't draft them specifically because they didn't have their top scouts see them enough. Particularly for the warm weather states that can be scouted in late January, area scouts' top priority is to get all top-five-round prospects turned in (a full report is written), properly ranked, and prioritized to be crosschecked as soon as possible. As we said, once that's done, then the scout can focus on making that player more draftable by getting to know them, their family, their agent, their medical history, seeing them play another half dozen times, etc. (Once this process is done and they've "finished" their area, some scouts will also use this time to branch out to see out-of-area players for personal growth.) Once draft time approaches, the area scout has a meeting with their crosscheckers to go over their list and prepare themselves for their more formal meeting in front of the front office to present their area and talk about every player they want to draft in an ideal world.

The Summer Showcase Circuit

The summer showcase season is a little harder to pin down far in advance. There are the tentpole events—the Perfect Game National Showcase days after the draft, East Coast Pro in late July, Area Codes Games in August, the televised Under Armour and Perfect Game All-American Games—but the details change a bit each year. The high school version of Team USA (the U18 squad) also has a couple stages of week-long trials, traditionally at its HQ in Cary, North Carolina, but that event (known as Tournament of Stars) changed in 2019, indicative of possible larger changes in the showcase calendar.

Showcase baseball has exploded in the last decade, increasing the reps and opportunities for players and the efficiency of travel for teams/scouts, but in less traditional team-focused environments. Pitchers are indirectly encouraged to throw to the radar gun in one- or two-inning stints and, of course, knowing that's what they're training for to kickoff this year of being scouted, these pitchers often train more for the gun than the game situation. Hitters, similarly, are sometimes more geared for batting practice homers than live pitching.

But the bigger issue is that kids have to pay hundreds of dollars to go to most of these showcases (run by for-profit companies), while the games-only tournaments put on by scouts are usually free. This is why MLB is stepping in, partnering with Team USA and the teams to put on more free and games-based events rather than letting companies like Perfect Game, The Baseball Factory, and Prep Baseball Report operate without any oversight in handling many future top MLB players. In 2019, Tournament of Stars was replaced by

MLB's PDP (Player Development Pipeline) three-week event in Bradenton, Florida, at IMG Academy, housing and training 80 of the top prep players both for the benefit of scouts and as a trials event for Team USA. IMG is one of the high school facilities that has a TrackMan unit, so teams got data from all of these games, subsidized by MLB.

Some summer scouting icing on the cake is getting to see top players at multiple positions, as rosters can get stretched near the end of events and if a top pitcher wants to take a few cuts in the game, the scouts running many of the events are curious. This is also where a lot of catcher conversions for prep players are first tried out.

Reds vice president of player personnel Chris Buckley advises to take these out-of-position moments in the summer or spring to inform a holistic view of the player: "When you go see top high school arms—[Roy] Halladay, [Adam] Wainwright, [Zack] Greinke, [Chris] Carpenter—there's a lot of lefty hitters, bats third in the lineup, plays shortstop or center field types. MacKenzie Gore, Hunter Greene, Rick Ankiel all fit this, too. They're baseball players, and you see a lot more specialization now. If you're going in to see Greinke, come in for two days to see him play shortstop, then pitch the next game; he was a real prospect as a shortstop. We took Tony Santillan and he was real at third base, Michael Lorenzen same out in center field. Then you know the athlete box is really checked before they even pitch. After two full games and two full pregames, you can see how cerebral, athletic, and prepared they are. Those well-rounded ones are the minority—three-sport DI guys like [Joe] Mauer, shortstop and closer like [Buster] Posey."

It's fun to talk about the best tools you've ever seen—Kerry Wood, Dwight Gooden, Tom Gordon, and injury casualty Terry Taylor were the answers we got when we asked about the top-of-the-scale, present 80-grade curveballs on the 20–80 scale that scouts have seen in high school—but noticing patterns, seeing players play different sports and both ways in baseball are the sort of things that are more often the separators, the things that seem most predictive.

Bridges recalls an instance where pattern recognition helped: "I'm at a wood bat tournament in Atlanta and Austin Riley hits one over the lights. I get it, he's a little overweight, everyone loves that he's up to 95 with a breaking ball on the mound—but that's over the lights. I keep watching him hit and I start thinking about a mistake I made years before.

"I was managing the East Coast Pro showcase team. There was a kid I wanted at the plate for [Team Georgia] against the Florida team. He hits a double that clears the bases and wins the game, against a loaded team that had Mat Latos and a bunch of others. He also pitched, but that spring was just 88–92, not the 95 I'd seen before. He could really pitch. Our national guy asked me what to put in a summation of his report when he saw the kid and I told him 'Hall of Fame because that kid's a winner.' I turned him in as a pitcher and he wasn't throwing hard, so we didn't get him. All he wanted to do in college was hit. I knew he could hit. Wish I had that one back. Buster freakin' Posey, man.

"So I've been down this road before. I send Roy [Clark] to the LaGrange tournament in Columbus, Georgia, to see Riley and he's never spent the night in Columbus but I tell him do it and stay for the whole tourney. Don't just drive in to see him pitch and leave, stay the whole time. He calls me after the tournament and he says, 'Now, on the mound, I don't know, but…' I stopped him right there and said I know what the bat is; now you saw it, too. We kept sending guys in there, we didn't know what other teams were thinking, we were told there were one or two others that had him in good and as a bat. Because of that Buster Posey mess before, we were on him, we did all the work, and when teams ran in late to see the bat, they didn't have the history on him and we did. They wanted to bring him in for workouts but he knew we'd take him high." The Braves took Riley 41st overall in 2015 and he made the big leagues in 2019, hitting 18 homers in 80 games.

The Basics of Working the Board

The draft used to be uncapped in terms of bonuses (with slot-bonus guidelines to anchor negotiations) until the rules shifted in 2012 to a mostly hard cap, but over a whole draft class rather than each individual pick. In the 2011 Draft, with clubs aware that a harder cap was coming the next season, some clubs asked ownership for more money in their budget and spent big, including the Pittsburgh Pirates, not just big market clubs.

Executives saw a chance to spend money to buy young talent without any punishment from MLB for going over slot recommendations and the stern words from MLB's commissioner's office would ring hollow with the rules changing the next year. With the shifting rules and a historic draft class (Gerrit Cole, José Fernández, Francisco Lindor, Trevor Story, Anthony Rendon, Javier Báez, Mookie Betts, George Springer, Blake Snell, Trevor Bauer), clubs spent $228 million in bonuses in 2011, which it took four years to top under harsher slot recommendations, once MLB was able to put its thumb directly on the bonus scale.

In the previous system, every pick came with a slot recommendation to act as the foundation of the negotiations as to the "true value" of the pick. MLB would take teams to task every time they went well above slot to the point that some owners wouldn't let their teams go over-slot at all, while most teams just had to pick their spots and take the tongue-lashing. In the new system for 2012, clubs got an all-in bonus limit that applied to the top-10-round picks. After the 10th round, clubs could spend up to $100,000 (later adjusted up to $125,000) without a penalty, but anything over that amount would count toward that top-10-round amount.

Clubs can go up to 5 percent over that all-in amount by paying a 75 percent tax on the overage, but anything over that amount (5–10 percent over) would trigger losing a first-round pick along with the tax, and going far over (10 percent or more over) would cost two first-round picks along with the tax. Most teams spend into the tax, some to within a few dollars of the 5 percent cutoff, but through the 2019 Draft, no team has spent 5 percent or more over their bonus pool to trigger pick loss.

ESPN's Jeff Passan wrote a speculative article about the circumstances where a team could try doing this, but ultimately deemed it unlikely to ever happen, which is the same conclusion we've arrived at. The biggest reason is that agents could hold a team hostage once they found out the team was going to spend wildly. If a couple players ask for double or triple their slot, to the point that the club doesn't think the player is worth the money, losing a few of those from a haul could end up making the loss of two first-round picks counterproductive. It would also be hard to keep it a secret with expanded budgets and the targeting of players for over a year in advance. Agents, rival executives, and rival teams would figure out what was going on before the draft and certainly after the first few picks.

In the new reality of the hard-capped draft, strategies shifted to make a dollar go further. It took a few seasons for most clubs to realize and use this strategy, but stacking low-bonus seniors in Rounds 5 through 10 saves money to spend later while still taking the best player in the top rounds. If a club is targeting a prep player to overpay at a later pick, ideally they would be able to wait until the 11th round, as $125,000 of the bonus wouldn't count toward their pool. If in rounds 5 through 10, the club took seniors ranging from $1,000 to $50,000 when the slots for each pick are at least $125,000, they could bank a decent amount of money and not really lose much talent.

In response to this, some clubs "play it straight," meaning they just take the best available player in rounds 1 through 10, which can be fruitful after the fifth round, with over half the league taking players who, on talent, shouldn't go in the top 10 rounds. When Kiley was in the Braves draft room for a couple years, they would front-load bonuses in their top few picks, then take seniors as early as any team would. It was excruciating to watch players that the room liked and thought should go in the fourth round end up lasting to the seventh round for unclear reasons, then sign for $150,000, far below what the team would normally pay, but the Braves couldn't take them because the bonuses had boxed them into a senior for no more than $5,000 at that pick.

Myriad draft studies show that the production of a draft comes overwhelmingly from the first two rounds; it's a "power law" if you'd like to see it visualized. A club thinking they are better at picking sixth rounders than another is kidding themselves, aside from maybe a handful of players per team per year where they have exclusive, key information other teams don't. Playing it straight in the top 10 rounds because a team thinks their eighth-round pick is actually a sixth-round pick value can seem attractive, but the benefit is marginal at best on any one pick. The opposite point of view would be that the whole draft is a crapshoot past the first few rounds, so take as many six-figure gambles as you can, rather than thinking anyone can nail a handful of picks so well as to have almost their entire draft pool spent by the fourth round.

The first year with hard draft pools was 2012 and the Astros, in their first draft under GM Jeff Luhnow, were in a unique position. There wasn't a slam-dunk top player, the Astros already saw baseball differently than the rest of the industry, and they were the first team to pick in the new pool structure, so nobody really knew what the best strategies were. Ultimately, the Astros drafted Puerto Rican prep shortstop Carlos Correa first overall, leveraging his status as possibly sliding to the seventh pick to negotiate a below-slot bonus of $4.8 million, creating savings to spend on later picks, which included Florida prep righty Lance McCullers. The next pick, Byron Buxton, the consensus top prospect in the draft, signed for $6 million with Minnesota.

We've had it confirmed by numerous sources that Houston didn't think Correa was the clear top prospect in the draft and thought it was close enough that they didn't have a strong opinion about whom to select. Instead, they decided the top tier of talent was Correa, Buxton, California prep lefty Max Fried, and Stanford righty Mark Appel, so they reached out to all of them to see who would take the lowest bonus at the first pick. They had decided to just take whichever of those four gave the lowest number. Correa came in the lowest, but we're told that Fried's number was incredibly close, within a few hundred thousand dollars, and if he came in a dollar below Correa, Fried would've been the No. 1 overall pick.

Draft Day Decisions

Pulling the trigger on a high pick is a rush. It's insulting to call scouting a crapshoot but picking a player, especially atop the draft, is like a high-stakes roll of the dice. Depending on how it plays out, it may be a moment you think back on and smile, keep trying to recapture, or a fear you spend years regretting.

Tom Kotchman, father of former big league first baseman Casey Kotchman and current Red Sox scout, is best known in baseball circles as one of the most legendary scouts of all time. When he was an area scout for the Angels, he had a legendary run of picks that turned into good big leaguers, often later-round picks and junior college players, like Patrick Corbin, Jeff Mathis, Scot Shields, and Darren O'Day.

Donny Rowland was his scouting director with the Angels. "His players always came as advertised," Rowland said. "He was one of the most thorough scouts I've ever worked with."

Arguably the best of those picks was Howie Kendrick, and, as you may have noticed, we've spoken with a number of people who worked for the Angels at the same time: Rowland and Bridges were the first two. The third was then-crosschecker, now-agent Hank Sargent. His partner is another scout-turned-agent from the Jason Heyward story, Al Goetz.

Sargent recalls how the Kendrick situation played out: "[Kotchman] asks me who the best hitting guy is in the state and I say Ernie Rosso at Brevard Junior College. Kotch goes to Brevard, writes up the team, and asks Ernie who the best hitter in the state is, if anyone had distinguished themselves in his eyes, and Ernie says it's Kendrick at St. John's Junior College. Now, you should know St. John's really sucked at this point—sucked beyond suck. They didn't have anyone, you'd see them once in the fall and then never go back in the spring. Kotch goes to see them and takes great video of Kendrick but doesn't turn him in until super late in the process.

"Only one other team even went to see St. John's and they didn't ask Kendrick to fill out an info card, so Kotch knows nobody is even considering this guy. If you get him a player ID for the draft, so you can pick him, every other team can see that he's on there as registered. Kotch didn't want any indications he was good to other teams beyond the player ID, so he didn't even want him crosschecked," Sargent said.

"He shows me video of Kendrick while we're in the draft room and I'm like, 'Why haven't we discussed this guy yet?' He tells me it's because we've only done top-five-round types so far. We watched the video as a room and we filled in scouting reports based off of that. There's some blanks, like run time, but we can get a decent idea. All the checkers put the OFP at 57 to 62 because the swing was so good. He was a 50 runner and the defense at second was a 4 or 5. Everyone went into alert and put these reports in so we had something.

"Kotch looks a little uncomfortable. He tells us he'd promised the St. John's coach that he'd only draft and follow Kendrick." Draft and follow (DNF) is something that doesn't exist anymore, but it allowed clubs to draft a junior college player and have almost a whole year to sign them. It could be risky if you do it with too good of a player. If you wait three months and offer $250,000 to a player that's worth $1 million, other teams may find a way to tell him (*ahem*, without directly tampering) to wait another nine months and he'd get four times as much. You would only do it on players where you're taking a flier on and aren't sure if you want them, so this allows you some time to have a firmer opinion.

Tim Wilken has a story about when Harold Reynolds was under DNF control of the Mariners, but he recognized Wilken at a diner across the street from a summer tournament and came over to say hello. Wilken knew there were enough scouts around that someone would see them talking and assume the worst, but he wasn't sure how to get Reynolds to leave his table. Like clockwork, his boss, then–Blue Jays GM Pat Gillick, called Wilken to chew him out because the Mariners GM had called to complain to Gillick.

Sargent brings us back to Howie Kendrick: "So Donny [Rowland] asks Kotch if he can get Kendrick done for $150,000. Kotch tells him he can get him for $100,000. Donny tells him, 'Then you're gonna have to find him another middle infielder so we can sign this guy.'"

As the scouting director, it was now in Donny Rowland's hands to navigate where to draft Kendrick, though it seemed pretty simple with literally no other competition. "So Kotch's report has him in the fourth round," Rowland said, "and the room settles on third or fourth round as his value. Come draft day, we're past the second round and I ask Kotch to come sit by me and don't move, to make sure we don't lose sight of Kendrick. In the fifth round we're about to take him and Kotch says, 'Don't take him here. We don't have to; nobody knows about him.' I ask if he's sure and he says, 'Yes.' We get to the 10th round and Kotch is like, 'Aren't you gonna ask if we should take him here?' And I said, 'Nope, because we're taking him here.' He said we didn't have to, but we did. He was the highest guy on the board for seven straight rounds."

Wilken's best and more successful draft story was when he got in a battle in the draft room and ended up landing a Hall of Famer. In the 1995 Draft, Wilken was a national crosschecker for the Blue Jays. Twenty-five-year-old Cuban righty Ariel Prieto was going to go straight to the big leagues, so scouting director Bob Engle had him first on his list, but had Roy Halladay, a Colorado prep righty, ranked second.

"Halladay didn't get out of the chute good in the spring," Wilken said. "There were 50 mph winds in a few games. He had a one-piece arm action; it helped him get over his knuckle curve, which was uncommon then. Normally guys move their arm slot via the delivery rather than just dropping their arm. Mel Queen said Halladay is the only one that's ever done that who he knows of. [Halladay] later got a traditional curve that Mariano Rivera helped him with.

"One of Halladay's mentors from age 14, Buzz Campbell, a part-time scout, told him to run more, so he joined the cross-country team. He finished third in the state. He had an energy-style delivery, his body control was really good, it was helped by cardio from cross-country in his senior year.

"I saw him in a tournament in Arizona, he was just fair, but he kept getting better after that. I saw his best game—right after I had the scariest flight in my career. He competed, he had feel, he had the breaker working, he threw strikes, he couldn't find any competition good enough to challenge him."

The whole room didn't have Wilken's conviction due to varied looks throughout the spring. He pushed hard for Halladay and got him in position to be the pick, but he also needed Halladay to last to the Blue Jays pick at 17th overall. "No one knew what Pittsburgh would do at 10. They were tied to Reggie Taylor; he fit their type. [Phillies scouting director] Mike Arbuckle told me the Phillies at 14 would take Halladay if Taylor was off the board." Pittsburgh took Chad Hermansen at 10, so Philly took Taylor at 14, which freed up Toronto to take Halladay at 17.

"We were fortunate to get [Halladay] there," Wilken said. "Some people in our room thought it was a great pick, but there was some heated disagreements leading to the choice, it was the pick begrudgingly for some of them."

Next season, for the 1996 Draft, Wilken was the scouting director for the Blue Jays. "People joked I was the director the year before, but I lost a few friends that year because of the Halladay process."

Halladay, of course, passed away in 2017 and was inducted in the Hall of Fame in 2019.

Two more great scouting stories came out of that Angels era under Rowland. In 2001, he had hired Marc Russo (who also eventually worked with Kiley with the Braves) away from the Cubs to be area scout for one year with the agreement that he'd be a crosschecker the next year. He covered the Carolinas and Virginia and did lots of crosschecking that first year.

"We're going around the room by group," Rowland said, "talking about all the potential group A's, A-minuses, then Russo brings up a kid he has as a B-plus. He had mono in the spring, has looked bad compared to the summer, and not a lot of scouts know he had mono, so they thought he had regressed. Russo thinks he can get him for $375,000 or $400,000 and thinks he'll still be on the board in the fourth or fifth round. I tried to go to my superiors to ask for money for an overpay in those rounds, but couldn't get it. Went back again and didn't get it again. We were poised to take him in the third or fourth, but we couldn't go over our internal budget and he wouldn't sign for that amount. Russo had him nailed and, as the director, I should've moved him up, had the money he wanted already slotted, like in the second round it would've worked."

The player was Justin Verlander. "The number one skill for a director is listening, not just living with his personal evaluation." We pointed out to Rowland that Bridges said almost the exact same thing to us. Rowland chuckled. "Hopefully he saw that modeled in the draft room and maybe he was still a little mad about the Scott Olsen thing."

The last Angels story was about the eventual Marlins sixth rounder in 2002, Illinois prep lefty Scott Olsen. Bridges was covering the area and it was his second year as a scout. He recalls that the Cubs (the late Stan Zielinski) and the Marlins (Scot Engler) were the only other teams that were on Olsen. They didn't know which of them would be there one night and Bridges saw Zielinski behind home, but they didn't see Engler. Later, they found Engler hiding in the bushes behind home plate, trying to not be seen, in case a fourth team was there.

Now Sargent, as a crosschecker, enters the story. "We get rained out on Olsen one day. I go from Chicago to Detroit, then that game also gets rained out. I come back to Illinois to see Olsen and this one lines up nicely. Bridges and I are riding to the game and we get in an accident while I'm on the phone rescheduling flights; a car sideswipes us and we end up on the shoulder. I can't get out because my door is jammed, I yell at Bridgey to go get the guy in the other car, he's trying to hit-and-run us after ending up in a ditch. An 18-wheeler and a cop stop. After the cop asks who we are and we explain we're trying to rush to a game, the 18-wheeler driver stayed to give documentation and the cop tells us to get to our game."

Now this seems like a great story about beating the odds to get to a game and land a player. But you already know the Angels didn't draft Olsen. "Jokes on us, Olsen hit 92, couldn't throw strikes, is falling off to shortstop. He didn't look like a top-five-round pick and in the sixth round, you weren't sure you could sign him."

On draft day, Zielinski tells Engler and Bridges that the Cubs are out, he can't get Olsen high enough on the board. Bridges pushed Rowland to take him, but can't get it done either. Eventually, Engler lands Olsen because his crosschecker, Joe Jordan, got in there and saw Olsen pitch better than Sargent did.

After covering the Marlins in spring training, Sargent called Bridges to apologize: "He's up to 96 and directional now." Rowland also felt that one: "Russo had Verlander nailed, Bridges had Olsen nailed. You've got to listen to them."

Owners

Then there's the issue of ownership. It comes in all shapes and sizes and can be a value add, or a haunting presence over the proceedings.

"We did our 2011 draft in Mesa, Arizona, at the spring training facility," Wilken, then with the Cubs, said. "[New owner Tom] Ricketts flies in on draft day, it's his first time seeing draft boards and that sorts of stuff. He's feeling kind of frisky. He sees Shawon Dunston Jr. on the board and asks if that's Shawon Dunston's son, because that was his favorite Cub growing up."

Then Ricketts drops the hammer, 20 minutes before the draft: "Tim, have at it. No one is unsignable."

"Our unsignable board was way over in the corner and we roll it to the middle of the room. We got Dunston [$1.275 million, 11th round], Dan Vogelbach [$1.6 million, second round], and Dillon Maples [$2.5 million, 14th round] off there.

"So I'm meeting with Tom about my contract after Jim Hendry was fired as GM. I had two years left of my deal and he said he was going to let the new GM decide my fate. I ask him about the draft for next year, we had just spent $13 million the year before, the highest we'd ever spent. He said he was thinking $18 million to $20 million and that had some wiggle room. But it never happened, because we got hard caps the next year."

Former Rays owner Vince Naimoli is infamous for being a terrible owner, both for meddling and penny-pinching. When Wilken was running the draft for the Rays in 2004, they took Rice RHP Jeff Niemann No. 4 overall and his teammate Wade Townsend went No. 8 overall but didn't sign and was again eligible in 2005.

Wilken wanted Florida prep outfielder Andrew McCutchen and his backup option was Florida prep righty Chris Volstad. Wilken went in to GM Chuck LaMar the day before the draft and pushed for McCutchen, but LaMar told him he didn't like how McCutchen played in a recent high school All-Star Game. Wilken reminded him of a great pre-draft workout at Tropicana Field to no avail. LaMar told Wilken he didn't have the votes for Volstad, so they were taking Townsend with the eighth pick.

It's not clear if this was LaMar's choice, or if Naimoli was dictating a "safe" college pitcher as the choice to LaMar, but Townsend was ultimately their choice. Townsend's highest level was Double-A, Volstad had a mediocre 3.1 career WAR, while McCutchen has posted 49.9 through 2019.

Naimoli's poor ownership acumen was clearer in another instance. Wilken relays that when the owners of Outback Steakhouse pulled out as minority owners of the Rays, the team was short on money. Nobody with the club could get a raise that year. Team executive Scott Proefrock told Wilken that Naimoli paid for Wilken's new contract by selling reliever Al Levine to the Royals during the 2003 season. Naimoli appeared to be doing what was rumored to be former Royals owner David Glass' approach to running a team—break even every year and make money on the appreciation of the team over time.

Agents

The last aspect of the draft puzzle is negotiations and dealing with agents. We talk to a lot of them and have some great stories to illuminate this aspect of the game, but it's pretty tough to get an agent to share details on the record. Scouting directors can dish on past picks and talk about the private parts of the process because the draft is a one-time deal. Everything is a secret, then you draft or don't draft a player, then the past can be public in most cases, particularly when it's a decade later and the reputation of everyone involved isn't on the line like it might be in the moment.

For agents, telling about a time when they were promised more money than they ultimately got in the draft because they couldn't maneuver and bluff their way down the board to the biggest payday could be used by rival agents (dishonestly) as a mark against this agent, as representation only ends when the player's career ends. Because being an agent is an ongoing hustle and the checks keep coming on top players for a decade or more, the stories with details can't be contemporary.

In broad terms, there are agencies of all sizes and specialties, but the business of representing players in the draft is tricky. You get 3–5 percent of the bonus, but often have been servicing the player and battling other agents to keep a player for two or three years by the time that first check rolls in. Agents don't get another check until their player gets to arbitration, since they don't take a commission when a player is making the league minimum (or close to it). For bigger agencies with free agent deals signed every off-season, they don't take on amateur clients unless they think the player will go in the top two rounds. Anything below that level gets to where it'll be a break-even proposition to represent a hypothetical high school player from age 16 to age 26 and only get one check in those 10 years.

The mechanics of deals getting done in the draft isn't that different than the sort of business you've already read about in this chapter. It's technically illegal to negotiate before a player is picked, or help coordinate someone to slide down the board to a pick with more money to offer, but this happens really often and both sides are incentivized to keep it happening to create more certainty about what will happen on draft day. There are still instances where unforeseen things happen, but it's common for agents to know that they have interest from, say, these four teams in a row, then nothing for five picks after that, and so they negotiate as picks come off the board to try to get as much as they can, then to perform damage control to get to one of those four teams before a free fall.

A complicated element of this is related to medicals. There will likely be a rule change in the new CBA to fix this, but currently clubs can ask for medicals pre-draft and often top agencies will not provide them. That means that after a player has been drafted and agreed to terms, if something comes up the club doesn't like on the medical, they can hold the player hostage and almost offer them whatever they feel like. Players have the leverage to not sign and re-enter the draft the next year, but many of them would do it as a college senior with less leverage, or be forced to go to school when they already decided not to.

There's belief that some teams will take advantage of this, feigning concern over a medical to leverage a kid into a lower deal than what they'd already agreed to. It's difficult for agents to juggle these concerns, because some teams will be less likely to draft you if you have a tough agent who won't agree to a pre-draft deal and withholds medicals, because teams like certainty when they're trying to put together a financial puzzle in a hard-capped draft setting. In most cases, agents tell us it's better to not provide full medicals, because that allows clubs to take you off or move you down the board, whereas keeping it a mystery enables the team that likes you most to take you, and the flunked physical discount will also be highest from them. This avoids a fall down the board with panic created by a bad medical that teams will sometimes chatter about amongst themselves, even though they're not supposed to.

There are all kinds of postures an agency can take. Boras Corp is known for being pretty difficult to get information from, negotiating very hard, having a big roster of players and employees, and Scott Boras himself will try to use the media (through the art of hacky quips) as a tool of negotiations. But this is a unique situation, and Boras is the best ever at his job.

Some agents are known for playing nice with clubs and communicating well, signing for slot, but most of them have also engineered a nice over-slot payday in recent years. It all varies by the specific situation. We'll often check with agents around draft day and they'll compare notes with us about where they think their ranges of interest are, and where they think they can find landing spots.

It's always more apparent on the agent side that baseball is just a business. No matter how strong an interpersonal relationship is it's pretty easy to put a dollar figure on a client and decide if they're worth your trouble. Ultimately, this is true on the scouting side as well.

When Stan Meek was describing to us how he drafted José Fernández, he covered all the bases in a few sentences. He instructed his area scout to not show interest to Fernández's camp because, given how much Fernández had been through and how much he loved baseball, Meek wasn't worried that he would be tough to sign. "He was going to the University of Baseball," Meek said.

The scout did all of his background work talking to coaches and teachers rather than the agent and the family. Miami was scared that Milwaukee, picking two spots in front of them and right behind them, may pick their pocket if they knew Miami had interest in Fernández.

Meek is also comfortable explaining how he landed Fernández at the 14th overall pick: "We really liked [Archie] Bradley and [Dylan] Bundy; both went up high. We liked [Danny] Hultzen, [Bubba] Starling, [Javier] Báez, [Francisco] Lindor, [George] Springer. How'd we get [Fernández] at 14? Lots of guys we liked were gone!"

José wanted to play for Miami and Meek was told that José asked his agent the morning of the draft if they were interested and his agent told Fernández the Marlins were not interested. When Meek talked to him on draft day, you could see the child-like joy from Fernández: "He said, 'I didn't think you guys would take me. I had no idea you guys were thinking about me!' José was shocked. He didn't know my name then, he always called me 'Boss.' Actually, he never learned my name, I was always 'Boss' to him."

CHAPTER 3

The Mad World of J2

November 12, 2015, was to be like any other day in the Dominican Republic for Kiley while he was working for the Braves. The team was set to sign a precedent-setting, pool-busting, tooled-up class of players on July 2, 2016, a group headlined by Venezuelan shortstop Kevin Maitán, who'd be getting a $4.25 million bonus. At the time, Maitán was considered to be the best international prospect since at least the 2009 class headlined by Twins third baseman Miguel Sanó ($3.15 million) and Yankees catcher Gary Sánchez ($3 million).

The Braves' amateur director and all of the domestic crosscheckers were also in the Dominican at the time, for two reasons. The first was that the international staff wanted them to see some of the players in the 2016 international class. The second reason was to compare the tools and profiles of players in a market they rarely see to the players at the top of recent draft classes. It also helps the domestic scouts to see some rookie-level prospects of the near future so they'll better understand the players competing for playing time with their own later-round picks in next year's draft. Seeing players like Maitán before they're signed makes them feel like a bigger part of that process, and having more stakeholders in a big decision is typically positive for org culture.

The group left the JW Marriott in downtown Santo Domingo at 8:00 AM, like most days, to get out of the city before traffic got bad and to allow us to see the players work out before it got too hot. We were set to drive over an hour to get to a private workout with one of the more notable Dominican trainers, Rudy Santin. Santin looks like a bouncer. He's big, bald, he's typically sporting facial hair Guy Fieri would approve of, and his look is cut with a hat from the Greg Norman collection. We'd already agreed to sign a couple players from Santin's group on July 2, including one of the top players in the class, switch-hitting SS Yunior Severino, to whom we eventually gave $1.9 million.

Santin is a former scout and perennially has top players, particularly hitters, coming from his camp. In just the last three years, Santin will have had two hitters receive seven-figure bonuses in the 2020 class (Starling Aguilar/Red Sox, Malvin Valdez/Reds), one in the 2019 class (Ismael Mena/Padres), and two more from the 2018 class (Orelvis Martinez/Blue Jays and Alexander Vargas/Yankees). There are generally about 20 such players per signing year across all of Latin America.

This trip was to primarily see Santin's 2016 players (who were to be a part of our big signing class) but also his 2015 players (who were eligible to be signed immediately). Since we had already committed to go over our 2016 bonus pool and pay the penalty tax, each additional 2016 prospect would only cost money, the bonus, and more tax on the overage, whereas clubs that were not poised to exceed their cap had to weigh player bonuses as part of their fixed-pool amount. We had already spent every dollar available to sign our 2015 signing class, headlined by Dominican CF Cristian Pache and Dominican SS Derian Cruz, so any 2015 signings would have to be at the pool-exempt price of $10,000, which is the price a team pays for DSL filler players with little chance to reach the upper minors.

The workout was pretty typical. It started a little later than expected, the trainer ran out many more players than were necessary for us to watch (Santin later did this at a workout Eric attended, as well), including many who didn't fit our limitations or needs. One 2015 player stood out enough to sign for the 2016 DSL squad: 18-year-old Dominican infielder Eudis Lora, eventually released after two DSL seasons. We also signed two pitchers for low six figures as part of the 2016 class: 17-year-old LHP Erick Abreu and 17-year-old Nicaraguan RHP Alger Hodgson. Abreu sat at 90–91, mixed in an average curveball, and had command issues, eventually leading to his release after two DSL seasons. Hodgson hit 97 mph once in this workout and mixed in an above-average changeup and fringe-to-average curveball. He was suspended for 72 games in 2016 for a positive PED test, and spent the 2019 season in short-season Danville.

We wouldn't be telling this specific story except for one detail that stuck with everyone at the park that day, especially the domestic scouts still getting their feet wet in this market. Before the workout started, Santin walked over to the group of Braves scouts and began his sentence apologetically, but confident.

"I know you guys are going over in 2016 and you're here to see 2016s and you won't have money to spend in 2017. But I've got a 2017 you have to see. We'll be quick, but you've got to see this." Our international staff starting groaning because they knew how this went. They'd schedule a private workout to watch four players that should take an hour or two to complete, and instead they end up seeing 30 players for over four hours. The trainer knows you're going to wait to see the players you came to see, but the international scouts dealt with this on a daily basis, and they were about to tell Rudy to get to the point.

Before that happened, the amateur scouts were confused. A 2017? That means he's 14 or 15. They'd never seriously scouted a player that age before. Rudy is a former scout, so he wouldn't just bring out a child for no reason. Eventually the group decided not to stop Rudy, mainly because the players we came to see were still stretching, so we had a few minutes.

The player came out and Santin was beaming like a proud father, pointing at him, making sure everyone knew who to watch, like it wasn't already clear that we were to be watching the only player on the field not playing catch half-heartedly in left field.

The prospect took grounders at short and looked pretty slick, showing good arm strength, actions, and footwork. He was a little short, but well-built, and some of the domestic scouts starting talking amongst themselves about how a high school freshman-aged player could possibly look and play like this. The international scouts knew that this was possible. At this early stage in a Dominican prospect's career, there has barely been process for verification of age and identity yet. Plenty of players around this age have a slick glove, but can't hit a lick, they're not strong enough yet.

Then the prospect grabbed a wood bat, took a couple dry cuts in the on-deck circle, and stepped in against a BP pitcher. The first swing was from the left-handed batter's box and it was louder than anything we'd heard that week in workout events. The next couple swings were just as loud and several of the balls were homers. He stepped out of the box to compose himself and then went into the righty batter's box and, thwack, just kept doing the same thing. Now the international and domestic scouts were on the same page. None of them had seen anything like this before.

Santin looked over at our group and the international scouts gave the signal to end this part of the workout, because they didn't want to waste the kid's time. He saw the signal, shook Rudy's hand, gave some of us fist bumps through the netting then trotted off to hop in a car and go home.

Kiley knew everyone would be asking who this prospect was, even though we had no chance to sign him with a maximum $300,000 bonus for his signing year, so Kiley walked over to Santin to get his name. Rudy fumbled around on his clipboard and handed me a roster from a recent game that this player was in, so we had the name and biographical info. He pointed at the name on the roster and Kiley traced his finger over to see the date of birth: March 1, 2001. He was 14 for another three-and-a-half months.

The name? Wander Franco, the current top prospect in baseball and top bonus ($3.85 million from Tampa Bay) from the 2017 international signing class.

Kiley worked in the front office at this time and wasn't in any department, helping each of them in different ways. We were set to spend between $25 million and $30 million on our 2016 signing class, with bonuses and penalties combined, while 2017 would later become the first hard-capped year.

After this showing by Franco, one of our domestic scouts pulled me aside and half-whispered a question out of the side of his mouth that he knew not to ask our international scouts.

"Is it too late to pull out of all these deals so we can get that guy?"

International Scouting Staff

In Chapter One, we covered the basic rules of the international market. Now we'll dive much deeper and explain how to run a department.

Latin American club scouting operations are based in the Dominican Republic, since that's where the majority of players who are signed come from. Since all 30 teams have academies and infrastructure there, many prospects with medium-to-high dollar potential from other Latin countries that produce less talent and draw fewer scouts will relocate, like Nicaraguan RHP Alger Hodgson from the preceding story. Venezuela's political and economic issues are so bad that run-of-the-mill citizens are fleeing, let alone pro baseball prospects. They're often only able to do this once a trainer takes interest in a player and can foot the bill for the player to move to the Dominican Republic.

From 2010 to 2014, we have signing info from every international signing (including the MLB deals to Japanese professionals) to illustrate the breadth of countries producing players:

2010 – 2014 All International Contracts		
Dominican Republic	2150	55.4%
Venezuela	1079	27.8%
Panama	122	3.1%
Mexico	102	2.6%
Colombia	99	2.5%
Cuba	82	2.1%
Nicaragua	43	1.1%
Australia	40	1.0%
Curaçao	32	0.8%
Others	26	0.7%
Japan	23	0.6%
Taiwan	15	0.4%
Netherlands	12	0.3%
Aruba	10	0.3%
Brazil	10	0.3%
South Korea	9	0.2%
Italy	7	0.2%
Germany	6	0.2%
Guatemala	5	0.1%
Haiti	5	0.1%
South Africa	4	0.1%
Bahamas	3	0.1%
Total	**3884**	

This shows that the 30 teams over five signing periods average just under 26 players signed per year. Given that over 60 percent of players signing will be scouted in the Dominican Republic and operations are based from each team's academy there, this is where most of the full-time area scouts are also based.

Again, it varies pretty widely from team to team, but most teams split the country up in zones, just like domestic amateur scouting groups do. That means roughly four to eight area scouts are the first level of talent discovery. Given the drastically different economic realities in developing countries, these area scouts often make close to the poverty level in terms of a salary in the U.S., but for a Dominican resident it's a steady, stable income with benefits.

Depending on a number of factors, teams will also have area scouts in other countries. This often means a few in Venezuela, then some combination of full-time and part-time employees covering the other countries of note, even though those may not have a prospect of interest every year.

The next level of employment would be a Latin American or Dominican scouting coordinator. For some teams, this role is that of a traffic cop who handles administrative duties. For other clubs it's the senior, Dominican-based scout who essentially crosschecks the island, and pitches in with academy operations.

Similar to domestic operations, the tier above this is international crosschecker; these may be the scouts who travel the most in all of baseball. They're responsible for seeing every signable player of interest in Latin America, which is basically year-round, given the tropical climates and open signing periods. For most teams, this job is only targeted on Latin America, with some events for Cuban defectors, or other outlier situations, in the U.S. (often in Miami).

For other teams, it can be global, with at least one trip per year to Europe, a few well-timed treks to Asia, as well as the locations of several notable, international tournaments. International crosscheckers are overwhelmingly U.S.-based and make about the same as domestic crosscheckers, but with a much bigger benefit in terms of airline miles (diamond medallion status on Delta is a lock).

Above the crosschecker would be the international director, who is the scouting decision-maker for most clubs, with some exceptions. The director is in charge of budgets, staffing, signing players, and, increasingly, the tech elements of the department like video, data, and various technologies like TrackMan, Rapsodo, Blast Motion (all covered in detail in Chapter 12). They usually live in the Southeast (U.S.) so they can take shorter flights to Latin America, and they're heading down there roughly every other week to either scout players or monitor progress of the DSL players at their academy. If they aren't fluent in Spanish, they are trying to be, or they know enough to get their point across and excel in other areas.

Speaking to the exceptions in the last paragraph, there's also a level just above the international director, often called special assistant or director of player personnel, VP of scouting or assistant GM, scouting. If this scout (teams usually have one to five of these focusing on some form of scouting) rose through the ranks doing a good bit of international scouting, their job will be just above or just below the international scouting director and see as many players of consequence as they possibly can in every market. Maybe they got this title when they were poached from another team where they were a director, so the title was made up to make the new job a promotion, technically.

This person is usually seen as the GM's *consigliere* when it comes to scouting, and often their opinion will trump the director's when it comes to significant, seven-figure expenditures, particularly Cuban defectors, for whom there's often missing or imperfect information available. It normally doesn't get to a point where the director's opinions are getting forcefully vetoed, or overruled, but if this higher-level evaluator gets a bad look on a premium prospect, he'll usually go see him again to get a more complete picture until both sides can come to an agreement.

The Academy

A little over 10 years ago, not every team had their own Dominican academy. A couple clubs split a rented facility while their own was being built. Now, every club has their own Dominican facility, with something like a quarter of them in rented facilities, while the rest are owned by the clubs. A handful of clubs had Venezuelan facilities to service their Venezuelan Summer League (VSL) teams, but given the political unrest, the VSL ceased operations in 2016 and all teams abandoned their facilities. Scouts still describe Venezuela as a dangerous place to travel, though there are some other places where you shouldn't be out or travel at night (Mexico, Haiti) or places where scouts could/may have been kidnapped (El Salvador, Honduras, Guatemala).

In 2009, the Rays announced plans to build a Brazilian academy in Marília, an athletic complex for which the local government would pay $2.5 million while the team picks up the tab for yearly operating costs (reportedly between $500,000 and $1 million) once constructed. In 2012, the plan was aborted and Pedro Moura, who was then with the *Orange County Register*, reported, "The plans were squashed for circumstances that have never been made fully clear. Most of what's known is this: the mayor of Marília and his secretary were arrested on charges of corruption."

Academies all have the same basic features. There's lodging for at least one DSL team (roughly 35 players) along with some staff and tryout players, a gym, cafeteria, coach and player clubhouses, training room, and at least two, full game-quality fields, with hitting cages and bullpens.

Outside of those core elements, they come in all shapes and sizes. The rooms for players can be bunk beds sleeping four (or even eight) to a room, often times with intermittent air conditioning, or they can look like something closer to a hotel room with two single beds. Gyms can be pretty bare bones, like the worst hotel gym you'd see in the States in terms of quality, or it can look more like the big box gym around the corner from your house. Food can be standard local fare like beans, rice, and chicken for almost every single meal or special-ordered organic food offerings designed by a nutritionist.

Rented facilities are at the lower end in terms of size and quality and usually come with a multi-year lease of between $500,000 and $1 million per year. This covers the facility, upkeep, maintenance staff, and food—basically everything you need is all inclusive.

The team-owned facilities are more of an upfront expenditure, and often cost even more for yearly upkeep, but the conditions are much better. Some of the top facilities with a larger footprint had to pay $1 million or more for their land, especially to be near other academies (shorter trips for DSL games) and/or hotels, airports, and major towns (shorter drives for staff, general convenience for deliveries, fewer/shorter power outages, etc.). It's anywhere from $4 million to $10 million for the actual building, and yearly costs creep closer to $1 million per year before you get to coach, trainer, and support staff salaries.

Teams can plan to have multiple DSL teams run out of the academy and in that case, they need, at minimum, some half-fields or a third and maybe fourth field along with at least 75 beds. Teams often go back and forth between having one and two DSL teams depending on team needs, but obviously expanding/contracting the academy itself isn't quite that easy.

Adding an extra team to an academy that's already equipped to handle the added players has some additional costs: player bonuses (you could sign a whole team to pool-exempt $10,000 bonuses for $350,000), player salaries (under $100,000 for a season for a whole team), additional equipment, transportation, and coaches/trainers. The tab for that extra team for one year is roughly $500,000 to $600,000.

At this point, the majority of academies are B-grade or better, offering some version of the better end of the scenarios painted a few paragraphs ago. One former scouting director's talent-centric, dissenting opinion regarding academies is to always rent and make sure you have at least a C-grade facility, because your best prospects never play in a DSL game, the money spent operating one could be spent on signing more or better players (especially in the old, uncapped environment) or things that directly improve them, and you want the player to be just uncomfortable enough to want to strive to leave and get to the GCL/AZL in the States.

The more common opinion on this topic is to own your academy because, in addition to what is typically a lower quality facility and quality of life for your employees, the lack of control of your day-to-day situation can be infuriating. If the access road is flooded enough from last night's rain that a bus can't pass through, your game is probably cancelled because the landlord isn't fixing that issue in the couple hours you have to get it done and still have a game. If the electricity is going on and off, or a power line goes down, same issue. The renting team can't improve or customize much about the academy other than painting their logo on it somewhere. The gyms are often substandard. The food is often subpar with no option to handle it in-house or use a company not owned by the landlord. The internet can be unusable.

If a team owner sees his international department as something that will be a key part of the organization for decades (and they all should, or else they're short-sighted or worse), spending $5–$7 million now so you can avoid most or all of these problems is a slam dunk. And if the owner wants to have an industry-leading, resort-looking facility, it'll probably cost about $10 million in Year One.

Player Development as Part of Scouting

Domestically, we treat player development as a completely separate and independent department to the scouting departments. In Latin America, these two become intertwined, and staff often overlaps for a number of reasons.

Since players agree to deals ahead of time—sometimes a year or more in advance—the trainer/agent has no incentive (though some generally accept responsibility) to keep the player in shape and improving as a ballplayer in the interim, but the team also has a hand in that. Trusting trainers/agents/ *buscones* is an enviable but often elusive thing.

Scouts tend to point to Ivan Noboa as one of the best at training young hitters, keeping them in shape after a verbal deal, and being accommodating so you can get the looks you need on the player to make a decision. Like Santin, Noboa always has good players and also a personality.

Per one international director, "He's as eccentric as they come, very chatty." He added, "The majority of trainers are good in the balance. A small minority are constantly trying to pull the wool over your eyes, or being immoral."

Many international crosscheckers and directors have a background in coaching or development, so when they first see a player, their evaluation is rooted in and colored by that experience and point of view. This is not only beneficial but arguably essential, because they're often scouting 14- and 15-year-olds who, in many cases, lack physical maturity, in addition to (outside of the top trainers) proper instruction, nutrition, and strength training. This alone makes development a much bigger part of the evaluative pie than when scouting a well-off, 18-year-old domestic high school player who has been on the showcase/travel ball circuit for years.

Some Latin kids will quickly put on 10–15 lbs of bad weight just because they don't know how to eat in moderation when there's suddenly a steady abundance of food for the first time in their lives. When with the Braves, Kiley noted they had players that, between his visits, would lower their body fat percentage but still gain roughly 10 lbs in just a month or two from proper nutrition and training. Rays VP of player development and international scouting Carlos Rodriguez has seen it firsthand: "The average player adds 40 pounds of man strength after we sign them. We signed José Alvarado at 160 lbs and he's listed at 245 now."

This is perhaps part of why Maitán has struggled early in his pro career, now with the Angels. As an amateur prospect he was likely to fill out, slow down, and move off of shortstop eventually, but nobody expected him to balloon to well over 200 pounds before his 18th birthday, while simultaneously losing the athleticism that made him an exciting hitting prospect. This is the sort of rare thing that can undermine someone who is deemed a generational talent, along with injuries for pitchers.

Amateur players can visit academies under somewhat complicated rules that have changed a few times in recent years. A source supplied us with this table that MLB circulated to clubs as the guidelines:

International Tryout Players: Eligibility to Enter Club Facilities

	1/1/19 to 7/1/19	7/2/19 to 12/31/19	1/1/20 to 7/1/20	7/2/20 to 12/31/20
2018–2019	**Eligible to Sign** Player may enter Club Facility for up to 45 days in any 90-day period	**Eligible to Sign** Player may enter Club Facility for up to 45 days in any 90-day period	**Eligible to Sign** Player may enter Club Facility for up to 45 days in any 90-day period	**Eligible to Sign** Player may enter Club Facility for up to 45 days in any 90-day period
2019–2020	**0–6 Months from Signing** Player may enter Club Facility for up to 15 days in any 45-day period	**Eligible to Sign** Player may enter Club Facility for up to 45 days in any 90-day period	**Eligible to Sign** Player may enter Club Facility for up to 45 days in any 90-day period	**Eligible to Sign** Player may enter Club Facility for up to 45 days in any 90-day period
2020–2021	**12–18 Months from Signing** Player may enter Club Facility for up to 7 days during this period	**6–12 Months from Signing** Player may enter Club Facility for up to 15 days in any 90-day period	**0–6 Months from Signing** Player may enter Club Facility for up to 15 days in any 45-day period	**Eligible to Sign** Player may enter Club Facility for up to 45 days in any 90-day period
2021–2022	**24–30 Months from Signing** Player may not enter Club Facility	**18–24 Months from Signing** Player may not enter Club Facility	**12–18 Months from Signing** Player may enter Club Facility for up to 7 days during this period	**6–12 Months from Signing** Player may enter Club Facility for up to 15 days in any 90-day period
2022–2023	**36–42 Months from Signing** Player may not enter Club Facility	**30–36 Months from Signing** Player may not enter Club Facility	**24–30 Months from Signing** Player may not enter Club Facility	**18–24 Months from Signing** Player may not enter Club Facility

This gives clubs the chance to see how the player handles game situations of their design, and coaches and staff can see how the player handles instruction, get a feel for makeup, social skills, aptitude, and other aspects of their young personhood. Some trainers are hesitant to let their top prospects be subject to whatever conditions teams would like to see. In this case, the club can go to the facilities of the player's trainer and bring their own pitchers (under-contract ones or more tryout pitchers they're interested in seeing) to get more than the allotted amount of days of game-type looks that they can control. This is usually only allowed by the trainer when the team is a serious bidder for their pupil.

Once a prospect signs a pro contract, they enter the academy and, aside from the top 25–50 players in the global signing class (who head to the U.S. in the fall for instructional league, if their parent club is doing it), will spend most of the time there until the next season starts, then live there through the next summer in their DSL debut season. The coaches and development-minded scouts who are in and out of the academy become mentors, confidants, sometimes even father figures in the players' first extended time away from home. The players are learning social and life skills and encountering challenges they've generally not seen before, in addition to more intense training, focused nutrition, and technical instruction. Many of them are also coping with a new level of professional and existential pressure.

From the team's perspective, this is a key point in the player's development as this first year as a pro is when they're educated about how to take care of themselves, and players' physical well-being (prospects often show up with minor, non-baseball-related, undiagnosed medical issues) stabilized, while baseball things can be taught and improved. With so little to distract them at the academy, there are tons of reps used to hammer home mechanical changes, far more than a domestic high school player or lower-level professional will ever get in a prep season. It's not unusual for prospects to get in hundreds of swings per day in a structured environment, monitored by instructors.

Another important element of development at the academy comes from the topics under the umbrella of cultural assimilation. Awareness of the benefits of preparing these players for the culture shock they'll soon experience when they head to the U.S. to play ball only started about 10–15 years ago, when clubs widely began offering English classes to players. For almost all teams, classroom activity has become more formal and now includes many more valuable elements, such as preparation for cultural situations (how to order food at an American restaurant, talk to customer service people) and financial ones (how to start/maintain a checking account, direct deposit, budgeting).

One of the clubs Kiley worked for about a decade ago had an issue with GCL players getting into trouble at the team hotel at night. The team found out the players were taking their checks to check-cashing places, because most of them didn't have bank accounts or even know they needed one. There was a strip club and a Denny's within walking distance of this hotel full of cash-flush teenagers and young twenty-somethings. After a couple weeks of complaining from the hotel manager, it was clear something needed to be done. Ideally, teams would prioritize player education for its own sake, but realistically it's incentive to avoid incidents like this that catalyze adjustments and improvements to the ways teams groom young men.

More activity like this should happen with domestic amateurs who, on the average, don't come from socioeconomic circumstances as difficult as their Latin American peers, but who are often products of a flawed, underfunded education system in the United States. Continued education for young American and Canadian ballplayers enables teams to rebut the "don't go play pro ball, enroll early at Random University and get an education" spiel college coaches use to get kids to campus.

Rodriguez traces the growth in this area: "Ten years ago, few teams had this squared away. Some were ahead, but it's exponentially improved—in the last five years it's really jumped. Clubs can pump resources into a holistic approach for cultural assimilation."

With this context, you can see why the predominant opinion about academies is to pay a little extra upfront to have control over the facility but also to make this period more comfortable, fostering quicker growth for players. Even the top prospects that sign for seven figures and never play in the DSL (debuting in the GCL/AZL, occasionally in the Appy/Pioneer League) spend over a month in the academy before signing, then two to three months before going stateside for instructional league, then intermittently over the winter before spring training in the States.

"WE HEARD ABOUT HIM RIGHT about when you saw him for the first time."

Rodriguez recalls when he first saw Wander Franco and he thinks it was around the time when Kiley and the Braves staff stumbled into seeing him at the Rudy Santin private workout.

"We had a deal with Rudy for [Dominican] RHP Rony Garcia for $125,000 for the 2014 class. He promised Gordon [Blakeley, a then-Yankees executive] a chance to see Rony before he signed, but we already had a deal. I rescinded our offer to Garcia because of that. I don't know if Gordon ever even saw Garcia. Rudy called back later to get the deal done, but I had to walk away on principle." Garcia eventually signed with the Yankees for $100,000 in the 2015 class and is now a bit of a prospect, spending most of the 2019 season in Double-A at age 21.

That may seem independent of Tampa Bay's later signing of Wander Franco, but the international market has a way of amplifying the effects of a team or individual's reputation and credibility. It's a tangled web of tit for tat, decisions, and deals that combine to either nurture or harm relationships that later have an impact on whether or not you acquire talent, which is the goal. The Rays later signed Jesús Sánchez (an eventual top 100 prospect whom the club would trade for late-inning reliever Nick Anderson) from Santin's camp as part of that same 2014 class that Garcia was originally supposed to be part of.

"This helped us develop a rapport with Rudy," Carlos said. Sources and some of our firsthand experience told us that Santin can be impulsive, so

Rodriguez setting boundaries on Rony Garcia in 2014 set the tone for the signing of Sánchez in 2014 and Franco in the 2017 class.

"We first saw Franco at a private workout with Rudy. Rudy was pumped about Wander and an outfielder that ended up being an early-peaking type player who didn't pan out, eventually signed for $10,000. We were fired up after seeing Franco once; we ran guys in to see him and they all were on board. [Special assistant to the GM] Bobby Heck was in, [then international crosschecker, now international scouting director] Steve Miller was in. We had the same concerns as most other teams. How will he trend going forward? What's the [defensive] position? How does the body develop? Where will the power come from? Who is the comp?

"We really liked the bat and just sat back and watched. We put our stuff down and just watched. He made all the plays. His baseball IQ stood out. The maturity, energy, and enthusiasm, it was all there."

Often, the answer is staring a scout in the face. It's a good test of perspective to focus on what a player can do rather than what he can't do. No player, particularly no amateur player, is perfect. Putting away the camera and the radar gun and the stopwatch for a while before you write the report is a good idea. Truly elite players are just elite all the time. Don't make it more complicated than it already is.

How to Run a Top-Notch Department

What specifically makes a club top-notch in the international arena? There are a lot of potential answers, but most of them can be reduced down to how they navigate the unique social dynamic of the market, how well they allocate their resources, and how good their scouting process is.

In terms of resources, the options for how an international director can spend their budget are almost endless—the Wonkavator of baseball evaluation processes.

You could get more scouts; pay them better; add to the crosschecker/special assistant level or area scout level; expand travel budgets; add support personnel to the academy; add analysts to handle data; upgrade/expand aspects of the academy; add a second DSL team; improve conditions/hire people to upgrade nutrition, training, education, or coaching; invest in more technology or buying stats and video from professional foreign leagues. As you can see, there are ways to invest in almost any area you'd like to improve or area you think is low-hanging fruit to gain a competitive advantage.

You may look at the preceding paragraph and think that MBA types or more corporate clubs would excel here, with a complex jigsaw puzzle of decisions that may best be solved with that method of analysis. You'd be right to think some clubs are doing this, but the international market is unique.

When we talk to clubs about who they think the best international departments are, we keep hearing the same teams over and over. The Yankees, Dodgers, and Rays come up the most, and the Indians, Red Sox, Phillies, Nationals, Padres, and Rangers all come up a lot of the time. The Diamondbacks and Giants are trending up recently.

It's pretty easy to watch what a team does with their big league team, trades, and the draft, and see what they value. We may or may not know what they actually value, or what their statistical models may emphasize, but, at some point, if their model emphasizes something but they never act on it enough for us to recognize it, then it doesn't really matter.

It's much harder to do this in the international market, since there isn't as clear a delineation between the types of players a procedurally progressive team would prefer compared to a traditional team, given the amount of projection, lack of statistical information, and asymmetrical distribution of information/intelligence.

That being said, we have a decent idea of where teams lean in the process. The Phillies, Nationals, Padres, and Rangers are seen as more traditional, scouting-driven international operations, with the Rays, Yankees, Dodgers, and Red Sox as moderate types, and the Indians are the most successful team with a progressive process. More on that later.

A foundational question for teams is what type of player they want their scouts to spend time scouting. Do you want to snap up any 14-year-old that you like and think represents a strong value? Do you want to save some money for later-blooming prospects? Or do you think you can beat every other team on 14-year-olds more than you can on 16-year-olds? Or do you want to pivot completely and not cut any deals until a month or two before signing day and focus more on passed-over, later-peaking prospects and late-arriving Cubans?

The Rockies are unique in that they don't really strike many verbal deals well in advance of signing day and wait to spend most of their money late in the process. Waiting until late and hoarding pool space is typically what more progressive clubs will do, but Colorado does it with more of a traditional scouting-focused approach.

With the bigger payroll teams come more resources. When you ask teams about size of staff, the Yankees always come up first, as they appear to have the biggest international contingent, while the Dodgers usually get mentioned next. Teams such as these place importance on all of the available information/data and also have the scouting bodies for blanket coverage on all fronts. They'll often have accumulated dozens of reports before signing higher-profile players. This also means they can afford a few more elite pairs of eyeballs, more support staff, more tech, more analysts, and a nicer academy with the option for multiple DSL clubs. It's not unusual for less successful, scouting-oriented clubs to make decisions based on just a couple of looks with few/no formal reports written.

When Kiley was a part-time writer trying to get to events in the Dominican, he stayed with a former boss who became an agent/trainer. This guy owned a new facility that was so good it was bought by a team years later and turned into their academy. Kiley was still pretty anonymous as a writer, and on days with no outside events to attend, he'd hang around the facility and watch the trainer's prospects work out. One day, a team came by with their international director, head Dominican scout, and an area scout, specifically to have a private workout and find some filler players for their DSL team.

Kiley was sitting a few rows behind them, the only other person in the half-dozen rows of bleachers, and the scouts didn't pay attention to him, likely thinking he worked full-time at the academy. They watched a few pitchers throw live to batters, then a decent prospect on the mound caught their attention. They wanted a filler-type to eat innings for their DSL team and the pitcher was throwing 87–90 mph with some deception and feel for three decent pitches, but he was 18 years old without much projection. This was essentially the Platonic ideal of the filler DSL pitcher that signs for $10,000 or so, plays for a year or two in the DSL, then gets released. Something like 10 percent of this type of player ever get to the upper levels of the minors, much less become a prospect.

When the pitcher appeared to be a potential target, the director sat up straight and asked his Dominican coordinator if his staff has seen this guy pitch before. It was pretty clear he hadn't, as he mumbled and flipped through a notebook and looked at the area scout for help and neither of them had answers. Then the coordinator said he had seen him before, a couple weeks ago, and that the pitcher looked the same as he did now. This was all the director needed to hear, but he was half-listening, focused on the pitcher. After about 30 pitches, the director had seen what he needed to see so he started talking bonus figures with the other two scouts. The director walked down to the dugout to meet the pitcher and tell him they wanted to sign him and were going to talk to the agent.

This was a pretty sloppy process. It was a new international director, who has since been let go, who only had a background in domestic scouting and got the job mostly because the new regime atop the organization liked his work domestically. A better process would have more reports, more history, private workouts at their facility to see him on TrackMan and other tech, before making a decision, rather than whatever you'd call this. Teams with sound processes almost never get into the position where they would go and one-look a pitcher that they need badly enough to sign him on the spot. It's worth noting this director signed a current elite prospect whom we're told he did the right amount of homework on, but everyone does homework on big-dollar signs; that's not what puts a department in the top tier.

This was the best example of the advice another international director with only prior domestic experience (since promoted) once told Kiley: "The biggest market inefficiency down here is paying attention and taking notes." They were at a major tournament-style event and Kiley was trying to take notes about what the notable prospects were doing in games that were going simultaneously on both fields at a team academy. The director tipped his notes toward Kiley so Kiley could see how much he'd written just from this game, Kiley showed him his notes and the director said, "Look around. There's over 100 scouts here, two fields of prospects playing games. How many open notebooks or active pens do you see?" It was a handful at most.

Part of this is because it was a couple hours into an all-day event and focus levels were waning, which is probably true at all jobs, but he had a point. Kiley was furiously taking notes because he was a writer who came down for about a week a year, so each day was a huge percentage of what he got to see from the amateur class, and he treated it as such. The director pointed out that this isn't true of himself, but he approaches each day like that—he has to—because any one of these players could be a difference maker and having detailed notes on 40 at-bats per prospect after 10 days of events instead of the handful most scouts there were recording is what separated him from them.

Unfortunately, the amount of detail that goes into MLB free agent contracts, trades, scouting minor leaguers, and setting up a draft board simply didn't exist in the international market until recently. Players didn't play enough games until the last 10 or so years. But the rise of independent and MLB-run prospect leagues has created enough game stats that they can be used as an indicator of something. Previously, an insufficient number of games to create reliable stats and a lack of radar-based tech limited the rigor and breadth of any potential process; it was eyeball-only.

Things you couldn't fathom occurring during a domestic-player workout—things you wouldn't know if you didn't ask or investigate—happen somewhat often in this market, like a kid having a bad private session because his shoes are three sizes too big. Combine that with the seemingly random, non-linear development of some players, *and* the huge gap between what these players are and what they could be, and for a long time it encouraged a gut-feel-focused, shoot-from-the-hip, Brett Favre style of scouting and acquisition. For a long time, the international market was largely exempt from Moneyball dogma and the corporatization of the game, and some whole clubs and lots of individual scouts still operate this way.

But, largely, that is not the case now. The best operations have many dozens of employees, and some top teams see it as a failure if they don't have multiple reports filed on every player that signs for six figures. We've heard stories of staffs getting aired out when this happens. This is especially tough in a world where more than a few teams are still signing players like gunslingers, after a look or two, thinking this gives them an advantage. We've heard stories about a current big league All-Star who got plucked out of an open tryout because he had a deceptively big extension measured by the academy's TrackMan unit, but otherwise was pretty similar to other pitchers in the workout.

There are plenty of ways to leverage this data in this market, like holding amateur events at your Dominican academy to get exclusive access to data on eligible players, or finding ways to pull a full video history of Cuban players as they defect (lots of amateur international events stream and are logged on the WBSC YouTube page) to build a deeper background before their open workout. The best organizations can beat you in multiple ways and spend their budget in a way that presses those advantages.

RESEARCH BY FANGRAPHS' CRAIG EDWARDS shows that Wander Franco would likely net over $100 million on the open market as he approaches his Major League debut, despite signing for just $3.85 million in 2017. If not for a big-picture change to the international market in December 2016, due to a new collective bargaining agreement, Franco very well could be a member of the Yankees organization.

Donny Rowland, the Yankees director of international scouting, is considered one of the top in baseball at his position. His reputation, recent track record, and the fact that GM Brian Cashman is constantly trading for additional international pool space reinforces the belief that the Yankees have one of the best international operations in baseball. When lining up the top prospects for the 2017 international class, he saw a chance for a special haul for the Yankees.

"We had a shot to get three of our top five players in the class for a good price if we acted early," Rowland said. "We had identified these guys and had done the work to be in a position to sign them. We had some choices to make and the CBA kinda hung over our heads."

What Rowland doesn't say is how far they'd gone to lay that groundwork. It was widely believed, reported, and confirmed by league sources before the CBA was announced, that the Yankees were likely to land Franco, and had planned to go up to $6 million if necessary, a plan that would change if the new CBA included hard limits on international spending. The new CBA included hard limits with a top pool of under $6 million, so the initial plan was scrapped just eight months before signing day.

When Rowland was with the Angels, he signed Erick Aybar, who happens to be Franco's uncle. Those sorts of advantages come to scouting directors with long histories, a little quirk of the international market that features more relationship-focused recruiting than many fans think, or any statistical model could account for. With the whole market based around early deals and teams having similar bonus pools, having a track record with a trainer and/or the family can be the difference. We've heard stories of families turning down offers of over $2 million more than their verbal deal, because the families value their word and they don't know or trust the team offering the bigger figure.

The Yankees could still chase Franco and potentially use most or all of their pool to land him, but post-CBA, the Rays became a bigger threat. In the new three-tiered pool system based primarily on market size that year (it now includes free agent signings as a factor), Tampa Bay was placed in the top tier at $5.75 million and New York in the bottom tier at $4.75 million.

An all-for-one approach, where a team spends their entire pool on a single player, includes considerable risk, according to Rowland: "We could push on Franco, but we didn't know how far Tampa Bay was willing to go. If we offer our whole pool and they top it, we don't get Franco and by the time it plays out, odds are a couple of our backup options have committed elsewhere too."

There was also the bit that Franco wasn't seen, at the time, as a can't-miss, generational talent, but merely the consensus best guy in the class, maybe best in the last few years. Some clubs wondered if his 5'10" frame would limit his power upside or if he'd have to move off of shortstop. He was just unusual enough, especially his helicopter swing, that you could poke a hole there, if you wanted to find a reason to spend less on a different elite prospect.

The shifting CBA landscape forced a decision for Rowland, changing from a potential situation of abundance to one of scarcity. "The CBA really affected our strategy. As a director working in a market with this much variance to outcomes, getting three of your top five guys in a hard-capped setting is almost unheard of. Franco looks like the top guy from the class now, so it stings and hindsight can be more unflattering because that's how it's played out so far. That's the way things go sometimes, things could also change from here. We still had [Franco] evaluated correctly, we made a strategic decision to go another way. We're really happy with who we got and the process. Without the CBA changing the rules, maybe we get four of our top five. Outcomes don't always mirror the process."

The Yankees spent $4.6 million of their initial $4.75 million pool (they eventually traded for more pool space) on three of their top five ranked prospects: Venezuelan outfielders Everson Pereira, Antonio Cabello, and Raimfer Salinas. Pereira and Cabello are both ranked in the 10–15 range among that signing class, with Salinas and lower-dollar signee outfielder Anthony Garcia in the 30–50 range, while five more prospects are talented enough to be written up somewhere on FanGraphs. Of players ranked and considered real prospects at FanGraphs, the Yankees' nine from the 2017 international class is tied with Texas for the most from that year.

Five clubs have had Top 100 prospects already emerge from that class of 16-year-olds (White Sox OF Luis Robert was nearly 20 when he signed and Angels RHP/DH Shohei Ohtani was 23) and are currently the top performing teams in this class, as those top prospects have so much more value than more speculative ones: Franco, Mets SS Ronny Mauricio, Indians OF George Valera and SS Brayan Rocchio, Mariners OF Julio Rodriguez, and Diamondbacks OF Kristian Robinson.

At this very early stage, those clubs have produced the most value from 16-year-olds in the 2017 class because one or more of their players have broken out quickly, in a significant way. The Yankees and Rangers depth of quality players has them next, and they have the potential to jump those teams with a couple breakouts with plenty of candidates to do so.

It's an impressive Yankee class, but those involved can't help but wonder if they were (holds thumb near forefinger) *this close* to signing an historic one.

The performance of new millionaire teenagers impacts one's job security and has nine-figure ramifications for your club, but that's the reality of working in the international market. It's about striving for perfection while living with outcomes that fall short of it.

THIS DYNAMIC OF THE STAKES seeming low but actually being high at all times applies to many areas. The Franco issue was a moment when tough, impactful decisions had to be made, and the people involved knew this at the time, but there isn't always an obvious decision, each year, for each team to make. There are a lot of dull moments, weeks on end when scouts only sleep, eat, and watch games, but still see very little pro-quality talent.

South Park creator Matt Stone has made nine figures, mostly off of *South Park* and the play *Book of Mormon*. By any measure, he and his writing partner Trey Parker are as successful in their field as any in the creative field. Stone said in a 2009 podcast interview, "You're always looking for things to motivate you. If you can use anything happening… to self-light a fire under your own ass, use it. It's all delusion anyway, because none of it really matters…. We just make a cartoon. It is that dumb. But you have to convince yourself you're saving the world, because it's hard to get up in the morning and go to work. You have to really pretend like it's super important, even though it's not…. I think a lot of Hollywood kinda loses their mind in that exact little gap. You have to always keep in mind you're just making television. You're not curing cancer, you're not fighting a war, you're not doing anything important. But if you think that, you'll never do anything good. So you have to kind of like trick yourself all the time into thinking you're really, really important and what you're doing is really, really important for the world… so you can actually make some good stuff. But you don't actually…. You have to think about it on grandiose levels to do a good job."

Scouting and signing baseball players fits into this realm of being a cool job, but ultimately not mattering.

Rodriguez, like Rowland and every other international director, has some regrets that come to mind as well. "In 2012, we went over and our targets were Amed Rosario, the Basabe twins, Luiz Gohara, José Castillo, and José Mujica. In hindsight, we should've gotten Rosario." We've had two other scouts tell us about the first time they saw Amed Rosario after their club had already committed to another player for a big bonus, feeling the same thing the Braves scouts did when they saw Wander Franco for the first time.

"We went over again in 2014 and our area scout was very close with [Kevin] Maitán in the next class, we ended up punting on him to get the 2014 class." The conversation shifts to Adrian Rondon, the weak spot in an otherwise sterling 2014 class (more on that later) but Rodriguez ends up reflecting on the process, how it has changed since then, and circles back to the sentiments from Stone three paragraphs ago.

"I'm not sure what we could've known to do a better job on there. We're constantly adjusting based on how things go. We're pretty progressive, pushing the process internally, not being glued to what others are doing. Our staff development focuses on scouts speaking English to write reports so analysis is easier. Josh Kalk was down here then, I talked with him, learning how to use technology in this setting. There's a level of humility the game gives you. But you have to have a level of confidence when you're evaluating and making decisions, weighing your opinion versus others you trust."

All of this is to say that having some semblance of work/life balance is important and leads to better job performance. But venture too far into comfort and a dozen teams will zoom past you and you'll be looking for a new job.

Having the constitution to focus at a time when everything is telling you to mentally pack it in led to the Rays signing an asset and recent playoff contributor. Trainers are often asked to bring players to an academy for a private workout, and pretty much every time the trainer brings a few extra players the team didn't ask to see. Rodriguez recounts one time in the Dominican when a trainer pulled a "sneak attack," as their staff calls it, with the agent bringing three or four extra guys to a workout. This one was particularly bothersome because it was at the end of a long week of all-day workouts which had yielded nothing. "We hadn't run into anyone to even consider signing for weeks. We were in a big time slump.

"We had tried to crack down on the sneak attack, telling agents to knock it off, that we wouldn't watch anyone who wasn't on the roster before the event begins. We were taking a beating with extra guys making every workout take an extra hour and the extra guys are almost always the worst players." The Tampa Bay staff—the whole department was there—had been doing three workouts a day for a week and had begun this day's third workout at about 3:00 PM after going to other facilities for the first two workouts of the day.

Thirteen pitchers had thrown live BPs of about 20 pitches each and none was worth following up on. The sun was literally and figuratively setting on the day. Rodriguez started walking from the fields to the office to recap the day with his staff, when he saw a player in a Yankees hat and pants. He was about to yell at the agent that the event was over and this player wouldn't be seen, but there were a lot of other agents in the stands and it's bad form to show up an agent in front of that many others at the risk of pissing them all off and having them withhold info from you.

Rodriguez rounded up his scouts to ask if anyone knew this player and the scout that covers Santiago said he had been invited but wasn't put on the roster since he didn't know if he would show up. Rodriguez recalls muttering that this last pitcher better throw 95.

"My job is to see the players. We'll watch them, we'll stay extra to see them all. This is the reason why." The pitcher's first pitch was 95; the next was 96. He'd turned 20 years old a few months earlier, so it's not like even then this was an elite prospect, even with big league velocity. "At that age, they're considered senior citizens down there. But it was present stuff, big stuff. Power breaker, chance for multiple plus weapons. And we hadn't seen even a good player in over a week."

The Rays officially signed RHP Diego Castillo a few days later, on March 5, 2014, for $64,000. He was added to the 40-man roster after the 2017 season and pitched in the big leagues in the summer of 2018. Over 2018 and 2019, Castillo has been a reliever and opener and has posted a 3.30 ERA over 125.1 big league innings, posting 2.1 WAR, or roughly $20 million worth of value, probably more when you consider that WAR value is non-linear and Castillo helped pitch the Rays into the 2019 playoffs.

You never know where they'll come from. Part of that is motivating, that every moment is precious and could be career-defining. The other part can be paralyzing. Committing to one player means you're indirectly passing on hundreds of others, a bunch of players you haven't seen and, in the case of late-bloomers or Cuban defectors who haven't defected yet, ones you didn't even know about when you signed your pool away.

Rodriguez knows this feeling. "We spend a lot of time going through multiple scenarios and forecasting potential outcomes. Crosscheckers, data people, the odds to get the player, projected cost, value. One of the keys is to not get too cute. There are 30 teams, they're all highly capable and there are dynamic evaluators who we're competing with daily. We try to do our best to prepare and get out in front."

Cruz takes the bird in the hand: "If you like the player, you sign him and you deal with the rest later. Maybe money pops up later and you're grateful for that. If you try to save money, you'll lose guys."

Failure runs parallel to letting your guard down. You could have a perfect process and perfect execution of that process and still fail most of the time if your bar is to be clairvoyant about the future of a 15-year-old. Rowland identifies with this feeling. "In doing my job that day at the park, I have to walk out of that ballpark 100 percent confident that I've nailed the evaluation. At the end of the day, we know there's a 90 percent chance of being wrong when you're trying to project an entire career before it starts."

Rowland continues, "This exists in all aspects of player acquisition, that's what creates thick skin as an evaluator. You can't live and die on every at-bat that comes in on the game report each night. That's what drives you to the insane asylum. How many transactions come with a half-dozen years of history on the player and after one season, they look like a disaster? [The teams] have almost unlimited information in some of those decisions. You have to be okay with failure, but that's why successes mean so much, to every person in the department."

In light of this peek behind the curtain, we're reminded of how, when reading an oral history of even successful movies, seeing all the raindrops they have to dance between, you wonder how a movie can even get made. Signing good players regularly seems like a miracle.

Scouting J2 events can be really tricky. Rodriguez has advice: "It's smart to have eyes wide open to all sorts of things. Some bats and balls at events are pretty obvious you should be skeptical. I'm not accusing someone of cheating, but having a healthy skepticism." It's common for scouts to walk the 60 yards before the prospects run to verify the distance, since it's common for trainers to make it 58 yards to improve their player's times. Some sloppy trainers make it 55 yards and the times are so off that everyone has to start over and run a newly-measured 60 yards. The same issues that exist in domestic showcases exist here, but the added variables of a developing country and kids that are a couple years younger serve to make it especially challenging.

Kiley did a study for one of the early teams he worked for, going over all of the international signings of all time, to spot trends and inform strategy. He was troubled by the Mets track record, but not because it was bad. They were actually in the top half of teams in terms of WAR produced in that period by international signees.

The problem was that if you took out José Reyes, who signed for $13,500 (the 319th highest bonus that year out of 835 league-wide signings), they went from the tier of the 10th–15th ranked teams to the bottom five. When he recounted this anecdote to international scouting directors as a setup for a question about how tough it is to cope with the randomness of outcomes, they all, to a man, took a long pause before speaking and said some form of what Dodgers international director Ismael Cruz told us: "It happens to everyone. The ball is round."

Reyes was the 18th highest bonus of 36 Mets signees in 1999 and signed in September, after sitting on the open market for a few months. A completely anonymous signing at the time—one player signing for a medium bonus—is the difference, even with over a decade of signings considered, between firing or extending an international director.

OUR YANKEES PROSPECT LIST FROM the 2018–19 off-season was 38 players long, included 23 international players signed first by the Yankees, and, among those, six were signed for $100,000 to $300,000, while four more were signed for $50,000 or less. Nine more Yankee-signed sub-$300,000-bonus prospects were added to the list during the 2019 season.

FanGraphs' research shows that any player who makes the prospect list is worth at least $1 million in asset value (which means they're all criminally underpaid), so you can see why Yankees GM Brian Cashman has been aggressive trading for additional pool space, with a short-term positive Return on Investment (ROI) in a market where many teams are hoping for only a long-term positive ROI.

The Rays prospect list has a similar, staggering short-term ROI over multiple years. From their 2014 signing class, where they gave $2.95 million to high-profile bust SS Adrian Rondon, the Rays signed five current prospects, with three making the top 100 list (2B Vidal Brujan, C Ronaldo Hernández, now-Marlins RF Jesús Sánchez) while those five cost just over $1.1 million in pool expenditure. This class, with a high-profile miss, cost the Rays just under $6.4 million in bonuses and just over $3 million in penalties. The group now has an asset value of $114 million.

In 2017, the Rays signed Wander Franco for $3.85 million, who is now worth about $112 million, according to Craig Edwards' work, and in the 2015–18 signing classes, they added 11 more current prospects alongside Franco. These players are obviously more than just the cold asset values, but money is a common denominator that exists across baseball and it's useful to use it to show the scale of success/failure in these arenas, the same way runs are the common denominator in many advanced big league metrics.

You could make the case that these two, the Yankees and Rays, are the best international scouting groups, but they're both certainly in the top five by any measure. It's unsurprising that they go about their business in similar ways, and often they're going after the same players.

"MY GUYS WERE RAVING ABOUT him. Telling me, 'You've got to see him right away.' I saw him the next time I was in the DR. After 20 minutes of watching him, I had no words, I was just watching."

Rowland's first time seeing the prize of his 2019 signing class, Dominican CF Jasson Dominguez, must have been electric. He talks about it like someone talks about being properly laid for the first time. "Our top guys walk over and I ask, 'Is that what he looks like every day or is this his best day?' They say they've seen better. Are you shitting me?"

But once the adrenaline wore off, once he had transitioned into a scouting refractory period of sorts, he moved to the practical: "Are we sure about age? Yes? PED? Yes? Let's double check. I want to see him again soon. When the hair on my arms started to stand down… then we started the in-depth process."

Rowland took the international operational processes that had taken years and tens of millions to build and focused all of it on Dominguez. One of the adjustments MLB has made that teams are happy with is conducting PED tests very early in the process. Clubs can see players as early as 13 years old and within days get a PED test administered by MLB, and have them conducted multiple times to ensure what they've been seeing is real.

It sounds silly and macabre to do this with kids of this age, but it was born of necessity. Always off the record, even the best clubs have told us about players they signed in the last few years who ended up being busts because they agreed to a deal when the kid was 14 and he didn't have to take a PED test until he signed at 16, so they had to essentially guess if the trainer was scrupulous or not; often the kid isn't even sure what the trainer is injecting. MLB wanted to keep cost controls in place on the market and, realizing this meant teams would find value with younger players agreeing to verbal deals earlier, opted to be realistic rather than lecture teams about how to sign players.

Within the last decade or so, changes have also come to age and identity verification. It wasn't common, but every now and then a player would sign and start playing pro ball in the States, and the team would find out his age or identity was materially misrepresented. Steadily, MLB and the clubs got things to a point where this barely ever happens, though some clubs don't have as thorough of a process on low-figure signings. We'll often hear about a player who looked like a top prospect in the class at age 14, but once he's been on the radar long enough that MLB has done a couple rounds of background checks, he turns out to be three to four years older and eventually signs, after his league-imposed, year-long suspension, for a meager bonus. This has happened in the past, usually six to 12 months before the player is eligible to sign. In this situation, the club doesn't have the whole market to choose from when their seven-figure deal dissolves, but that's part of the risk in committing to a player early in the process, and why your scouts ideally will spot this before a formal background check. It happened in 2019 to a prospect whose age was adjusted to about a year older and the seven-figure deal remained intact.

Dominguez quickly had a thorough background check and multiple PED tests due both to his amazing talent, but also because his style of talent (mature-bodied, muscular, quick-twitch) is often the type that scouts flag as potential age fraud, since those physical qualities usually come later, if at all. If LeBron James was Dominican, fans would be saying he was older than his posted DOB on a daily basis. Outlier talents look weird next to their peers.

"He was even better when I saw him two days later. The game was on, it was a no-brainer. I asked the group, 'Are there any other 2019s that compare to him?' They said no. I repeatedly asked everyone, all the veteran guys, what their thoughts were. Victor Mata [the Yankees' supervisor of Dominican scouting] has been doing it for years and he said he's the best J2 guy he's ever seen. Several others said the same thing."

He doesn't mention the kid's name for tampering reasons, but this is notable because 2019 Dominican shortstop Robert Puason was considered the prize of the signing class a few years in advance—the best player since Wander Franco. He became famous outside of international scouting circles when, as part of its investigation into the Braves international malfeasance, MLB determined Atlanta had an illegal deal set up with Puason where they had essentially put a down payment on his bonus by overpaying marginal players from the same trainer in earlier classes, ahead of a bonus that was going to rival Dominguez's.

The Braves were barred from signing Puason when he was eligible, but that was more of a punitive punishment, as their total bonus pool for 2019 was reduced to $0, with only pool-exempt $10,000 bonus signings allowed.

The industry consensus is that Dominguez was the top player in the class, but some scouts still preferred Puason, a somewhat common level of disagreement in a market where many teams don't see top players for over a year before they sign, disappearing from 29 other teams after a verbal deal is in place. Oakland ended up signing Puason for $5.1 million (the same bonus as Dominguez), tops in the class.

Once again, Rowland processes the scouting opinions, then turns to practicality. "Okay, let's walk through the process thoroughly and in complete detail to make sure everything is covered before we dump all or most of our bonus pool into one guy. All the i's dotted and t's crossed.

"It was 70s and 80s [on the 20–80 scouting scale] any given day, across the board. Hit tool projection is obviously tough with anyone that far away, but all the measurables were all 70s and 80s. If and when he gets to the big leagues, let's see if it's all 70 and 80 grade level skills. Given the love for the game, makeup, intelligence, and competitive nature, I'm surely hopeful and think he'll be a hell of a big leaguer, or I wouldn't have done what I did. He's just one of those guys where you see it and you're like, 'Holy shit, is this real?'"

Rodriguez found himself, once again, ending up in the same place the Yankees staff did. "I felt similar seeing Franco for the first time as I did seeing Dominguez the first time. [Dominguez] had one of the craziest workouts I've ever seen."

Jasson Dominguez signed with the Yankees for a $5.1 million bonus on July 2, 2019, almost all of their $5.398 million bonus pool. We ranked him as the 61st best prospect in baseball the day he signed, whereas Franco was in the 100–150th overall tier the day he signed. Per Edwards' research, the 61st overall prospect is worth about $27 million on the open market.

The overlap between the Rays and Yankees doesn't end there. As part of the 2019 class, the Yankees were long tied to Dominican outfielder Jhon Diaz and sources indicated they had a deal in place contingent on the Yankees trading for more pool space to afford the agreed-upon low-seven-figure deal. It took the Yankees a little longer to do this than expected and, about a week before they got the necessary money, the Rays swooped in and signed Diaz for $1.5 million. Rowland has noticed that trading for additional pool space had gotten harder: "There's not as much trade money floating around as in the past. There's no penalty box now, so more teams want to invest and sign players for themselves with their own pool."

Rowland sees more than just a coincidence between the Yankees and Rays: "My guys and I, the decision-making group, were talking about this the other day. We ranked our top five competitors. Us and Tampa [Bay], we're always on the same players. I don't have an answer as to why. I'm a thousand percent confident our scouts aren't sharing notes. I can only attribute it to the fact that, through the course of time that people procure their process, their philosophies and ours have melded similar to each other. We have developed an attraction to some of the same processes."

Rodriguez see the same thing: "I don't know if they feel the same, but it seems like we're constantly competing with the Yankees on players, and not just on the top guys."

There's also the issue of budget for Rowland: "We have higher revenue, which we have used to have a bigger staff. We highly value scouting personnel and scout training. I think Tampa Bay does too. Part of our process is to get as many looks at a prospect as we can. Tampa Bay's guys work their asses off, I know that."

Rodriguez concurs: "The Yankees and Dodgers staff size is a place where the muscle stands out. Teams have choices on how to spend their money… the best way we can provide more long-term impact could be by an extra analyst or new initiative to add value across the board. Tech had exploded in the last five years in terms of analysts, video guys, TrackMan-type devices, Blast Motion, video scouting, etc. Some clubs are still in the exploratory phase, others have it as a big part of the evaluation process. We're constantly thinking about how to allocate budget for staffing, travel, academy, tech, and also a Jasson Dominguez, Wander Franco type vs. lots of players in one class. We won't take from the player-bonus budget under any circumstances but otherwise we keep an open mind."

How does Rowland approach spending his budget and getting the most out of his scouts? "Where do you spend money? First having a quality staff. We're fortunate to have the resources of a big, quality staff. You hire proven winners and pay them well. Or you hire potential A's and train the daylights out of them. We try to do a bit of both. We have a formal framework for that scout-training process. I'm sure Tampa Bay does a similar thing."

Ultimately, Rowland finds the keys to success lie in things like the rather boring daily admin work of managing a staff. "We also have a formal process for our scouts' schedules, vetting rosters, and attending various events, which are happening almost every day, all over the world. The only way to do it is to follow all these processes. Even then, we know it's a failure business."

IT MAY SEEM UNUSUAL, WITH all this talk of process, budgets, and modern business terminology applied to international scouting, that successful teams put a lot of value on the gut feel of a scout and intangible things like morale. Some organizations mostly ignore those things. Some organizations think morale is created by having success, as if Fleetwood Mac started getting along after *Rumours*. But it's probably important to note that none of the clubs described as being miserable to work for are Top 10 in terms of generating results from scouting departments by any measure.

"Our staff and I wake up knowing every day they could run into a big leaguer and they can sign that player," Rowland said. "It's an empowering feeling. It's long days and massive amounts of sacrifice in your personal life." This is how working in baseball really is. Longer hours than a normal job, often lower pay overall or at least lower pay per hour worked than a normal job, but the intangible feeling of accomplishment when you see your player on a big league field is indescribable.

In the previous chapter, we discussed how draft models are quickly growing in influence around the game, and in future chapters, we'll spend a lot of time talking about the general corporatization of organizations. Another area where these two topics come together is in the international realm.

Hearing it from Rowland, Rodriguez, and Cruz, international scouting is a stew, combining scouts, data, analysis, and other facets into a process that's a little better than other teams. One of those things carries the day for them, particularly in the international scouting arena. A few paragraphs ago, Rowland said the first thing that he prioritizes his budget on is a quality staff, a sentiment which all the people interviewed for this chapter hold.

This means that your scouts and what they think are paramount. This maxim is becoming less common in the game as teams are helmed by corporate baseball separatists, but the further away you get from stable big league data, the more important scouts become. International amateur scouting is the furthest you can get from the big leagues; prospects gestate for a long time before you get true feedback about how good they are. In 2019, the average age of someone making their big league debut was 24. Decisions about how much to offer or whether to sign the best international talents are made when the players are 14 or 15. Colleges can recruit kids at that age, but it's only a verbal commitment until at least age 17 and they're on the field ready to contribute at 18.

The tech-driven alternatives that cost-cutting orgs seek to apply across the minor leagues and elsewhere don't really exist in the international market, at least not with the blanket uniformity of other realms. Sure, teams have TrackMan units and the like at their academy, but these players' bodies and physical characteristics are going to change quickly and so will their outputs as measured by those devices. We've been told many forms of widely-used data for pro players is kinda useless for 15-year-olds.

Athleticism and physical projection are the two chief evaluation elements at this level and neither of those is quantifiable. Fostering and nurturing relationships with players and trainers can be the difference between signing a player and not, as can a certain type of charisma that appeals to young male athletes. There are game theory applications that can be applied to how a team chooses to target players, but that kind of strategy needs a foundation of intelligence provided by bush-beating scouts who can pref the players correctly and connect big league teams to those players. None of this stuff can be modeled and experienced scouts have a big leg up.

So it seems incredibly obvious that getting the best scouts, paying them well, keeping them happy, and empowering them to drive the process (with other elements, including data-driven ones, also included) is the most important in the international realm, the best recipe. "It's the last bastion of grassroots scouting," Rowland told us. "Obviously many other factors contribute to the final evaluation, but it's the last place where the process of forecasting a future value has to be driven by traditional scouting."

Not every team sees it this way, but they'd never admit that publicly. In the past, some racist owners just didn't want to invest in an international department in any way, and sometimes teams failed in this market because of this (luckily that point of view has left the game, but more recently than you may think) or some other factor entirely out of their control. Some GMs are fixated on their job security (people respond predictably to incentives) and the big league team, so they focus their capital on decisions with a short-term return. If you're a GM on the hot seat, are you going to be funneling resources toward talent that will take several years to contribute to the big league teams or possibly even appreciate into trade value? These GMs treat the international department budget like corrupt politicians treat education funding—like a piggy bank. Other teams see international scouting as an area to put second-tier people and thus they aren't aggressive about spending capital, and their director has trouble attracting and keeping top scouts.

Corporate-style GMs are more likely to think that scouts are replaceable and only worth what their track record can prove they've accomplished. Ironically, demanding results in order to pay a scout above a median salary means the scout is at risk to leave for a team that notices the scout's talent before the first team feels comfortable evaluating them at all, since they have to wait for the players on a pref list to develop before evaluating the scout. If you only have below-average scouts because you lose the good ones due to org culture, of course your data is going to say scouts aren't useful.

Further, this point of view, if taken to the logical extreme, would say that every player is a total crapshoot, gut feels of scouts are useless, and makeup reports will only serve to complicate the process of signing talented players. They see players as objects with an asset value and see a signing class like a hedge fund manager sees a basket of stocks.

This may sound ridiculous to you, to think that the GM of your favorite team sees "good" scouts (read: more expensive, seeking action to respond to their opinions) as a waste of money, but we've both heard plenty of stories to support the industry belief that there's more than a few GMs who openly talk like this in meetings. The international realm is an area where this point of view sometimes ends, given how the process differs from domestic operations, but some teams are bringing it into this market as well.

Teams like this don't spend big money at the top of the market, both because that's where the biggest misses are, but also because high-profile misses are how you get fired (or not promoted). And if the market is a crapshoot to be optimized, why take a big swing when you don't have to? Many decision-makers for teams like this are trying to fast-track themselves to be a GM and often don't have much international experience.

At first blush, separating clubs into two camps—no top-tier bonuses, ROI-focused bang for the buck, generally corporate approach vs. a more scouting-focused, bang-seeking approach—would seem too binary. After all, some MLB All-Stars signed for bottom-tier bonuses and some top-tier bonuses were given to marginal players.

Upon further inspection, the investment posture of the international department, across dozens of decisions every week, has to lean, at some level, into one of these two camps. Is the organizing principle of decision-making a fear of making a mistake (and staying out of the top of the market) or trying to find impact talent wherever it is (and responsibly seeking risk in search or reward)? Is the market a crapshoot that needs to be modeled and positive ROI zones identified or should scouting opinions drive the process? Eventually, you'll be forced to pick one, because the market will offer every conceivable situation, and more quickly than you'd think.

Is getting a quick positive result—a DSL batting title from an older non-prospect, making non-prospect pitchers throw more than 50 percent breaking balls in the DSL to juice their strikeout rates and try to create trade value in rival club's models—baseball's version of whatever flavor or financial hokem you detest most: pump-and-dump stock schemes, private equity takeovers–turned–bankruptcy, management consultancies like McKinsey or Bain, high-frequency trading and other create-no-value-but-get-rich scenarios? Is it shocking to see corporately modeled MLB teams with people who have worked in these industries trying stuff like this in a setting where almost no one is paying attention?

Rowland knows where he stands: "For me, getting bang at the big league level, the kind that wins championships, is what matters."

Similar to how the efficiency of choosing players in the draft improved after high school showcases became a staple, more elite prospects from the international realm are getting top bonuses, due to the prospect leagues holding regular games. Recently, the top international prospects on Top 100 lists included Yoán Moncada, Vladimir Guerrero Jr., Gleyber Torres, Rafael Devers, Eloy Jiménez, Wander Franco, Amed Rosario, Juan Soto, Fernando Tatís Jr., and Ronald Acuña Jr.

Seven of those 10 got bonuses in the top few of their class, Soto got $1.5 million, Tatís got $700,000, and Acuña is the outlier, signing for $100,000. If you dig a little deeper on the lists, Ozzie Albies and Victor Robles also signed for six figures and became elite prospects and good big leaguers, but the principle still generally holds. There's been a shift in efficiency since the advent of prospect leagues, with teams often giving the top bonuses to the top eventual pro performers.

It's worth noting that this applies mostly to hitters, as hitting development is mostly linear. Pitching development is often not linear, but tied to when physicality and arm speed develop, which is more random, but typically comes with age. This effect exists domestically and later in the development process, but it isn't as dramatic the older players get. This is the reason that the vast majority of seven-figure bonuses go to hitters internationally, since they're easier to predict at the ages at which clubs are agreeing to verbal deals. Thus, the predictability of bonuses to big league WAR for pitchers is less direct. If you count just 16-year-olds, pitchers make up 9 percent (7 of 79) of seven-figure bonuses in the last three signing classes.

CHAPTER 4

The Changing (But Still Mad) World of J2

"Everybody knew the name and had seen him. He was easy to see. The way he was hitting at his age was blowing us away," Ismael Cruz, then international director of the Blue Jays (now at the same position with the Dodgers), said, recalling his earliest memories of seeing Vladimir Guerrero Jr. before he signed him.

Everyone had seen Vladito. Kiley even saw him in early 2014, at a multi-day Dominican Prospect League event in Boca Chica for 2014 prospects. There was a brief showing of 2015 prospects at the end of the event, about 18 months before he was eligible to sign, before he had a deal. Cruz saw the same player that Kiley saw at that stage: "The body worried you, he might balloon in pro ball. At age 14 he was about 6'1", 215 or 220, with a 40-grade arm. Everyone said maybe start him in the outfield, but he may be a DH." After a very short showcase look, Kiley didn't think Vlad Jr. was a top tier prospect, but mainly because there wasn't a game portion to the event and there's where Vlad's elite skills were concentrated. A year later when Kiley saw him again, it was obvious he was a special player.

This is where our exploration of the more corporate approach to the J2 market comes into play. Kiley has done the full study of every international signing of all time for a club he worked for. It was pretty clear that, other than David Ortiz, players that were corner-only, non-third-baseman as amateurs basically had a success rate of zero. Every notable corner position player in the big leagues was an up-the-middle type as an amateur and usually at least a few years into pro ball.

Vladito looked like he fit into this danger zone, where both scouts and even more so analysts didn't want to spend big money. Despite his elite hitting skills, teams weren't lining up to spend their whole bonus pool on him like they did with Wander Franco or Jasson Dominguez, up-the-middle players with at least plus speed.

That's where the on-the-ground knowledge that comes from experience shifted things for the Jays. Cruz and his boss, then Jays GM Alex Anthopoulous, who is Canadian and worked for the Expos when Vlad Sr. was playing, had a meeting with Vlad Jr. and his agent/uncle, former big leaguer Wilton Guerrero. Anthopoulous asked Vlad Jr. what position he wanted to play in pro ball and Vlad Jr. said third base. Wilton jumped in to correct him and say that Vlad Jr. is an outfielder. Anthopoulous asked Vlad Jr. again, if that's really where he wants to play. Vlad Jr. says yes, "the dirt is where I feel comfortable," Cruz recalls, and then Wilton corrected him again, saying he hasn't even played in the infield.

Cruz says this stayed with him and his boss after the meeting, but they decided to not bring it up again when talking to Wilton or with Vlad Jr. when they had private workouts. "We wanted to avoid jeopardizing the signing and going against the uncle." When searching for a comp to hang their hat on, Cruz recalls his boss coming back to the same one: "Alex kept bringing up Sanó as a comp for Vlad Jr. Vlad had better plate discipline than Sanó, Sanó had a better body at signing."

Cruz added, "We went back and forth on the money, trying to get it down so we wouldn't go into the penalty just to sign him. We eventually got it to where we'd get a one-year penalty. That was the best we could get." Vlad Jr. signed for $3.9 million, within 5 percent of Toronto's pool, to land in the lower penalty bracket, after trades for more pool space to help them get there.

"Alex told our player development folks to try him at third base in the first workout after he signed. We never saw him play third base until we had him signed. At that point, I doubt anyone had. But we thought he had the raw skills to do it and he's done even better than we could've expected."

THE EFFICIENCY OF BONUSES WASN'T quite this stark before prospect league games were widespread, but now WAR-based studies will start showing the market is different than it used to be. Choosing to stay out of the top of the market precludes you from much of the impact talent, so you'd have to have a risk-averse analysis to tell you to never spend $2.5 million or more, which some teams appear to be actively employing as a strategy.

We spoke with an international scouting director who recounted a conversation he had with a rival director of a club that has this more corporate point of view. His recollection of this conversation: "They said paying top dollar, even for clearly the top talents in the class, is insane. They're completely risk averse, only searching for undervalued assets. He said they are looking for undersized position players, contact oriented, so they come out of the gate and have good stats. It's for trade value and also so they can get contract extensions or promotions due to good early results. Contracts are renewed yearly or every couple of years; it isn't clear if a player will be good until a couple contracts after you sign a class. DSL batting titles don't make the big leagues. They're scared of losing big, letting fear drive their decisions."

As you may have guessed, Houston is perceived as being at the forefront of this movement and rivals believe they have a significantly smaller scouting staff in Latin America than the Dodgers, Yankees, Rays, and other top programs. Cleveland appears to subscribe to this point of view in terms of how to spend their bonus pool, but notably appears to value both quantity and quality of scouts more in line with other top programs. They're also seen as the only corporate/progressive international program that's in the top tier in terms of process and results, and even though they seem to approach things this way, their backfields have been flush with talent for the last several years. The Indians club record international bonus is $2.1 million and the second highest is $1.5 million. Since Jeff Luhnow's arrival in 2011, the Astros top bonus to a 16-year-old is $2.25 million and the next highest is $1.8 million.

An interesting Houston-specific wrinkle is senior scouting advisor Charlie Gonzalez. He is based in south Florida and worked for Luhnow when he was the scouting director in St. Louis, landing players like Jon Jay and Kevin Siegrist. Gonzalez does a number of things for Houston, but primarily focuses on Cuban players, helping out in other departments as needed. Industry sources indicate that Gonzalez is one of the few scouts who isn't directing a department whose opinion Luhnow truly trusts. It's arguable that Houston's best international moves under Luhnow have been signing Cuban pitchers Cionel Pérez and Rogelio Armenteros and trading for DH Yordan Álvarez just after the Dodgers signed him. Cruz was the signing scout for Álvarez: "There were a few teams with interest, no one was pushing that hard. I later found out Charlie was on him."

The other factor of interest around Houston is their front office structure. Before Mike Elias left to be GM of the Orioles in 2019, he was Luhnow's number two and was in charge of player development, pro scouting, amateur scouting, and international scouting, starting in 2016. Houston seems to be leading the charge with this sort of structure, having an assistant GM in charge of all non-big league operations and, if they have director titles below that number two, they are less powerful than with most other clubs.

Invariably, this means the head of a few departments has no specialized experience in that department. After Elias, whose background is in domestic amateur scouting, left for Baltimore, Luhnow promoted Brandon Taubman to this role, whose background is only in the office, in administrative roles. Taubman was fired during the 2019 playoffs for an outburst at female reporters during the ALCS victory celebration in the Astros clubhouse.

This isn't to say that Cleveland has a bad or incorrect approach to international scouting. They're clearly getting above-average results and doing some things that other clubs aren't doing. We advocate for finding an unexploited approach in player selection and to keep pushing it until other teams start copying you, then to go find the next one. The issue is Cleveland is the best at this general approach and other clubs like Houston appear to be taking this mindset to its logical extreme, seeking efficiency and cost savings ahead of finding impact talent, all when the cost savings of a smaller staff are negligible, compared to getting an extra prospect per year. More on this issue is coming in later chapters.

Some international scouts take this dislike of more corporate-minded teams even further. Some think that the clubs with fewer scouts and scouts with fewer years of experience in the market are getting onto players once they see the top scouts for more successful clubs bearing down on them, peering over their shoulders while they take a test they've studied for. One top scout from a top-tier international club specifically detailed an instance where a club with an international director from a second-tier club, with a background in administration and no scouting background, suddenly became interested in a player once the top-tier team made an offer. The trainer later told the scout that this second-tier club hadn't talked to him about the player until the top-tier club made the offer. This is much more common in the international realm, as there's fewer markers (public rankings, college scholarship offers) of who the good players are early in their exposure to scouts. Seeing top scouts from top clubs bearing down on a player is a good predictor of quality if you aren't positive what you're looking at.

The stakes for fine-tuning your international process and yielding top-tier results are massive. In a study Kiley did at FanGraphs, we estimated the value created by each yearly signing class (the value in WAR, translated to dollars at the free agent rates for WAR, over the six to seven controlled years) as a whole at around $1 billion (adjusted for time value of money and of WAR), while bonus expenditures, now hard-capped, for all teams are at about $150 million. Team-specific annual variable expenses like staff, travel, a DSL team, and academy upkeep run about $2–$3 million per team. Multiple sources, who agreed with the broad strokes of this math, said that this proves that every team can afford to invest heavily in the international market; some just choose not to.

That puts the ROI of an international dollar spent, all expenses included at over 300 percent. Those returns don't have to take 10 years to accrue, when the six controlled big league seasons have happened. If a player shows potential a year or two after he's signed, he can be traded for the implied dollar value of that future return, to a club more interested in a future return than a current one. You can see why GMs from top-tier international programs see this market as one of the best investments they can make, regularly trading for more pool money.

There are still very few hard and fast rules when it comes to managing a baseball organization, as even Houston appears to be empowering and listening to at least one of its international scouts to positive effect. Particularly when it comes to international scouting, it pays to value scouts and their opinions. Rowland sums it up from his point of view: "Ultimately, it comes down to listening. If I've surrounded myself with a quality staff of highly trained evaluators that I respect, I would be an idiot if I didn't listen to them." We've seen many examples where this principle extends to GMs and owners as well.

CHARLIE GONZALEZ AND YORDAN ÁLVAREZ are a good example of what can be done by scouts who focus on the Cuban market. Most teams have a designated scout that mostly focuses on Cuban players, as there's now always high double- or triple-digit Cuban players that are free agents after defecting, usually based in the Dominican to maximize the scouting looks they can get.

Most of them never sign pro contracts. There's also numerous potential targets still in Cuba, playing on the various international traveling Cuban teams for each age group. Having one experienced scout that can put together history with these players and develop methods to quickly come to conclusions, often with limited information available, is key to succeeding in this market.

We covered the rules and potential changes to the rules regarding Cuban players in past chapters. Cuban signings have been governed many different ways over time, and the effects of the changes can be seen by looking at the pattern of the ages of the defectors. Long gone are the days when Cuban veterans like Orlando Hernández and José Contreras were leaving for the states in their prime, or just past it.

When the World Baseball Classic began early this century, teams could finally scout Cuban talent against elite competition. Contreras' initial deal was sizeable ($32 million) and likely motivated younger players to defect. Aroldis Chapman (21 years old when he left the island), Yunel Escobar (22), and Kendrys Morales (21) all split. Yasiel Puig and Yoenis Cespedes left Cuba earlier than their predecessors. At some point it became clear to Cuban prospects that the amount of time they had to sign before MLB tried to cap international spending was growing short. Now Lazaro Armenteros, Yoán Moncada, and others in their late teens began to leave before a hard cap was put on international spending.

It was an exodus of talent that left pro ball in Cuba relatively devoid of talent. At this point, all of the top-tier players over 20 years old have left and the only notable known quantities are veterans either over 30 or past their peak. The best Cuban players hitting the open market now are typically those with little profile, who defect after a good showing at a 15U or 17U international tournament, right when they can first be scouted in earnest outside of Cuba.

Rather than knowing, for years, that exciting players existed in Cuba who might soon defect and reach MLB quickly, now the level of discovery is at the teenage level. The best prospects on the top Cuban national teams are in the 19–22-year-old range and project as platoon players or potential low-end regulars, the best potentially worth low seven figures, but elite players still regularly pop up in the 15- to 16-year-old age range. The challenge scouts face in this reality is that Cuban players are harder to pin down on the evaluation.

RHP Yadier Álvarez was completely unknown and defected to no fanfare. Then rumors of mid-90s velocity were circulating when Kiley was in the

Dominican for FanGraphs to see Hector Olivera's workout in 2014, along with nearly 100 scouts. Álvarez threw two innings at the end of this event full of Cuban players who never signed, and hit 97 mph with preposterous grace and mechanical ease. He threw a handful more times privately for clubs, then the Dodgers gave him $16 million on July 2, 2015, which came with a matching $16 million tax penalty paid to MLB. Álvarez got onto top 100 lists early in his pro career and has fallen off of them as he's struggled in pro ball amid the Dodgers' public, growing dissatisfaction with his work habits. Cruz joined the Dodgers from the Blue Jays to helm international scouting a few months later.

Regardless of the process, making that decision with that amount of information is tough, and the range of outcomes is much wider than when scouting even 14-year-old hitters that you can follow for years before they sign.

These challenges are nothing compared to those that the Cuban players face. Many of them try to defect, fail, and are thrown in jail, only to keep trying until they succeed. Some are thrown in jail or put on house arrest when they're suspected to be plotting to defect. Both the Marlins RHP José Fernández (at age 13) and Dodgers/Angels 2B José Miguel Fernández (in his mid-twenties) are among the many that have had a form of this happen to them.

As detailed in the harrowing 2014 *LA Magazine* piece by Jesse Katz, among other accounts by other writers, Yasiel Puig was snuck out of Cuba on a speedboat by a drug cartel. After exiting the country, he was essentially kidnapped, as the drug cartel held him for ransom until an agent or other middleman appeared to pay cash for the service the cartel had done.

This is not an unusual path, though Puig's high-profile nature and potential big payday also caused him to be treated more like a financial asset than a human being, with more severe conditions than most other players encounter. There was some hope, briefly, in 2019, when MLB and the Cuban government reached an agreement for a posting program like Japan and Korea have with MLB, where the Cuban government would get a cut of players sold to MLB teams. The Trump administration decided this was in violation of the embargo against Cuba since money would be going from U.S. companies to the Cuban government, and stopped it. Reports indicate at least a dozen players defected from Cuba in the weeks after the posting program was scuttled.

It's also a risky area for agents to get involved. The line between representing a player's interests by helping negotiate a contract after they've defected from Cuba and the label "human trafficker" for helping a player actually leave the country can sometimes get blurry. Does the agent know about the player's intentions before the player defects? If the agent is simply in the country where the player defects to, it sets off alarm bells to investigators.

It's also proving to be risky for teams. What if a scouting director happens to be in the Central American country with little baseball culture right when a Cuban player defects there? That could seem suspicious, or enterprising that he's got a leg up on other teams in creating history and a relationship with the prospect.

The Department of Justice has launched an investigation into possible wrongdoing by MLB teams in this area, with reports mentioning the Dodgers, Braves, Padres, Hector Olivera, and one-time agent Rudy Santin among the entities of interest. This investigation appears to be centered on corruption, specifically if MLB teams bribed government officials in the process of clearing Cuban players to sign, but there are no clear results of this investigation yet.

MLB has sent memos to clubs in the past outlining the federal laws that apply to Cuban players. Even talking to a Cuban player when at an international tournament and telling them that they could make good money if they defected is a federal crime, as that sort of casual advice gets really close to enticing human trafficking when the player is still residing in Cuba.

Once the players defect, it often takes weeks or months to get paperwork in order, then months to get the player into ideal shape. It was common when older Cuban players defected to not be available to scouts until they got into insane shape, months after defecting, getting the top-tier training and diet that often isn't available in Cuba, and certainly not as they're cooped up in a hotel room, hiding, for weeks on end. Scouts would refer to a linebacker-looking prospect as a "Cuban physique" because it was common to go to the first open workout of a Cuban player and see them in skin-tight performance gear to show off the 20 lbs. of muscle they added since their last appearance for a Cuban club. This isn't as suspicious as it would seem otherwise, given where they were coming from. Context is important.

In some of the older cases of more mature players defecting, this allowed clubs to use their data, video, and scouting advantages to have a clearer opinion of the player. When an unknown 16-year-old defects, every team is getting basically the same information at the same time. When Yoenis Cespedes defected in his mid-twenties, there was a long history of video from games in Cuba's top pro league; statistics from that league; and video, stats, and scouting looks from international tournaments for close to a decade.

Before the bonus pool period, there was an odd mystique around Cuban players. There were a couple waves of talent where seemingly every one was an All-Star and the Cuban premium started to get out of hand. We heard from an agent that one Cuban player that signed a modest big league deal that his next best offer was a minor league deal for millions less. Exactly one team thought there was still a big Cuban premium and there weren't enough players on the market often enough to have direct comparisons to know they were wrong. Right about when the soft bonus pools began and the clear straight-to-the-big-leagues Cubans and clear prospect types were separated financially, teams started figuring out that a 16-year-old Cuban that's been scouted in two international tournaments isn't any different than a 16-year-old Dominican you've been seeing in more casual games for a year or two.

We spoke with a director from one of the aforementioned top-tier teams and he said before his club streamlined the process for international decision-making, that his club's office analytics people were overruling him on mature Cuban players on the basis of their statistical performances. Eventually, the players had less track record as the defectors got younger and the office realized that there was enough intangible makeup and scouting history to make the scouts' opinions a bigger part of the decision-making pie. This director thinks he would've landed multiple Cubans that eventually became All-Stars if left to his own devices. He summed up that mistake: "In the draft, you can run the draft completely off a model and do pretty well. Internationally, you can't."

"THE BAT WAS ALWAYS ADVANCED, every time we saw him. He was similar to Vladimir Guerrero Jr. in that way, they were both monsters at the plate."

Cruz recalls the defensive skills of Yordan Álvarez. "We saw him four or five times, put him in left field, right field, center field, first base. We knew it was a bat-only type; Vlad Jr. was definitely a better defender."

"He's a great kid, the makeup was there. He wanted a lot of money, came out after the Cuban frenzy in late 2015. We spent some money on younger guys and he wasn't in the picture." Lots of teams went over their international budgets in 2015 and had earmarked that money far in advance, like the Braves at the beginning of this chapter. While teams could technically spend as much as the wanted, they were running into internal budget limits when Cuban players kept popping up, after seeing money being spent wildly.

"He was a DH type and there wasn't a ton of money in the market at that point, so half the teams were out. We saw him at a workout at Killian High School in Miami and he was putting balls on houses in right field. That's where the deal was done."

Álvarez was signed for $2 million (plus a $2 million penalty) on June 15, the last day of the 2015–16 signing period and was traded to the Astros just over a month later for reliever Josh Fields.

Around the World in 20–80 Days

An overwhelming ratio of MLB talent, let alone international talent, comes from the Dominican Republic and Venezuela, but it is a global game with growing reach and cultural relevance elsewhere. The depth of baseball's roots in each culture, as well as how refined MLB's process is for mining talent there, varies depending on which country we're talking about.

Mexico and other Caribbean-satellite islands like Curaçao and the Bahamas are middle-tier talent producers. Curaçao would be in the top tier if it weren't limited by its size and population. The island, which is in the southern Caribbean, about 40 miles off the northern coast of Venezuela, has a population of about 160,000, roughly the size of Clarksville, Tennessee. And yet Curaçao has produced several All-Stars, and it's the highest per-capita producer of MLB talent.

Cruz told us about the first time he saw Jurickson Profar as an amateur player in Curaçao. "Lots of people are laid back and kinda lazy there. Profar was like that. Don't think he had a deal yet at this point. He was wearing flip-flops to the field, coming from school. He didn't run well, was kinda lazy, didn't have infield actions, looked like more of a pitcher. Every country is different. You've gotta be patient and do the homework and know the context." It's common for kids in Curaçao to go to school until they sign (most Dominican kids stop at around age 12), and know three languages: English, Spanish, and Papimiento.

Most ballplayers from Mexico come from the Western portion of the country. It churns out a lot of pitchability pitching prospects and middle infielders with bat-to-ball skills.

Japan loves baseball and it's deeply ingrained in the culture there, so much so that Nippon Professional Baseball (NPB, the top pro league in Japan) seeks to keep top domestic talent in Japan for as long as possible before they come to the MLB. This led to the institution of a system MLB and NPB have agreed upon, in which players who'd like to play in MLB must either wait to have played nine pro seasons in Japan before they sign with an MLB team as a free agent, or else be subject to "posting."

Players without the requisite nine years of professional experience to gain international free agency can request to be "posted" for Major League clubs. Under posting rules that were instituted in the 2018–19 off-season (these rules have changed several times in the last decade), the "release fee"—an amount that an NPB club must receive in the event an agreement is reached between a posted player and an MLB team—depends on the value of the contract a posted player signs.

MLB clubs have a month to negotiate with a posted player. If no agreement is reached in that timeframe, the player returns to his NPB club for the following season. He cannot be posted again until the next off-season.

Previously, Japanese clubs set a release fee that could be as high as $20 million, and before that there was uncapped, sealed bidding for players' negotiating rights. Unlike other forms of MLB talent acquisition, the NPB posting system has trended in a player-friendly way. Yu Darvish was posted during a time of uncapped bidding for exclusive negotiating rights, which meant the teams benefitted from a free market in which all 30 teams could bid for those rights, but the player could only then negotiate with the team that won. For example, the Rangers bid $51 million just to talk about a deal with Yu Darvish, and signed him for $60 million over six years.

Under the following set of rules, with a $20 million posting fee cap, during which all teams who bid $20 million for negotiating rights could talk to the player, Masahiro Tanaka got seven years, $155 million because he was allowed to negotiate with all the teams who had bid $20 million rather than just one. He was the beneficiary of a market rather than his NPB club.

Now, the "posting fee" is called a "release fee" and is a scaled percentage of the deal the player ultimately agrees upon with any MLB team, determined after the player signs rather than before. So now the player's market dictates the release fee given to his former NPB team, rather than the other way around.

MLB's goal is to acquire talent for as little money as possible while, in this relationship, NPB's goal is to preserve the quality of play in their league and bolster national pride, which is great for marketing (flag flaps in the wind behind red-white-and-blue beer cans). NPB wants the best Japanese players to hang around for a while and sell tickets and jerseys, rather than leave baseball in Japan in a talentless stupor like what has happened in Cuba. But this means the players coming over from Japan are older, and they've accumulated a lot of statistics at a high level of play. They've also performed in front of tech that measures their physical abilities (there are TrackMan units in Japan), so teams take an approach to scouting Japan that's similar to how they'd scout Double-A and Triple-A.

Japan has a specific baseball culture, with lots of native players that have an active, slappy swing like Ichiro and a couple North American players in each lineup, typically power hitters. There aren't a ton of changes made by either camp in terms of development. On the pitching side, a number of 4A-type North American pitchers have gone to Japan and dramatically improved with subtle changes, leading to a payday back in the States. The general differences in Japan include more throwing on the side, longer bullpens at lower effort (sometimes 200 pitches), throwing starters once a week for more pitches, and a focus on fastball command, to the end of a lack of wasted pitches, which will often improve command. Also, the splitter is a much more common pitch there and is often learned.

While Japanese players now enjoy something resembling a free market for their services under the new posting/release agreement, players from South Korea, which has seen baseball grow in popularity quite significantly throughout the past decade, are subject to posting rules from the stone age and are allowed to negotiate only with the MLB team that submitted the highest posting bid.

We've spoken with international scouting sources who suggest that Korea is one of the countries with the most potential for growth as far as baseball-talent output and actualization is concerned. Not only has South Korea made significant, and fairly recent, economic strides, there's also been a groundswell of cultural relevance baseball has enjoyed since the 2008 Summer Olympics.

"After Korea won gold in Beijing, it changed things," an international scout told Eric as he was sourcing opinions about free agent Korean hitters for an ESPN Insider piece in 2015. "They then did well in the subsequent World Baseball Classic, won the Asian games the year after that, [and] baseball took off."

From that piece:

> While the game is seemingly growing in Korea, the people are as well. A 2015 report from University of Oxford economist/researcher Max Roser shows that South Korean men are becoming physically bigger at a staggering rate. Korean men born in the 1950s had an average height of 168.6 centimeters (about 5'6½") at adulthood, while South Korean men born in the 1980s average 173.8 centimeters (about 5'8½"). Meanwhile, the height of the average American adult male has risen only two centimeters during that same time frame. The same phenomenon is occurring in Japan, where the average male born in the '80s is eight centimeters taller than in the '50s.

Australia and Korea have produced comparable flows of talent to MLB. The new CBA rules dictating players must be well into their mid-twenties before coming to MLB from a foreign country might help cultivate baseball there, as good homegrown players like Robbie Glendinning become stars in the Australian Baseball League before potential transition. The ABL was only founded in 2009, so baseball Down Under is still in its infancy.

Taiwan has a history, like South Korea, of top high school players signing in the J2 period when they finish high school. Because of this extra development, some heavily scouted international tournaments, great in-game feel, and the leverage of college options, bonuses normally are inflated a bit in Korea, Taiwan, and Australia relative to the pure tools for what you'd get in Latin America. Players do not get posted from the top Taiwanese professional league due to a long history of meddling by organized crime and match fixing, casting doubt over the true ability of players in the league. Any players with MLB potential in that league go to Korea (KBO) or Japan (NPB) to get to the U.S.

Another potential sleeping talent giant is Brazil. The Association of Nikkei and Japanese Abroad estimates that 1.9 million people of Japanese descent are currently living in Brazil, the most in a country outside of Japan, and with them they brought Japan's love for baseball. The game has gripped the culture enough to make rock stars out of Yan Gomes and Paulo Orlando. The country has a population of just over 200 million, and a handful of sports (jiu-jitsu, basketball) vying for the space in the public consciousness behind soccer. The Blue Jays signed Brazilian RHP Eric Pardinho, who has Japanese heritage, for $1.4 million in 2017.

China's population size also makes it intriguing as a place to search for talent. Milwaukee signed a pair of Chinese pitchers recently and at least one of them—teenage righty Lun Zhao—has a real shot to make the big leagues. Just one big leaguer would probably be huge for baseball's popularity in China, which might snowball into more dudes.

There is some baseball in South Africa and various parts of Europe. The potential for growth in Europe may be limited by space. There isn't sprawling, flat, vacant land on which to put many baseball diamonds. Twins outfielder Max Kepler hails from Germany and an Italian shortstop named Marten Gasparini got $1.3 million to sign with Kansas City several years ago. It's likely that continent will spit out a real talent once in a while, but it isn't likely to show significant growth, in part because cricket already has such a hold on the culture in many European countries. Same goes for India and countries in the Middle East.

RODRIGUEZ'S VOICE LIGHTS UP WHEN we ask about the signing story that stands out the most in his mind. "It's my craziest story for sure. The cook at our complex found us a prospect, maybe even a big leaguer! Everybody around there loves the game.

"Every now and then, we have tryouts for friends of the academy, neighbors, local kids, that sort. Not on a regular basis at all. Our cook recommends a guy and that kid brings two other guys from the same program. The main kid wasn't that good, pure rock thrower, all over the place, threw hard, but everything was to the backstop. The other guy wasn't that good, either.

"The third kid was 5'11", 135 lbs. But he was 88–89, pretty clean, diminutive frame, and the kids were kinda making fun of him; they gave him a nickname because of his bad teeth. He was the best one. We brought him back to play in the Tricky League and he's 89–94, so we sign him. Then he gained eight pounds and a year later he hit 97 mph. In 2019, he was up to 101."

The player's name is Joel Peguero; he's been on our Rays prospect list for a couple years and has a good chance to reach the big leagues as a reliever.

The Rays had another unusual signing whose genesis was also in the Tricky League, but he was playing for the Astros squad. "There's an interesting lefty, sitting 83–85 and one of our supervisors, Danny, asks who that is. I'm looking at him more closely and I'm like, 'That's a tryout guy; look at his busted shoes. They wouldn't let one of their players on the field like that.' Danny goes looking around the field for the agent, invites him back to our place in a couple days and we signed him for $35,000. We were hoping he'd turn into a 90–94 type control guy, but now he's in the upper 90s."

He's since been traded to the Cardinals, but that's how the Rays signed Genesis Cabrera.

EVERY PROGRAM HAS SUCCESSES AND failures and some have good processes but bad results for stretches. There are also clear moments when the wrong thing has been done.

Given the amount of autonomy international departments have over choosing their players, there's also a greater chance for rule-breaking. In 2008, the White Sox fired two scouts and senior director of player personnel Dave Wilder for a scandal that involved bonus skimming. Skimming is the practice of inflating the evaluation of a player in scouting reports to create a paper trail of false pretense, then paying the player more than he's worth (but in line with the false report) and splitting the difference with the player's agent, who is in on the deception and taking a cut. This is a way to steal money from a team when you may be in charge of a $10 million international budget, but can't just write yourself a check.

Given the wildly divergent opinions about the ability of teenage prospects, it's hard to prove this is happening. Rumors circulate around baseball of international scouts doing this even to this day, on a very small scale (like skimming $10,000, the max amount of cash you can take through customs, off of something like a $200,000 bonus) to where it's almost impossible to prove unless someone is sloppy. We've heard rumors of a scout suspected of doing this (since fired) who was rumored to always be on the grift, including having a half-dozen rental cars stolen in one year in the Dominican.

There was another notable skimming scandal in 2009 when Nationals GM Jim Bowden and special assistant to the GM (and former big league pitcher) José Rijo resigned. This scandal centered around alleged 16-year-old Esmailyn Gonzalez, to whom the Nationals gave $1.4 million, who then turned out to be a 20-year-old named Carlos Lugo. There were also some lower-profile scandals at the time, according to a March 1, 2009, *New York*

Times story about Bowden and Rijo by Joshua Robinson and Michael S. Schmidt:

"Last July, the Red Sox fired their Dominican scouting supervisor, Pablo Lantigua, for what was presented as a violation of team policy. A month later, the Yankees dismissed their director of Latin American scouting, Carlos Ríos, and their Dominican Republic scouting director, Ramón Valdivia, when similar accusations of bonus skimming surfaced. Baseball officials also made referrals to the F.B.I. in those cases."

Like with steroid and identity problems in later years, MLB has almost completely snuffed out skimming. But other issues arose. About a decade later, during the advent of bonus pools, teams began packaging players. In 2016, the Red Sox were caught inflating the value of players as a way to work around the $300,000 limit put on them for exceeding their 2014 bonus pool to sign Yoán Moncada.

The Red Sox signed a bunch of players from the same trainer to deals that included a $300,000 signing bonus. Some of them were barely pro prospects who other teams wouldn't have come close to offering $300,000. Others were better than their $300,000 price tag and getting those players for that price is what set off alarms around the industry.

An MLB investigation revealed the money was being redistributed to the better players later, behind closed doors. This way, the Red Sox got access to players they shouldn't have been able to land. All of the players involved were deemed free agents, the Red Sox couldn't sign an international player for a year, and the two notable prospects at the center of the plan, outfielders Simon Muzziotti (Phillies) and Albert Guaimaro (Marlins), got second "amateur" bonuses after playing a summer for the DSL Red Sox.

The biggest sanctions yet, perhaps ever, came in 2017 when Braves GM John Coppolella was fired and banned for life from baseball for a larger packaging scheme. Since the highest-profile players signed in this period weren't packaged, MLB decided that since the Braves had packaged players on a smaller scale (underpaying young players subject to bonus pools, overpaying Cuban players from the agents that aren't subject to bonus pools, all to avoid going into the penalty zone) in 2015 before their big expenditure in 2016, that all of the players signed in 2016, though not packaged, were acquired through circumvention of the rules.

This meant over $15 million worth of prospects (plus another roughly $10 million in penalties for exceeding their pool)—headlined by Kevin Maitán (Angels), Abrahan Gutierrez (Phillies), Yunior Severino (Twins), Guillermo

Zuniga (Dodgers), Yefri Del Rosario (Royals), and Livan Soto (Angels)—were taken from the team, hit the open market like the Red Sox players did, and collected a second "amateur" bonus soon after the first one.

It was also alleged that the Braves had entered into a similar packaging scheme with 2019 prospect SS Robert Puason (later signed by the A's), already putting a down payment of sorts on players from Puason's trainer ahead of the 2019 class as part of a deal. In addition, the Braves were set to sign Korean SS Ji-Hwan Bae (Pirates) to a contract that hadn't yet been cleared by MLB, that was alleged to include a bonus packaging scheme. The Braves were barred from signing either of those players, as well.

The punishment was a firing for Coppolella and a lifetime ban; a firing for special assistant to the GM (and international department head) Gordon Blakeley and a one-year ban; along with losing all of those players, the penalty payment from signing the players, the rights to signing two more, being able to sign no players above $10,000 through the 2019–20 international period, and a halved bonus pool in 2020–21.

International scouts were shocked at the extent of the punishment for Atlanta, particularly for their first offense, though conceded the extremes the team went to were unique. International department heads were scared that this meant MLB would enforce other rules that hadn't previously been enforced, like agreeing to verbal deals before the July 2 period began, but MLB made it clear to clubs that it was/is only punishing packaging deals to circumvent the pools, not early deals.

There have also been plenty of examples of mistakes in the international market that aren't due to malfeasance, but simply hubris. Scouts will tell you about times when teams decided they wanted to "make a splash," often after opening a new academy, and jumped in the deep end of high-dollar players without much prior experience.

One example that comes up often is the 2008 Padres signing class. They spent over $5.9 million, signing prospects for bonuses of $2 million (Venezuelan RHP Adys Portillo), $1.25 million (Venezuelan OF Luis Domoromo), $1 million (Dominican RHP Jorge Guzman), and $500,000 (Australian OF Corey Adamson). The class of 16 players yielded no big leaguers and the previous highest bonus for the organization was $750,000. The Padres announced a new Dominican academy in 2007 and it opened in 2008.

Another notable example of international malarkey, known widely in the industry, was stumbled through by former Arizona Diamondbacks brain trust chief baseball officer Tony La Russa, general manager Dave Stewart, and senior VP of baseball operations De Jon Watson. La Russa was a former successful manager. Stewart was one of the better pitchers of the late 1980s, then became a pitching coach and executive before becoming an agent. Watson's previous job was eight years with the Dodgers as head of player development, rising to the title of assistant GM before joining Arizona. Before that, Watson had been the director of pro scouting for Cleveland, a pro scout for Cincinnati, the domestic amateur scouting director for Cincinnati, and an area scout for the Marlins.

Watson had experience in domestic amateur scouting, pro scouting, and player development prior to joining Arizona, and with the D'Backs he was in the high profile role of—according to his D'Backs executive bio—overseeing "the franchise's professional, amateur, and international scouting as well as all player development functions. Along with general manager Dave Stewart, he advises chief baseball officer Tony La Russa on all key decisions." As the de facto number three in the organization, one step below the GM, Watson had risen to a level where he was in charge of every non–Major League department with the team, but he had no real experience in one of those areas: international scouting.

None of them did. Watson joined the D'Backs in September 2014, alongside new GM Dave Stewart, and left the team in September of 2016. In the interim, they made some ill-advised decisions.

As their first big splash in the international market, according to sources, the D'Backs struck a verbal deal with Dominican SS Wander Javier, one of the top players in the 2015 class, for a bonus between $3 million and $4 million. That wasn't a mistake, as Javier was clearly one of the top players in the class to any scout at that point; his pro career has been a bit below expectations due to injuries, but that's besides the point.

In the months leading up to the 2015 signing period, Javier ultimately signed with the Twins for $4 million because of what the D'Backs did next. Watson wanted to find some impact talent that was closer to the big leagues and fell in love with Cuban RHP Yoán López, who is currently the D'Backs set-up man, but that's not really the point. In January 2015, six months before Javier was set to sign with the team, the D'backs signed López for $8.27 million.

The bonus rules at this point were a soft cap: a number you could exceed, but the penalty for going well over it was a dollar-for-dollar tax on any overage and two years of no signings over $300,000. López's bonus was about double the D'Backs pool, so his signing came with another couple million in penalties on top of the bonus, it voided their verbal deal with Javier since they'd now be locked out of the next signing period because they exceeded their pool this year, and they'd be in the penalty box again the following year, in 2016. Due to their poor performance on the field, the D'Backs were set to have the No. 1 pick in the next draft (Dansby Swanson) but also the biggest international pool, room for Javier's big bonus and then some.

This still could be seen as a change of plans on Javier and a shift to favoring López. But that wasn't how it happened. Multiple sources that worked in the Arizona front office and multiple sources from other teams confirmed that Watson, who is listed as López's signing scout by Baseball America, signed López both without knowing there would be a penalty on top of the bonus and not knowing that it precluded him from signing Javier. It seems ludicrous to think Stewart—whose wife, Lonnie Murray, would later become López's agent for a time—didn't sign off on the deal somehow, which would indicate he was either unaware of, or simply not properly weighing, the total costs, monetary and otherwise, of the deal.

Two scouts told us about walking up to Watson at the first major international event after López signed to ask if it was fair game to go after Wander Javier now, since the D-backs clearly couldn't sign him. Both scouts recount that Watson was confused by this question and a D'Backs source confirmed that Watson didn't run the signing by the full front office, which included people who specialize in the rules and would have immediately known the implications.

Six months later, the team essentially sold 2014 first-round selection Touki Toussaint to the Braves in exchange for $10 million in salary relief. This was an NBA-style salary dump, where Bronson Arroyo was due a little over $10 million and was injured, Toussaint was a top 100 prospect and the D'Backs return, infielder Phil Gosselin, was an end-of-roster bench player. Toussaint was attached to Arroyo to get someone to take his contract and sources indicate this was to balance the $8 million tax penalty paid on López's deal, as first reported by Keith Law in an ESPN Insider column.

If viewed together, some combination of the D-backs front office paid an extra $6 million to effectively swap Touki and two years of activity in the international market, for López. They either didn't know the rules or had no idea how to value players.

Diamondbacks ownership bears some of the blame for putting La Russa and Stewart, who both deserve to be remembered for other accomplishments

(Stewart's playing career and foundation of Sports Marketing Partners agency, La Russa's managerial career and animal advocacy), in positions they were clearly ill-equipped to handle. The D'Backs declined an option on Watson's contract after the 2016 season, but he was hired to be one of the Washington Nationals' assistant general managers the following January. He got himself a World Series ring in 2019.

In his Diamondbacks bio, the club recapped Watson's tenure as such:

"Since joining the D-backs, Watson has increased the franchise's focus in the international market, playing a key role in the team's signing of Cuban free agents Yasmany Tomás and Yoán López."

THERE ARE SOME POTENTIAL CHANGES coming to the market in the next Collective Bargaining Agreement (CBA), possibly sooner. We cover it in the first chapter, but it's worth a slightly longer discussion here. If the international draft is instituted in a form similar to what's been proposed so far, there's an opening for domestic amateur draft–style models to be a huge part of the international draft process. This level of analysis is only a factor for a handful of teams at this point, and usually in a limited universe of players they are actively scouting.

Given the amount of homogeneity in a potential international draft— all players would have to register, have uniform background checks, steroid tests, physical combine-style tests, have the chance to play in MLB-affiliated prospect leagues—teams with smaller staffs could get an edge with players and data being easier to come by, and relationships and historical knowledge/ connections would become less important. Teams with more analysts (and better analysis) will excel by running burgeoning international data through similar systems they use to partially or wholly automate MLB advance scouting, pro scouting, and domestic amateur scouting.

Rodriguez is still confident: "I think we're set up to be able to handle different scenarios. The Yankees have Donny, who used to run a draft room, most guys have some level of involvement in a draft in their past. Our new international director, Steve Miller, used to be an area scout and crosschecker, and one of our international crosscheckers was a national crosschecker before that."

Rowland is as well: "The teams that have shown an ability to get an edge in this market are the most likely to get an edge in a draft setting, even if it doesn't appear to advantage them directly at first."

GMs will likely get more involved with trading of international picks likely a part of the new system. This means big leaguers and wholesale rebuilds could be leveraged in the international market, thus more public scrutiny, and for us specifically, more rankings, movement, scouting looks, and draft rumors.

A director went off the record to discuss these proposed changes: "There will be more senior-level evaluators doing crossover work, both international and domestic, to have more consistent ways to apply evaluations. There will be more front offices getting involved. Everyone will have some type of modeling, different things that give you a way to get more consistent in evaluations across departments, since they're more linked and have more in common now."

An underrated change is in a draft, instead of merely needing to be right about the players that you sign and hoping you saw all the players that matter, you need to know and have an opinion about every eligible player. Having standardized information from a set player pool and the ability to trade up and down means every pick by any team is a decision by all 30 teams, even passively. This still means that bigger staffs can scout players for future classes and have almost exclusive history on players before they enter the more standardized system in the year that they're draft eligible.

The latest proposal for a 20-round draft is too many rounds for most scouts, as the picks are compelled and hard-slotted in the current incarnation, meaning you have to pick a player to give $100,000 to at a certain pick if you can't trade it, even if, in a non-draft scenario, you'd rather sign a couple players for lower bonuses that total $100,000. There will also be a host of unintended consequences. Some may be obvious right when the new rules are announced, but there will certainly be more that emerge later in the process.

The draft will, in whatever form it takes, lower overall costs, put a cap on the top of the market, and likely smooth the middle-tier bonus. Scouts think whatever MLB ends up implementing will move lots of $10,000 type players that take less due to odd timing in the year-round period when players can sign, moving up to $100,000 to satisfy hard slots, and some mid-six-figure types will slide down into that range.

Another director went off the record to discuss these potential changes: "The draft will make evaluations get better due to more information. It'll enable teams to invest money better since they'll know a lot more, could run smaller staffs, and pay about the same for the players. That's the goal of the owners. They want to spend more of their pool on top-end players, know more about the players, and avoid big cost increases, saving where they can."

It's also rumored the new CBA could reduce minor league affiliates in the short-season and low minors in exchange for higher minor league pay and a more robust independent league. For teams that like to have more players than others in their minor league system, that could mean more DSL and GCL/AZL teams to handle the players, but flexible enough to be cut or added year to year without other, fixed commitments like in the Appalachian or Northwest Leagues.

THE INTERNATIONAL MARKET IS CONSTANTLY changing. We have some opinions about how we'd spend an international budget, but we also may change our minds in a couple years if the market shifts again. We'll be brief with this, since this chapter may have spanned multiple trips to the bathroom for most of you and you've already got the opinion of plenty of seasoned experts on the topic so far.

The things you pay a retail price for in the J2 market are current raw power, current velocity, and current bodies. Scouts love to project, but when there's no projecting, things get easier. Often these types of prospects are universally drawing multiple retail-priced bids since there's a carrying tool that's easy to see, but that usually overshadows some real issues in the background, like contact ability, or command, that are essential to success.

Thus, the sorts of hitters we'd stay away from are now-body, power-over-hit types at the top of the market; this group is littered with busts. The sliver for exceptions in this group are prospects with elite athleticism, but even then, there aren't many of these. Bad makeup is a killer and especially if it comes with a bad body, bad swing, or bad delivery, because the bad makeup makes it less likely adjustments can be made, even to seemingly fixable things. High-effort pitchers with below-average athleticism are total stay-aways, except for the lowest (like $10,000) bonuses.

On the positive side, teams still get discounts, even at the top of the market, with players that are hit-tool first, that perform in games and have instincts, but lack elite physicality, projection, or standout tools. Going back to the section where we mention Cleveland's style of player, this is the type that they tend to target, that they rightfully think is undervalued, and that they've done a good job with so far. We would also target this player as part of our overall approach.

On the pitching side, deep projection, low-cost, lottery ticket–type arms would be most of our signees, but we'd also go into the low-to-mid-six-figures at times to get a premium version of this. Along those lines, the one-tool projection hitters with good makeup are another low-to-medium budget target for us. Typically, this will be a kid with athleticism and one standout tool, but nothing else really, and you're banking on one having dormant skills that emerge and your development crew can fine-tune what's already there.

Going back to the bang vs. bang for the buck discussion, we'd also target the very top of the market, for the truly special player every year or two. When there's a Wander Franco or Vladimir Guerrero Jr., we need to get in there early enough, identifying them at age 13 or 14, to where we have a shot to build the relationship and sign them if they are a truly elite prospect with elite tools, skills, and makeup. Much like the top players in the NBA, the constraints on bonuses in the international market make the best player or two in the international market great values, even if analysis says that top-dollar players in general are overvalued.

CHAPTER 5

Prose About Pros Scouting Pros

You're the new director of pro scouting for a team who finished the previous season at the bottom of its division. It's known, publicly and throughout baseball, that your primary task is to lead a rebuild that will yield a competitive team three or so seasons from now, depending on how well ownership and the young, doe-eyed GM who hired you perceive you to be executing.

You know your current big league roster has three or four veteran pieces who have varying amounts of trade value, including one All-Star-caliber player whose contract has three years remaining, set to expire when he's 33 years old, just as your team is expected to be competitive again.

The team's previous GM had a background in finance and didn't really care what scouts think, so a few years before their club bottomed out, they resurrected the corpse of Al Dunlap to come in and lay a bunch of them off. You need to restock your department with competent eyeballs and structure it in a way that best prepares you to collect information on rival prospects for the coming fire-sale. What do you do? Let's talk about building and structuring a pro scouting staff.

Know Thyself

There are 30 orgs to cover, including yours, which is arguably the most important group of players to know about, especially if your team is a contender looking to add big league pieces, which means being asked to part with prospects in a trade. For this reason, the decision-makers in your organization should be the ones most ardently tasked with seeing your

123

club's players. Earlier in the book, we mentioned that geographic location and proximity from the big league team play a significant role in how teams choose their affiliates, and this is part of why.

Ideally, the GM and other members of the organizational brain trust can drive to and from the affiliate whenever they want to, easing spontaneous trips to your affiliates when one has the time, allowing for flexibility when you want to watch a rehabbing big leaguer to see how they look coming back from the IL, so those with the most organizational weight can have cogent opinions about your own players. Front office members near the top of the org are the ones most likely to see players under multiple umbrellas.

It's also typical for teams to have the bulk of their scouting staff, both amateur and pro, see their own players. It's sort of a treat and team-building thing for the amateur staff to see the fruits of their labor on the field. The pro staff typically gets a *prix fixe* look at the best guys in the org either sometime during minor league spring training when the team has org meetings at the spring training site, or during fall instructional league.

Teams also know much more about their own players' personalities than other teams do, as the player development and coaching staffs are interacting with them constantly. When top execs visit an affiliate, it's unusual if they don't go into the clubhouse most days, sit with the coaches, and interact with some players. They gain feel for how hard the guys go in the weight room, what they're eating, how intuitive the on-field minutiae is for them, and other aspects of their personhood that could impact professional success. Sure, opposing scouts can show up for batting practice and leave with some notion of how attentive players are to their monotonous daily routines, and the best-sourced scouts know how to ply sources within other orgs about their own players' makeup, with varying degrees of subtlety. If a player is a douchebag, their parent club is the one most likely to know and people like ushers and radio play-by-play guys are likely aware. Knowing this is paramount. A talented player may not be a good target, or perhaps can be had for a discount, if you think his makeup issues are fixable or even conditional, like a combative young manager trying to assert himself.

Blanketing the Minors

Now that your own org is being covered, what about the other few thousand players in the minors? Most pro side departments are staffed with 12–15 scouts, spread throughout the country, tasked with seeing them. While there aren't exactly a bevy of different styles and structures of pro scouting coverage, the pro side has more flavors than the league-wide approach to draft scouting, which is quite uniform throughout baseball, aside from a few exceptions.

If pro scouting is a carton of Neapolitan ice cream, then the artificial-looking, petunia-pink strawberry ice cream is the growing, data and video-driven minority (covered in a later chapter), while the other two are the chocolate and vanilla. All have distinct advantages and drawbacks.

The vanilla pro scouting structure is "org coverage" which, for scouts, entails top-to-bottom looks at a team's entire minor league system, as you may have guessed. We don't mean "vanilla" pejoratively, as if to say this department configuration is bland, just that it's the most common. In fact, if org coverage is vanilla, it's a lovely French Vanilla flecked with black bits of vanilla bean.

The coverage most commonly encompasses Triple-A down through Low-A (all the full-season clubs), but may include looks at the short-season guys during fall instructional league or the top short-season team. It's less common for scouts to have summer coverage of those lower-level prospects, as it would really blow up the schedule. Complete coverage of the short-season clubs is tough since the rosters are bigger, there are more timeshares, and they're unlikely to have any history to help with incomplete looks. Typically, late-season looks aren't scheduled ahead of time because it's largely for seeing players that weren't seen early (those promoted or injured earlier in the year), getting September looks at the youngsters on the big league team to see how they adjust, and special assignment work, focused on pending free agents and trade targets.

Scouts with org-based coverage are typically assigned three teams' prospects to see, though some are tasked with as many as five, which means between 12 to 15 full-season affiliates to cover. At about a week per affiliate—all five starters, sometimes six, plus an off day—that leaves little wiggle room to get all your coverage done well ahead of the trade deadline.

Scouts develop multi-year backgrounds with players this way, which gives them a better shot at nailing the makeup. They've also seen their bodies develop over several years and may be better equipped to extrapolate and project on players' builds. Their Twitter follows are the beat and minor league writers for those organizations, so they're on top of injuries, promotions, and other reports, unlike more random coverage. Theoretically, good scouts should also be the first to spot when players have changed, because of their background with the players. Swing changers, pitchers who've tweaked their repertoires, and players who have remade their physiques should all immediately stand out to scouts who've been given this context because of the coverage type. Gathering makeup is often done chatting with pitchers that are in the stands charting the game and some pitchers may know opposing scouts assigned to the org just as well as scouts from their org that drop in once or twice a year.

Baseball's global uniformity might lead one to believe that assessing the talent of those who play it is also pretty uniform. The bases are always 90 feet apart, the mound always 60'6" away from home plate, which is always the same width (the scouting embodiment of Gene Hackman's measuring tape bit in *Hoosiers*). In actuality though, there are sizeable differences, depending on who you're watching and where. Context is important, and when you're scouting pro ball, there are countless details that help one evaluate a player with the proper context, and there's also ample opportunity to fuck it up.

Org coverage can be bad for travel. While some clubs' affiliates are located within a few hours of one another, some sprawl to all corners of the country. Baltimore's affiliates are all packed along I-95 near the big club's home city, most of the Phillies system is in eastern Pennsylvania and New Jersey across a distance that takes just five hours on tree-lined highways to traverse from end to end. Get stuck covering the Giants though and you'll spend time in northern California, Georgia, Virginia, Oregon, and Arizona, and a hell of a lot of time getting from one place to the next. This also makes doubling-up more difficult—if all three of your orgs have teams in the same league, you can knock out two affiliates in five days when they match up and make sure to see one team when they're playing one of the others. Like in French Vanilla, this is the egg yolk that makes this sort of coverage a little too rich for some.

There's also a bias and report-diversity problem with org coverage. The team is relying entirely on one scout for their reports on an entire org. Because of the sheer volume of players the scout is tasked with evaluating, it's likely they're wrong about a couple of them, or just missed seeing some due to injury or promotion. It would be advantageous to have multiple sets of eyes on the same players to draw from a more diverse well of opinions. This would also protect against elements of human nature that harm the quality and accuracy of reports. Like anyone else, scouts can be stubborn and less inclined to alter their initial report on a player, an admittance that they were wrong. But most scouts get accustomed to and comfortable with being wrong and have no qualms about altering their reports. They also get bored with seeing the same players and drawing similar conclusions about them every year, perhaps impacting their level of engagement, or just not liking one sort of player. For this reason, most organizational-coverage-focused pro scouting departments change the scout/org connections every two to three years.

If these issues strike you as severe, then you might want to consider chocolatey Regional Coverage. Regional coverage is pretty self-explanatory: your scouts cover affiliates near where they live. This avoids some of the pitfalls of org coverage. The bloated travel schedule disappears, and now your club naturally has a few sets of eyes on players who have been promoted to a new affiliate during the season. These players are arguably the most important guys to see during the year, because the promotion means they're playing well, and their parent club wants to see them challenged against better competition, and this is exactly the type of player you want more than one scout to see.

But this setup means anytime you lose a scout, you need to replace them with a scout in the same location to avoid sudden holes in your coverage. That means either limiting your pool of potential replacements to scout candidates who already live in the area (which would be stupid) or paying for new hires to relocate to that region, which defeats some of the cost-related advantages that regional coverage affords, as it relates to travel budgets.

Regional coverage also leads to scouts watching a lot of the same level or two of baseball. Scouts in the Northeast and Carolinas will see all kinds of different players at various stages of development, but most of the rest of the country would only end up seeing two minor league levels. In California, you'd see High-A and Triple-A. In Texas, Double-A and Triple-A, in the Midwest, almost entirely Low-A. Even Florida really only has High-A and Rookie-level complex leagues.

This is bad for your scouts' development because they're no longer exposed to a variety of bodies, player ages, levels of procedural competence, nor an array of maturity. It hurts their feel and understanding of all-important context. Effective scouts are good at pattern recognition and deductive reasoning; exposing people with those skills to a thin slice of the minors makes it harder for those traits to play, and regional coverage affords scouts less opportunity to forge meaningful relationships with people in rival orgs, which means they're less likely to have interesting off-field intel, increasingly important in the age of TrackMan doing many things that only scouts could do in the past.

Downward Pressure

One of the quickly disappearing aspects of pro scouting is Major League advance scouting. A lot of orgs still give their scouts big league teams to see because it helps calibrate their eyes and remind them what it is they're supposed to be looking for while they're out seeing minor leaguers or amateurs, but scouting big league clubs for the purposes of identifying player-by-player weaknesses and tendencies is going the way of the horse and buggy, and data and video is the car.

There are still teams who employ an explicitly named advance scout. Washington has one, Boston has two (one of which is a former West Point grad and minor leaguer), Kansas City's used to be their bullpen catcher, the Giants had two for several years leading up to this book but let one go at the end of 2019, shortly after a regime change. Clubs are now doing the job with the overwhelming amount of video available to them, with heat maps, spray charts, data related to pitch sequencing, and visual machine learning capable of stealing opponents' signs and identifying when pitchers are tipping pitches. If there's a growing reason to deploy an advance scout, it's to see how opponents might be learning about your team in real time, especially at their home park, so you can try to combat it. There are a few big league parks at which road teams show a heightened level of paranoia about sign stealing, and you'll see them taking in-game precautions, such as having their catchers using multiple signs even though nobody is on base.

In general, data and video have funneled in-person scouting resources down to lower levels of baseball, both amateur and professional. There are several reasons for this. For one, the majors and the upper levels of the minors are more stable competitive environments (except perhaps for the Pacific Coast League, which has several cartoonish offensive environments due to altitude, exacerbated in 2019 with use of the suddenly more explosive Major League baseball), and thus teams are more comfortable with statistical performance at those levels. Individuals who reach those heights almost always have sufficient talent, technical proficiency, or some combination of the two, to play competitive baseball there, whereas the on-field competency of lower-level pro baseball talent (think teenagers in the DSL, AZL, Pioneer League, etc.) is more variable, player to player.

As a result, statistical performance is much more reliable the further up the ladder you go, allowing teams to more confidently incorporate it into their player evaluations. The player has also generated multiple years of data at that point. This, combined with the proliferation of TrackMan and Statcast metrics in pro baseball (almost every minor league park in the country has a TrackMan unit now), means that a growing number of teams feel that they have a firm grasp on upper-level players even if those players are not seen as much by scouts. Some organizations have even begun to de-emphasize in-person scouting at these levels, though some view it as more important because they know fewer teams are doing it, and they seek to be the first ones to know when players tweak a swing, learn a new pitch, or change for the better in some way. But allocating scouts more heavily toward the lower levels of the minors makes sense because performance is less meaningful, and more focus should be placed on bodies and athletes.

But as we'll continue to mention until it's seared into everyone's head, context is an important part of scouting, and perhaps most relevant with famous youngsters playing at the lowest levels. This is especially true late in the summer, when a pro scout gets their first look at a hyped, high school draftee, and absolutely crushes him in their report. In our experience, this happens surprisingly often for, in our opinion, a number of reasons.

First, there is some factionalism between the pro and amateur departments, and seeing a top pick with holes in their game is an easy chance to call a seven-figure decision dumb. Secondly, the scout usually has never seen the player before, so a tough week isn't dismissed as a tough week like it can be by a scout that has seen them perform before, and knows why they were a top prospect. Thirdly, high-profile prep prospects who just signed have just finished playing more baseball than they ever have in their lives in the 18 months leading up to the draft, and they aren't used to playing every day, for a whole summer, in either sweaty Florida or hellish Arizona, against the best competition they've ever seen, while having daily instruction, so they're usually struggling, or fatigued, or tinkering with mechanics, etc. We're much more likely to listen to positive reports on new draftees, or negative reports if they include a marked change in physicality or athleticism, suggesting the player is either hurt or has undergone a relevant physical change.

The Complexes

Based on what we've discussed so far, how are you inclined to answer the question we asked at the beginning of this chapter? Most of the problems presented by org-based coverage can be solved by having good, open-minded scouts and owners willing to have a proper operational budget, and because those are two reasonable boxes to check, if forced to choose, we think org coverage is the best foundation for a pro department's structure. But the problems of time constraint and scout bandwidth still remain, so in our opinion the right answer is to get creative and do a little bit of both.

If we give three orgs to each of 10 scouts, and task them with covering all full-season affiliates, that means our team will have comprehensive coverage of Low-A and above by early July. That leaves extended spring training (which lasts through May) and the rookie and short-season affiliates (which begin play after the draft and continue through the end of August) as uncovered pre-deadline. This is a problem we'd employ a more surgical, regional setup to solve.

Having a couple dedicated scouts in Arizona, Florida, and the Dominican Republic gives your department extra reach while also patching some of the holes associated with org coverage. In addition to having more complete coverage of the entire minors, you also now have at least one other scout filing a report on any given player. Having scouts planted in these locations for long periods of time also means they make connections with baseball ops people from many different orgs.

Because the baseball that occurs on the complexes in Arizona and Florida lacks the same regulation and expectation of public information, you need to have a scout who can source schedules, rosters, lineups, rehab schedules, and various other ephemera specific to this realm. It's easier to get this done when you're a familiar face, getting to know the loose-lipped coaches, the frantic and fastidious video intern, or the bored kid running the TrackMan laptop. All of them will tell you things you need to know to best do your job.

Of course, asking a single person to cover the entirety of these locations alone while they simultaneously navigate all the little geographic and social intricacies specific to these places is unreasonable, so it makes sense to limit these scouts' scopes a bit and focus on players that make more sense to see. It's unrealistic to expect rebuilding teams to part with their younger prospects via trade. Those teams are the ones trading their big leaguers for prospects, not the ones looking to unload their best 19-year-old arm in extended spring training. It's logical to either omit those clubs from coverage entirely or just have a short list of targets for your Arizona, Florida, and Dominican scouts to see.

Conversely, contending teams have incentive to part with players several years from the big leagues in exchange for guys who can help them win right now, even if it means paying a premium by parting with a high-ceiling player. For this reason, those clubs' prospects are must-see at the complex level in case your team's season goes sideways and you find yourself selling at the deadline.

Teams attempting to shut the door on a division or thrust themselves into playoff contention with a mid-season trade are typically not going to let a prospect who is anywhere between three and five years away from the big leagues stand in the way of adding the big league piece that pushes them over the top.

There are some clear recent examples of these forces at play. The Cardinals and Pirates recently began some version of complex-level coverage, with Pittsburgh sending a few scouts back and forth from Florida to Arizona to see targets for potential trades, while St. Louis now has a scout focused solely on Arizona. In anticipation of losing big leaguers to free agency and with the knowledge that ownership was not inclined to patch these holes with big contracts for proven hitters, the Cleveland Indians were willing to part with several interesting, very young prospects for players who had lower ceilings, but were ready to help the big league club immediately. They traded beastly teenage OF Jhon Torres to St. Louis for perfectly fine starting CF Oscar Mercado, and converted pitcher Tahnaj Thomas to Pittsburgh for power-hitting platoon OF Jordan Luplow. Both Luplow and Mercado contributed to Cleveland's wild card push the following year. Meanwhile, Torres was sent to full-season ball very quickly, flopped, then raked when he was sent down to a level that was more age-appropriate. Thomas' stuff exploded and he was touching 101 with his fastball during the summer. Cleveland got what they needed, but gave up two potential impact talents.

We've been told that the Braves had the prototypical discussion ("Some rookie ball kid can't keep us from making this deal," a decision-making executive said at the time) when they included 19-year-old Neftalí Féliz (in the short-season Appalachian League at the time) as the third piece in the 2007 Mark Teixeira deal with Texas. Féliz never quite delivered on his promise after exploding as a prospect in full-season ball, but he still posted 4.7 WAR in his first four MLB seasons as a reliever, delivering over $25 million in value in that span, per FanGraphs.

Of course, contending teams are aware of this issue and so some of them find clever ways to hide players, especially pitchers. Because young pitchers are typically on relatively conservative innings limits anyway, these types of prospects can be shelved before the trade deadline and still get in most of their year's workload throughout August and Instructional League in the fall. It's good for teams when the other clubs like their prospects, and they're typically pretty accommodating of scouts when it comes to providing information about when/how to see their players, but undoubtedly there are prospects that a given parent org thinks have real growth potential, that someone who might balance a trade as a second or third piece today (and they may not be able to say "no" currently) but may be the centerpiece of one next year.

Occasionally there are scouts whose explicit duties involve hybrid coverage, with another responsibility beyond coverage complexes for minor league spring training in March, extended spring training April through early June, then short-season leagues June through August. During slower times of year for their core beat (the short-season portion), some teams offer an interdisciplinary program designed to give the scout a different perspective on their market. A frequent example: scouts from the amateur side picking up some short-season coverage after the draft. For example, Four Corners area scouts may pick up AZL or Pioneer League coverage in July or August, when school is out and their usual beat is slower. They're well-equipped to scout short-season guys, who are often in the same age range as the high school and college players they see regularly. Another is complex-oriented scouts seeing some high school tournaments or a stateside international amateur showcase, as both are often happening on complex backfields and include players of similar polish and skill level.

Because there's little else going on, there's a lot of staff flexibility when it comes to covering the Arizona Fall League and Fall Instructional League. The Arizona Fall League (aka Fall League or AFL) is almost like prospect finishing school. Each of the 30 MLB teams send half a dozen prospects there to fill six total rosters, and those six teams compete over about six weeks in a league focused on scouting and development. There are plenty of high-profile players there—top 100 list, famous types—but the most important evaluations are of the guys on the Rule 5 and 40-man bubble who might represent low-cost roster upgrades for you in the winter.

Fall Instructional League games often take place at teams' spring training facilities in September and early October, after the minor league season has ended, and it typically includes a cross section of the youngest, most-inexperienced players in the org, and also the ones the org most wants to see and subject to extra development. Instructional League rosters also have that summer's international free agent signees, so this is often the place high-profile Latin American players make their domestic pro debuts. For full instructs programs, teams play at least a few games per week against other local instructional league teams, with camp days (intersquad games, practice) on the other days. This is a very rich cross section of talent that would be valuable to send your org scout in to see so they can build a foundation of looks at the young players they'll see trickling into their full-season scope over the next few years.

Fewer and fewer teams are doing traditional instructional league (only six Arizona orgs did so in 2019: White Sox, A's, Rangers, Padres, Royals, Dodgers) as teams use the fall to work with players outside of game environments in a classroom setting and in the weight room.

Some teams take advantage of the loose structure of instructs to get creative with the format. The Dodgers often have players either playing defense or offense on a given day, not both.

Some teams do some intersquad work, even if it's just a couple of innings, and some have moved baseball activity to January. The Giants had instructs in January 2019 and players took infield and outfield, then used a high-speed pitching machine to play simulated games. It wasn't as valuable a look as a normal slate of games, but those in attendance got the first domestic look at the elite bat speed of Marco Luciano, the precocious power of Luis Toribio, and lots of others because, at that time, it was the only game in town.

Shapeshifters

Again, what we've described so far is boiler plate pro scouting with some shades of what we think are best practices. But teams are innovating around these circumstances either with the budget in mind, or to spackle over little holes in the coverage, improve the quality of the reports, or the quality of life for scouts.

Some teams use a dynamic coverage that allocates scouting resources where it makes sense, based on where the big league team is on the competitive spectrum. Contending teams shift resources to the upper levels, looking for players who can contribute in the short term. These teams are often looking for pitching depth to protect against a rash of injuries, and sometimes they're looking for these arms because they've already suffered a few casualties. There are even a few teams that have scouts who specialize in scouting pitchers.

This type of incentivized thinking and scouting is what leads to a lot of non-blockbuster trades. The Yankees acquiring Luke Voit, Garrett Cooper, and Ryan McBroom within the span of a year is evidence of this kind of approach. All three were Triple-A performers at first base who were seemingly acquired to be depth behind oft-injured 1B incumbent Greg Bird. All three of them either played meaningful time for the Yankees in place of Bird, or were flipped in trades for something else.

This type of logic applies in other ways. Trade discussions start, stop, gestate, and change sometimes over a period of several months before a deal's consummation, and during that time orgs typically send extra sets of eyes in to see that team's players. Deals that don't quite come together before the trade deadline are often revisited in the off-season, which gives those teams the late summer and fall to fixate on each other's systems. This is where special assistants and special assignment scouts get involved. Special assistants are often former directors or VPs on the off-ramp to retirement in terms of a full workload, but still are top-notch evaluators with deep Rolodexes. Other times, it's a vague title so a team can steal a director-level employee from another club without offering a clear promotion (which would usually require a VP or assistant GM title) but often offering better quality of life, flexibility, money, or length of contract.

Teams also shift around scouting personnel based on experience. Older scouts may eventually settle into a role that minimizes travel and maximizes application of their contacts. Entry-level scouts may be tasked with lower-stakes coverage, both to minimize harm they might cause as they make mistakes of inexperience, and for their superiors to see how attentive they are to the work. Let's say you have a pro scouting opening that you'd like to fill with a promising intern who has no scouting experience beyond what they've done as part of their fellowship/internship. Limiting that person's scope or assigning them coverage of teams that your club is less likely to have meaningful trade discussions with is a good way to get their feet wet in year one.

In pro scouting, you may go long periods of time without making a high-profile transaction because the opportunity to trade for prospects rarely presents itself. It takes the right situational brew—two teams motivated to trade who also like each other's players, and yours is the one rebuilding. It's different than amateur scouting because everyone has an opportunity to take players every year, which helps keep the staff motivated, focused on mundane but necessary paperwork, and armed with the relevant gossip needed to navigate the draft well. If you're a pro scout covering an org that's rebuilding, and therefore unlikely to trade prospects, it can be irritating to spend that week in Idaho Falls watching mostly non-prospects play 4½ hour games with 25 combined runs while staying in a lower-tier chain hotel, eating at lower-tier chain restaurants.

The Rays coverage structure is unique and almost indecipherable from the outside. Their pro scouts do a lot of crosschecking one another (focused on targets rather than whole teams), their pro scouts do more in the Dominican Republic than is typical, and they have a higher concentration of scouts based in Arizona and Florida than most other orgs.

Understanding Equilibrium

Another angle to work when it comes to pro talent acquisition is the 40-man fringe. Teams are constantly on the lookout for upgrades to their 40-man roster. A better backup catcher, pitching improvements of any kind, defensive versatility. Some teams, usually the worst ones in baseball, are active on the waiver wire as they try to build viable depth. Conversely, there are teams so flush with talent that they have a surplus of 40-man-eligible players who either need to be rostered or else be exposed to various forms of claim by other teams.

Teams with an especially high number of rostered players under contract for the next season as well as many prospects who will need to be added to the 40-man roster in the off-season, lest they be exposed to the Rule 5 Draft, have what is often called a "40-man crunch," "spillover," or "churn," meaning that team has incentive to clear away the overflow of players via trade for something they can keep—pool space, comp picks, or typically younger players whose 40-man clocks are further from midnight—rather than do nothing, and later lose players on waivers or in the Rule 5.

Teams with good player development, or with absurdly deep farm systems due to a well-executed rebuild, are the ones most likely to make a surplus of good players who become of interest to teams. So the Yankees, Dodgers, Astros, Rays, and Padres are the ones who've been churning the most in the years leading up to this book's publication.

Some teams are clearly taking opportunistic fliers on players who fit this description. Toronto has done so most frequently over the past several years, acquiring players who have been squeezed out of other, deeper orgs' big league picture. Billy McKinney, Brandon Drury (both from the Yankees), Teoscar Hernández, Derek Fisher, David Paulino, Trent Thornton (all from Houston), Brock Stewart, Randal Grichuk, and Breyvic Valera are all recent examples of this. The Jays were trying to have most of the periphery of their next competitive roster in place for when Vladimir Guerrero Jr. and Bo Bichette arrived, it seemed. It's an interesting approach to team building during the middle stages of a rebuild and, in perpetuity, a good way of identifying likely trade partners.

Using Rules as a Potential Competitive Advantage

We covered basic roster rules in Chapter One, with details on options, Rule 5 eligibility, 40-man vs. 26-man rosters, and outright waivers. These come most into play when it pertains to pro scouting, in terms of manipulating your 40-man roster and juggling payroll, so we'll go one step deeper on the basic rules of rostering players here.

Outright waivers is the most common form of waivers and the version we're referring to in Chapter One. It's the waivers for when a team is trying to outright a player off their 40-man roster but doesn't want to lose the player.

Churning is the term for when a team wants to claim a player on waivers, but doesn't want to use the 40-man roster spot, so they claim the player on waivers to be on their 40-man, then immediately outright them, hoping no other team claims them and they end up with the player's rights, but not on the 40-man roster anymore. A player will be called "outrighted" on MLB Trade Rumors when they've been taken off the 40-man roster, cleared outright waivers, and have been sent to the minors, off the 40-man roster. They are paid a higher salary than the typical Triple-A player, and the team paid $50,000 to claim them, so it's basically just purchasing depth without using a 40-man spot.

This is how some players get claimed a half-dozen times in one off-season, as multiple teams try this exact thing, often trying to time when they outright a player around when teams have more full 40-man rosters. This has become more common with more clubs adopting similar progressive valuation techniques, so many of them are trying the same maneuver due to the same evaluations on the same group of players.

A recent example of this is RHP Oliver Drake and the Tampa Bay Rays. In January 2019, Drake settled as outrighted off the Rays 40-man, *after* switching organizations seven times in nine months and pitching for five MLB teams in one season (an MLB record). His 2019 performance after being added to the Rays 40-man and then-25-man rosters in late May 2019 (once injuries hit and cleared a spot): 56 innings in relief, 3.21 ERA, 0.5 WAR, or roughly $4–$5 million in value. This ended up costing the Rays a $50,000 claim fee and the prorated portion of the league minimum salary ($550,000), or something like an additional $380,000.

This may seem like small potatoes, but micro-payroll teams like Tampa Bay ($64 million payroll in 2019) need at least this sort of positive net value on every player on the 25-man roster (roughly $4 million net value on Drake, times 25 roster spots = $100 million) to have a chance to compete with a team near the luxury tax ($206 million in 2019), especially considering their division rivals the Red Sox and Yankees exceeded it in 2019.

Another term you likely read on MLB Trade Rumors often is when a player is designated for assignment, or DFA'd. This means the team is taking a player off their 40-man roster, usually to make room for a player that's just been added, and they have 10 days to either release, trade, or waive the player. I didn't learn this until I worked for a team, but a team can only use the DFA (rather than outright waivers) when they're already at a full 40 on their 40-man roster.

The value of a DFA is when there's a player coming off the 40-man roster that has some value and either the team is: 1) taking him off the roster quicker than expected, so you want to buy some time, rather than just put a player on waivers, and/or 2) you think there's a strong chance the player is claimed, so you want a couple days to find a team to pay more than $50,000 (the waiver claim fee) or a low-level prospect to trade for him.

This is why some teams have players out for the season and they leave them on the 10-day IL (on the 40-man roster) and don't move them to the 60-day IL (off the 40-man roster, referenced in Chapter One), until they're forced to when adding new players, since that takes the player off the 40-man and takes away DFA as an option.

Release waivers is for when a team wants to release a player (usually an underperforming veteran on a big contract) and the claiming price is only $1, since players are almost never claimed through this process. This is because, once the player with his current (usually large) contract clears waivers, he becomes a free agent and would then play for the league minimum in future MLB stints (while his last contract is still active, since MLB contracts are guaranteed).

When a player with a guaranteed salary is released, passes through waivers, and then signs with a new team, we have what's called an "offset." So, let's say we have a player who's due $5 million that season (last year of his deal) and is released in spring training and signs with a new team as a free agent on Opening Day. The new team pays him the league minimum ($550,000) and the team that released him then pays $4.45 million, so that his combined salary stays at $5 million. If the player had positive value to where he was worth a claim (and paying the full $5 million), then he would've been traded before going to release waivers. It's common for these sorts of players to have multiple offers of an MLB deal for the league minimum, or (more commonly) minor league deals with an opt-out date (can request release if not in the big leagues) after a few weeks. This way, the team has a chance to see the player in their org before guaranteeing money that comes with a promotion to the big leagues.

There's some negotiated perks that can come with minor league deals like opt-outs, foreign language (terms to opt out of a deal if a team in Japan/Korea make a big offer), a spring training invite (free agents expecting a guaranteed MLB deal that settle for a minor league deal get guaranteed time with the MLB team in March), and various performance bonuses and salary (above the league minimum) for if/when they are in the big leagues that don't come with non-negotiated MLB deals, i.e., any young player under team control.

Some younger players playing for the league minimum get put on release waivers when the team tries to trade them, there's no interest, and they tell their club they will elect free agency if outrighted. This also sometimes happens when a team needs a 40-man slot in the off-season and a player has been disappointing, so the team cuts a deal for a minor league contract (off the 40-man roster) with a 40-man roster level salary (far more than most minor league deals) already agreed to ahead of time.

Players can elect free agency when they've been outrighted for the second time, or the first time if they have three or more years of MLB service. A big league season is 186 days (give or take a few in any given season) for service-time purposes, with any number over 172 days on the MLB roster counting as a full season, with MLB injured list time counting. Young pitchers that have arm surgery are fortunate in a small way if the injury happens while in the big leagues (White Sox RHP Michael Kopech is an example), since they accrue MLB pay and service time while injured, while some that get it just before they will be called up (Rays RHP Brent Honeywell) are hit especially hard, losing over a year of MLB service time and pay during rehab.

Service time brings us to another topic that's become mainstream recently: service-time manipulation. It's common with top prospects to call them up roughly two weeks into the season, to put them at 171 days of service at the end of the year. Service time is expressed as "Years.Days," so 0.171 rolls over to the next season as that same number, but 0.172 (an in-season figure) rolls over to 1.000 for the next season. This is why Kris Bryant and Ronald Acuña Jr. were held down a predictable number of days when they were probably big league ready at the end of the previous season: skipping the September at-bats and the first couple weeks of April (with a few more off-days than usual) yields an extra year of control at the end of the six years of control, when they're likely in their prime.

We referenced the six years of control, because that's the amount of service time before free agency, unless a player is released or non-tendered. With one exception we'll cover next, players make the Major League minimum ($550,000 currently, sometimes a bit more if they're accomplished at the MLB level) until their service time hits 3.000 or more. This could take far more than three seasons to occur if a player is demoted/promoted a lot, but for a player called up on Opening Day that never gets sent down, this would be after their third season. (Internally, 0.xxx service time for season one is called "0+" for short, followed by "1+" for season two and "2+" for season three.)

Players that are classified as 3+ in an off-season are eligible for arbitration for the first time, with 4+ and 5+ the second and third times, and anyone that has 6.000 or more of service time in the off-season is a free agent, if they aren't already under contract in a negotiated multi-year deal. Arbitration is a process where players get paid more than the minimum, but less than their market value for three seasons until they hit free agency and presumably get paid a market rate.

The arbitration system is complex, with all kinds of odd and arcane details, but ultimately it's a comparables-based negotiation using basic performance and service time, with well over half of cases settled between the agent and team before even getting to the arbitration hearing. A minority of cases (usually one or two dozen per year out of well over 100 potential cases) do go to a hearing. The arbitration panel is three labor arbitrators that aren't baseball experts, so comps, simple comp-based arguments, and old-school baseball-card stats dictate the hearing. The outcomes are often hard to predict, even for experts in the field that are in the room, listening to both sides present their case. This also means advanced-stats darlings, like defensive standouts, hit-unlucky hitters, or pitchers on poor teams with inflated ERAs and low win totals, will be unfairly underpriced, making them more likely to sign extensions. On the other hand, one-dimensional sluggers with big homer totals and mediocre relievers with big save totals tend to get overpaid relative to the market.

It's a battleground for MLB's labor relations department and the MLB Players Association, who heavily advise and influence the cases that the teams and agents present, in terms of setting precedents for salary inflation, particularly with top players. Not every top player goes through the process, as extensions (with fixed salaries through arbitration) for top young players are more common, as a cost-certainty move for clubs that also serves to take potential precedent-setters out of the arbitration pool. Agent Scott Boras, notorious pro-player labor figure (among other things) is known for making a point of taking his top clients through arbitration and to free agency expressly to set the market at each stop. The general discount on the market value of the player is 30 percent of market value in their first arbitration year (3+), 50 percent in year two, and 70 percent in year three. Elite players will make over $20 million in their last arbitration year, mapping somewhat to top players getting $30 million or more per year in free agent deals.

Another common time to call up top prospects is to try to manipulate Super Two arbitration, the exception to the above scenario. Some players that are in the 2+ class in service time are eligible for arbitration and could thus go through the process four times. Super Two allows for the top 22 percent of players with 2+ service time to be eligible, so the exact cutoff is a little different each year, but can be predicted reasonably well. It's moved up in 2019, with the cutoff under 2.115 (catching Milwaukee's Josh Hader in arbitration by a few days) when it's been as high as 2.134 in recent years. So, while the mid-April callup to get an extra year of control is very easy to nail, the Super Two cutoff is a little trickier. The players that got the mid-April callup like Bryant and Acuña will easily qualify for Super Two unless they are sent down for nearly two months (the gap between 171 days and 120 or so). Super Two means that the first year of arbitration (as a 2+) is a little cheaper than the typical first year for most players (as a 3+), but the team ends up paying a bit more in the next three years with that extra year serving to inflate the following totals.

Lastly, there's a period just after the season ends each year when players can be non-tendered. For example, if a player looks poised to earn $5 million in arbitration and the team either doesn't think he's worth that much, or would rather him hit the open market (where he'll likely get that or less) and decide on his salary/roster spot later, they effectively release him to join free agency by non-tendering him. This is meant for teams to have a process to get out of paying arbitration figures for every player that's eligible, but since you can effectively release a player without passing him through waivers, it can be used on non-arbitration-eligible players for a different use, which we cover below. Plenty of serviceable players get non-tendered, sign an incentive-laden make-good contract, have a bounce-back season, then become assets once again.

There are lots of obscure examples outside of the scope of this book to manipulate these rules in ways that weren't intended. For example, one is to draft a previously outrighted young player in the Rule 5 Draft, with the express intent of outrighting them before Opening Day. (Remember, if a player has been outrighted twice they can elect free agency.) So in this case, the idea is that the player would declare free agency and then adding the young player becomes a bidding war rather than using a finite 40-man roster spot for an entire season in the standard Rule 5–retention method. Kiley discussed this possibility internally with one of the teams he worked for, but we aren't sure if it's ever happened. A Rule 5–eligible player with a prior outright that's worth getting in a bidding war over is a pretty rare situation.

If a team wants to take a player off its 40-man in December, but doesn't want to subject him to waivers (he's good enough to likely be claimed), they can non-tender then re-sign him to a minor league deal. In-season, outrighting takes the player to waivers, but the non-tender deadline provides a mechanism to immediately take any player (though it's designed to be used on arbitration-eligible ones) from the 40-man roster to free agency, where a pre-arranged, high-salary minor league deal can be signed in the same sitting.

This was successfully done by the Yankees with former first-round pick and top prospect OF Slade Heathcott in late 2014 and they tried to do it again in late 2016 with LHP Jacob Lindgren, a 2014 second-round pick who'd just had Tommy John surgery after getting to the big leagues in 2015. While Kiley was working for the Braves, the team jumped in between the non-tender and signing of the new minor league deal with an even more attractive minor league deal and signed Lindgren. Losing a bidding war is the clear downside to this strategy.

That big minor league deal led to the rebuilding Braves adding an asset for what appeared to be a discount while Lindgren rehabbed an injury. Unfortunately, the rehab didn't go to plan and Lindgren never pitched in 2017 or 2018, or for the Braves at all. Lindgren made out well, with another payday and MLB service time before signing a minor league deal two years later with the White Sox, where he pitched in the minor leagues in 2019.

CHAPTER 6

But I Wanna Be a Ballplayer

If you're a player who hopes to play at the next level, then many decision points lie ahead of you, and we're constantly asked—almost every week in our chats at FanGraphs—to help families new to the process navigate these issues. We talked to a number of experts who dwell in this specific realm of youth baseball—college coaches, agents, players, independent trainers—to get a more complete picture of how to approach issues from the point of view of young athletes. It's not the primary aim of this book, but probably applies, in some way, to many of the people who read it. To those for whom it applies immediately, we wish you luck, good health, and the poise to move on with grace and maturity should you realize you're not talented enough to level up. Know that that feeling comes for every single one of us at some point, whether it happens at 16 when you get cut from the high school team or in your forties when you can't catch up to 92 down the middle anymore and get heckled by an over-served guy who was cut from his high school team at 16.

How to Get Seen

Most obviously, play for your high school team. Beyond that, one-size-fits-all recommendations get tricky and it depends on what caliber of player you are, how open your schedule is, and what sort of resources you and your family have.

The first choice outside typical varsity play is to play travel baseball. Being a standout player at top events or just playing on a top team is an easy way to get noticed by college recruiters and scouts. This route is also pretty costly, usually many hundreds of dollars per player, per event, plus the travel and lodging are costs on top of that. Play serious travel baseball and you'll find yourself flying to Southern states several times per year, watching your parents buy an umbrella at a pharmacy after your mom got sunburned on the first day, then not knowing what to do with the unpackable umbrella once the week of games is complete.

Another choice comes with regard to showcases. Many companies run these NFL Combine–style events, but Perfect Game, Prep Baseball Report (PBR), and The Baseball Factory are the main national companies, with other regional players also putting on worthy events. These are focused on showing your talent, mainly outside of a game situation, with a bullpen or a game inning or two for pitchers, and a full workout for position players: 60-yard dash, infield/outfield, batting practice. There's usually, but not always, a game toward the end of the event, sometimes with loose team affiliations; some of the coaches may work for MLB teams in some capacity. These events also run in the hundreds of dollars and usually run for one day, occasionally two.

The other main decision to make is related to training. You can handle this on your own in various ways, go to a local batting/pitching coach or go to one of the more progressive data-driven places that are popping up around the country, like Driveline Baseball (Kent, WA), Cressey Sports Performance (Jupiter, FL, and Hudson, MA), Texas Baseball Ranch (Montgomery, TX), and others. These are also expensive and for some athletes they can involve a pretty intense shift in lifestyle (eating and sleeping habits, weight training, etc.).

College coaches advise to do what makes the most sense for you, given your goals and resources, because no one of these is the magic bullet to make you improve, get a scholarship, or get noticed by pro scouts, and several of them will take up lots of time and prevent you from playing other sports, which most scouts/coaches consider a mistake. If you don't have much money to put toward these things, there's ways to do bootstrap training on local fields or a backyard, with friends, using training plans that you find online, using the camera on your phone instead of buying a specialized one, etc. You don't need to do travel ball or showcases at all if you have a good sense of where you fit in the recruiting landscape. And, if you don't, we'd still send you to the same place.

The under-publicized—and arguably best—choice for most players to get seen by the right college coaches are college camps. Colleges hold them on campus in the off-season and they're usually promoted pretty well, as they're both a key source of off-season funds for the program (volunteer assistant coaches working for a stipend or free grad school as their salary often get to keep the camp revenue) and a great place for the coaching staff to get familiar with potential recruiting targets. For data-driven programs, you'll also perform using their tech (TrackMan, Rapsodo, etc.), so they'll have more info on you than they'd get from other events in addition to them getting to know you better as a person.

If you're with a travel ball organization, don't go to events that are too expensive or play for a team that threatens to cut you if you don't go to enough events. Those are signs of a team being run for the coach's profit and not the best interest of the players. Do research on what tournaments have college coaches in attendance from schools you think fit your talent and pick your spots. Both of these things will also help inform where you stand in the recruiting pecking order and further refine your methods.

Driveline CEO Mike Rathwell has another rule of thumb to get a sense for where you fit in the recruiting hierarchy: "For pitchers, look at the bullpen and see if you're better than the fourth best guy in the bullpen. If you are, then you have a shot. Look at the depth chart, who's the backup at this position? If you can beat them, then give it a shot." The back of college rosters are filler types, often freshmen that need to improve and/or players that soon end up leaving the program due to lack of playing time. If you want to be a target for that school, shoot to be at least in the middle-tier of their talent, where this membrane of coming and going exists.

Rathwell does not see value in paying lots of money to showcase: "There's an inverted signal: the less you pay to attend an event, the more value there is. If you're invited to go to an event for free, you should go. Kids aren't paying to be in the Under Armour All-America Game. There's usually low value in events that cost lots of money. They may be using your fee to essentially pay coaches to attend to then attract more kids." One way to do this is to hire an assistant or staffer from a college to write reports on players at the event in return for the head coach attending. If the budget is tight, the head coach is getting his staffer some side money and may find a player.

The cost of college camps is well below showcases and travel ball, and you can approach it like college admissions, picking high-, middle-, and low-end schools of interest in your area to get a sense of where you fit in the recruiting hierarchy talent-wise, while also doing a conventional college campus tour. The process of driving to the campuses, getting tours, and talking to coaches during camps, cuts out the middlemen in your process, while saving time and money, and allowing you to interview them, pick their brains, to see if this is a good fit for you. This is your career and education, after all, it should be a good fit.

We've talked to college coaches who admit, off the record, that they've been put on prospects they'd later sign in some unexpected ways. We heard one story from a Power 5 assistant about a kid showing well at a camp, and the one school who saw him pitch became interested. But eventually, word of that interest got out, and at his next start for his travel ball team, assistants from most major schools in the Southeast were there to chase the rumor about a pitcher they'd never seen before.

Another coach told us about seeing a video on Twitter, retweeted by a mutual friend, of a kid pitching with a radar gun in frame that showed him hitting 89 mph, enough to get the coach to go see his next travel ball start. The school eventually landed a verbal commitment from the player. Both stories are from perennial top 25 teams in major conferences.

Don't spam coaches with highlight videos. If you're a pitcher, make a video showing each of your pitches from the catcher's perspective, with a radar gun in the frame (finding someone with a gun might be the toughest part of this), and record a couple pitches from a side angle so folks can see your mechanics. This video can be less than 30 seconds and be shot at any field or training facility, and if you can't find someone with a radar gun who'll help you out, good-enough pocket radar guns are as cheap as about $100 now, and facilities or higher-tier teams usually have them as well. We don't have quite as clear of an answer for hitters, but showing your hitting mechanics from the open side is essential. Ideally, some measure of power, like possibly a max exit velo off a tee, could also be included if you're trying to DIY a recruiting video.

Put it on social media where the coaches and recruiters are, usually Twitter, and send it to accounts like @FlatGroundApp that have a big following and repost videos like this. You don't need to hire a company or pay an extra fee at a showcase for an edited or slow-motion video to show to coaches. The amount of interest you draw from this 30-second, social media video will help give you an idea of where you stand. If you're getting direct messages from D2 and D3 schools when you're expecting an SEC offer, this is an indication of where you stand. Like everything, this alone won't dictate your path, but Rathwell calls it a "useful part of a balanced portfolio."

Anything with music cues, long highlight compilations, or non-game situations like pulldowns (pitchers running/throwing at a screen with a gun behind the screen) aren't compelling enough for many coaches. If you can hit

102 mph in a pulldown, every coach would rather see 93 mph on a mound. They need to see some sense of your physicality, mechanics, and power/velocity all in the same, short video, showing a skill that could translate directly to a game situation. Anything other than that could do more harm than good.

Another important factor is to not be seen until you're ready to be seen. Playing in a showcase or on a top travel team when you're fatigued will do more harm that good. If a coach first sees you playing at a level below what you're normally able to do, they'll write you off. Everyone has bad days, but do what you can to put yourself in a position to succeed. We've heard comedians say that it's also key to not move to New York or Los Angeles until you've gotten good enough that the agents and executives that see your first performance on the big stage would actually want to see you again. More exposure isn't always better.

How NCAA Rules Factor In

You also have to be aware of the "closed period" and "quiet period" of the recruiting calendar. It's easy to Google and find out specifics, but generally, every few months there's up to a week when coaches can't make any in-person contact with recruits or their families, but can communicate digitally (dead period), or almost one-third of the year, when a recruit can only speak to coaches in person on the college campus, or digitally, but the school can't interact with the recruit otherwise or watch them play (quiet period).

The periods not covered by the quiet/dead label are called contact periods, where coaches can visit the high school, the home, and generally scout/recruit athletes freely. The exceptions for this are based on which year the recruit is in high school. Generally speaking, a coach cannot initiate contact with a recruit before they start their junior year of high school. The way around this is if the recruit initiates contact, and high school or travel ball coaches are often the intermediaries for these introductions. An athlete can also initiate an in-person meeting with the coach before this time via an unofficial campus visit, scheduled via a planned phone call, made by the athlete that's communicated via a third party (the high school/travel coach). If your parent is your high school coach, this is a somewhat common situation that allows colleges to directly contact a player's father when they wouldn't be able to, if he wasn't a coach. If this sounds convoluted and silly, that's because it is.

Any showcases or tournaments during the dead or quiet periods should be avoided, as they're likely to just be calendar-fillers and revenue-generators for the organizer, since college coaches can't attend. The quiet period is a good time to do an unofficial campus visit and get a sense for how the program runs, ask to attend a practice, etc. In some cases, the camp is the only way for you to get face time with a coach and assess your fit, personality-wise.

If you can afford it and want to do it, do some research and see what showcases and travel ball tournaments are typically attended by the types of coaches you want to be seen by. A couple hundred dollars to be seen by 20 coaches whose program could be a fit for you can be a solid investment and is more efficient than going to 20 camps. But remember to check if the event is being held during a closed period, when coaches by rule can't be scouting you.

September of your junior year is when the restrictions are lifted for contact, aside from the quiet/dead periods. One assistant coach estimated that about 10 percent of the desirable players for top programs are still uncommitted at that point and the schools are acting accordingly. He said it's common to "timeline" a player around this time—make an offer that expires at some point in the near future—to ensure that they can fill up their class to their liking, usually with one spot saved for late pop-up prospects or kids that decommit after a coach gets fired, or some other circumstance.

All you need to do is get the attention of the schools that you want and that may also want you. Playing travel ball for a couple summers for five figures and going to showcases just because you feel pressure to is often eyewash when the most random thing, or just showing up on their campus, can directly make it happen. Pick reach schools and safety schools, go to their campuses, do whatever else you can afford and spread these things out so you don't have bad showings when you're fatigued.

Doing Homework on College Programs

Rathwell points to the example of Shohei Ohtani as the ideal way to handle learning about a school before you commit. From a *New York Post* article:

"The memo, released in the name of Nez Balelo, co-head of CAA Baseball and Ohtani's lead agent, asks each suitor to evaluate Ohtani's talent as a pitcher and as a hitter; to explain its player development, medical training, and player-performance philosophies and facilities; to describe its minor league and spring training facilities; to detail resources for Ohtani's cultural assimilation into the team's city; to demonstrate a vision for how Ohtani could integrate into the team's organization; and to tell Ohtani why the team is a desirable place to play."

This can easily be adapted to apply to colleges and speaks to the questions that would yield the sorts of answers that tell you what you need to know about an employer. Force everyone involved to show their hand rather than let the process dictate terms to you. If you're a top-tier player, you are the one in control throughout the process and, even if you aren't, coaches are much more used to inquisitive recruits that want to know if a coach intends to tweak his mechanics, or their opinion on weighted balls.

Don't be ashamed to ask about these things, because you don't want to be misled and find out as a freshman when you've already been boxed into the NCAA's corner and can either stay at this school with the coach you don't like, leave for a JUCO, or miss a year of time as you transfer to another DI school. Ask to watch practices and if a coach won't let you and doesn't give you a way to learn what you need to know, consider that there may be some things going on that they don't want you to know.

Attracting MLB Scouts

Getting on the radar of pro scouts isn't that different. We've heard plenty of stories of kids getting turned in by a scout for the draft (shorthand for recommended to their team to be drafted), or even getting taken in the top few rounds where a scout found out about them by accident, or had written off a kid in the summer and then wrote him up after running into him in the spring when targeting someone on the other team.

Getting invited to scout-selected showcases (East Coast Pro, Area Code Games are the top-tier national events, though most regions have smaller ones, organized by area scout regions) is a great way to get on the radar, as these events are cheaper or free (Perfect Game and Prep Baseball Report are businesses that profit off players and parents, MLB clubs are not, though they are exploitative in other ways), and you get face time directly with the scouts, who coach the teams. Often these rosters and the pre-event tryouts are chosen from commitment lists, travel teams, and showcases.

If you're truly on the level where scouts should be watching you, even if you can't get the attention of a school you like, it won't take long for you to be known to the scouts, who have incentive to know about you. Some college coaches will intentionally try to keep under-the-radar commits away from events with pro scouts. If you play in one event in front of a handful of scouts and you're that kind of player, word will get out very quickly, because scouts get fired for not knowing about every notable player in their area and they talk a lot to make sure this doesn't happen.

The thing to remember is even if you're one of those worst-case-scenario players who are good enough to sign with a pro team out of high school but is missed by scouts is that a pro contract is merely a few years away (do your best to stay healthy), when you'll then get a bigger bonus if you keep performing similarly. Lots of prospects are either lightly scouted in high school or simply not well-regarded, then explode early in college on the way to stardom.

Washington Nationals/NC State shortstop Trea Turner was very lightly scouted in south Florida and once told Kiley he couldn't get Florida State, his dream school, to scout him. Kiley was with the Pirates the year they drafted Turner out of high school, but couldn't meet his price, partly because NC State was all over him when he made the leap during his senior year, assuring him he'd have the platform to increase his value in college. Turner was a first rounder three years later out of NC State and was second in MLB Rookie of the Year voting two years after that.

Turner narrowed his scope down to one dream school, and that's risky because any one school can treat you incorrectly. Rathwell sums up our most common answer when a parent or prospect complains about a lack of recruiting attention: "The correct answer, over enough time, is become a better baseball player. The ways scouts and recruiters find you are way more democratized than they were five or 10 years ago." When a top draft prospect is at a Division II school, there's always a reason, like he got kicked off the team or had no grades or punched a teammate. The process isn't perfect, but it's pretty efficient.

Making the Decision

The bottom line is to take your time and make the right decision for you, ideally on your timeline. Facilities are fun, swag is great, and a campus visit with a few parties and a football game may appeal to your epicurean nature, but you're deciding where to spend four key years of your life and those things don't matter in the grand scheme. Don't worry about your teammates, travel coach, Twitter, or other external pressures. The sooner you start becoming an individual and making decisions with that in mind, the better off you're going to be.

When talking to coaches about how the program works, if you're someone who identifies with the more progressive player development practices of using advanced tech, figure out by talking to players and going to practices if the coaches are really practicing what they preach. There are a lot of schools putting out videos and paying lip service to this stuff because they know kids pay attention to it, hoping they won't find out they do it three days a year, when a camera crew is around. An unsexy mid-major program without a big budget, top-notch facility, or fancy tech, but with a track record of making players better and getting some drafted highly may be a better fit for you.

The same thing applies to agents and MLB organizations, if you're the sort of player talented enough to have to make those sorts of decisions. We've spoken with agents and teams that tell us kids are now setting different signability numbers for different teams, based on who has the best development track record and transparency about their methods for development. When meeting with potential advisors, find one who isn't tied to your decision (i.e. is buddies with a college coach recruiting you) and do research about who they've repped in the past, how it's gone, and if they stick to their word. Some agencies seek the spotlight and don't communicate much, while others are more workmanlike and have a family atmosphere. All the major agencies have done big deals and messed others up, so find the qualities that matter to you.

Is Showcase/Travel Baseball a Good Thing?

We go into this in the draft chapter and we beat around the bush a little bit above. People in and around the game complain about showcases because of:

- Cost vs. benefit for the players and the profit-seeking motives of some showcase organizers
- It encourages kids to focus on batting practice power instead of in-game hitting ability
- It can slow, or at least doesn't aid in-game instincts due to lack of competitive games
- Pitchers often sell out for velocity since short outings encourage that, while longer starts require a different kind of competence

These are fair critiques, but are also a bit reductive. There are some predatory companies and events out there, but it's also on the kid and family to do the research, since some of them are pretty obvious, or would be after asking around about a company/event, emailing coaches, etc.

Kids should practice for BP since it's also a key part of scout-driven events. We want to see game hitting talent ultimately, but we're projecting a decade into the future and if you don't have the raw tools (i.e. power, bat speed, etc.) to reach the big leagues, or can reasonably project them, your hitting ability in games does not matter. In-game instincts are important, but showcases don't keep you from also getting game reps elsewhere.

For better or worse, velocity is the single most predictive quality to success and an MLB career. Every recruiter or scout or even media member is looking for multiple other qualities, but velocity speaks to quick-twitch movement, arm speed that would help you improve a breaking ball, and velocity to create separation for a changeup to work. It is the one quality that affects everything else you do. Even if scouts only saw pitchers in competitive games, they would scout them the same way; because some coaches/showcase operators may suggest to pitch in a short-sighted way isn't the fault of the showcase industry at large.

Travel baseball has a different set of issues, mostly revolving around the cost, year-round nature, and pressures that come with both of those. As we said above, if you're interested in a travel program and they're requiring huge upfront payments before any games are played, or require you to go to a certain number of events or you're cut, then odds are that's probably not a good program in the first place. These programs widen a socioeconomic gap. Rich kids from New England can fly JetBlue to Florida as often as they need to play in a showcase, but a poor kid from Biloxi can't do that as easily, so the latter player doesn't get seen as much and might fall on that showcase's player rankings from the lack of attendance.

The pressure to "keep up" and play year-round so you can "be seen," even if you have unlimited resources, is peer pressure from an industry that you don't need to succeed. It's the showcase's way of advertising to you, preying on your fear of missing out on something they've created. If you are a non-elite player with limited resources, this probably isn't an option for you, but there are plenty of ways to work around it, so it's not the loss that many may make it out to be.

Both systems have their problems, but there are companies and events that are doing it right, and plenty of alternatives that you can opt out of both and not seriously or even materially affect your outcome. Ideally, the whole showcase/travel system would be free for every player that could benefit from it, but that isn't the case and never will be. The amount of free events or ones with scholarship options (usually, but not always, for elite players that don't really need exposure) are increasing, and the events that MLB and scout associations put on are pretty much universally cost-effective and efficient for you, if you're invited (or can talk your way into a tryout) and fully healthy.

We don't feel like there are any for-profit companies that universally are completely unproblematic enough to give a blanket recommendation. Even the most reputed companies have events or practices that seem to be run for profit first or to fill the calendar. It's up to you to do the homework and make a good decision, but we've provided the framework to make those decisions. We're also pretty easy to reach online via email, social media, and weekly chats at FanGraphs if you have a specific question.

Some of the Unsavory Parts of the Recruiting Process

We don't feel like showcases or travel baseball are inherently evil. We wouldn't call the NCAA evil, but the well-being of the student athlete, across multiple sports, is less a priority than it should be. Luckily, the most egregious examples are tied up around transfer rules, coach pay, and player compensation in higher-revenue sports, sports with no option to sign out of high school: basketball and football. The recent, non-passing of a rule that would have allowed baseball programs to have a paid third assistant coach (which the schools/conferences voted down), and the completely absurd 11.7 scholarship limit are examples of how the NCAA is problematic for athletes in baseball too.

Similar to the international signing period for MLB teams, college coaches find themselves in an arms race of sorts when it comes to recruiting. With the influx of cash to the SEC and, to a lesser degree, the ACC, via huge television rights deals, this means new facilities, uniforms, and tech are brought in to entice players. The overall efficiency of talent actualization is on the rise as programs become more professional and corporate, like the top football programs in the country. Coaches at top programs are also getting multiple verbal commitments, sometimes a half-dozen, from kids before they even play a high school baseball game, similar to how 13-year-olds are getting seven-figure guarantees in Latin America, three years before they can sign a contract.

This is happening for the same reason that NFL coaches are hesitant to go for it on fourth down as much as analytics/historical outcomes suggest they should: NFL coaches get ridiculed if they do an unconventional thing (go for it on fourth-and-1 on their side of the field) and it fails, but they don't get ridiculed or even fired for failing at a conventional, but unwise thing (punting from the opponent's 40-yard-line). The discourse around this is shifting, but mostly in the Twitter echo chamber of like-minded people. For college baseball recruiting among top programs, if you don't commit any players until your main competition already has a half-dozen or more of the current top prospects, that is the same situation the NFL coach finds himself regarding fourth down decisions. If you're "behind" in recruiting and have a bad season on the field, the money at top programs is enough that you could get fired just for that, ignoring a multi-year track record of success up to that point.

At some level, this allows recruiters to demonstrate evaluation and recruiting skill by identifying and committing players earlier, so it can be seen as a positive, from a distance, to let the market decide these things as it wishes. In reality, coaches privately tell us that they don't want to be doing this, but one of them will commit these players early, so they all feel like they have to. We've been told that kids are getting SEC offers off of a bullpen or an inning or two and very limited in-person makeup evaluation, since NCAA rules restrict communication.

Judging young hitters at this earliest stage is more heavily based on tools and projection, rather than performance, since that gives margin for error in the evaluation, similar to the July 2 market early commitments. Judging pitchers is similar, where a sophomore in high school that sits 87–89 mph is already throwing hard enough to survive mid-week in the biggest conferences, so not that much projection is necessary, even though lots of things will change in the next few years.

One coach told us that if we each saw a 14-year-old pitcher one time, pitching one inning one week apart, we'd have at least as much evaluation ability and overall information as many top-tier programs do when they commit a recruit to their school. It's getting more popular for colleges to hire former scouts to be their recruiting coordinators, but there's still only a handful of those. With the rising assistant salaries at top schools and stagnant scout salaries in MLB, it will likely be happening more.

It's no surprise then that, as many coaches have also pointed out, these extremely early commitments often lead to nothing. Kids can plateau early, get hurt, continue improving and turn pro, or turn out to be a little better or a little worse than implied by the early commitment. The way these verbals get unwound is pretty unsavory. The coach doesn't want to be labeled as one that goes back on his word, so he tells the family that Timmy probably won't get any playing time as a freshman, because of his development and the returning roster, as a way to drive Timmy to decommit so the coach can reclaim the scholarship percentage he offered a few years ago.

This also happens to players once they are on campus. Kiley was once at a fall scout day for one of the top programs in the country and the college's legendary head coach was sitting in the scout section, chopping it up with scouts and letting his assistants run the event. Kiley realized why this was happening once the event began, because the coach was announcing to anyone who would listen that the role player junior taking BP right now would sign for a $125,000 bonus in the upcoming draft and that he was a real attractive prospect with good makeup. The coach was doing this because he wanted an MLB team to sign him and free up some scholarship money, as the player wasn't the core regular that his scholarship percentage—negotiated as a sophomore in high school—suggested. He'd rather push the player to sign than to be known as the coach that reduced a scholarship percentage for a contributing player. The head coach was making over $1 million at the time, as something like six to 10 college head coaches now do.

Some top programs that excel because of their recruiting get about half of their impact players by flipping later-blooming high school prospects initially committed to lesser college programs, or scooping up new, free agent recruits that reopen recruiting when a coaching staff they initially committed to got fired. Clemson lost catcher Cal Raleigh (Florida State/third round to Mariners) and pitcher Jackson Kowar (Florida/first round to the Royals) very late in the recruiting process when they fired head coach Jack Leggett in June 2015.

Imagine, as a recruiting coordinator, committing two elite prospects as sophomores in high school. They both put out big enough signability numbers for the draft that there's a good chance they can get to campus and then perform well enough for three years in college to go high in the draft three years from then. Think of it: three years of prep to get them committed, three years of their contributions on campus, the legacy of elite alums, all blown up because Clemson had lost two straight regionals, going two-and-out. Those two players could have easily been the difference makers to put the program over the top for the next three years.

It's a common refrain amongst scouts in Florida when they see a prep prospect who is committed to a mid-tier school take a big step forward, that it's a matter of days before he commits to Florida, one of the clear top-five programs in the sport. In the handful of days between when we were writing and proofreading this chapter, this exact thing happened.

There's been some recent early commits with real talent who never got to campus because the school got too lucky with recruits not signing pro contracts. Mississippi State had the incredibly unlikely outcome of two recruits drafted in the first both not signing in 2018: righties J.T. Ginn and Carter Stewart. Ginn was able to get to campus after the Bulldogs shuffled scholarships around late. But sources told us they couldn't clear enough money to make a spot for the eighth overall pick in the country, Stewart, who ultimately went to junior college.

Elijah Cabell has legit 70 raw power and plus bat speed and had been committed to LSU for years, but ended up not getting a pro offer he liked and, when LSU had a number of draft-eligible players somewhat unexpectedly opt to come back for one more year, Cabell was released from his commitment because LSU didn't have room for everyone. He eventually landed at Florida State.

In the same way that international scouting directors have to worry about the unknown opportunity cost—if you lock down a 14-year-old verbally, you're taking a hypothetical, unknown Cuban player that may defect a year from now off the table, or maybe you aren't if they never materialize—colleges have to wonder how to deploy their limited scholarships. If a recruit reclassifies when he's particularly young or old or academically advanced or behind for his class, it blows up all your math. There's some merit to saving a couple spots for when coaches get fired and Kowar or Raleigh hits the market later, or a Trea Turner pops up late, but that means you're purely picking over the leftovers and you're removing yourself from the early elite talents, who are often the elite talents in college baseball.

So, how does the NCAA solve this situation? Does it need to be solved? The clearest answer would appear to be making early commits binding and/or adding earlier signing dates, with opt-outs if coaches get fired. If top programs knew that their less rigorous recruiting commitment processes would be binding and whatever happened to this prospect over his next three years of high school was their problem, there would be far fewer early commitments. Fewer early commitments means less movement to decommit, flip, and recommit elsewhere, and that means a longer evaluation period and better decisions by all parties involved. Opening up camps and direct contact to even younger-aged players would allow this longer recruiting process to get started earlier, at the choice of the player. Some coaches suggest outlawing any sort of contact with younger players, but the counterargument is that a player shouldn't be kept from making a decision or starting the process if he wants to.

This seems unlikely because this doesn't exist in basketball or football, so why would the NCAA make a baseball-specific adjustment and not any other sport, with baseball being a second-tier revenue sport? The reason this problem is biggest in baseball is that skills are more important in baseball relative to physical tools. Football programs aren't committing more than a few players longer than a year or two in advance because physicality is more important, so they have to wait later to make decisions, even if they're non-binding. This also applies to basketball, not because of the contact but the overall athleticism required to be a key player at a top program.

Baseball obviously requires some physicality, but the most gifted athletes don't even get to campus, they get drafted early, so colleges often target the most skilled players early in the process, and hope they don't get too physical to draw a seven-figure offer from a Major League team. One exception to this is quarterbacks, arguably the most skill-based position in football, and QBs are notorious for, almost across-the-board, committing much earlier than their peers at other positions.

On the positive side, there's more money for the biggest schools in the biggest conferences and this directly has been going to head coaches, assistants, tech, and support staff in those programs. In recent years, the top college pitching coaches are being paid the same or more than MLB pitching coaches and the list of coaches interviewing for MLB pitching coach jobs include more and more college coaches, specifically for roles with more progressive MLB teams.

This is happening because there are pro-level monetary resources at these top college programs. Unlike MLB teams, where a farm system is a collaboration between dozens of people, college programs have comparable tools, especially at the top-level programs, and one or two coaches control an entire scouting, analytics, and development pipeline. This means recruiting eighth graders all the way up to fine tuning workload management for a 23-year-old senior and hiring developers to make an app for pitchers to record their workloads on their phone.

You can see why, if a college pitching coach appears to excel in the right areas after given this level of autonomy and interdisciplinary skill, that this is the best breeding ground for finding the next elite MLB pitching coach, but also to make top-tier money while doing it. Top-tier assistants in college make in the $250,000 to $500,000 range while slowly moving up in pro ball means making $40,000 to $100,000 coaching at a minor league affiliate, moving into the low six figures for minor league pitcher coordinator or director of pitching roles.

When we specify the role of the assistant coach, you may have noticed we keep saying pitching coach. This is because hitting development at the college levels lags far behind, for some clear reasons. Kiley wrote about this on FanGraphs in 2019 ("Swing Changers: Spurning College to Get Pro Development"), but the basic message is this: hitting development takes a more linear path since pitchers dictate the action, so making drastic changes takes time and colleges don't have enough time to necessarily take the time to do what's best for your career since it impacts winning games in the short-term.

Take that and combine it with the weaker defenses and high stakes for head coaches hoping to make millions, so bunting and hitting groundballs is a better short-term strategy to win game, but not to improve your career. When it comes to pitching, the way to win in college is pretty close to the way you win in pro ball (maybe except throwing lots of pitches and lots of breaking balls in key games) and changes can be made quickly, so pitching coaches in the SEC and MLB are doing pretty similar things.

College coaches tend to think that the recruiting calendar and player development rules around days/hours of coaching have all improved in recent years and aren't a problem at this point. Transfer rules have recently loosened, which is good for players and good for most programs.

How to Train

We'd love to give you a handy table with all the pertinent measurements, to say what sort of hand speed, bat speed, exit velocity, attack angle, launch angle, etc., that you need at each level of baseball and easy ways to measure them. Many things like this exist if you Google around and, if you get them from reputable sources, they're usually fine as a general guide. We wouldn't recommend relying on it too much because there's a dearth of public information in this area—either lots of Statcast data on big leaguers and nothing below that level, or Blast Motion bat sensor data, mostly on non-professionals from independent trainers—and there's also all kinds of secondary, game-specific skills that can nullify any advantage you gain in this area.

One thing we can tell you is that if you aren't able to hit a 90 mph fastball at least 100 mph, you will not play in the big leagues. Here's the table from the chapter on how to scout hitters:

Grade	Max Exit Velo (mph)	Average Exit Velo (mph)
80	118 (Vlad Guerrero Jr., Aaron Judge)	95 (Aaron Judge)
70	116 (Ketel Marte, Ronald Acuña)	93 (Christian Yelich, Joey Gallo)
60	113 (Tommy Pham, José Abreu)	90 (Mookie Betts, Juan Soto)
55	111 (Matt Olson, Ryan Braun)	89 (Buster Posey, Anthony Rizzo)
50	110 (Max Muncy, Lorenzo Cain)	88 (Willy Adames, Colin Moran)
45	108 (Todd Frazier, Anthony Rendon)	86 (Austin Barnes, Juan Lagares)
40	106 (Raimel Tapia, Eduardo Escobar)	85 (Albert Almora, Omar Narvaez)
30	103 (Tony Wolters, Eric Sogard)	83 (Jarrod Dyson, Garrett Hampson)
20	100 (Billy Hamilton, Tony Kemp)	80 (Victor Robles, Roman Quinn)

The players whose power is their weakest tool and is also the weakest amongst all big leaguers still hit the ball 100 mph. If you're in high school or earlier, you've got plenty of time to add strength and see better velocity to get to this level. Plenty of players can do this and still don't make it, but this is a nice reality check if you want a concrete thing to wrap your head around.

This brings us to the first piece of advice about training. We'll let Rathwell explain it: "The basic mistake people are making is being underdeveloped physically for the level they aspire to and thinking playing more games will solve the problem. If a kid thinks he's going DI (but doesn't have an offer) and he can see that he isn't hitting the ball as hard at kids at D2 and below, he either needs to be Andrelton Simmons with the glove or get stronger and improve the bat." He also points out that the opposite of this issue, a weightlifter with no feel for the game, does sometimes happen, but is much less common because playing games is fun.

As much as we don't want to be the guys to tell you that if you can't do one certain physical thing that you can't play at a certain level, that is generally true. It is a sorting mechanism that recruiters and scouts use and it's only getting more that way as data becomes a bigger part of scouting and player development.

Knowing where you fit in this continuum, relative to the level you're trying to get to, will dictate if you need to focus more on weight training, mechanics, practice repetition, or game situations. The right answer is almost certainly a combination of all of these things and, if you aren't getting the results you want on the field or in recruiting, weight training is probably your biggest need. There are all kinds of resources online for whatever specific needs you have and Driveline recently made their TRAQ training software free to try, covering hitting, pitching, and strength programs along with templates for year-round training.

In terms of speed and defense, we also don't want to be the guys to tell you it doesn't matter much. The reality is it's becoming less and less a part of evaluation, but depending on your specific situation, it could either be holding you back from getting recruiting attention and/or it could be low-hanging fruit to differentiate yourself from a number of similar players. In these cases, it makes sense to prioritize speed training and defensive practice reps.

For the pitchers, we'd also once again like to be the guys to tell you velocity doesn't matter as much as people say and honing your overall craft and execution is key, but that's not true. If you aren't strong and flexible, you can't throw hard, and if you don't throw hard, it's a real uphill battle for you. You'd better have some easily identifiable elite secondary characteristics to get someone's attention, or have elite athleticism and physical projection. Rathwell has advice for a 15-year-old throwing harder than most of his peers: "Many things are separating you from MLB success, even when you can blow it past guys at 87–89 mph. The main difference is that Major League players are a lot stronger than you."

So, similar to our hitting advice, prioritize being physically strong via weight training. Talk to your high school training staff and/or your physician about how you should proceed. Invest time in finding someone who is good enough locally to help you with strength training. Rathwell points out that, especially in the earlier stages of your career, to focus on doing it, and not waiting until you can find a pro-level guy so you can match Justin Verlander.

Once you get your strength level and basic mechanics squared away, arm care is your next priority. You can't throw year round and pitch in every game you're asked to. "Our arm care uses J-Bands, wrist weights, weighted balls, and a small trampoline," Rathwell said. "Yours can be that simple." In addition, listening to your body and your arm and deciding how often to throw and throw in games is an individual enough decision that we won't bother to break down all the various choices and programs you could use.

There's no clear correct blanket answer to this, so do some research and figure out what works for you.

A good rubric for making these decisions is to envision your career in an 8–10 year horizon. Is selling out for a big velo number at a camp in two months the right way to reach your potential five years from now? Rathwell continues down that road: "Is jumping at a Power 5 preferred walk-on offer better than a scholarship at a mid-major with a good track record of developing pitchers? Is it worth taking a slightly smaller signing bonus to sign with a club that you know aligns with your thoughts on throwing programs, pitch design, and arm care? It depends—it's individual to each athlete."

We hear a lot of different opinions about playing multiple sports. You hear it come up most often with elite athletes that are top-tier DI and pro-potential types in multiple sports because their recruitment and ultimate choice become newsworthy. How should a potential DI athlete, but not necessarily a pro prospect, handle this?

It depends what kind of athlete you are. If you're the skills-over-tools type player we referenced earlier, you may need to focus on baseball only, or maybe just heavily, earlier to get the reps to develop those skills to make up for your lack of physical gifts. If you're already getting the type of results you want in baseball while playing other sports, then keep doing that as long as you can do it.

Scouts tend to give the benefit of the doubt to multi-sport athletes both because they tend to be more athletic, but also if they're on a pro scout's radar while splitting time, they'll likely improve when playing just one sport. One approach is to pick sports that complement your baseball skills and position when you're taking a break from baseball. If you're a shortstop and want to work on quick feet and change of direction, soccer and racquet sports make sense and cross country makes less sense. For a catcher working on leverage and balance, wrestling makes sense. It's all part of a complicated, very personal path to making it to the level you want to achieve.

CHAPTER 7

How to Scout

We're not professing that once you digest what you're about to read you'll be able to head to the field and effectively pan for big leaguers. A lot of scouting is developing experiential knowledge that takes several years to develop. You will fuck up booking travel, your notes or video taking, eating on the road, how you deal with stretches of social isolation, family re-immersion, and countless other little details that will snowball and make you worse at scouting until you learn to be better at everything.

We can't replicate that in these pages. So much of what makes a great scout good at their job is how they've refined their approach and eye in ways that are often specific to where and what they're scouting. It's the little things, like knowing the gate code to a spring training complex's backfields, noticing cameras set up at a secondary field means a sim game might go on over there later, noting who's charting today means they're likely to pitch the next game, noticing scouts going down the side to watch a hitter means he's a prospect, knowing the good places to eat near a ballpark, etc.

It also takes time to build a proper context for evaluating individual skills. In order to properly evaluate physical tools, a scout needs to see what kinds of bodies, athletes, and swings play in the big leagues, learn what an effective big league repertoire looks like. Watch only high school games and the kid sitting 87–91 with a curveball he can throw in the strike zone is going to look like Kerry Wood. Go to a big league game and spend nine innings watching fastballs no slower than 94 mph and it will change your perspective on that high school kid. Without having some idea what it is they're supposed to be looking for, scouts have impotent eyes.

Proper evaluation skills are just one necessary trait. The other, of utmost importance, is report writing and communication skills. Scouts need a way of communicating with one another across an organization, they need to be speaking the same language. Over time, systems of measure and communication have evolved (and some are now antiquated) to enable scouts to not only communicate amongst themselves within an organization, but so they can move freely from team to team in search of employment without a ton of new verbiage, sort of like heading to a new football team that uses the same scheme. That system of communication, infamous and immortal, is the 20–80 scale.

The Scouting Scale

It may be apocryphal in the same way Thomas Jefferson is often credited with inventing mac and cheese, but the invention of the 20–80 scouting scale is often credited to legendary executive Branch Rickey (80 eyebrows), and it was maybe the third-most important thing Rickey ever did, as he also pioneered player development through farm systems, and was instrumental in Jackie Robinson breaking the color barrier. Assuming two scouts have well-calibrated scales, you can read their reports on two separate players and know which of the two you prefer without having seen either one. It's part evaluative measure, part language, a mix of objectivity and subjectivity, an intersection between science and art.

Areas under the normal curve that lie between the 1, 2, and 3 standard deviations on each side of the mean

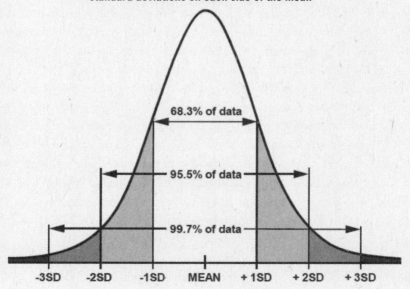

68.3% of data

95.5% of data

99.7% of data

-3SD   -2SD   -1SD   MEAN   + 1SD   + 2SD   + 3SD

Whether he intended this or not, the 20–80 scale mirrors various scientific scales. A 50 on the scale is the mean, the average. Then, each 10 point increment represents a standard deviation, better or worse than average. In a normal distribution, three standard deviations in either direction includes 99.7 percent of your sample, so that's why the scale is 20 to 80 rather than 0 to 100, as anything outside the 20–80 range is likely statistical noise.

Imagine if Usain Bolt decided to play pro baseball. While he'd certainly be the fastest baseball player on the planet, he'd still just be graded as having 80 speed, since his talent is so exceptional that it's unlikely to ever be seen again as to necessitate another notch on the scale.

It's important to note that 50 represents Major League average, not the average across all of professional baseball. The distribution of tools isn't a perfect bell curve for every tool, but is somewhere close to it for most of them because the player population is so large. Let's go through some well-known examples of hitter tools on the 20–80 scale so you can begin to build a foundation of context.

Grade	Player and Tool
80 (aka elite)	Michael Brantley's hit tool, Andrelton Simmons' glove, Joey Gallo's power
70 (plus-plus)	DJ LeMahieu's hit tool, Francisco Lindor's glove, Eloy Jiménez's power
60 (plus)	Ronald Acuña's speed, Rhys Hoskins' hit tool, Trevor Story's power
55 (above-average)	Nick Castellanos' hit and power, Eduardo Escobar's defense
50 (average)	Matt Chapman's hit, Andrew Benintendi's power, Buster Posey's arm
45 (fringe)	Xander Bogaerts' speed, Mike Trout's arm, Adam Eaton's power
40 (below-average)	Yoán Moncada's hit tool, Juan Soto's defense, Jean Segura's defense
30	Cesar Hernández's power, Jake Marisnick's hit tool
20	Late-career Chris Davis' hit, Brian McCann's speed

Most large populations of things show a normal distribution and create a visual bell curve when you plot out the data on a bar graph. If, for instance, we were to apply the scientific scale to the length of Great White Sharks, a shark in the 13- to 15-foot range would be a 50 since that's the average range for adult White Sharks. The 20-foot behemoths among the largest ever caught would be an 80, and the fictional 35-foot shark from *Jaws* would be noise.

Because so much of any population is typically packed close to the middle, near the average, scouts often use 45 and 55 to describe skills and tools that are just shy of or just above average, respectively. Values 35 and 65 are sometimes used too, but less often, and lots of scouts think it's chickenshit to use either of those and would rather you make a call on whether something is a 30 or a 40, or a 60 or 70 instead of splitting the difference. We've been told a story from a team's draft room where a scouting director told two scouts who both put a 65 on a tool grade to pick 60 or 70 at the count of three. They both said 60 at the count of three and a former first rounder and big leaguer in his first draft room said, "Wait, so that's how you guys picked me?"

These half grades like 65 and 75 don't have separate terms because many teams use a 2–8 scale rather than 20–80 and 2–8 is the scale that was predominant when many of today's top scouts were starting out. Now 20–80 is more commonly used, but often you'll hear older scouts at the ballpark call someone a "six or seven," while we might call that a 65 here. It helps in our situation to have more numbers to describe things when we're trying to differentiate between literally hundreds of prospects that have 50 or 55 power grades, for example.

Though some teams have scouts grade each of these components, it's the five core scouting grades that are paid attention to universally. It's common practice in scouting reports for scouts to explain in the comments when, say a 55 fielding grade includes some 60 or higher components (range, hands, instincts, etc.) and some 50 or lower components, but often a 55 means a number of average to above skills and doesn't merit much additional explanation. Scouts also use present and future grades for each tool. Present grades often are 20s for high school players while, in the upper levels of the minors, the gap between present and future grades is very small.

Just so we're clear in a housekeeping sense about shorthand: a present 20 and future 50 grade on a tool is noted as 20/50. This is not the same as the present and future grades on a player's overall ability, which we call present value and future value. We'll go into more depth on that process in another chapter.

You can apply the scale to nearly anything, either objective or subjective. Kiley likes to apply it to produce to add Consumer Reports–level precision to a grocery store visit. If we were going to draft Batman movies and we'd only be able to watch these Batman movies for the rest of our lives, this is how Eric would have them all evaluated:

20: *Batman & Robin*

30: *Batman v Superman, Batman Forever*

40: *Batman Begins, Batman: Gotham Knight*

45: *Dark Knight Rises, Batman: The Movie* (1966)

50: *Batman Returns, Mask of the Phantasm, The Dark Knight Returns Part 2*

55: *Batman* (1989), *Batman Beyond: Return of the Joker*

60: *Batman: Year One, Batman: Under the Red Hood*

70: *The Dark Knight*

80: *The Dark Knight Returns Part 1*

The Dark Knight is probably at or near the top of everyone's Batman movie pref list, so in a sense it's objectively excellent, but exactly where you have it on your pref list will have a huge impact on whether or not you end up with it in the draft, so the subjectivity on the margins is very meaningful. Also, if you don't recognize some of the above titles it means Eric knows about more Batman movies than you, giving him a better chance of leaving the draft with more good movies, the same way good scouting departments can separate themselves from others in the middle rounds of drafts.

The Tools

Scouts head to the field looking to evaluate—using the 20–80 scale—the core physical abilities needed to play baseball, and these abilities are called "tools," as you probably know. The five tools for position players are: 1) Hitting, 2) Power, 3) Running, 4) Fielding, and 5) Throwing. Yes, this is overly simplistic and should bring about several pertinent questions in the minds of most readers because it plainly ignores several aspects of baseball. Scouts apply 20–80 grades to all kinds of traits beyond those five (like athleticism, which is a 20–80-scaled attribute we'd like you to keep in the back of your mind for later in this chapter), but for now consider just these traditional five.

In the past, scouts would slap a 20–80 on each tool, then calculate the average of the five tools and the resulting number would be the player's OFP or Overall Future Projection (or Overall Future Potential). This is a terrible way of going about it because it weighs all five tools equally, when in fact they are not, varying wildly by position. Here's an example:

Player A: 30 hit, 20 power, 80 speed, 80 fielding, 50 throwing = 52 OFP

Player B: 70 hit, 70 power, 20 speed, 30 fielding, 20 throwing = 42 OFP

Using the Old Testament OFP, our department would greatly prefer Billy Hamilton (Player A) to David Ortiz (Player B) and we'd all get fired.

This misguided form of aggregation has been scrubbed from the game, and now scouts are more often tasked with evaluating all the tools individually, then putting an overall 20–80 grade on the entire player's profile, which is informed by the tool grades but not derived from a faulty equation, more from an overall consideration of his value.

Because the 20–80 scale is scientific in nature and we have such a huge sample of big league players generating statistics, we can pull stats generated by big leaguers to both set the lines of demarcation that comprise the scale, and also give scouts an idea of what they're looking at. Let's start with a relatively simple tool to evaluate: speed.

Click-click… Click-click

The traditional means of evaluating speed is with a stopwatch, specifically one of the many Accusplit models, which come in a variety of colors. In a showcase environment, scouts are timing a 60-yard dash, which is a straight-line speed measure akin to the NFL Combine's 40-yard dash. You start your watch when the player makes their first move, and stop when they cross the finish line, which is typically where all the scouts are standing.

Scouts also take runners' times from base to base, most often when the hitter is making a max-effort sprint from home to first. This is a more accurate form of data generation as the scout can anticipate both when the hitter will make contact with the baseball (start the watch) and when he'll make contact with first base (stop the watch). Often scouts use their raw times to grade a player's speed on the scale (frequently comparing them with nearby peers to verify accuracy, especially if someone runs a blazingly fast time) but sometimes they'll round up or down based on weather or field conditions, or how good of a jump out of the box the hitter gets, a full swing or a drag bunt, etc. Some hitters have a natural "jailbreak" out of the box which favorably alters their home-to-first times to a grade or two above their true speed. (Ichiro and Rickie Weeks are two recent, prominent examples of this.)

The scale for 60-yard dashes and home-to-first times, along with some examples, looks like this:

Grade	60-Yard Time	LH Home to 1B	RH Home to 1B	Example
80	6.3 or less	3.90 or less	4.00 or less	Byron Buxton
70	6.5	4.00	4.10	Dee Gordon
60	6.7	4.10	4.20	Ronald Acuña
55	6.8	4.15	4.25	Albert Almora
50	6.9–7.0	4.20	4.30	Yasiel Puig
45	7.1	4.25	4.35	Carlos Correa
40	7.2	4.30	4.40	Jason Heyward
30	7.4	4.40	4.50	Joey Votto
20	7.6 or more	4.50 or more	4.60 or more	Brian McCann

The actual average home-to-first time in baseball is about 4.4 seconds, but that number is dragged down by glacial runners at the bottom of the league. Though less mathematically correct in the purest sense, the traditional scale above is better, we think, at assessing relevant speed. There's also a way to perform a sanity check using a broad rubric: an average runner with an average jump hitting an average ground ball to an average fielder with an average arm should be a bang-bang play.

Right-handed hitters have a greater distance to run to first, so their times are, on average, a little slower than lefty hitters. Righty batters hit the ball to the left side of the infield more often, which means longer throws for the defense and more potential opportunity for high-effort sprints to first because of this, but we're not sure how that impacts the data beyond giving us a more reliable sample for righty hitters.

In the past we'd have considered a selection bias to be possible for lefty hitters since they're the kinds who would've been bunting for hits when that was more common, and so it may have been more important that the lefty hitter have speed and that big league teams would select for that, thus creating a bias. But those parts of the game are less pervasive now and so we're less worried about lefty hitter data being dirty. The tenth-of-a-second gap between the left- and right-handed batters is the industry-accepted delta, though independent research Eric conducted while at Baseball Info Solutions indicated the average gap between handedness is actually closer to two tenths of a second, and that the average for left- and right-handed hitters, respectively, is closer to 4.15 seconds and 4.35 second per run to first. We're fine with the speed scale times being slightly off what they're technically supposed to be, mathematically, because there's big value in communicative ease and this is the scale scouts have been using forever. Moving away from it to an altered scale may go the way of the American adoption of the Metric system.

Not So Fast, Sprint Speed

The popular, modern, public-facing way of measuring big league speed is with "Sprint Speed," a Statcast metric that quantifies quickness by measuring how many feet per second a player runs in his fastest one-second window of movement, essentially measuring top, or peak speed. While this is an interesting piece of data, it isn't solely what we'd lean on to evaluate players' speed. It ignores important aspects of running, like acceleration, entirely, and it only encompasses roughly one fourth of the event that occurs as a player runs from one base to the next in that one-second window. Here are some examples of what tool grades would be if we used Sprint Speed as a means of evaluation for big league players, with the player's home-to-first time-based speed and its corresponding grade in parentheses after their name. We've intentionally included players with discrepancies to illustrate our point.

Grade	Sprint Speed (feet/sec)	Example
80	31.6	None
70	30.1	Mike Trout (4.28 to first, 50)
60	28.7	Andrew McCutchen (4.32, 50)
55	28.0	Matt Chapman (4.40, 40)
50	27.2	Jonathan Schoop (4.52, 30)
45	26.5	Franmil Reyes (4.60, 20)
40	25.8	Eugenio Suárez (4.71, 20)
30	24.3	Willians Astudillo (20)
20	22.9	Brian McCann (20)

There are lots of hitters who have exactly the same Sprint Speed as another player but their home-to-first times are significantly different, and if all else is equal, we'll take the guy who can haul ass down the line, as that's the speed actually impacting the game. Running from home to first is the most common event in which a player's speed is relevant. It's the difference between being out and safe, and the difference between making an out and not is significant when you only have 27 to spend over the course of a game. Measuring times from home to first encompasses a combination of the player's top speed as well as their acceleration, and it can all be measured by a light portable device with a seemingly everlasting battery that can fit in your pocket.

This is painfully straightforward compared to other tools. Time the runners from home to first, check the handy scale for the applicable 20–80 grade, and voilà. Skepticism regarding the accuracy of a given run time should be tempered by the frequency of trials and the eventual realization that every scout gets pretty good at starting the watch at point of contact and stopping it when the runner steps on the bag. Hitters who make a lot of high-quality contact are less likely to need to run full tilt to first base and sometimes those guys are tougher to get a time for, so scouts also take times with the turn, which means stopping the watch when the runner hits the bag even when he's taken a turn toward second base. Typically, times with the turn are .3 seconds slower than times straight through the bag, and scouts make the easy conversion. There's some judgment, with .1 or .2 deductions for less-than-typical turns.

Baserunning skills, instincts, and good jumps out of the batter's box are also folded into the run grade when scouts see enough of a player to have an idea of his abilities in this area.

Lasers and Leather Wizards

Now that you know how to tell not just who is fast and who is not, but exactly how much faster or slower one player is than another, you need to level up and consider defensive abilities, including arm strength.

Scouting arm strength sounds very easy, like it should be much the same as scouting fastball velocity with a radar gun. This is mostly true for outfielders who crow hop and step into their throws most of the time. Statcast has measured throws from the likes of Aaron Hicks and Brett Phillips in excess of 100 mph, and that's what an 80 outfield arm looks like. Outfield arms are fairly easy to scout during pregame defensive drills when outfielders are making throws to third base and home from their respective outfield positions, assuming that they're all trying to throw hard. This is the type of thing that takes a while to gain feel for as a scout; you just need to watch a lot of guys throwing from the outfield to polish your eyes up and be able to identify the 50s and those on either side of it. Just a handful of nudges from a seasoned evaluator sitting next to you ("Hey, that one was a 50") can quickly calibrate your scale.

Some scouts have a rule of thumb for evaluating outfield arms based on the number of hops it takes on the way to the plate (they adjust based on the arc; no slow-but-bounceless rainbow to home is going to garner a good grade, even among scouts who do this), but we suggest starting your arm-strength note taking by listing the players in order of best arm to worst arm. Two throwers too close to separate from one another? Good, list them side by side rather than on top of one another and, as you collect more and more throwers, you'll start to see a bell curve emerge, like this fake example:

RF Timmy DeLaser
RF Marcus Zipp
CF Chuck Fine, RF Viyabell Brazo
CF Armie Soft, LF Raul Tirarlento
LF Larry McWetnoodle

Things get a little more complicated for infielders, who just don't have as many opportunities to make clean, strong throws. When they do have that kind of time to gather themselves and make a max-effort throw to first it's because the runner is slow, or because the ball was hit right at them, and often in these cases they have no reason to reach back and let it rip. On rare occasions, players like Carlos Correa and Fernando Tatís Jr. have uncorked throws around 93 mph from shortstop (Correa threw one measured at 97 mph in high school), and that's what the top of the scale looks like if we want to measure infield arm strength in this way. Though, 2020 Draft prospect Sabin Ceballos threw a ball 99 mph across the infield at a 2019 high school showcase, so maybe Tatís and Correa are 70s in this regard, not 80s.

It's common at high school showcases where there's grounders hit, for scouts to scatter in the seats behind first base with their radar guns just to collect velos on the throws to first. Accordingly, of course, the throws will often miss wildly, sometimes three or four times in a row, all in pursuit of a big velo number that has nothing to do with playing the position.

That's why we think this type of measure, while notable like sprint speed, is insufficient. Like we just said, it's not often that infielders can set themselves and throw to first the way Tom Emanski would like them to. Most of the time, they just have to chuck it over there as quickly as possible. Often, this is happening from weird athletic platforms, like when infielders charge to field high hoppers and have to throw while running in, or when shortstops throw across their bodies after making plays on balls up the middle, etc. The same way some quarterbacks are better at throwing on the run while others have bigger arms standing tall in the pocket, some infielders have great set-and-throw arms but can't make All The Throws, and vice versa.

We call this concept "Arm Utility,"™ and it's really a function of how an infielder's athleticism enables his arm to play in game situations rather than in a way that can be measured by a radar gun. Remember earlier in the chapter when we asked you to remember that athleticism is typically 20–80'd? This is the first of several instances where two measurable skills intersect and have some kind of impact on one another, creating a double counting of sorts. And again, we ask you to put a pin in this concept for later in the chapter.

Throws like these don't have a vapor trail coming off the back of them, but they are great throws. Infield drills force players to make a wide-enough variety of throws that you can get a good idea of raw arm strength, but ideally a scout would see the player get enough game action to have some idea of arm utility, as well. Here are some examples of big league arms on the 20–80 scale followed by what we think their arm utility is. We've intentionally chosen players for whom we think there's a gap, or who best help illustrate the concept. The 20- and 30-grade arms are either in left field or DHing.

Grade	Raw Arm Strength	Arm Utility
80	Carlos Correa	Fernando Tatís Jr.
70	Fernando Tatís Jr.	Nick Ahmed
60	Abraham Toro	Freddy Galvis
55	Nick Ahmed	Carlos Correa
50	Freddy Galvis	Kolten Wong
45	Ryan Mountcastle	Abraham Toro
40	Kolten Wong	—
30	—	Ryan Mountcastle
20	—	—

The notion of arm utility is new enough for the two of us that we haven't decided whether/how to explicitly fold it into our work at FanGraphs since arm utility is a harder thing for us to collect at a global scale without an entire staff of scouts. Throwing accuracy is folded into the throwing tool grade, and most scouts think poor accuracy is fixable, particularly when athleticism is present.

Catcher Arm Strength

Much like run times, scouts use a stopwatch to evaluate catcher arm strength. They start the watch when the pitch hits the catcher's mitt, and stop it when the middle infielder catches their throw. The average big league catcher pop time is two seconds, flat. Again, as is the case with run times, the stopwatch is measuring a couple of different things. The catcher's arm strength is part of it, but so is the "exchange," aka the amount of time it takes the catcher to get rid of the ball after he receives it. Catchers with inefficient economy of movement may have more projection on the arm if scouts think their mechanics can be polished up and they can shave a few fractions of a second off of their exchange. Here's the 20–80 scale for both pop times and raw catcher arm strength along with some examples. As usual, we've highlighted players who would fit in a different tool tier depending on which you used. We prefer the pop times.

Grade	Pop Time	Example	Arm Strength	Example
80	1.88	J.T. Realmuto	90.5 mph	Jorge Alfaro
70	1.91	Jake Rogers	87.4 mph	J.T. Realmuto
60	1.95	Jorge Alfaro	84.3 mph	Tom Murphy
55	1.97	Mike Zunino	82.7 mph	Austin Romine
50	2.00	Isiah Kiner-Falefa	81.2 mph	Mike Zunino
45	2.02	Sandy León	79.6 mph	Jake Rogers
40	2.05	Tom Murphy	78.1 mph	Sandy León
30	2.10	Austin Romine	75.0 mph	Isiah Kiner-Falefa
20	2.15	Stephen Vogt	72.0 mph	Vogt (he's at 73)

Scouts also take note of arm accuracy and know to note whether an infielder came off the bag to receive an inaccurate throw and how that might have impacted a pop time. It generally adds 0.1 seconds to the time until the tag if the ball is delivered at the fielder's head, rather than on the bag. Typically, they cut the ball off well before the bag if they have no chance of getting the runner, which can deflate pop times and mislead less fastidious scouts.

In showcase settings, catchers often cheat to throw, since in a game you also have to catch the ball, stay behind the hitter, and don't know until later if the runner is going. They also don't have a hitter in the box and don't wear full equipment, so those pop times can be essentially useless. One prominent showcase company has three or four stopwatches going for every 60-yard dash (along with a laser timer) and all five pop times and just takes the lowest, even if it's clearly a mistake. Scouts have agreed that taking 0.3 seconds off of the 60-yard dash time on the website is usually the correct adjustment, while the pop times aren't as easy to manually adjust.

Defense and Reductionism

Now we're starting to get into more complex and important territory. Speed and arm strength are relevant, but less significant than what we've yet to cover, and also far less complicated. Evaluating defense is about 20–80ing the player's ability, but more importantly it's about first gauging where the player fits on what is called the "defensive spectrum." This means determining what positions they're athletically capable of playing.

It further complicates things that positional requirements are changing in the big leagues, particularly middle infielders, due to the effect of shifts. Because the players being scouted are often very young, there's a lot of variation between what position/s a player might be fielding now and what position/s the scout thinks they'll be playing upon arrival in the big leagues and throughout the bulk of their careers thereafter. Even if you've never set foot in an amateur or minor league stadium, you've seen this happen. Ryan Braun and Albert Pujols came up as third basemen. Carlos Santana once caught and played third base. Hanley Ramírez was once a 30/30 shortstop. Throughout their big league careers, all of them tumbled down the spectrum to lesser positions as they became unable to play their original spots.

The concept of the defensive spectrum, a phrase coined by Bill James but not a concept introduced by him, is that there's an ordinal ranking of defensive positions by difficulty. James used it to track player movement across the spectrum during their careers. Some positions are more athletically demanding than others, and therefore more valuable. This is grounded in common sense and proven by looking, somewhat ironically, at the offensive performance at those positions. Think about shortstop and second base.

Both positions require a lot of the same things, except the shortstop needs to be able to make throws farther away from first base. And so, there are some players who meet all other requirements but lack the arm for shortstop, and so they need to play second base, but everyone capable of shortstop can hypothetically play second.

Here's a version of the OG Bill James defensive spectrum, from the most difficult position to the least, along with the minimum, prerequisite traits scouts would traditionally be seeking in order for someone to play there, though of course there are exceptions. You can see the requirements for each position withering away as you descend.

Catcher: above-average arm, all kinds of things so specific to catching that it arguably shouldn't be on the spectrum, though most agree it's the hardest.

Shortstop: above-average arm, plus speed/range, plus footwork, average hands/actions.

Second Base: below-average arm, plus speed/range, plus footwork, average hands/actions.

Center Field: below-average arm, plus speed/range, feet/hands/actions barely matter.

Third Base: above-average arm, 30 speed/range, average footwork, average hands/actions.

Right Field: above-average arm, 40 speed/range, feet/hands/actions barely matter.

Left Field: 30 arm, 40 speed/range, feet/hands/actions barely matter.

First Base: 40 arm, 30 speed/range, 40 footwork/hands/actions.

Designated Hitter: none.

Said in a more objective way, here's the positional adjustments we use at FanGraphs to calculate WAR. This is assuming a full season (162 full defensive games) for a starter, played only at this position, so this is the amount to move the WAR figure up or down. According to these adjustments, 10 runs basically equals 1 WAR or 1 win, with some variance year-to-year, usually between 9 and 11.

Catcher: +12.5 runs

Shortstop: +7.5 runs

Second Base: +2.5 runs

Third Base: +2.5 runs

Center Field: +2.5 runs

Right Field: -7.5 runs
Left Field: -7.5 runs
First Base: -12.5 runs
Designated Hitter: -17.5 runs

These component parts eventually combine to result in a 20–80 grade on the player's overall fielding ability, but it's much more important to draw conclusions about where they can play. Splitting up defense into its component parts is another perhaps unintentional application of scientific principles, this time the idea of methodological reductionism, which means we're breaking up the whole (a player's defensive abilities) into component parts (feet, hands, action, etc.) in order to better understand it.

Scouts will 20–80 each of these skills—sometimes in their notes rather than explicitly in a box on their sheet—which they've become adept at from watching thousands of hours of baseball. We've already talked about arm strength and speed (and here's your second instance of several attributes intersecting and modulating one another), but the others help make up most of the Fielding tool grade. "Hands" means something similar to what it does in football: How well does the fielder catch the ball? Infielders with good, soft hands field everything cleanly, deep in their mitt where the webbing meets the palm, and they successfully adjust to bad hops. Infielders with lesser hands are obviously more mistake prone, but they can also be identified if they're making plays with the ball clanging around in their glove.

Footwork is about positioning yourself to field and then throw the ball quickly and accurately to first, properly gauging the length and tempo of your paces, as well as your path to the ball. Some will include the entire lower half in this part of the evaluation since bending at the knees and waist is important for infield defenders' success.

Actions are all the little basebally things not encompassed in the other categories. It's the stuff that happens between when an infielder catches a ball and sends it onward to another base, it's how quickly and precisely they lay a tag on someone, and all kinds of other little things that frequently make a difference between getting someone out or not.

Instincts is the catchall term that can help all of these abilities play up or down, whether it's reading the pitch/location/swing and moving to the spot as the ball is hit, or knowing your 50 arm won't work deep in the shortstop/third base hole, so you circle the ball to get your momentum moving toward first base before uncorking a throw, like David Eckstein.

As players lose a step throughout their careers, these skills erode away and they have to move down the defensive spectrum. If they can hit, they stick around at newer, lesser positions. Hanley Ramírez, Miguel Cabrera, Victor Martínez, and Daniel Murphy are all good recent examples of this.

This impacts how prospects are valued. If a college center fielder lacks the speed to play center field in the big leagues and is viewed as a future left fielder, he'll be competing against not only the 30 starting left fielders in baseball for a job, but also all the best-hitting center fielders who are slowing down as they age. And so the best hitters typically filter down to the less athletically demanding positions, raising the bar for offense at that position and making it harder for the younger player to profile there. This is how 4A hitters get squeezed out of big league jobs: downward pressure on their profile from big league mashers tumbling down the spectrum and into their positional bucket.

It's also worth noting we haven't gone into a ton of detail in terms of how to grade an outfielder's defensive value. This is one area where the average fan can do a passable job as-is. While that fan may overrate the arm strength grade on a rainbow throw that's right on the money, they'll probably be close on arm utility grades since it's more focused on outcomes. Instincts and first-step quickness are important, as is closing speed, route efficiency, and initial positioning, and it's pretty easy to watch a replay and see all these elements.

This is also an area where computers can passably replace much of what scouts do, since scouts will often get a five-game look at a player and may only see one or two plays that actually show the best of these qualities per player. Statcast can quantify every element we just went over instantaneously for every MLB play in excruciating detail. It's almost impossible for technology to properly replace a scout's grade on a shortstop's "hands," as scouts define it, but replacing those handful of representative outfield plays per series is already happening.

The Shifting Spectrum and Components

We can illustrate this by looking at the average offensive performer at each position. The below table has the average wRC+ at each position dating back to 2012. wRC+ is a rate stat that attempts to credit a hitter for the value of each outcome (walk, double, home run, etc.) rather than treat all of hits/walks evenly, like OBP does. Baked in are controls for park effects and the current run environment. wRC+ is scaled so that league average across baseball is 100 each year, and every point above or below 100 is equal to one percentage point better or worse than league average.

Year	C	1B	2B	3B	SS	LF	CF	RF
2019	86	105	95	105	98	102	94	107
2018	84	105	93	102	95	102	96	106
2017	89	113	94	102	88	100	100	103
2016	87	108	101	106	93	97	96	101
2015	85	113	93	101	85	99	101	107
2014	93	109	88	100	87	103	103	101
2013	92	110	91	97	86	99	99	105
2012	95	107	88	100	86	103	101	104

For the most part, what was considered the defensive spectrum for the last few decades still holds true. Catching is hard to come by, and the offensive bars at the corner positions are much higher and harder to clear than those up the middle of the diamond.

But note the two significant shifts within catcher and shortstop during this stretch. Those years of more prolific offense among catchers might be explained by the presence of Buster Posey, Joe Mauer, and in-his-prime Yadier Molina as part of the sample. But that's also when there was a breakthrough regarding pitch framing (the catcher's ability to make pitches near the edge of the strike zone look like strikes to the umpire), and suddenly a skill everyone knew to exist was now quantifiable and the John Jasos of the world moved to new positions.

Upticks in wRC+ at the middle infield positions began to climb around the advent of ball-in-play location data and defensive shifts. Improved defensive positioning de-emphasized lateral range as a defensive skill, and so bigger, stronger bodies have ended up playing those spots in recent years. Corey Seager, Carlos Correa, Paul DeJong, Xander Bogaerts, Max Muncy, and Mike Moustakas have all seen a lot of time at middle infield positions. This concept applies to the entire infield.

The movement is significant enough that the lines between some of these positions has blurred. Catcher is still the most valuable (though, who knows how much this will change if electronic strike zones are eventually implemented), but the up-the-middle positions have become more clumped together; left field is performing up to expectations, while third base is exceeding them. If we're going to extrapolate using these wRC+ trends (perhaps some teams haven't yet realized how to hide offensive-minded shortstops and second basemen with good defensive positioning but soon will), then the speculative defensive spectrum looks like this:

C - 2B - SS - CF - LF - 3B - RF - 1B - DH

We think quite this much change is unlikely, but there's clear evidence that things are shifting and teams have become more open-minded about the kinds of athletes who play the middle infield, perhaps the infield in general. Lateral range has become less important because that shortcoming can be better hidden by shifting and more precise defensive positioning, and so bigger, stronger bodies are playing shortstop and second base, and there's now more offense at that position.

This is, we think, one of the areas where teams are questioning old dogma and making different decisions. If you have the opportunity to acquire one of two players who are the same in every way, except one plays left field and the other plays third base, which are you going to choose? It's possible third base offensive performance is being skewed by a currently historic group of talent (Bregman, Chapman, Machado, Suárez, Devers, Moncada, Arenado, José Ramírez, Guerrero), and the best long-term bet is still to take the third baseman.

What if instead you're deciding between a second baseman and center fielder? Does shifting actually make second base harder to play because they have to make more throws from shallow right field and from deep behind the second base bag? Or will the Travis Shaw/Max Muncy stuff at that position become more common? It's an interesting area to think about when trying to predict what types of players might be undervalued, and there's some evidence for this kind of anticipation. Here are some contemporary examples of all the component parts woven into some defensive grades. Opinions are ours.

Player	Pos	Feet	Hands	Actions	Range	Raw Arm	Arm Utility	Overall
Nolan Arenado	3B	80	55	50	60	70	80	80
Cody Bellinger	1B	60	70	70	70	60	60	80
Carlos Santana	1B	50	80	70	40	45	50	70
Scott Kingery	2B	50	45	50	80	55	45	60
Mike Moustakas	3B	60	60	60	45	60	60	55
Max Muncy	2B	50	55	60	40	50	50	50
Yoán Moncada	3B	40	40	40	70	60	50	45
Vlad Guerrero Jr.	3B	50	50	45	30	70	55	40
Josh Bell	1B	40	40	50	50	50	40	30

How to Scout Hitters

To this point we've slowly introduced scouting concepts and practices with growing complexity and underlying intersectionality. It brings us to hitting, which is a messy and difficult thing to evaluate. It's also the most important aspect of evaluation by a wide margin, as it's almost impossible for someone to be an impact player without producing on offense, or a big leaguer if he has no hitting ability. If a scout could project pitcher health and hitting ability as well as other aspects, they would be shockingly close to perfect in their evaluations. Since no one is likely to be solving pitcher health any time soon, let's focus on evaluating offense using some of the concepts we've already outlined, like reductionism, to see if we can arrive at better conclusions.

For scouts, offense is divided into three 20–80-able categories: hit, raw power, and game power. Let's start with the power categories. Conceptually, raw power is how hard or far a player is capable of hitting the ball. Traditionally this is something that has largely been evaluated during batting practice, and that's still a useful way to do it. Depending on the scout, this standard process could include one batting practice or sometimes as many as three to get a feel for the broad abilities the player brings to the table and what it looks like as they go about their business in a slow-paced setting, with different priorities and effort levels on every swing.

When we were advising former FanGraphs managing editor Carson Cistulli on how to scout (he now works in the Blue Jays front office), Kiley shared a rubric for grading raw power that he learned from his first boss with the Yankees, now-Angels GM Billy Eppler:

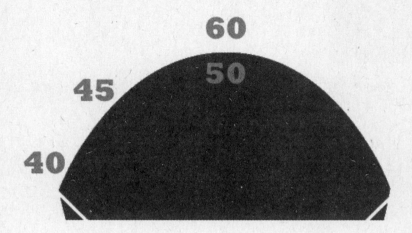

All things being equal (like effort level, baseball quality, wind, etc.), if a hitter's farthest couple hits in BP are homers that just get over the wall to his pull side, near the foul pole, that's 40 raw power. If it's a wall-scraper in the pull-side gap, it's a 45; if it's a non-homer to the warning track in center field, it's a 50 and if it carries the 400-ish foot sign in center field, it's a 60. If the ball goes well over in any of these places, or you're adjusting for swing effort, wind, baseball quality, etc., that's how you land on the other numbers. Consistent homers to the opposite field gap is usually a 55.

Guys that Kiley has put a 70 on typically carry the center field wall by 30–40 feet, which was done by guys like Kyle Schwarber and Gary Sánchez while minor leaguers. To get 80 raw power would mean hitting it 50-ish feet or more over the wall in the middle part of the park, which describes the minor league versions of Giancarlo Stanton, Aaron Judge, Joey Gallo, and former Tigers one-dimensional slugger Steven Moya.

It's important to note that the extenuating circumstances mentioned above are key and one of them is almost always relevant for any given swing. Most times when a notable prospect hits a BP bomb, it's either a non-repeatable softball-type home run–derby swing (saved for the last round of hitting when most hitters are doing this) or they could've hit it even further. Judging raw power from BP is one of those things one gains feel for through lots and lots of reps and by occasionally running into the 70- and 80-grade types so you can see what the top of the scale looks like. Eric doesn't love the above guide (he's typically at least a half-grade stingier with raw power grades than Kiley), but Kiley notes that there's still plenty of art in even this appears-to-be-objective process. At the very least, it's good for beginners to start with this before they move to constructing their own system.

If you ask scouts for a short list of the things they're looking for in hitters, the list would include 1) athleticism/looseness, which includes an ability to rotate; 2) bat speed; 3) some feel for precision with the bat head; and 4) some sense of a plan at the plate, recognizing pitches/adjusting, and other plate-discipline-type things. This is especially true for amateur hitters, because that's the level where stats mean almost nothing due to the wild differences in pitcher quality, and scouts are purely looking for raw abilities that can be developed.

In batting practice, you'd like to see an easy swing with low effort looseness, quick hands, and some pop to all fields, with the ability to turn on a pitch and yank it out of the park, but something more varied than pull-only, home run–derby approach. Many hitters show you all of their raw power in BP and some seem to go out of their way to just hit low liners gap-to-gap. You'd like to be able to grade raw power and have some inclination as to how you might grade the hit tool after BP, but some hitters make that harder on the evaluator than others. These sorts of hitters, when they hit a monster shot in a game, often elicit, "He never showed me *that* in BP!" from scouts that are hastily erasing the pregame raw power grade.

But apart from purely visual scouting, once the whole enchilada of raw power evaluation, some of the technology used in player evaluation has forced teams to consider if there are objective measures. A player's average exit velocity and maximum exit velocity are two logical places to start. Average exit velo is affected by the quality of contact and hit tool components, so perhaps that's not as good a measure as max exit velo. If we're applying the mathematical concepts of the 20–80 scale to these measures, it looks like this:

Grade	Max Exit Velo (mph)	Average Exit Velo (mph)
80	118 (Vlad Guerrero Jr., Aaron Judge)	95 (Aaron Judge)
70	116 (Ketel Marte, Ronald Acuña)	93 (Christian Yelich, Joey Gallo)
60	113 (Tommy Pham, José Abreu)	90 (Mookie Betts, Juan Soto)
55	111 (Matt Olson, Ryan Braun)	89 (Buster Posey, Anthony Rizzo)
50	110 (Max Muncy, Lo Cain)	88 (Willy Adames, Colin Moran)
45	108 (Todd Frazier, Anthony Rendon)	86 (Austin Barnes, Juan Lagares)
40	106 (Raimel Tapia, Eduardo Escobar)	85 (Albert Almora, Omar Narvaez)
30	103 (Tony Wolters, Eric Sogard)	83 (Jarrod Dyson, Garrett Hampson)
20	100 (Billy Hamilton, Tony Kemp)	80 (Victor Robles, Roman Quinn)

Physical Projection

Obviously, we want to look at fully realized big leaguers differently than we do physically immature hitters in their teens. The cement is dry on the bodies of most athletes well into their mid-twenties, while younger guys have a better chance to add strength and muscle to their frames, growing into raw power as they do. This is why scouts watching lower level minor leaguers or amateur players need to "project" on the body and the power. Projecting means making an educated guess as to how any given attribute will evolve for a given player. A huge percentage of this has to do with anticipating physical growth. If two 19-year-old hitters have 50 raw power right now and are otherwise the same in every way, but one is a broad-shouldered, 6'2", 170 pounds and the other is a squat, 5'9", 185 pounds, you're going to prefer the kid who has more room for growth on his frame. By the time he's done filling out and growing, he might be 6'3", 200 pounds, and have plus power. He might not, but his chances are better than the kid whose body is maxed out already.

Projection applies to everything, from physical ability to refined baseball skills, especially when the player has an atypical background. Again, if two players are exactly the same in every way except one has been playing baseball for his whole life and the other has only been at it for two years, the newer player likely has more room for growth as a ballplayer; he may only be scratching the surface of his ability.

This most often applies to two-sport athletes. Kyler Murray barely played baseball between his senior year of high school and junior year at Oklahoma due to injury, his football commitment, and then his transfer from Texas A&M to Oklahoma, so some teams went justifiably nuts projecting on his skills once he were to focus solely on baseball (and we wish we were living in the timeline where he would have decided to play baseball). This also applies to two-way players (position player and pitcher), with Jacob deGrom a great example of a converted pitcher who justifies this type of projecting.

Projecting is inexact and harrowing business, impacted by what the player's parents are built like and what the scout thinks of the player's work habits. Where raw power is concerned, bigger frames typically generate more aggressive projection, though a foundation of athleticism and bat speed/an ability to rotate is necessary. A common rule of thumb some scouts use is that calves and butts stay the same size, but the rest of the body grows so those are in proportion, like a puppy's paws. You could also apply this to shoulders (the hangers of the body, ideally broader and thicker for a stronger build or more projection) and feet.

Again, raw power is how hard/how far a player can hit a ball. Game power is a measure of power production in games and it's a very difficult thing to assess and project upon because it's impacted by so many other variables. Some players have monster raw power but have severe strikeout issues that prevent them from ever getting to it in games. Others have flat swings and can't lift the ball in the air enough to hit for in-game power. Some hit a bunch of homers, but could hit more if they swung at better pitches. Player development has improved so dramatically over the last five years that, anecdotally, issues like these are more likely to be remedied now than they were for most scouts' entire careers.

And this is another one of those areas where we, and many teams, have some unanswered questions about how to proceed in this realm. Some teams have such excellent player development that their scouts and decision-makers may more confidently project on things like game power. The Dodgers, for example, have an excellent track record of tweaking swings (Justin Turner, Chris Taylor, Max Muncy, etc.) and thus probably view talented hitters with swing issues differently than teams who aren't as good at molding swing mechanics.

We struggle with the idea that, in our work, we should rank or value players more highly based on what team they play for. When Baltimore hired Mike Elias away from Houston to be their GM, he brought with him the knowledge generated by perhaps the best pitching development organization in baseball. Should we suddenly value their pitchers more highly across the board than we did before Elias was hired? If a player is traded to a team with better or worse player development, do we alter our overall evaluation in that moment even though the player has not changed? We're still uncertain how to handle that and tend to think if a team with better dev gets hold of the player, we'll alter our evaluation more quickly than usual if/when the player improves, given the Bayesian implications.

Because game power is a performance-based evaluation, we've had statistical measures for it for much longer than we have raw power. Often, this is through home run output. Dingers all come from quality of contact and power, while stats like Slugging Percentage and Isolated Power, or any other measure that includes extra-base hits, are somewhat impacted by a player's speed, which may enable them to take extra bases. Isolated Power does a better job of, uh, isolating power, so let's look at how these older performance measures look on the 20–80 scale. The few seasons leading up to this book's initial publication included a hyperinflated home run environment due to manufacturing changes to the baseball itself, so we're using multiple years of statistics to derive the scale you're about to see. We just don't know how this might change in the near future if MLB decides some action needs to be taken to change the run-scoring environment.

Grade	HR per 650 PA	ISO	SLG Percent
80	43 (Gallo, Stanton)	.300 (Gallo, Trout)	.580 (Trout, J.D. Martinez)
70	35 (Sanó, Arenado)	.260 (Story, Encarnacion)	.523 (Bregman, Goldschmidt)
60	27 (Correa, Braun)	.217 (Betts, Springer)	.475 (Gurriel, Soler)
55	23 (Votto, Rendon)	.195 (Pham, Castellanos)	.460 (Ozuna, Puig)
50	19.5 (Hosmer, Altuve)	.174 (Brantley, Semien)	.433 (LeMahieu, Kendrick)
45	16 (Posey, Swanson)	.150 (Freese, Merrifield)	.410 (Pedroia, Span)
40	11 (Wong, Segura)	.129 (Heyward, Cain)	.380 (Maybin, Cervelli)
30	5 (Aoki, DeShields)	.095 (Sogard, Iglesias)	.345 (J. Dyson, A. Escobar)
20	3 (Gordon, Revere)	.070 (Jay, Hamilton)	Under .330 (Hamilton)

As with raw power, TrackMan proliferation brings with it the ability to measure things that we couldn't before, and some of those could be used to 20–80 scale game power. Average exit velocity is once again a candidate, but hitters need to lift the ball to hit for power too. It's useful to measure average launch angle for hitters to see if they're lifting the ball, but that ignores how hard they're hitting the ball. The Statcast metric "Barrels" attempts to measure a combination of both exit velocity and power-relevant launch angle, with the angle necessary to classify a ball as a Barrel changing depending on how hard the ball is hit.

We also have public access to big league data showing a percentage of balls hit above 95 mph, frequently referred to as "Hard Hit Rate." Teams have proprietary metrics generated from TrackMan data collected and shared, but these public-facing measures are a good starting place for the scale. We don't advocate for simply mapping similar minor league metrics to tool grades, but this is what big league versions of this stuff looks like, and knowing that helps scouts parse through what they're seeing at the field, as another layer of checks-and-balances.

Grade	Hard Hit Percent	Barrel Rate
80	60% (Aaron Judge)	20+% (Miguel Sanó, Joey Gallo)
70	52% (Nellie Cruz, Joey Gallo)	16% (Pete Alonso, Bryce Harper)
60	45% (Trout, Brandon Lowe)	11.7% (Bo Bichette, Austin Meadows)
55	40% (Eugenio Suárez, Matt Thaiss)	9.7% (Rhys Hoskins, Nick Castellanos)
50	36% (Gleyber Torres, Marcus Semien)	7.5% (José Altuve, Francisco Lindor)
45	32% (Willians Astudillo, Adam Eaton)	5.2% (Michael Brantley, Alex Verdugo)
40	28% (J.P. Crawford, Wilmer Flores)	3.3% (Albert Almora, Omar Narvaez)
30	20% (Luis Arraez, Nicky Lopez)	1% (David Fletcher, José Peraza)
20	13% (Billy Hamilton, Jon Jay)	0% (Billy Hamilton, Wilmer Difo)

Even the most miserly stat people we've spoken to agree these scales are all mostly agreeable for informing what we're trying to do, and it's comforting that most players who show up at or near the top of any one measure are also near the top for all the others and pass the common-sense eyeball test nearly all the time.

Of course, there's not a comprehensive public source of minor league and amateur TrackMan data (beyond the little bit we source and publish at FanGraphs) for us to compare to these metrics and, as we said, the players we're interested in evaluating are subject to physical changes, which means we'd be projecting on this data even if we had comprehensive access to it. Much of amateur baseball doesn't get played in front of a TrackMan unit, and aside from the colleges that have units (there are about 60), an insufficient sample of data is generated to draw confident conclusions about measurable aspects of talent.

And so visual evaluation remains a very important part of gauging and projecting game power in amateur baseball and at the lowest levels of the minor leagues. These visual evaluations are more important the further we get from the big leagues, thus the more physical projection and various adjustments can't be quantified as well by data.

Scouts are looking for lift in the swing path and a consistent and seemingly intentional ability to make impact with the bottom of the baseball. Extension through contact (think Ken Griffey Jr.'s swing) is a popular way of assessing a hitter's ability to rotate fast and generate a bunch of power, and seeing the end of the bat's path can help one interpolate its life in the hitting zone, but physics-based studies conducted by renowned baseball researcher Alan Nathan show extension through contact to be meaningless, and players with abbreviated finishes (think Chase Utley's swing) can hit for power too. We'll talk more about mechanical components while/after we discuss...

The Enigmatic Hit Tool

The two of us have about a quarter century, combined, working in baseball, and, as is likely the case for you if you're holding this book, our period of watching the game with a level of attentiveness such that baseball goes beyond entertainment spans longer than that. And evaluating hitters still gives us absolute fits. The hit tool is generally defined as "how much contact the hitter makes," but there are some problems with either this definition or the way the hit tool is measured, and despite the deep dive you're about to undertake, we're probably still only scratching the surface of hitting. What follows includes the framework of a rubric that we (and, to a degree, scouts) use to grade hitting ability, and all the many components of it, on a sliding scale. It's all about long track records, sample sizes, raw tools, and proving (via performance against good pitching) how much a hitter is getting out of his raw tools.

Traditionally, big league hit tools have been assessed with batting averages, but most readers will have instantaneous issues with this. Batting average is impacted by all kinds of things that have nothing to do with the hitter's ability to put the bat on the ball, including sheer randomness. Faster hitters are more likely to run higher BABIPs and therefore higher averages, and pure bat-to-ball abilities can be undermined by an undisciplined approach at the plate, which can tank someone's average even if they're a talented hitter, and we don't want to lose those guys in the shuffle. Also plate discipline isn't a physical tool that's graded 20–80, so we can't even traditionally grade it separately to point this out.

We can also think about the hit tool as, "How tough is this player to strike out?" But, once again, strikeout rates are impacted by the hitter's selectivity. They're all relevant, if flawed.

Grade	Batting Average	Strikeout Percent	Swinging Strike Percent
80	.335 (Luis Arraez)	6% (Willians Astudillo)	2% (Luis Arraez)
70	.307 (Betts, Trout)	11% (Yuli Gurriel, Jean Segura)	4.5% (Joe Mauer)
60	.279 (Ozzie Albies)	17% (Kolten Wong, Martin Prado)	7.6% (Albert Pujols)
55	.265 (Denard Span)	20% (Juan Soto, Josh Bell)	9.1% (Howie Kendrick)
50	.251 (Paul DeJong)	23% (Kris Bryant, Bo Bichette)	10.7% (Freddy Galvis)
45	.237 (Randall Grichuk)	26% (Bryce Harper, Jorge Soler)	12.3% (Mallex Smith)
40	.223 (Lucas Duda)	29% (Fernando Tatís, Isan Díaz)	13.8% (Steven Souza)
30	.195 (Ryan Schimpf)	35% (Derek Fisher, Wil Myers)	16.9% (Franmil Reyes)
20	.168 (Lewis Brinson)	40% (Chris Davis, Keon Broxton)	20% (Jorge Alfaro)

Strikeout rate also ignores the quality of the contact a player makes, it only cares about how often the player makes contact. José Iglesias has routinely had one of baseball's lower strikeout rates during his excellent career as one of the world's best shortstop defenders, but he makes such low-impact contact that he can't be considered a good hitter, even if he's making a lot of it. At the big league level, everyone's tool grades are just informed by what their performance is (regressed where it's logical to do so), and despite lots of noise created by other physical abilities, batting average is still the most popular measure scouts bear in mind when assessing the hit tool.

Since there's no obvious, entirely sound substitute, we again try to go to the field with *components* of the hit tool in mind, rather than just try to no-scope the hit tool in its entirety. We split hit into three components.

Plate Discipline

This is the easiest one to understand at this point. Most fans understand that you need to have an idea at the plate, be able to recognize balls and strikes as well as different types of pitches. What hitters swing at and when informs this aspect of scouting. For amateur players, you typically have to learn about this stuff when a hitter faces a guy throwing around 90 mph, which explains why it's sometimes hard to suss out this skill before guys get to pro ball, when the pitching gets better and we start to have a larger statistical sample to aid in analysis.

Does the hitter chase fastballs above the zone or breaking balls far off the plate? Does he offer at the first pitch of an at-bat even though the pitcher has been wild for the preceding couple of hitters? Does his body language indicate his takes have been easy and comfortable, or have there been a lot of half swings at pitches that other hitters would yawn at as they hummed past?

This type of mental skill is hard to scout. You need to see a lot of the player in various situations to get a good feel for his approach and plate discipline as a scout, and over the typical week-long look one has at a player, you're not always presented with the entire picture. This is an area where statistical analysis—especially more granular analysis on minor leaguers than the public has access to—is extremely helpful, more so than for the other hitting components we've talked about so far.

Sometimes scouts will talk about how "the game was too fast" for a hitter. This is the sort of thing you notice when you have a big library of hitters in your mind to consult and compare to what you're seeing. That phrase is a catchall for "the hitter looks uncomfortable," "he seems to be guessing on pitches," "the pitcher is dictating the at-bat to him," etc. The real-world effect of this is that he'll likely struggle at the next level without further adjustment. Some hitters look uncomfortable at each new level and then, like clockwork, figure it out after a month or two as they continue their march to the big leagues. Every hitter is a snowflake once you recognize all the different categories.

Most scouts stick behind the plate the whole game at pro games to focus on the pitchers, while some scouts, particularly on special assignment to see a few players rather than a whole team, will go down the side to see the open side for some at-bats. In most cases, after four or five games there's not much marginal benefit from seeing another game or two and a scout would be better off getting those couple extra games four to six weeks later, rather than tacking on more at-bats at the same time. Getting early and late looks on a player in the same season is much more valuable than knowing intimately what he's like at just one point, as the hit tool is all about history and track record, not a snapshot.

In the amateur world where scouts are often just focusing on a couple players and hitters can have raw mechanics due to the lower level of pitching/coaching talent, it's not unusual for scouts to spend the whole game down the side. In pro ball, and specifically at Double-A and Triple-A, it's almost impossible to hit over .250 with mechanical problems unless you have huge bat speed or raw power to make up for it. At those levels, evaluators are much more experienced and can pick out the more subtle swing flaws quickly from behind home plate, which most scouts agree is a harder place to assess hitting mechanics.

Sometimes pro scouts will chat with players on other teams to size up their hitting sentience, communication skills, and general demeanor. It's tough to do this without plausibly being accused of tampering, or in a way in which your intentions aren't obvious, so some clubs like to comb the internet for quotes from the players whose hitting approaches they're interested in learning about. One writer who churns out lots of interviews with players that drills down into this stuff is FanGraphs' own David Laurila, and this quote from an old interview with All-Star 1B Adrian Gonzalez is particularly good:

DL: What do you see when the ball comes out of the pitcher's hand?
AG: I see rotation. I can pick up on what the pitch is as soon as the pitcher lets go of it. Most of what you see is innate. If you ask some of the great hitters, they won't all say the same thing. Some just see balls. Some guys see speed out of the hand. I can't recognize speed, but I can recognize rotation. Some guys can recognize speed but not rotation and some guys just see a ball and swing. They just let their abilities take over and that's not something you can teach.

It may seem too subjective for that sort of thing to be an integral part of an evaluation, but it's amazing to me how often a quick observation like that will be backed up by a hitting coach, the stat line, later at-bats, and often the player himself telling you he was out of sorts. This is very common at the amateur and low-professional levels with hitters that look good in a uniform but haven't produced. Often, if a scout gets that impression about a player in multiple games at different points in the season, particularly a player that's been in pro ball for years, it's an indicator of a real problem.

Great hitters don't all see the same thing, don't all see the ball in the same way, and they don't all describe the hitting process the same way. Great hitters come in different packages and some, like Gonzalez and Joey Votto, like talking about it and describe it pretty well, while others can't really put their finger on why they're great. Some of it is elite vision (which most big leaguers have, so that's really more of a prerequisite) but it's mostly an innate ability to process a specific type of information quickly and efficiently, with some hard work mixed in as well. There isn't a perfect way to identify it (there's physical ability to consider as well) and it doesn't seem like you can learn it, generally speaking, you can only unlock what you already have.

What we're saying is we don't really understand it at all. *Mysterious!* (Smoke bomb explodes, authors disappear.)

Some useful stats that we have access to for big leaguers and that teams have access to for minor leaguers are Walk Rate (BB percent), and various stats indicating how often a hitter swings at a pitch in or out of the strike zone. Low O-Swing percent (out-of-zone swing rate) is an indication that the hitter lays off stuff that's not a strike. Conversely, a higher Z-Swing percent (in-zone swing rate) indicates a hitter attacks strikes. Each player's swing results in stronger contact at different parts of the zone, and smart teams have used a combination of pitch location and batted ball data to identify where an individual hitter "does damage," and many of them have proprietary metrics that show how good a hitter is at not only attacking strikes, but attacking strikes he can crush.

Some hitters, like 2019 White Sox first rounder Andrew Vaughn, are so obviously good at attacking pitches in this way that scouts can indeed see it, but it's one of the more difficult attributes to assess.

Grade	Walk Percent	Zone Swing Percent	Out-of-Zone Swing Percent
80	16.4% (Cavan Biggio)	83% (Freddie Freeman)	15% (Biggio)
70	13.7% (Yasmani Grandal)	78% (Eddie Rosario)	20% (Joey Votto)
60	11% (Giancarlo Stanton)	73% (Miguel Andujar)	25.5% (Justin Turner)
55	9.6% (Marcus Semien)	70% (Eric Hosmer)	27.9% (Manuel Margot)
50	8.3% (Gleyber Torres)	68% (Cody Bellinger)	30.7% (Nelson Cruz)
45	7% (Dom Smith)	65% (Yoán Moncada)	33.5% (Miguel Cabrera)
40	5.6% (Kurt Suzuki)	63% (Elvis Andrus)	36.3% (Scott Kingery)
30	3% (Tim Anderson)	58% (Matt Carpenter)	41.9% (Brandon Phillips)
20	<3% (W. Astudillo)	53% (Dan Vogelbach)	46% (Francisco Mejia)

How much plate discipline can be taught? Tools for educating players and helping them manifest mental adjustment on the field are improving, but many of the scouts we've talked to think a lot of pitch recognition and plate discipline are inherent skills you can't teach. Some of them think it can be learned, be it genetic or *learned* through years of reps with travel/high school teams, but not *taught*. Kiley once did a study for one of the clubs he worked for and the basic takeaway was that, among above-average regulars in the big leagues, less than 10 percent of them materially improved or regressed their plate discipline numbers once they got into pro ball. A growing number of team personnel we've spoken with disagree with this traditional wisdom, but they won't say why, for obvious reasons.

Kiley also has a theory that plate discipline is like concrete and it dries after a couple years of high-level experience. Carl Crawford (three-sport prep athlete with limited baseball reps) improved in the minors, whereas showcase-circuit-stalwarts Delmon Young and Josh Vitters didn't. It's hard to prove this is true, but there's likely some truth to it.

Bat Control

The idea behind bat control (also sometimes roped in with "plate coverage," or called "feel for the bat head" or "barrel accuracy" among other phrases) is the hitter's ability to change their swing to match the pitch that's being thrown, a mid-ball-flight, baseball-specific, fine-motor-skilled athletic adjustment. Can the hitter drop the bat head and square up a pitch at the bottom of the zone in one at-bat, and then whack a pitch at the top of the strike zone the next? Was their timing clearly disrupted by an off-speed pitch, yet they managed to foul it off to prolong their at-bat? Then they probably have good bat control. Ichiro and Vladimir Guerrero Sr. are examples of 80-grade bat control and they're a pain in the ass to get out. As with most of the positive traits we've covered, better athletes typically have better bat control.

This is a good time to mention that we also make delineations between baseball athleticism and football athleticism. Football athleticism is size, speed, and strength, as measured through combine-type measurements, without any regard for even the finer skills needed for football, like flexible hips, etc. Baseball athleticism is quick twitch and forearm-to-fingertip strength, without the need for bench-press strength, 40-yard dash long speed, or hulking mass. You'd like to have both (Yoán Moncada is a clear version that has both types), but there are plenty of Hall of Fame–type baseball players that would never be allowed in the NFL Combine. We call bat control a "mid-ball-flight, baseball-specific, fine-motor-skilled athletic adjustment" because the football athleticism type may look great in a uniform and have a better chance to do this than the general public, but all of the baseball athleticism types can do this.

The antithesis of bat control is a "grooved" or stiff swing. Grooved swings just slice through the same path, over and over again. Lots of minor league sluggers, even plenty with good numbers, have grooved swings that work up until they start facing pitchers who are better at executing pitch locations. Sometimes these kinds of hitters are referred to as "mistake hitters" or described as "sit and spin" because they wait for a fastball, then swing as hard as they can, without another move in their toolbelt.

Every good hitter crushes mistakes, but the Platonic ideal of a grooved swing guy *only* hits mistakes. A grooved swing can often be picked out quickly in batting practice, particularly when your batting practice mental library has reached a critical mass (usually after a year or so of daily games). This type of hitter is stiff, almost always strong and the swing almost always has some steepness to it, since they'd like to lift the ball when they do make hard contact, but it also looks exactly the same every time. Having the bat in the zone a long time gives you a chance to hit balls that you don't time perfectly. A grooved, stiff swing means you have to time the ball perfectly and have it come right into your wheelhouse (the limited areas you can make hard contact). Bat control comes from fluidity of movement and this guy doesn't have it.

If we want a simple, standalone bat-control metric, our best bet is probably In-Zone contact rate, or Z-Contact, which is the percentage of pitches in the strike zone that the hitter impacts, per swing.

Grade	Z-Contact Percent
80	97% (Willians Astudillo, Michael Brantley)
70	93% (Mookie Betts, Andrelton Simmons, José Iglesias)
60	89% (Oscar Mercado, Cesar Hernández, Charlie Blackmon)
55	87% (Joey Votto, Vlad Jr., Marcus Semien, Bryan Reynolds)
50	85% (Nick Castellanos, Amed Rosario, Dexter Fowler)
45	83% (Wil Myers, Kris Bryant, Pete Alonso)
40	81% (Fernando Tatís Jr., Jorge Soler, Giancarlo Stanton)
30	77% (Khris Davis, Luke Voit, Keston Hiura)
20	73% (Joey Gallo, Keon Broxton, B.J. Upton)

Swing Efficacy

This category includes bat speed, raw strength, and the basic structure and foundation of the swing. Maybe you'd say strength and bat speed are more a part of the power tool, but it's an indelible part of hitting. The swing path (steep, level, uppercut, etc.), the type of hitter (power/contact, flyball/line drive), the load (pre-swing hand movement), and the lower half (stride length, direction) dictate how well the physical-talent attributes (bat speed and strength) generate results.

Let's start from the ground up and talk about how some different "looks" to these parts impact swing efficacy. It's important to be open-minded about an individual's swing mechanics. There are no universal goods nor bads and plenty of hitters with ugly, horrendous swings (Hunter Pence) end up having better careers than guys with immaculate cuts (Josh Vitters). There's still a lot about hitting that we don't know, because it's so complex and involves cognitive processes. We don't profess what you're about to read is gospel, but it's what we've found works for us.

A hitter's footwork can impact their timing, their general explosiveness, and even their vertical plate coverage. You might hear broadcasters talk about hitters "getting their foot down early" so they're not late on good velocity. It's true that lots of hitters have enough strength in their hands to do damage with a relatively conservative stride that includes planting that front foot early, but others benefit from big leg kicks and long strides back toward the pitcher, as it's a significant component of the coiled kinetic energy the hitter aims to unleash on the baseball.

Josh Donaldson and José Bautista added big legs kicks and broke out. Generally, the bigger-leg-kick and longer-stride hitters are the ones who take big hacks geared to hit for power. But, as is generally the case for all the parts of hitting, the more noise in the swing, the harder it is to time and maintain. Being an above-average athlete is essential to make an acceptable amount of contact with a swing like that.

Longer-striding hitters often exhibit some combination of a front-knee bend and/or backside collapse. Flex in the lower half helps hitters adjust their vertical plate coverage without drastically altering the way their hands work, swing to swing. A pitch near the top of the zone may require almost no bend in the legs to impact, while a pitch at the bottom or below it may require a lot to square up (think of Adrián Beltré famously homering on a swing he took from one knee, perhaps the most extreme example of this). A backside collapse means some part(s) of the rear leg dip(s) in a significant way, creating loft and uppercut in the swing.

Lots of the current Dodgers hitters have similar swings that include overt examples of this particular thing, many of which have been altered to include this type of lower-half usage. Chris Taylor, Max Muncy, and Will Smith all once lacked in-game power sufficient enough for them to be impact regulars, but had their swings tweaked by the Dodgers and got better. Corey Seager's swing also often includes this type of lower-half usage, and Joc Pederson and Cody Bellinger's have had it in the past, but it eventually toned down to cut down on whiffs. The better the athlete, the better-suited they are for this type of cut, since it's the mechanical equivalent of wielding a bazooka.

The way the hips work as the hitter swings, and their posture throughout, are also notable. A hitter's hips need to rotate as part of overall body rotation, which is very important, and they need to fire before the hands do. Sometimes they'll rotate more than others. It's hard to rotate them on pitches away from the hitter while, on inside pitches, it's almost necessary to rotate and clear them just to get the fat part of the bat on the ball.

Swing-to-swing variation, when appropriate, is a good sign, because it means the hitter can adjust their body to impact a pitch and it means they're making that adjustment as the pitch is in flight. Beware of the "bucket strider" whose front foot drifts toward their pull side, causing the hitter's hips to open up too much at times, impacting their plate coverage. These hitters get eaten alive by breaking stuff away from them and have pull-heavy ball-in-play profiles, they're typically shiftable. Conversely, there are players who "dive" and end up very bent at the waist, with swings geared for hitting balls away from them. They can be vulnerable to being tied up by pitches inside, though some, like José Altuve, have such deft hitting hands that they can get the bat to inside pitches anyway. Longer-lever hitters (typically any hitter over 6'3") are especially vulnerable to this. Some advanced big league hitters have markedly different swings for inside and outside pitches, since one swing can't impact both kinds of pitches (as measured by exit velocity) in the ideal way for power output.

And so we move further up the body and arrive at the hands. This is the area where we think talent most drives effectiveness. The best hitters all have a sort of unteachable explosion and life in their hands (some scouts call it "handsy looseness," which maps well to bat control) that help generate much of their quality of contact. That's not to say coaches and player dev personnel can't affect change; they can. And watching players with that in mind is important, but things like bat speed are generally regarded as unteachable.

Scouts aren't great at evaluating bat speed on a granular level and lining guys up in the exact order, from fastest bat to slowest (we know of a team who pitted their scouts' eyes for bat speed against objective measures, and they didn't do very well) but they are pretty good at determining it at a binary level—who has good bat speed and who does not. Some unsurprising examples of elite, 80-grade bat speed would be Javier Báez, Clint Frazier, Mike Trout, Gary Sheffield, and Ronald Acuña.

All of these hitters either have or had some version of a bat waggle (Sheffield has the biggest, most notable one of all time), which is often used by players with big bat speed as a way to time their swing, because their bats can be too fast to the zone early in their careers. The waggle creates a longer swing path (Báez's worst minor league performances came when, at pitch release, the top of the bat pointed at the pitcher, elbow pointing to the sky) so the time from the decision to swing to contact takes the same amount of time for a hitter with normal bat speed and hitting mechanics.

How the hands work is often as important as how fast they are, and hand paths vary a lot, hitter to hitter. Hitters need to "load" their hands, drawing them back toward the umpire and catcher like the string of a bow. This load typically occurs as the hitter's front foot strides forward toward the pitcher, and this combo is often called "hip and hand separation" or just "separation." The height and depth at which the hands load is important. The depth, or how far back they go, influences how short or long a hitter is back to the baseball. The deeper the load, the longer it takes for the bat to enter the hitting zone. The deeper load is what traditionally leads to a swing being called "long" or "loopy," or the swing has "a hitch," or a "hole inside," since a deep load can lead to being late, which would most impact results on inside pitches.

But longer swings typically enable more scoop and lift, while shallower loads enable the hitter to get back to the ball quickly, but often result in the hitter chopping down at the ball without much power. If a hitter loads their hands so deep that their front arm lacks bend at the elbow, this is called an "arm bar," and scouts dislike the stiffness and lack of bat control this causes, though like everything we're talking about here, there are examples of hitters who are so talented that little mechanical blemishes simply don't matter. It takes longer for scouts to get on board with a hitter that does it an unusual way, but scouts will change their tune quickly if the tools are there. Scouts will get on board much less quickly if the tools aren't there and it looks unlike other successful big leaguers.

Load height is also important. Hitters who load high (Dilson Herrera is an example of a "lift load" that goes primarily up, rather than primarily back) are typically a little shorter back to the ball but, again, end up chopping downward. Low load types have big natural loft in their swings, but they often struggle to catch velocity at the top of the zone and swing underneath it. Hitters who load their hands higher, up around their shoulder, are arguably in a better position to deal with the increased rate of high fastballs thrown by pitchers in recent years, but will often struggle to lift them, with Nick Markakis as an example.

The best big league hitters tend to be relatively level bat path guys (leaving the bat in the zone a long time for a better chance at contact with more pitches) who are so physically gifted that they can muscle a ball out of the park, or their feel for impacting the bottom of the baseball is so good that they lift it without much uppercut in their bat path. This is what you have in guys like Albert Pujols and Miguel Cabrera. There's also some like Mark McGwire that have some steepness to their path to create loft but have such compact/efficient mechanics and superior bat speed that they also hit for average and power.

Having big raw strength (baseball-specific, so mostly in forearms, not biceps) allows for big power from a short load, which is what many elite hitters have (the "strong" type, like Cabrera or McGwire). Others have huge bat speed (the "loose" elite hitter) that allows them to wait longer to decide on a pitch and their power derives more from the longer bat path (long on-ramp to accelerate the bat) that their elite bat speed allows for, like Ronald Acuña.

There's also an increasing amount of a specific kind of outlier that the traditional scouting of hit and power tools evaluate incorrectly. The best current example is White Sox C/1B Zack Collins. Some club-side analytics types grade his plate discipline as an 80 (more on how to do this in the data chapters, but essentially it grades swing/take decisions) and his raw and game power as 70, but his hit tool and bat control are well below average, maybe both a 30. Because of Collins' excellent plate discipline, he only swings at good, driveable pitches and because of his power and lofted path, he hits a lot of homers. The walks also drive his OBP higher than his raw hit grade would suggest, but the lack of bat control makes his power tool have trouble showing up against MLB pitchers with plus command that pitch to the corners. There's clearly a lot of extreme things going on here, with the traditional grading system basically ignoring them.

At the end of the 2019 season, when Collins reached the majors, the Steamer projection system had Collins' current true talent level as a .212 batting average (a 20 on the traditional, batting average-only hit tool scale) and a .322 on-base percentage (the implied OBP of a 50 hit tool) with above-average power metrics. With more lofted swing planes and true-three-outcomes (strikeout, walk, homer) hitters looking to do damage by maximizing exit velocity, this sort of hitter is becoming more popular, but ultimately isn't an everyday player unless they have elite speed and defensive ability. José Cruz Jr. is a less extreme type of this player, from an earlier era, playing from 1997 to 2008.

Another example of why assessing swing efficacy is important is the career of Yandy Díaz. Díaz had amazing peripheral stats coming up through the minors and his initial big league foray showed that he was also generating premium exit velocities, but visual evaluations of his swing made it clear this guy, despite other skills, struggled to hit the ball in the air. Barring a significant swing change, he was unlikely to ever hit for much power. Díaz got bulkier and lost some of the athleticism necessary to make such a change, so the cement on the swing is probably dry. He has everyday player physical ability but, because the swing doesn't work great, he's a limited, part-time player.

Five-Tool Players

You've probably heard this term thrown around a lot, which is problematic because there really aren't many five-tool players. Five-tool guys are average or better at all of the five tools we've just detailed, and some folks in baseball think it should only apply when all the tools are above-average or better. The list of players throughout baseball for whom this applies is shockingly, infinitesimally small. Mike Trout doesn't even qualify because he has a mediocre arm. Even some of the toolsiest guys of all time (Bo Jackson was an 80 run, 80 raw power, 80 defense, 80 arm player with a below-average hit tool; Ichiro was 80 everything but power) aren't five-tool types, which should tell you that, while fun to think about, the designation is arbitrary and, ultimately, meaningless.

The ones who are true five-tool guys are athletic marvels and typically among the better players in the game, unless they have horrendous plate discipline (which isn't a tool), and it makes for great bar conversation. Here is a non-complete list of who we consider to be five-tool players: Ketel Marte, Mookie Betts, Francisco Lindor, J.T. Realmuto, Christian Yelich, Cody Bellinger, Ronald Acuña, and Javier Báez.

Projecting, and Some FanGraphs Prospect Methodology

Bodies play baseball and they are constantly changing. The age of the players you're scouting and the way they're built should influence how you think they're going to develop over time. If two teenage players are exactly the same in every way, but one is wiry and skinny while the other is bulky and physically mature, the way those two players will grow and change as they enter their twenties is probably very different. Putting a present grade on the tools, then projecting on them based on the body, athleticism, makeup, etc., is necessary, especially when scouting amateur players.

Earlier, we mentioned the theory that guys who enter pro ball with very little baseball experience—often two-sport athletes like Carl Crawford or players who come from cold-weather locations where they play less baseball, like Mike Trout—have fewer habits and are easier to mold as ballplayers. Conversely, guys who are playing a ton of baseball and become known to scouts and other people in baseball as early as age 14 or 15, such as Delmon Young or Josh Vitters, might have more concrete skills, for better or worse, when they sign.

Latino players are perhaps the best evidence in support of this notion because they often don't see much game action until after they've signed, but they're most often the ones who show dramatic, rapid improvement and race to big league stardom at younger ages than the industry expects. Nationals outfielder Juan Soto played fewer minor league games than every other teenager to debut since Alex Rodriguez and, while his game has some holes on defense, he became an offensive force with relatively little in-game experience.

There are plenty of counter-examples to the Crawford/Young/Vitters observation above. Royals OF Bubba Starling was a toolsy, two-sport athlete in high school and a high draft pick who never really panned out. Jeff Francoeur was a relatively raw, multi-sport prospect like Crawford, but never developed a shred of plate discipline. For every Trout there are several Anthony Hewitt types in the Northeast, who beat up on bad high school pitching in their geographic area and have no chance of hitting pro-quality pitching.

Putting a present grade on a hit tool for a teenage player is hard, so hard that we think it's foolish to bother really trying. No amateur scout sees enough big league baseball nor enough of a high school player against good pitching to have any idea how that player would hit if he were dropped in a big league lineup today. Our way of dealing with this issue has been to standardize hit tool grades based on a combination of age and polish. Raw or neutral teenage hitters all have a 20 present hit tool grade on our website. Advanced teenagers have a 25. For college-aged hitters (they don't have to be in college, it could be a 20-year-old pro hitter) it's 30 or 35, respectively. Once a player reaches Double-A, that's when we start to consider how he actually might perform in the big leagues. This isn't perfect, and we haven't come up with ways to use similar logic for other tool grades, but we think this communicates something where there used to be nothing.

In a July 24, 2019, chat with FanGraphs readers, Kiley was asked why Luis Robert wasn't in the top tier of prospects and took the opportunity to break down some of our behind-the-scenes thinking with the lists, illuminating ways in which we could be more precise (slightly edited for clarity):

Josh Nelson: What do you need to see from Luis Robert to give him a FV 60+?

Kiley McDaniel: This goes back to a conversation I have with fantasy baseball dynasty friends that ask me which hitting prospects to pick up when they're promoted. I tell them generally to take the lower K rate ones because their game translates to the big leagues easier (better performance from day 1) and they'll reach their upside faster, even if it's lower.

Then, a friend didn't want to bug me and assumed using K% as a guide that Lewis Brinson (18 percent in AAA in 2017) was a better bet than Cody Bellinger (20 percent in AA in 2016, 27 percent the year before that). In retrospect that seems silly, but you can see there are limits to this approach.

I had to explain that Brinson was a swing-and-miss type with crazy tools that had a lower K rate because his tools didn't allow him to be tested until MLB, so his AAA K rate makes him seem lower risk than he is. And Bellinger is power-focused, does it well and is an athlete with bat control (important distinction), so his approach was a conscious tradeoff and was mature in that it would work in AA similarly to how it would work in MLB. This is not obvious even from reading our reports closely, though you may pick up that sort of nuance if you're a long-time reader.

I bring all this up to say that while I'm not saying Luis Robert is Lewis Brinson, his issue is similar in that he's so toolsy he can't be challenged in AAA. We've heard from analysts and scouts that his pitch selection is still an issue (particularly off-speed) and he'll need to figure that out in the big leagues, which could be painful and slow (Brinson) or go quickly because his tools are also elite in MLB and that it won't challenge him for more than a couple months (Ronald Acuña).

Another recent White Sox super prospect, Yoán Moncada, had an issue somewhere between Bellinger and Brinson, in that he was a little stiff and didn't have elite bat control, but had a good approach, so he just needed to dial in his approach to do maximum damage when the right pitch was there and realize he probably wouldn't be a career .300 hitter. It took Moncada about 900 PA to make an improvement (he's been pretty BABIP lucky this year, so the improvement is a little overstated) but we've said before that we'd much rather have a Moncada-type because the pitch selection and power means you'll always get to the power in games since you can pick pitches to drive, you just may hit .250 or whatever (but w/ solid OBP).

The other type of player, Brinson/Robert, will have trouble getting to the power in games against elite pitching due to poorer pitch selection, also not walk much, so at least until an adjustment is made (if it is made), it's empty batting average driven by bat control and people waiting for the breakout.

Explaining this in detail a few times makes me think we should grade plate discipline and bat control when elite hitting prospects are in the upper minors to help classify which sort of hitter each guy is.

So, the much shorter version is that Robert probably won't be a 60 FV for us because to prove that he's clear of the Lewis Brinson trap will probably take most of an MLB season to prove, given that we don't think he'll change in Triple-A (thus he will have graduated the prospect list when/if he proves it).

We started grading pitch selection, bat control, and athleticism on the 20–80 scale for the next winter's prospect lists. None are "tools" in the traditional sense, but grading those skills and doing it on a consistent scale helps communicate this without needing a long chat answer for each instance. And plenty of teams have/still do grade non-tool qualities, like a delivery, on the 20–80 scale.

Closing Thoughts

Why did we start thinking about hitting in this way?

From being wrong a lot.

We have public opinions about thousands of players and many of them either supersede or fall short of our very specific expectations, and upon reflection we've been able to identify why. Yoán Moncada is a good player, but he has below-average bat control and less arm utility than is needed at the middle infield positions, and so he has ended up with a less spectacular offensive profile than we hoped, and also began to play third base. (Eric would like to see him in center field, where the offensive bar is lower.) Again, he's a very good player and considering his physical talent and presence, we think amateur scouts were right to be gaga for him when he first left Cuba, but better understanding his shortcomings would have helped us place him more accurately on the minor league continuum (somewhere in the top 15–30 minor leaguers before he debuted) than we did. (Eric and others ranked him as the best prospect in baseball before he graduated.)

Reflection and refinement of process is key to improvement. Open-mindedness about the way you and your team go about evaluating players will make changing much less painful and improve how you line up players and assess their abilities. Stubbornness will get you fired.

CHAPTER 9

How to Scout Pitchers

Things get a little easier now. It's often the case that people who pursue scouting get a feel for evaluating pitching before hitting, probably because they're seeing pitch after pitch in succession for several innings at a shot, while you can go several games without seeing all of an individual player's hitting and fielding components on display. You're also not only making your own assessment of pitch quality, but you're being reinforced by the hitters' reactions to every pitch, their ability to deal with the pitcher's stuff.

A crosschecker once told one of us, "Watch the hitters, they'll tell you most of what you need to know about how good a pitcher's stuff is," and we agree that hitter comfort level and swing decisiveness are telling, especially when someone's stuff wouldn't otherwise impress you in a vacuum, and would seem ordinary if not for all the ugly swings. If a pitcher is throwing 93 and still absolutely blowing dudes away (in pro ball), it's probably because something else is going on, something relevant. Seeking out and identifying the other forces at play are part of what separates actual scouting from someone just doing glorified data entry.

While we think pitching is a little easier to scout, it's harder to predict. Who will get hurt? Who will throw harder as they enter their physical prime? Who will retain that velocity into advanced age? Whose command or secondary pitches will improve? These are slippery central questions for which we still only have vague, perhaps apocryphal answers that apply across the pitching population as a whole, partially because, now more than ever, so many of those answers are dependent on player development. If we knew with 100 percent certainty about the future of any specific player's hit tool or pitcher health, scouting would be significantly easier.

We'll get to that stuff later in the chapter, but let's again start with basic principles and applications of pitching to the 20–80 scale.

Heat

If you're reading this you probably need no hand-holding when it comes to fastball velocity. You've probably seen so many fastballs and their corresponding velocity on TV that you have a crystal-clear idea of what's hard and what's not. It's likely you can guess how scouts measure velocity at games too. Almost all of them have a radar gun fixed on the pitcher for the entire game, save for the times someone clearly isn't a prospect, or when the stadium's scoreboard radar gun has shown itself to be accurate early on in a contest.

More novel and entertaining to monitor than the velocities themselves are all the ways scouts come up with in order to avoid holding their radar guns for three hours. Peeking over their peers' shoulders, sliding the gun's handle through the bottom of a cup-holder with its nose trained toward the mound, using a hotel towel to swaddle the gun and nestle it snuggly between the backs of two seats, attaching an intricate array of steel clips (a supposed, MacGyverish, radar-gun-holding invention of former Astros and Phillies GM Ed Wade) to the seat in front of them. Holding a radar gun in one hand while writing notes with the other with only your lap to support your clipboard or hugging the gun under one armpit to do some writing after each pitch both get old really fast.

Kiley still does a move he saw a crosschecker do once in 2012, only doable when no one is sitting in front of you: cross your leg to create the outline of a table in your lap, put your notebook and pen on the leg that's touching the ground and balance the radar gun on the knee area of the folded leg, precariously propped at the perfect angle to register velos. Scouts are great at refining everything they do through trial and error, including how to travel and work in comfort.

Like we said, this part is simple. Fastball velocities are measurable, concrete. The velocity of each of a pitcher's offerings, fastballs and otherwise, will vary over the course of their outing. Sometimes fastball ranges span an octave or more during a start. We think it's important to note, specifically, if a pitcher loses gas from the stretch, or later in their outing, or in an inning after he sat in the dugout forever during a long rally. Otherwise, keeping a simple histogram of velocities suffices for this slice of scouting. Here's the current 20–80 scale for fastball velocity.

Grade	Velocity (mph)	Player
80	>99	Andres Muñoz
70	97–99	Noah Syndergaard
60	95–97	German Marquez
55	94–95	Justin Verlander
50	92–94	Shane Bieber
45	91–92	Matthew Boyd
40	89–91	Rick Porcello
30	87–89	Yusmeiro Petit
20	<87	Sergio Romo

League average fastball velocity among starters with at least 50 innings pitched in 2019 was 92.7 mph; among relievers it was 93.7 mph. We considered splitting the two, as many teams do, but the line between the roles of starters and relievers has become blurry enough that we think it now makes more sense to lump them all together. You could do the same with righties and lefties and the velo gap from relievers down to starters. Righties down to lefties descend almost 1 mph at each notch; some teams have four separate velo scales like this. Across all of baseball in 2019, the average fastball hummed in at 93.3 mph.

Those averages are way, way up above velocities from just a half decade ago, and the gap is even more significant when we reach back to 2003 (the farthest back fastball velocities go on FanGraphs).

2013 Grade	Velocity (mph)	Player
80	>98	Aroldis Chapman
70	96–97	Craig Kimbrel
60	94–95	Homer Bailey
55	92–93	Yu Darvish
50	91–92	Cole Hamels
45	90–91	Mike Leake
40	88–90	Wandy Rodriguez
30	86–88	Jered Weaver
20	<85	Mark Buehrle

2003 Grade	Velocity (mph)	Player
80	>97	Billy Wagner
70	94–96	Eric Gagne
60	92–93	Kelvim Escobar
55	91–92	Kevin Brown
50	88–90	Dontrelle Willis
45	87–88	Ted Lilly
40	85–87	Greg Maddux
30	83–84	Tom Glavine
20	<82	Jamie Moyer

A lot of scouts have been employed for this entire span of time, which means they've been asked multiple times to alter the scale they use to grade velocities—or they work for lousy teams. There's an argument that, because the scale is a communicative tool, it's better to avoid creating the possibility of miscommunication by using new nomenclature or measures. But while there may be an adjustment period for an individual scout changing teams, or a staff of them with a new boss, the same way there's a change in verbiage when a football team learns a new playbook, it's just better to be correct.

With several, quickly changing variables throughout the game (the baseball itself, knowledge and implementation of coherent pitch design, weighted ball training, swing changes, three-batter minimums, robot umps, etc.), we think constant reassessment of the scale is not only necessary, but especially important during this volcanic phase the game is experiencing.

The Other Stuff

But what about that 93 mph fastball that whizzes past guys at the letters with regularity? Surely Colin Poche, who has an 18 percent swinging strike rate (league average, for all pitches, is 11 percent) on a fastball that only averages 93, doesn't only have a 50 fastball. So what are some components that enable a fastball, or any pitch, to "play up" above its basic, superficial grade?

There are several. One is movement. Directional (horizontal and vertical) movement, covered a bit more in the data chapter, can be identified with the naked eye and, where applicable, with technology, like TrackMan. Horizontal or lateral movement (aka cut for glove-side movement and tail, wiggle, run, arm-side run, or just generally described as "movement" for arm-side) is much easier to see in the scout section behind home plate than vertical movement due to the effects on our field of view caused by the theater seating angle behind home plate. In our experience, vertical movement is less obvious to the naked eye from scout seats' vantage than lateral movement. If this is true then it's possible the industry, as a whole, was biased toward running, tailing fastballs for a long time. We had been underrating vertical movement in our fastball evaluations until it became clear that many pitchers whose fastball results were outperforming what we expected given their raw velocity, had a lot of upward vertical movement (aka ride, life, rise, lift), and because we noticed teams started targeting players with that attribute via trade.

These are indeed measurable qualities (vertical movement is often called "Z-break" by analysts, not scouts, since that's the nomenclature in a TrackMan readout), but they can be scouted with the eye, despite the limitations of scouts' physical point of view in a ballpark. If your line of sight were in the space between being level with home plate and level with the umpire, you'd probably be able to better identify vertical movement with the naked eye. But the hitters, umpire, and catcher would all be obstructing a clean look at the baseball at least some of the time, which is why scouts almost always like to be up off the ground a little bit, so they can see over the top of them.

With the naked eye, the things to watch for that would tip you off that a pitcher's fastball may have lift are a) missing bats near the top of the strike zone and seemingly locating there intentionally, b) a vertical or north/south arm slot, or c) hand position that alters spin direction without an obviously vertical arm slot. Fastballs with northward, vertical movement work best at the top of the strike zone, and you'll see a lot of Astros pitchers working up there.

The rate of spin, direction of the spin, and seam uniformity while the baseball spins, are all variables that influence how much a pitch moves, and in what direction it moves. You can't see a bunch of that stuff without a high-speed camera, or measure it without a piece of technology, but you can make some inferences about spin direction based on arm slot and hand position.

The closer to true north a pitcher's arm slot is (think Oliver Drake, Clayton Kershaw) the more likely they are to create pure backspin on their pitches as they release the ball, and that's one of the components of vertical movement. As an arm slot approaches true sidearm, pitchers tend to generate more horizontal movement, but hand position can augment this. Josh Hader, for instance, has a lower arm angle but he throws with his hand positioned in such a way that he still gets behind the baseball and creates backspin and vertical movement, rather than sidespin. You'll see a lot of Astros pitchers (Rogelio Armenteros, José Urquidy) doing this too, though not typically from an arm slot as low as Hader's. Orioles RHP Mychal Givens is notable for hand position because he throws a cutter from a nearly sidearm slot, where basically every other sidearmer throws a sinking, running fastball as their hand is oriented sideways like their arm. Givens does this by getting his fingers pointing more up than to the side.

The lower the arm slot and lower a pitcher's natural spin rate, the more likely they are to be suited for working with a two-seam fastball or sinker. Four-seamers are thrown with an orientation that enables the maximum amount of seams (four per ball revolution) to rotate uniformly into the air through which it's moving. A two-seam fastball rotates such that only two of the seams encounter the airflow; the smooth parts of the ball encounter the air. They're less "sticky" and worse at fighting gravity, so two-seamers tend to sink and get ground balls. Not everyone's fastball is suited for the four-seam, "up-in-the-zone" approach, but it's currently in vogue, and it's how most dominant fastballs miss bats right now. An approach throwing a two-seamer with sink and run down in the zone is more contact-oriented and thus draws less strikeouts as the plane of the pitch more directly matches the plane of the average swing.

This makes intuitive, visual sense when you think about it. The closer to the top of the strike zone a hitter is whipping the bat through, the more parallel to the ground the barrel of their bat. Of course, pitches with illusory north/south movement are better at missing those barrels than something moving laterally which, at the top of the strike zone, just has more bat to run into.

The opposite is true at the bottom of the strike zone. Hitters need to drop the bat head to whack pitches in the bottom of the strike zone, so their bat is more vertically oriented as it traverses the zone. Hence, you're more likely to miss bats at the bottom of the strike zone with pitches that move laterally, and conversely the middle-to-bottom of the zone is where "rising" fastballs go to die. It's where they're most vulnerable.

Keep this concept stashed in the periphery of your consciousness for a couple of pages.

You also have all sorts of other tertiary components that impact how a fastball plays. Some pitchers are naturally better at hiding the ball from hitters, keeping it back behind their bodies until it suddenly appears out from behind their head. Pitchers with lower arm slots are often especially tough on same-handed hitters because they release the ball in a place that's harder to see, back behind the hitter. Opposite-handed hitters get an extra long look at the ball from these pitchers, which is why so many sidearmers are lefty or righty specialists (facing only same-side hitters, often one or two total per appearance), depending on their handedness.

Some pitchers create tough angle on their pitches because of their stride direction. It's typical for most pitchers to stride from wherever they stand on the rubber straight toward the plate, but setting up at an extreme end of the rubber and/or striding at an odd angle can also create deception, or make it so a hitter needs to see a few pitches from that hurler before they're comfortable.

If a pitcher strides short of the imaginary line that runs perpendicular to the pitching rubber and toward the plate (often referred to as "throwing across his body," or "cutting himself off"), they're more likely to have a lower arm slot (think Freddy Peralta, Madison Bumgarner), while those who stride dead ahead often have a more traditional look to them. Some pitchers, like Ubaldo Jiménez and Chris Devenski, stride past that imaginary line and really open up their front side, and they almost always have a north/south arm slot and stuff profile.

Like all of these things, each decision comes with a cost. Throwing crossbody is an easy way to add cut to your fastball (you're forced to "follow through" more) and deception (easier to hide your arm behind your body, same-side hitters have the ball starting behind them) and often pitchers will do this to help them locate pitches to the glove-side more often. On the flip side, you're giving away extension by taking stride length and moving it sideways rather than straight, it's harder to throw a changeup and there's a long history of pitchers getting hurt when they throw crossbody, like Kerry Wood and Danny Hultzen. Our stance is this makes more sense to only start doing in Triple-A or the big leagues to enhance your stuff, deception, or command, because doing it earlier than that could make you a worse pitcher with bad habits.

Vertical approach angle of a pitch probably matters too. If two pitchers with the exact same fastball (velo, spin rate, etc.) locate it in the exact same spot, but one pitcher is a 5'10" guy with a lower slot and the other is a towering 6'7" with a higher slot, those fastballs are flying to that point at very different angles, so they will play differently. In general, from the pitcher's perspective, you want a high fastball to be as flat as possible (short pitcher, low slot, "rising" fastball, long stride down the mound is the most extreme example) and a low fastball to be as steep as possible (tall, high slot, sinker, short stride).

This concept is basically around the idea that, if you assume hitters collectively have an average swing plane, you want to be as far from an average pitch plane as you can, all else being equal. This is less important if you throw 100 mph, have plus command, a plus slider, etc., but that basic concept also applies to fastball spin and location—the middle ground is death.

Fastball spin rates, on their own, can't be 20–80'd because there are times when more spin is worse. High spin causes rise, but low spin causes sink, and plenty of heavy, grounder-inducing sink is a good thing. It's the average-spinning fastballs that rotate at about 2200 rpm that don't really do much moving, either way. Fastballs averaging 2500–2600 rpm are near the top of what's been measured so far (Corbin Burnes, Phil Maton, Gerrit Cole) while the 1800–1900 rpm realm (Justus Sheffield, Sean Manaea) is the bottom.

There's also the concept of spin efficiency, or active spin, where a 2500 rpm fastball might only have 1500 rpm of active spin and a 2000 rpm fastball might have completely efficient spin. Raw spin rates (the ones referenced online or on broadcasts) generally point in the right direction, since people usually aren't comparing two pitchers' raw spin that have 0 percent and 100 percent spin efficiency, but this can be important on the margins. A fastball with 100 percent efficient spin would be pure backspin, no sidespin, think 12 o'clock on a clockface, which means hand/finger position needs to be vertical. For a curveball, 100 percent efficiency would be pure downward spin (six o'clock on a clock face).

There are varying opinions among in-office analysts and decision-makers with data access as to whether or not their boots-on-the-ground scouts should see and use the data. Those opposed think it poisons the well of objectivity, and that scouts will draw predetermined conclusions about players based solely on the data once they've been indoctrinated, and that's something they can do at their desk without ever setting foot in a ballpark. Others think arming open-minded scouts with this knowledge will better enable them to see how and why pitchers with non-traditional stuff are succeeding as they map on-paper measurables to their visual evaluations, and that they'd be better equipped to see how their own player development staff might be able to change pitchers for the better once acquiring them.

Breaking Balls

This is not necessarily the case for breaking balls, though. Fastballs are either fighting, or working with gravity to create lift or sink. Breaking balls are almost always working with it, so more spin is going to generate more movement, all else being equal.

We're defining breaking balls as anything that has horizontal, glove-side movement (the Platonic ideal cutter), anything with directly downward movement (Platonic curveballs), and anything with some combination of the two (sliders). (By the way, we use "glove side" and "arm side" to describe movement and location because the pitcher's glove side and arm side are static descriptors. No matter your perspective on the action, no matter the pitcher's or batter's handedness, that description is applicable.)

The way breaking balls are classified depends on a combination of pitch velocity and shape of movement. Pitchers' hands and fingers are either coming around the side of the ball to create some amount of horizontal movement toward their glove side, or over the top of the ball to create downward movement. Cutters are going to be harder, approaching and sometimes overlapping with a pitcher's fastball velocity range. They have short, sharp, glove-side movement. Sliders will typically be a little slower than that, often with as much as 10–12 mph separation from someone's fastball velo, but the more important thing to note is the shape of the movement.

Sliders will have longer, more obvious, sweeping, two-plane (sink and cut) movement than cutters. They'll still have action to the pitcher's glove side, but they'll also have some amount of descent. Curveballs primarily have humpback vertical movement, arcing toward the strike zone like rainbows from hell. They're typically the slowest of the breaking pitches, though some pitchers have power curveballs in the low- to mid-80s that are faster than the sliders of soft-tossers.

Harder curveballs tend to be a variation of the typical curveball grip. The standard curveball grip yields a 12–15 mph gap from the fastball and has the index and middle fingers lined up behind a seam to make it easier to generate spin. This is the type of pitch that is the big-breaking curveball, sometimes as much as 20 mph slower than a fastball, what you probably imagine when you read the word curveball. A "spike" curveball or, more confusingly, a "knuckle" curveball means you start with the same curveball grip, pull your index finger toward your palm ("spiking" that knuckle) and by dint of the ball only rolling over one finger instead of two, it comes in more like 10–12 mph slower than a fastball, usually with less break.

Breaking ball movement can be described, from the vantage of the scouts' seats, as moving from one point on a clock face to another. A 12-to-6 curveball drops straight down, while an 11-to-5 curveball has a little bit of tilt, a 10-to-4 curve has even more, etc. Lefty breaking balls start on the opposite side of the clock. There are exceptions to this. More and more pitchers have sliders in the low-90s, pitches that would have been described as cutters not long ago. There are also some sliders that break straight down, like those of Brad Lidge, Greg Holland, and Liam Hendriks.

Exceptions are ripe for technical misidentification, which we think is fine. There's a spectrum of pitches from cutter to slider to curveball with examples at almost every stop, but the vast majority fall in three meaty clusters on the spectrum. Jonathan Papelbon tried to identify a pitch he threw as between a slider and a cutter, calling it a "slutter," to no one's surprise. So long as you're describing velocity, and movement, it's fine if you call it a cutter but the pitcher calls it a slider. Often scouts will ask a pitcher when he's charting in the stands how he holds a pitch so they can identify it in their report on the grip and action, not what he calls it, which can be "wrong."

In addition to a breaking ball's shape, you'll want to consider how much it's moving ("length" for sliders, "depth" for vertical curveballs, as if you're describing the amplitude of a sound wave) and how sharp the movement is (breaking balls that "bite" have sharp, surprising, impactful movement and can totally freeze a hitter, while others may have a lot of length or depth but be "blunt" or "loopy," and easier for hitters to track and adjust to in mid-flight).

Loopy means long break, but slow and "rolling" or moving along a predictable parabolic path. Bite, to most scouts, means breaking from that sort of path, a result of lots of active spin affecting the trajectory. A "hump" is hard to describe without a visual, but it's when a curveball looks like it goes up out of the hand before it goes down. This is bad and fits mostly with softer, loopier curveballs, essentially never with hard, biting spike curveballs. Some scouts describe the best version of a curveball—no "hump" out of the hand, sharp, downward movement and bite—as having "bend." There's a zillion ways to describe a curveball, but the key is making sure the person you're communicating with understands you.

You can probably deduce that arm slot, and the other mechanical components discussed in the fastball section, influence shape and effectiveness of breaking balls. We're about to show you the 20–80 scale for measurable breaking ball spin, but just as it is for fastballs, spin axis and seam uniformity and direction also have an impact on how good a breaking ball is, so you can't really tell how good a breaking ball is just by looking at its measurable spin. Prospects like MacKenzie Gore and Ian Anderson have low-spinning curveballs, but both deliver from straight over the top, creating an efficient, forward-tumbling spin that creates enough depth for the pitch to work even though it's not spinning very fast.

Grade	Spin Rate (rpm)	Player
80	>3000	Dustin May
70	2950	Sonny Gray
60	2700	Justin Verlander
55	2575	Aaron Nola
50	2450	Jack Flaherty
45	2325	Edwin Jackson
40	2200	J.A. Happ
30	1950	Archie Bradley
20	<1900	Amir Garrett

One old piece of scouting dogma is, "A pitcher either has a curveball or he doesn't," or some variation of this, indicating that you can't teach someone to throw a better curveball than the one they have naturally. Turns out, this is true. Driveline Baseball studies have concluded the ability to spin a baseball isn't malleable; it's a talent one either has or does not. Aside from the application of topical substances, or if the pitcher has no clue how to hold or grip the ball to begin with, it can't really be improved. There are band-aid solutions, like adding a cutter or designing pitches to try to fill holes in the arsenal, but not having a curveball or bigger-breaking slider has held back what would otherwise be long big league careers.

So how can you tell how good a breaking ball is? You just need to see a lot of them, and build a mental catalog and feel for correctly grading pitches over time. It's important to remind you that a 50 on the scouting scale is Major League average, not average for whatever level a scout is observing, and that means the average breaking ball you'll see at any level is going to be worse than the ones you see from MLB arms. This makes it difficult to truly learn what a 50 is. It's time consuming, a lot of sifting through galaxies of 88–91 mph fastballs searching for life.

The quickest path to calibration is watching a bunch of big league games from the scout seats, but that's not financially feasible for anyone. Instead, we'd encourage those with scouting aspirations to try to see pitchers at Double-A and Triple-A and supplement that with viewing big league games on TV, especially when the pitchers you've seen in person have been called up. If you've seen someone at Triple-A who gets called up to make a spot start, comparing how their stuff looks in relation to the other big leaguers in that game will help you start to triangulate pitch grades in person. Some MLB TV angles are awful (too far from center or too high), so the scouts seats are still the best angle to see a pitch like a hitter does.

But it's going to take time. Limiting your scope of thought early is fine. For instance, rather than worry about what's exactly 40 or exactly 70 on the scale, just try to assess whether something is clearly above, below, or clustered around the average. Precision will come with time. Ideally, having a scout tell you "that one was a 50," right after a pitch is thrown is the easiest way to get this. We've both spent years thinking about the same curveball a scout once told us was a 50. Kiley still remembers the Sean Gallagher curveball in High-A in 2006 that he used as a rubric for years once a scout told him it was a 55.

Changeups and Splits

There are many ways to grip and release a ball in order to generate movement that either juxtaposes or complements the things we've discussed so far— either the vertical movement of backspinning four-seamers, the tailing arm-side movement of two-seamers and sinkers, and the glove-side and/or downward movement of breaking balls. Any of the many different kinds of "off-speed pitches" can accomplish this, though that nomenclature is becoming obsolete. Most hitters miss because of location, not timing, so while disrupting a hitter's timing with pitches of different speeds may certainly impact their quality of contact, it's better to have pitches that move enough to miss lumber.

This has impacted how we think of changeups and their split-fingered cousins in a few ways. First, changeups are becoming less integral for a lot of good pitchers. Many pitchers simply have a couple different breaking balls that, when located properly, are perfectly suitable for dealing with opposite-handed hitters.

Traditionally, the thought has been that starters, who need several pitches to deal with the same hitters three or more times during a game, need a changeup to neutralize opposite-handed hitters. Because old (true) wisdom was also that breaking balls could not be taught, pitchers with a combination of velocity and natural breaking ball talent were targeted in the draft, and then taught changeups.

Changeups are "feel" pitches requiring delicate, precise use of a combination of deception (make it look like you're throwing a fastball by maintaining that arm speed) and dexterity (the ball actually has to float out of your hand like a puff of smoke) to be good. Even if you're talented, that takes time. High school pitchers, especially, have no reason to use changeups in the prep season. Why gift a 79 mph change to the kid who plays tenor sax in the marching band when you're better off blowing 90 mph past him three consecutive times?

As such, lots of premium amateur arm talents enter pro ball with zero changeup feel. If they can spin a breaking ball already, it's probably easier to teach them a second breaking ball, taking advantage of their natural proclivity for spin by simply altering grip and release to create a different shape, than it is to try to hammer a changeup into them over the course of several years. About half of the top 30 (by 2019 WAR) starters in baseball throw a changeup less than 10 percent of the time. The pitch is being de-emphasized across the game.

Because a slider has more glove-side movement (away from same-side hitters), it has a big platoon split (i.e. opposite-side hitters whack it around because it's coming toward them). So, if a pitcher has a fastball, slider, and curveball, then the curveball gets used as the changeup (i.e. versus opposite-hand hitters) since it's mostly vertical, like how most changeups are mostly vertical.

The types of changeups we're seeing are changing, as well. The notion that it's imperative to have a sizeable velocity separation between a pitcher's fastball and changeup is, traditionally, overstated. The power changeups of Félix Hernández and Zack Greinke were effective because of how they moved, not hitters' mistiming them. We love a good, string-pulling, touch-and-feel circle changeup, but there's a species of *cambio* growing in popularity, especially among orgs who seem ahead of others when it comes to developing good pitchers. Let's talk about the various kinds of changeups and how they move.

The change we describe above, the Old Testament changeup, has some arm-side action and "fade," "bottom," "depth," or sinking action. Hitters end up swinging over the top of them, both because of the movement and because the pitcher sells the hitter's eyeballs a fastball out of the hand and the hitter's timing is impacted. Many pitchers with this sort of changeup use a circle grip, in which the thumb and index finger make an "okay" sign that squeezes the ball on one side while the other three fingers cradle it. On release, the wrist pronates inward and the hand cuts across the top of the baseball, creating soft, arm-side action on the baseball. This type of change is best embodied by Cole Hamels' changeup, perhaps the best of this century.

Next you have the two-seam grip/spin changeups. Rather than turning over the top of the changeup, two-seam-style changeups are released in such a way that their spin is similar to a two-seam fastball, creating arm-side movement similar to that of a two-seamer. Reds righty Luis Castillo uses a circle grip to throw his changeup, but his release creates action on the pitch more accurately described in this paragraph. So, he and Cole Hamels have similar changeup grips, but their pitches are actually quite different.

Then we have all the splitter variations. Splitters, or split-fingered fastballs, are held deep in the index and middle finger of the throwing hand. What happens on release is a little more chaotic here. Often, splitters barely spin at all (but often sideways), and they have hard, heavy sinking movement, garnering swings and misses down in the dirt. Sometimes their spin direction varies depending on the release. For instance, if someone throwing a split "pulls it" across their body, as if to locate it to their glove side, that often creates a slider-like spin (in axis/direction, not in spin rate) and movement that can confuse viewers into thinking they've seen a slider or cutter when, in fact, they've just seen a variation on a splitter. Some changeups also have accidental cutting action at times, due to release variation. Think of the splitter as the spike curveball of the changeup realm—it's faster and breaks less, often making sense for a power pitcher without much finesse.

Again, it takes time and reps to assess the quality of these pitches. Splitters, or any off-speed pitch predicated on late bottom (late trapdoor action, falling off the table, etc.) are dependent on location. Their flight needs to start in a place that the hitter will see as a strike, then dip beneath where he can make contact with it. That's a pretty narrow band in which to work, so it takes a fair amount of precision. The ideal movement for a changeup, in terms of getting maximum movement, is sidespin. With the super slo-mo from most MLB broadcasts, you can see the changeups with less movement basically spinning like a two-seam fastball, backspin with some tilt, while the more active changeups come out with pure sidespin (like the best two-seamers that get called "sinkers").

True changeups need to be located in a similar fashion, and they also typically need to be set up by a fastball, especially if they're the type of changeup that serves to disrupt timing. The hitter needs to see 94 first if they're going to be early on 84 the following pitch. Ideally, both are located in the same spot and there's deception, in that everything about how the pitch is delivered is the same. An old veteran trick for more deception is to grunt when throwing a changeup, in the couple moments per game when you need an out on a changeup, making the hitter think you're muscling up for your best fastball in a key spot. All of this works even better when you have a good breaking ball, so the hitter doesn't feel free to guess on pitches and location, undermining otherwise good execution.

Given that changeups rely more on location and deception than pure movement, they can stand to benefit most from the concept of tunneling. The idea is that, when certain pitches with similar characteristics are thrown back-to-back in ideal locations, they will travel almost identical paths, staying in the same "tunnel" and diverging either close to or after the "decision point" for hitters. Certain pitches fit together well mathematically in this and they are classic combos you've probably seen many pitchers use over the years: sinker/slider, four-seam fastball/curveball, four-seam fastball/splitter, etc.

The New Testament changeup works similarly to the Hamels/old-school style above, in which most pitchers employ a circle grip and finish the pitch by turning their wrist over to create a sort of side spin. The difference here is that this is a test-tube pitch thrown by test-tube pitchers, and lots of test-tube pitchers have the vertical slot or hand position discussed above, which means their hands tend to rotate around the back of the ball rather than on top, creating more lateral, arm-side movement than fade and sink on some pitches. This species of changeup requires less impeccable sleight of hand and can kind of be brute-force installed into lots of pitchers. Their release is a little more telling, but the pitch still generates movement sufficient for garnering swings and misses.

Pitch Design

Let's take a leap back into the Stone Age of problem solving as it pertains to pitchers so that we're grounded in common sense before we start combining multiple elements from this chapter. Pitchers are the tip of the spear of run prevention. The best way to prevent runs is to limit the frequency and quality of contact by the opposing team, and causing them to miss pitches based on location is the best way to do that. So, how can we most frequently trick hitters into thinking a pitch is going to end up in one place when, in fact, it ends up somewhere else?

Based on how teams who have had the most success developing pitchers have gone about this, it involves cultivating repertoires that feature pitches with a cohesive variety of movement shapes. The boilerplate version: a fastball, a laterally oriented breaking ball (cutter or slider), and a vertically oriented breaking ball (curveball). Assuming they can locate those three pitches where they want, a pitcher should have no issue dealing with any broad subset of hitter.

Clayton Kershaw, Chris Carpenter, Walker Buehler, German Márquez, Justin Verlander, Charlie Morton, Lance Lynn, Jack Flaherty, Trevor Bauer, Dustin May… this list goes on forever. These guys don't throw many changeups if they throw one at all, and a good many of them had a career renaissance once they added the second breaking ball.

But why? Think back to earlier in the chapter when we introduced the concept of pitch movement and location in relationship to the barrel of the hitter's bat. This pitch mix enables perpendicular interaction with the bat in a few locations (fastballs up in the zone, the laterally-oriented breaking ball down-and-in to lefties) and presents hitters with enough to think about, and they can't just sit on one pitch and react to the other. These three ingredients fit together in a way that is sufficient for success.

That's not to say this is the best or only way to get hitters out. It's just to illustrate that for every pitcher there's probably an optimum recipe of pitches to deploy based on their inherent physical characteristics (arm slot, ability to spin, etc.). The breaking ball–centric approach we just talked about is best for high-spin four-seam pitchers. Sinkerballers are better suited for changeup use, and those with a naturally good changeup should incorporate a two-seamer into their pitch mix, since the two have similar-looking shape, with some combination of sink and tail. Sinkers, sliders, and changeups naturally fit together in this way, which is why "sinker/slider righty" rolls off the tongue as shorthand, just like "singer/songwriter whose songs all sound the same."

Former Blue Jays prospect Aaron Sanchez seemed to have top-of-the-rotation stuff as a minor leaguer—a heavy, sinking mid-90s fastball and nasty 10-to-4 curveball—but those two pitches didn't mesh together well. The curveball came out of Sanchez's hand up high; the sinker, which worked best at the bottom of the zone, came out low; so it was easy for big league hitters to parse them immediately. Sanchez's changeup usage shot way up in 2018, when the Jays finally realized this.

We think it's beneficial to understand that pitchers are being developed this way so they can have an informed opinion about how a pitcher might improve by adding a specific type of pitch, or creating more separation in movement between two pitches (Tigers RHP Casey Mize's slider and cutter became more different-looking after he got to pro ball) or whatever serves this general pitch design philosophy that a variety of movement is good, and pitches that look similar out of hand are good. This is a key, of sorts. Pitchers still need to slide it into the lock and turn it through proper location.

Control vs. Command and Pitch Execution

This dovetails into ways to evaluate and describe control and command, two words that may be used interchangeably during broadcasts or in other literature, though we suggest that they should not be. We consider "control" to be an ability to throw strikes and avoid walks. That's it. The control scale is below and can basically be automatically filled in by a macro that pulls walk rate.

Grade	Walk Rate	Player
80	2%	Josh Tomlin
70	4%	Shane Bieber
60	6%	José Berríos
55	7%	Tanner Roark
50	8%	Lucas Giolito
45	9%	Trevor Bauer
40	10%	Luis Castillo
30	12%	Matt Barnes
20	<14%	Jeurys Familia

"Command" we define as a pitcher's ability to throw *good* strikes, or to throw pitches where they want to. How do we know where the pitcher *wants* to locate a given pitch? Watch how/where the catcher sets up and whether or not the pitcher hits those spots consistently.

So while walk rates or strike percentages are an okay snapshot of a pitcher's control, visual evaluation, which gives you a better idea of intended location, is better for assessing command.

That's not to say there aren't supplements to this. Big league pitch locations can be viewed on heatmaps at FanGraphs. If you pull up Shane Bieber's heatmap and limit the display to include sliders alone, you'll instantly see he has incredible slider command because all the pitches are concentrated in the same part of the zone. This isn't possible for the public when it comes to minor league and amateur players, but teams probably have some ability to see this stuff internally.

Also, consider where the pitcher misses when he fails to hit those spots. For example, we'd much rather Justin Verlander miss up, above the strike zone with his fastball, where it's a ball, than miss down toward the bottom of the zone, where it's a strike but very hittable. Same goes for his slider, which we'd rather miss off the plate to his glove side than miss several inches to his arm side, where it'd be hanging, waiting to be hammered, in the middle of the zone.

"Pitch execution" is the term for this, one we're starting to prefer rather than "command," because command implies strikes, while "pitch execution" doesn't have that sidecar attached to it. Balls are not bad, especially when the count allows for them and when they show signs of sentience, signs the pitcher knows how his stuff works and is aiming to locate it where it plays best.

For high-spinning four-seamers, like Verlander's, that's at the top of the strike zone. Sinkers should be down. Glove-side execution of sliders, in a place where they're too enticing for same-handed hitters to lay off, but far enough off the plate that they can't be hit, is paramount. Look for backdoor sliders that start off the plate, away from opposite-handed hitters, then tilt over the outside corner. Backfoot breaking balls (can be curves or sliders) tilt across the strike zone and finish with movement in the direction of the hitter's back foot, out of the zone. Changeups should be down and they're typically away from opposite-handed hitters, though arms who have a really good one also work them down and in to same-handed hitters. It's rare, but sometimes pitchers can backdoor changeups to same-handed hitters, running them back over the outside corner.

If you're seeing some combination of this stuff from a pitcher, then they can execute their pitches, and that's going to enable their stuff to play. Similar to readers' likely feel for fastball velocity, you probably come primed with some notions about how big league pitchers need to clear an acceptable strike-throwing bar, and how pitchers with vanilla stuff can be successful thanks to precise command.

This is true, but impact command more often enables big league pitchers' careers to stretch into their mid-thirties as their stuff fades than it makes a prospect. A lot of pitchers never throw harder than they do at 18, because their seasons get longer, they start pitching every fifth day instead of once a week, and their bodies start to atrophy. Those whose command improves from years of honing and tinkering give themselves a better shot of having continued success, but we remain fixated on stuff when it comes to prospects.

Deliveries

This is the area where it's important to remind you that there are no absolutes when it comes to assessing mechanics. Like the Hunter Pence example we drew upon when discussing hitters, many pitchers do things their own way and, ugly though it may be, it works for them. Lots of scouts thought Tim Lincecum, Max Scherzer, and Chris Sale were going to have injury-riddled careers, and lots of scouts were certain that Mark Prior's delivery was immaculate. Different bodies and athletes are capable of doing different things, so there's probably a range of mechanics for each individual that both enables that individual to be effective and also gives them the best shot at staying healthy.

We're going to run down the parts of a pitcher's delivery, because you're going to want to describe what's happening, mechanically, to whomever is reading your report. The entire body goes to work, starting with forces generated by the lower half (legs, glutes) and culminating with rapid rotation of the upper extremities. It's violent, beautiful, and we're going to start from the ground up. Much of what we're about to describe is more thoroughly and scientifically explained in various, peer-reviewed journals of exercise science and in the treasure trove that is the online Driveline Baseball archive.

The forces generated by the legs and trunk of a pitcher play a large role in the generation of velocity, and they, as well as other parts of the body, help carry a load otherwise burdening tissue in the shoulder and elbow. A pitcher lifts his lead leg to its apex (some guys barely lift it at all while Orlando Hernández and Dontrelle Willis are extreme, knee-to-chest examples of the other end of the spectrum) and his center of gravity is placed over the rear leg (this is called the Balance Point), then his weight shifts and pedals toward home. Watch how deep the bend of the rear knee is during this time, how close to the ground the ass and hamstrings are. This is called "getting into your legs" or "loading the legs" and we consider it a sign of athleticism, or at least an indication that the rest of the delivery is going to be pretty explosive.

Next, the pitcher's front leg is headed toward home, and this is called "the stride." We've already talked about how stride direction can impact the way a pitcher's stuff works, but the length of the stride is also important. Short striders tend to stay a little bit taller during their delivery, creating more downward angle (or "downhill plane") on their stuff. This was traditionally considered a positive trait, the thought being a fastball descending with angle would be harder to hit than one entering the zone more level to the ground. But while a lot of modern pitching assessment has confirmed old wisdom, this is not universally the case with downhill plane.

Longer striders tend to "drop and drive," meaning they get lower to the ground as they stride home, which is often necessary if you're going to have a longer stride since the pitcher needs to propel himself way off the rubber, á la Tim Lincecum. Drop-and-drive pitchers tend to have flatter-planed stuff, which is totally fine, and arguably beneficial for some pitchers whose velo/spin/axis/secondary pitch profile is best-suited for flatter plane. Julio Teheran is an example of a drop-and-drive style pitcher with a repertoire (mostly a sinker and changeup) that's not great for missing bats from a flat plane, while Gerrit Cole's stuff is.

At some point during the stride, the pelvis/hips start to rotate. This is an important thing because it catalyzes a corkscrewing of the upper body that eventually finds its way to the arm and ball, and it's during the stride portion of the delivery that you should prepare yourself to look for it, but we're going to stay fixated on the lower half for a few more sentences.

The pitcher's front foot eventually needs to come down, plant in the ground, then support all the weight and power created by the rest of the delivery as the pitcher's torso hurdles over that front leg. When that front foot touches down it's called "foot strike" or "front foot contact," and scouts often use this as a visual checkpoint for other parts of the delivery.

If a pitcher shows balance, flexion, and stability in their landing or "blocking" leg as they finish their delivery, this is also something we consider a sign of athleticism and body control. Balance over that front leg is important. In fact, force-plate studies done by Driveline Baseball indicate that the ground forces generated by that front leg are more strongly correlated with velocity than the leg that pushes off the mound. Think of it as keeping the momentum generated in the earlier parts of the delivery alive. That built momentum can be diffused by a weak blocking leg.

Back to the hips and everything above them. During the stride, the glove hand and pitching hand break from one another, and the glove arm moves toward the plate, almost mirroring the swing and timing of the lead leg as it strides home. During this time, the throwing arm is in "early cocking phase," swinging back behind the body and preparing for its most intense part of the process. The lead arm extends outward, then starts to fold at the elbow. This movement, in which the lead arm folds and clears the way for the rest of the upper body to rotate, is called "disconnection." At front foot strike, the hips/pelvis have typically begun rotating, and their rotation is ahead of the torso and upper body, squared toward the plate. Disconnection has already begun at this point, and now the torso begins to follow the hips as well as the disconnected lead arm.

The throwing arm is typically up around the pitcher's head at foot strike, the forearm pointing ideally at the plate, or maybe just one frame away (in a slowed-down video) from getting there. If the hand is pointing to the center fielder, that's a problem (most teams don't like arm actions with this feature) and if the arm hasn't gotten vertical yet, with the hand pointing down, the arm is "late." This is often the thing scouts are looking for at foot strike to determine if a pitcher's arm is "on time." If the arm isn't vertical yet at foot strike, it's considered "late." Jake Peavy is a notable starter whose arm was late and eventually it caught up with him.

No one understands how to predict pitcher injuries, but being "late" correlates to injury, as well as to lesser command. The arm ideally hits these checkpoints and delivers the pitch, but if the arm is late, the body is already trying to deliver the ball and drags the arm along in a way that's hard to control and increases arm torque in many cases. It's a cheap way to create velocity, but often without anything else improving.

There's also the concept of an inverted arm action where, at foot plant, the pitching elbow gets above the pitching shoulder. There's some scholarship on this topic and also some snake oil salesmen on the internet who think they can predict injuries only on this. John Smoltz did it and he needed Tommy John surgery, but also made the Hall of Fame. Stephen Strasburg also does it, he also blew out and he's also really good. Scouts thought Tim Lincecum's body would explode due to his delivery. Most less athletic pitchers would and eventually Lincecum declined due to hip problems, but he also won two Cy Young Awards in the interim. One-size-fits-all approaches to scouting or developing pitchers is a really quick way to tell people you don't know what you're talking about.

If a pitcher's hand/arm action were to leave behind a trail of light as it traversed its path during a delivery, most light trails would resemble a corkscrew, or spiral staircase. The length of each pitcher's arm action can naturally vary, and can be changed. Look at Lucas Giolito in 2018 versus 2019 to see the difference between shorter and longer arm actions in the same guy. Madison Bumgarner's pitching hand stabs way back away from his body before his torso rotates and his arm comes through, while Trevor Bauer's elbow stays bent and he holds the ball closer to his body. Again, there are no absolutes.

During the arm spiral, there are several parts of the arm that are rotating, accelerating, decelerating, then accelerating and decelerating again. The point of the delivery that is most graphic is the point of "maximum external rotation," when the pitcher's shoulder has rotated back and their forearm is parallel to the ground. The type of flexibility that allows for this is important for pitchers, and it's such an incredible physical feat that we struggle to show people, in person, what is meant by external rotation because we lack that kind of flexibility.

At this point of maximum external rotation, the chest is squared to the plate and the torso has begun folding over the front side. "Internal rotation" occurs and the arm slings the ball toward home.

That's a lot of stuff while, at the same time, it's not a thoroughly detailed breakdown of what's happening, biomechanically, during a typical overhand throwing motion. If we had to boil it down to the few most important things to consider and note, they'd be: 1) power and balance in the legs, especially the blocking leg, 2) the sequence of rotation up the body, and 3) the looseness/flexibility/efficiency of the arm action on display during maximum external rotation.

It's also important to consider whether or not a pitcher repeats his mechanics. Again, there are exceptions, such as when a pitcher intentionally varies his arm slot to alter the shape of a pitch or just to disorient a hitter, but typically, varied mechanics means inconsistent control/command/pitch execution and lesser athleticism or body control. It can be a chronic issue for some pitchers, or something caused by fatigue that manifests later in starts.

Bodies, Athletes, and Projection

The ability to anticipate how bodies and tools/skills will develop over time is called "projecting," and it is perhaps the most important part of scouting. Projecting is like trying to guess what stock prices will be five years from now, except instead you're trying to guess who will have grown into big power but not gotten so big that they've had to move off of shortstop. Assessing the present ability of players is important, and that drives the evaluation of older players in the upper-minors. But that portion of the player population is typically low variance. They're fourth starters or fifth starters, they're a marginal 40-man relief upgrade, they're a viable platoon partner for an aging vet in a contract year.

Low variance does not mean low impact. Gleyber Torres was arguably a low variance prospect once he reached full-season ball; he was either going to be good or very good. Younger players with unrefined skills and physicality are almost always high-variance prospects, meaning there's a bigger gap between their reasonable ceiling and floor.

No team is trading you Fernando Tatís Jr. when he's at Double-A and his parent club feels certain he's going to be a stud, and probably very soon. But at the dawn of his pro career, when he's barely faced pro-quality pitching and might be a half decade away from the big leagues? That's when you have a shot to get that kind of player.

It's pretty easy to project on bodies. Young, skinny, broad-shouldered ballplayers are likely to fill out and get stronger as they mature, and that added strength will interact with all of their tools. For hitters, that means more power, sometimes less mobility. For pitchers, that means more velocity and that arm speed usually manifests in sharper breaking balls. But pitchers have some natural opposing forces to fight even as they fill out because, in pro ball, they're throwing more frequently across a longer season than they did as an amateur.

We caution against relying heavily on measurables (height and weight) to project on bodies, because even two bodies with identical measurables can have different composition. Players with square-shouldered, flat-backed torsos, high waists, a strong butt and thighs should be considered differently than a player with hunched and rounded shoulders and a flat ass, even if they're both 6'3", 180 pounds. These more subtle visual differences are easier to identify watching basketball. The athletes are long, their features telescope out and are more obviously variant, person to person, and the garb suits seeing and describing the human form more than other sports. So, in the same way art students have to paint nude models, we suggest aspiring baseball scouts work on describing physical characteristics by watching basketball players.

Projecting on skills is a little more complicated than bodies. We mentioned earlier that pitchers who already have one good breaking ball are increasingly likely to add a second. Pitchers with shorter arm actions are typically more able to develop viable changeups and, because *cambios* are a "feel" pitch, young arms who've had more reps typically come with better ones. This is also true of control/command/pitch execution and, for hitters, bat-to-ball skills. These are things that improve with reps, so high schoolers who live in locations where they play baseball year-round are typically better at them, earlier.

And so, we're more apt to project on baseball players' skills when they're from a cold weather part of the country, or when they have elite athleticism, or when the player's time has been divided amongst several sports, or they were a two-way player focusing on a lone task for the first time, or whatever else may have robbed them of reps up to that point. If a college pitcher spent his freshman year in the bullpen, then missed a season due to Tommy John and came out at the start of their junior year struggling to throw strikes, we'd be more forgiving of the strike-throwing situation, given the player's circumstances than we would if he had been healthy and starting for three years. Context is important.

A newer concept we're considering is "reverse projection," the idea that thicker prospects can reshape their physiques and improve, athletically. This is especially true of amateur prospects who are for the first time starting a Division I or pro athletic training regimen. Stephen Strasburg and Alec Bohm were each heavy when they went to college, but each reshaped their bodies and improved. Forrest Whitley's velocity spiked after he lost about 50 pounds during the winter between his junior and senior spring. Bo Bichette was a little doughy and couldn't maintain his swing as well as a prep underclassman.

Don't confuse a walking Abercrombie ad in spikes with athleticism. We'd define athleticism as a combination of explosion, grace, and body control, and plenty of baseball players are athletic even though they're built like Bartolo Colón. Colón looked like a toad but was so flexible that he could bend at the waist and put his forearms flat on the ground. Kiley noticed that late-career Adam Dunn, while at the on-deck circle, could casually bend at the waist, lock his knees, and his wrists would touch the ground while holding the bat, all when he was 6'6", 245 lbs.

Many scouts describe baseball strength as forearms to fingertips; jacked biceps are usually bad for pitchers because of their impact on flexibility.

We will often separate baseball athleticism (easy actions, baseball strength, quick-twitch, body control) and football or combine athleticism (size, bench press strength, 40 time, and also quick-twitch). Elite baseball athleticism can include ordinary-looking guys, but football athleticism essentially includes only physical specimens.

Good athletes show balance, coordination, they'll do obviously amazing things once in a while, and they're the ones who can best map instruction to their physical actions, altering a swing when a coach says to, and tweaking a release point when tech tells them it'll make their stuff play better. Other than predicting pitcher health, the most predictive thing you can know is a pitcher's ability to make adjustments.

CHAPTER 10

The Tricky Job of Summarizing

So far we've talked about individual tools, pitch grades, attributes, and what we consider best practices for evaluating them and learning how to evaluate them. What we haven't done yet, and perhaps we've buried the lede a little bit here, is tell you how we meld that stuff together to create an overall evaluation of the player and why we do it that way. After all, the problem we're trying to solve, the questions we seek to answer by scouting players is, "Which of these guys is going to be good?" and, more precisely, "*How* good are all these players going to be?" and, "How much better will some of them be than others?"

For big leaguers, we already have a pretty sound statistical way of doing this via Wins Above Replacement, or WAR. We're not going to evangelize about stats, or turn this chapter into a math lesson (go to the FanGraphs glossary for that sort of thing), but we ask readers inclined to be preemptively dismissive about our methodology because they're skeptical of WAR's veracity to be open-minded as they read the next five paragraphs, and that's it. Those who are already on board can skip these next few paragraphs, and meet us at the start of the next section.

Baseball is a fairly individualistic sport in which much of how your performance is measured comes from two matchups: batter versus pitcher and defenders versus balls-in-play hit near them. It's not completely immune from luck or the effects of teamwork, but the nature of the game makes it less beholden to teammate-related statistical noise than other sports (quarterback effectiveness depends upon the offensive line, wide receivers depend upon the QB, running backs depend upon the OL, quality of play-calling, etc.). This is part of why the statistical revolution struck baseball first; it was just easier to individualize everyone's accomplishments, with the vast majority of the game being a discrete battle between two players.

Run differentials (the difference between a team's runs scored and allowed) are very, very strongly correlated with won/loss record. There are a few formulas (Pythagorean Record is one, which is well-defined in the FanGraphs glossary) in which you can just plug in a team's run differential and it will spit out something very close to what their record is. And, in fact, run differentials are better at predicting how well a team will do the remainder of the season than their record is to that point. Twenty teams in 2019 finished with a record within three wins of their expected record based on run differential; it's sound math.

Because of this, we have a good understanding of the relationship between runs and wins. That understanding is that every 10 runs a team scores more than they allow is worth an extra win. So, the 2019 D-backs scored 70 more runs than they allowed, so we'd expect them to finish seven games over .500. They finished eight over. The Tigers allowed 330 runs more than they scored, so we'd expect them to finish 33 games under .500, and they finished 34 under.

We feel pretty good about knowing how runs lead to wins. We also feel pretty good about how all the individual, in-game events (singles, homers, caught stealing, etc.) contribute to, or detract from, runs. And we have metrics that weigh each of those properly, like wOBA and wRC+ for measuring hitting on a rate basis, rather than a counting one. The volume of statistics created by baseball's long history and the immense number of measurable events that occur during a game help give us a high degree of confidence in all of this math.

And so we can get a fair idea of how many runs a player has generated, and therefore how many wins they've generated. And we can compare that amount of runs/wins to those created by the population of bench/call-up/replacement players to get Wins Above Replacement. It's not a perfect measure, as defensive quality specifically has a larger error bar than the other inputs, and there's some margin for error (we wouldn't declare a player who generated 3.1 WAR to be certainly better going forward or even necessarily in the moment than one who generated a 2.9 WAR) but it's a good, all-encompassing stat for measuring player quality, the best single stat for such a thing to date.

What Is Future Value?

While we like WAR as a measure for player talent at the big league level, it's impossible to apply it to minor league players for a number of reasons, especially because of how impossible it is to define "replacement player" in the minor leagues. We would, however, like to anticipate how many WAR a prospect will generate once they reach the big leagues, since WAR is the best currently available catch-all for measuring big league talent. We have to find a common denominator between big leaguers and prospects in order to do this, and that common denominator is the tool grades. Just like we're generating present and projected tool grades for prospects, we can have tool grades for big leaguers (aided by the metrics we've outlined in the pitching and hitting chapters before this) and we can see how those tool grades translate to production, including WAR.

For example, Juan Soto is a 65 hitter with 65 power. He has elite, 80-grade plate discipline, which isn't a tool but heavily informs his offensive stats (traditionally created by the hit and power tools). Plate discipline is definitely the quality that affects WAR more than any non-tool. He's a bad defensive left fielder, at best a 40 on the scale, even though he's a serviceable, 45-grade runner. If we were to project these exact tool grades for a given prospect, then we'd expect that prospect to generate about 5 annual WAR, just like Soto did in 2019.

But we don't want to just use an expected WAR value as a way to line up prospects, because in addition to their tool grades, there are elements of their prospectdom that impact the likelihood that they reach those projected tool grades (like injury, or bad makeup, or the volatility of lynchpin tools) and impact the speed with which they actualize. If we have identical evaluations on two center fielders, but one is a 23-year-old in Double-A, on the 40-man roster, and poised to debut this year, and the other is a high schooler yet to be drafted, those two players should not have the exact same grade. If two pitchers have the exact same stuff, but one has never been injured and the other has a history of shoulder trouble, we should have some way of rounding down on the porcelain arm. You can think of dozens of scenarios like this where players have similar talent, but shouldn't be *valued* the same.

Our solution is to use the 20–80 scale to solve this problem. We can map the scale to WAR production to use as a baseline rather than WAR itself, and then round up or down, subjectively, when the circumstantial aspects of the profile dictate we should. The term we use to describe how we distill each player's scouting evaluation into this singular expression is what we call "Future Value." This moment where we say the name of the book feels momentous, like when Sean Connery tells Nic Cage, as if you somehow didn't know the name of the movie you're watching, "Welcome to The Rock."

Can we soundly map WAR production to the 20–80 scale? Kind of. It's an easy concept to apply toward the very top of the player population, where there are clear, distinct layers of talent. It gets harder toward the bottom of the big leagues, where you have a lot of part-time players and guys on the roster fringe. Remember that 20–80ing something requires a normal distribution, which means we'd need the number of players of lesser talent to dwindle toward the bottom of the big leagues, but instead there are more and more of them. We can't 20 a big leaguer, since even the worst bench player in the big leagues is probably not two standard deviations worse than the 40s, who are also bench players. To solve this problem, we think of big leaguers as kind of the tip of an iceberg that extends down into the minors, and we extend the Future Value scale into the minors, as well.

Here is fresh math from the 2018 and 2019 seasons regarding WAR distribution of hitters mapped to the 20–80 scale. Eric calculated it twice, first by using all hitters with 200 plate appearances (which produced a sample of 355 players, or approximately every team's starting lineup and its three most-used bench players) and then the best 255 players from that sample (effectively, the starters). We would say the players in the below tables have "Present Value," since they're fully actualized big leaguers, and that helps us map prospects who project to have their skill sets later, hence "Future Value."

Grade	WAR Range	Role	Examples
80	>7	Elite, MVP candidate, Top 5 in MLB	Mike Trout, Mookie Betts
70	5 to 6.9	Superstar, Top 20 in MLB	Ronald Acuña, Nolan Arenado
60	3.4 to 4.9	All-Star level	Bryce Harper, Ozzie Albies
55	2.5 to 3.3	Above-average regular	Matt Olson, Trea Turner
50	1.6 to 2.4	Average regular	Mike Moustakas, José Abreu
45	0.8 to 1.5	Low-end regular, utility/platoon	Kevin Pillar, Freddy Galvis, Seth Smith
40	0.1 to 0.7	Bench players	Adam Engel, Guillermo Heredia
35	Approx. 0.0	Up/down, 40-man fringe	Steve Wilkerson, Pedro Florimon
30	< 0.0	Org guys, upper-level MiLBer, 4A players	Mason Williams, Matt Skole
20	—	Non prospects	

Pitching is a little more complicated because pitching standards and roles are changing. Velocity and strikeout rates are higher than ever. Starting-pitcher innings are lower than ever. Whatever the shifting variable, here's how 2018 and 2019 starters shake out based on WAR distribution. For this, Eric's first pass included all starters who threw at least 50 innings (which ended up being 180 pitchers, essentially starters No. 1 through No. 6 on each team) then the top 150 pitchers from that sample (all 30 teams' starting rotations).

Grade	WAR Range	Role	Example
80	>6.5	Ace, No. 1 starter, Top 5-ish arm in MLB	Max Scherzer, Gerrit Cole
70	5.0 to 6.4	Top-of-the-rotation, Top 10 in MLB, No. 2	Chris Sale, Stephen Strasburg
60	3.5 to 4.9	No. 3, All-Star, Top 25–30 arm in MLB	Aaron Nola, José Berríos
55	2.7 to 3.4	No. 3/4 starter, Top 50, mid-rotation arm	German Márquez, Jon Gray
50	1.9 to 2.6	No. 4 starters, Top 75, average	Kyle Gibson, Tanner Roark
45	1.1 to 1.8	No. 4/5 starters, Top 125	Zach Davies, Mike Fiers
40	0.4 to 1.0	No. 5 starters, backend starter	José Ureña, Trevor Cahill
35	Approx. 0.0	Spot starters, up/down arms	Tom Milone, JC Ramírez
30	< 0.0	Emergency depth	Ross Detweiler
20	—	Non prospects	

The pitcher and position-player WAR curves are similar enough that, especially when we consider WAR's margin for error, it's reasonable to round and combine the two scales if you want to, so that they overlap exactly. But changes to the way pitchers are being used has started to cluster everyone closer to the middle, and things might continue to trend that way, so we're presenting a more exact version of the pitcher scale here in anticipation of this distinction soon becoming more important.

Relievers are punished in any WAR-based measure because they throw fewer innings. The best relievers on the planet typically yield about 3 WAR, while really excellent relievers are 1.5–2.0 WAR players, which caps their 20–80 grade in the 55–60 range, max. Some clubs do consider elite relievers to be 70s or 80s and think WAR-only analysis of relievers ignores too much of the leverage component of their jobs, and this is fair criticism.

For now, we bucket single-inning, middle-relief-type prospects as 40s, and we put a 45 FV on prospects we think will pitch toward the back of a bullpen, in traditional set-up or closer roles, or modern high-leverage rules. Most elite closers are failed starters, so we think most of the 50 and above FV relievers are graded as such on our lists, they're just starters waiting to be moved to the bullpen. Sometimes marginal starting pitcher prospects become elite in the bullpen, and we'll just tip our caps to them.

All teams ask their scouts to put an all-encompassing grade on the players they see, and often that's done using the 20–80 scale. Some teams (a lot of teams run by branches of the Theo Esptein executive tree like the Cubs and D-backs) adopted a system that is concerned with roles and uses letter/number designation (B2 is an average regular, A1 is an elite player) to put players into buckets, which might be okay if your staff isn't fluent in WAR. Other teams might call their overall grade an OFP, short for Overall Future Potential, which uses the 20–80 scale to put a grade on a player's ceiling, defined more precisely, at least according to Baseball Prospectus, which uses OFP, as a 75th percentile outcome for the player.

One way to test these different methodologies to see where they fall short and can be improved is to present some test cases and see how they do and where holes might be. We should always be able to work backwards with a big league career and have a pretty firm idea of how an oracle would have graded them.

Ceiling-based forms of evaluation are going to struggle with Carlos Gómez and Matt Duffy–type players, players who have a peak year or two way up above the rest of their career. Gómez had an MVP-caliber season in 2013 when he swiped 40 bags, hit 24 homers, and played great defense in CF. The rest of his career was somewhere between frustrating and fine. If you had his ceiling as a 70, were you wrong? No, but he shouldn't be on an even footing with someone who generates 6+ WAR year after year even though they have the same ceiling.

To solve this problem, we use a window of time during which WAR production is measured and averaged. So to further define it, Future Value is a grade on the 20–80 scale that maps to anticipated annual WAR production during the player's first six to seven years of big league service. Why the six-to-seven year boundary? We think basing rankings on multi-year projection for a player is more useful than a single-year peak, but we like our projections to be bound by some amount of time because, in the absence of such a constraint, we'd just be projecting career WAR. In that case, we'd have to consider who might still be playing into their late thirties and forties and what kind of players they would be at that time. That's ridiculous.

We love Bartolo Colón, Julio Franco, and LaTroy Hawkins, and cherish big leaguers who stick around forever, but it's a fool's errand to look at a high school prospect and try to decide if he'll play into his mid-thirties, or beyond. The six-ish year interval we've chosen lines up with the six years of service time players are forced to accrue before they hit free agency. During that time, players are being re-evaluated for free agency by means that are so vastly different than when they're prospects that it actually makes sense to view them as separate processes. When trading for prospects, teams often refer to them as having "six-to-seven years of control" since that's how many cost-controlled years they have, depending on how you manage service time. It makes sense to map the WAR horizon to that figure teams are constantly judging players by.

A finite scope also forces us to be more specific about defensive projections and decline phases. It's easy to look at Vladimir Guerrero Jr. and say that he'll eventually outgrow third base and move to first, but it's more useful to think about when that will happen with more specificity. Prospects who are older or whose bodies are the type that tend to have precipitous athletic decline earlier than most of their peers (Mo Vaughn types) also get their FV rounded down in anticipation of them declining during the six-ish year window.

Time Value of Prospects

For many reasons, we value proximity to the big leagues and attempt to bake it into FV. If there are two minor leaguers who are exactly the same in every way, and one is in Double-A and the other is in the GCL, it makes sense that the player closer to the big leagues would rank higher on a prospect list than the one in Rookie-level ball. There are some 50 FV players in our rankings who we think have a chance to be 60s or better in the big leagues, but the risk/proximity aspect of their profile needs to be captured in FV somewhere. The amount we deduct for things like risk, due to injury or player demographics is subjective, and we don't have a guideline to share for deducting FV when someone has a surgery or gets busted for PEDs. We're okay with that because so much of the scouting process is already subjective. We're not poisoning a well with this idea.

Different teams on different ends of the competitive spectrum might feel differently about this. A team looking to make the playoffs that needs an outfielder who can play tomorrow would, logically, value someone at Triple-A more than they would a comparable player in rookie ball. You can just look at the trades MLB clubs make for clear evidence of this. Recently, Cleveland has made several, like when they sent high-ceiling, power-hitting teenage OF Jhon Torres to St. Louis for solid, big league ready CF Oscar Mercado, and when they traded young conversion arm Ignacio Feliz to San Diego for big league pitching depth, including Walker Lockett. In both cases, Cleveland swapped players with higher realistic ceilings, but also higher risk of total bust, for stable, mature players. Torres is a physical monster with big power potential and Feliz is an ultra-athletic righty who's new to pitching. They definitely have ceiling above who they were traded for (Mercado's range of potential outcomes span from fourth OF to average regular, Lockett is maybe a fifth starter) so clearly there's some risk and time horizon assessment going on here.

Conversely, a rebuilding team may be more keen to acquire a player several years from the big leagues, whose arrival coincides with a more competitive big league roster. This makes logical sense, but there's no concrete transactional evidence of it happening, and most executives don't have the kind of job security that would enable them to act that way. We've seen some clubs in resets, or quick rebuilds, that prioritize prospects in the upper levels of the minor leagues, like Cincinnati (Aroldis Chapman trade) and Seattle (James Paxton trade).

One interesting wrinkle in the time value of talent topic is one Kiley has used for years to get at how an evaluator thinks about players. He would ask, if we knew their complete future baseball careers and you were acquiring them on the day of their big league debuts and only have them for their controlled years, would you take Aramis Ramírez or Ben Grieve?

Ramírez had a later-peaking career, with 38 career WAR, but, in his controlled years, he posted WAR of -1.0, -0.2, -0.8, 4.7, -0.9, 2.1 and 3.7, for 7.6 total WAR in his cost-controlled seasons. His first three years after his controlled years totaled 11.4. He had lots of WAR and a high ceiling, but it was distributed terribly for those looking for value when he was cheap.

Grieve was the opposite. Grieve put up 4.2 WAR in his three seasons playing at the league minimum, another 2.2 WAR in his first two arbitration years, then was out of baseball three years later, for a career figure of 6.7 WAR. After those first three seasons at the league minimum, Oakland may have known what his future held, because they traded Grieve to Tampa Bay in a three-way deal.

For value created over salary, or surplus value, Grieve is the easy winner, producing 4.2 WAR vs. Ramírez's 1.8 WAR in the period where they both made the league minimum. Grieve then had trade value, which Oakland capitalized on, while Ramírez reached his projected ceiling after hitting free agency and being available to the other 29 clubs.

Almost every scout picks Ramírez, and after looking at this data, almost every front office person picks Grieve. Each side doesn't really get how the other side could come to that conclusion. If an executive picks Ramírez, it's because they think they'd have a shot to extend him and capture his most valuable years, which is outside the scope of the question. Ideally, our system would project their production in controlled years closely enough that it would be clear it's a bit of a coin flip for that time horizon.

Variance, Helium, and Roles

Let's go back to the Carlos Gómez hypothetical. If, during his first seven years in the big leagues, Gómez accrued 21 WAR, peaking at 5–7 WAR some years and playing very poorly in others, while a second player, Rigoberto Regularium, also accrues 21 WAR but was good for 3 WAR every year. It's more correct to have a 60 FV on both of them than it is to have, say, a 70 OFP on one and a 60 OFP on the other, but FV doesn't explain that these players are different in a way that matters.

For this, we use the term "variance." Carlos Gómez was a high-variance player, whose year-to-year performance was volatile, because Gómez's impulsive, free-swinging approach at the plate made him an inconsistent offensive performer. There are prospects who exhibit similar traits who we'd anticipate to be high-variance players, or who have high-variance prospect profiles (like risky high school pitchers). We consider it like a gene that modulates consistency, so in addition to an FV, everyone gets a variance rating. We just use "high," "medium," or "low," but it's possible studies could be done to see if clusters of annual WAR standard deviation derived from common traits exist, which might tell us how many buckets there should be rather than the rudimentary three we're currently using.

We've spoken with clubs that tell us they pick through the minor league free agent class—generally the misfit toys of baseball—with variance as a guiding principle since there's so many players to choose from. Low payroll clubs that can't afford elite players are signing players to minor league deals and targeting high variance, hoping that they may find a Carlos Peña (a post-hype prospect that signed for a minor league deal in 2007 with Tampa Bay before a 5.9 WAR season) for free that they otherwise can't afford. Every team would like to do this, but some contenders are specifically looking for reliable depth, guys that can sit in Triple-A for a high minor league salary, but are of fifth-starter or bench-player quality, rather than org guy status. These teams would target lower-variance players, because they may need two fill-in starts at a random time in the season and need to know they can count on a 30-year-old veteran to not melt down.

We also wanted a way to identify players who we were especially optimistic about, or players who had a weird trait or background that was so exceptional and potentially impactful that it separated that player from what his typical FV evaluation would be. For this reason, we add a little + symbol to the back of some players' FV and move them to the top of that FV tier. For example, Colin Poche's surface-level evaluation is that of a middle reliever (40 FV), but his fastball is dominant in a bizarre and exceptional way that we need to round up on him a bit, just not so much that we group him with the elite relief-only prospects (45 FV), so he gets a 40+ FV.

He's probably a 40, but there's something going on here that might make him better than that, something we can't totally grasp because there isn't much precedent for it, and we want to capture that somehow. Twins, uh, catcher? Sure, we'll say catcher. Twins catcher Willians Astudillo is like this. His surface-level evaluation was that of an up-and-down player (35 FV) but his ability to put the bat on the ball was elite, totally exceptional, and ideally we'd notice that and put a 35+ on this type of player to show that there's a chance this guy blows up and becomes something pretty good. We only use the plus modifier on players outside our Top 100 (so 45 FV players and below). This is also helpful because we have over 1,200 minor league prospects ranked at any given time, so any extra tiers of FV make it easier to separate everyone.

We get critical feedback from people in front offices about our work, and this is true for Future Value as a term and methodology. Perhaps the most consistent criticism is that FV clusters players together too broadly, especially as we move down the scale. Lots of the 40 FV prospects in our work are risky young players who might be really good one day but might also be nothing, while several of our 40 FV players are near-ready back-end starters or limited role players. Some folks in baseball think an FV number and variance don't sufficiently describe how different a lot of the players within the same FV tier are.

Typically, our team sources want us to add a player's "role" to the marquee of their evaluation. Consider the Mercado-for-Torres trade we just discussed.

They had similar FVs at the time of trade, but we thought one was a safe, lower-ceiling player (Mercado's role would be "low-end regular") and the other was a high-risk/high-reward player (Torres' role would be "above-average regular") and we understand how it's informative to present that information at the forefront, rather than only in a player's long scouting writeup.

But some of these differences are already captured in the variance rating, and it's also difficult to describe the myriad roles in a concise way. Internally, the two of us are split as to whether or not we start incorporating role titles at the forefront of our player evaluations. Kiley thinks the existence of variance makes doing it kind of redundant, and that roles are shifting such that we'd have to define some from scratch and in ways that aren't concise or reader-friendly. Conversely, Eric wants to try to invent role terminology that describes, say, what makes Cody Bellinger different than most first basemen (his defensive versatility) but also what makes him different than Ketel Marte (who is also versatile, but in a different way).

Using the Draft as a Sanity Check

One of the most useful phrases we utter to one another as we're attempting to line up hundreds of players is, "Where does this guy go in a draft?" There is copious research about the draft. Rany Jazayerli's work on the relevance of prospect age is essential, supplementary reading. Sky Andrechuk, Victor Wang, Matthew Murphy, Jeff Zimmerman, Anthony Rescan, and Martin Alonso have all laid a foundation for public understanding of the draft in various ways. The most recent study applicable for our global predicament is another Craig Edwards piece at FanGraphs, in which he attempted to put a monetary value on each draft early pick.

There are some caveats when it comes to converting WAR to dollars, but much like a common denominator of runs helps us compare apples to oranges when analyzing player performance, converting things to dollars lets us compare things we wouldn't be able to any other way. Cash is exchanged in trades, so are international bonus slots, player's contracts are paid down so a team can get a better prospect in return, teams regularly give up draft picks to sign free agents, receive extra draft picks when they lose free agents or reside in a smaller media market, and some picks can be traded. Understanding draft picks and prospects in this way shows how underpaid minor leaguers are (and it would behoove the MLBPA to take these values to the bargaining table when they sit down for the next CBA negotiations), and it helps us better understand why teams make the decisions they do regarding those picks.

Craig's separate analysis of the draft and prospect lists in general found the following value for picks and Future Value tiers, respectively.

Future Value	Approx. Monetary Value
70	$85–$112 million
65	$60–$65 million
60	$55–60 million
55	$35–$45 million
50	$21–$28 million
45+	$6–$8 million
45	$4–$6 million
40+	$3–$4 million
40	$1–$2 million

Draft Pick No.	Present Value of Pick
1	$45.5 million
2	$41.6 million
3	$38.2 million
4	$34.8 million
5	$31.9 million
7	$27.4 million
10	$23.3 million
15	$18.4 million
20	$14.8 million
25	$12 million
40	$7.6 million
50	$5.9 million
Round 3	$3.8 million

From this, as well as other studies on what kind of return to expect at each draft pick, we can see that the top prospect in each draft is typically a 55 FV prospect (there's going to be year-to-year variation here, as some years are lean and some years there's an Alex Rodriguez–type player atop the draft). The top 10 picks are mostly 50 FV types who will be in discussion for the overall top

100 list once they sign, while the back of the first round is comprised of 45 FV prospects bleeding into 40+ FV players as we get into Round 2. Most of the gap between these two can be explained by the signing bonus; the pick value is if you were to auction the pick, whereas you'd still have to pay the bonus to the player after you bought the pick.

A lot of the players we're evaluating in the minors are either close to 18 (high school draftee age) or 21 (college draftee age), so we can make age-based, apples-to-apples comparisons between a minor leaguer in question and someone who was either just drafted or who is about to be, as a way of gauging what their FV should be. We think a lot of public-facing prospect work underrates young, Latin American talent that compares favorably to domestic amateur talent just because we don't have as long a history of scouting them. A 17-year-old high school kid touching 95 at Area Codes is a big deal, while a similar talent in the AZL does not get the same fanfare. There are hundreds of scouts critically watching a teenage pitcher's handful of showcase outings, while there's often just a handful at an AZL or GCL game, and some teams are completely absent from all outings for that team. Thinking about comparing players in this way helps us to correct that in our work.

More evidence supporting this can be seen in any trade that involves a one-for-one, compensatory-pick-for-player swap. The Brewers traded a comp pick (at the time of the trade the pick's exact spot was not yet known, due to free agent compensation picks ahead of it) that was going to be close to the 40th overall pick in the draft for lefty reliever Alex Claudio. The 40th overall pick is typically a 45 FV type player that will take a long time to mature into a big leaguer. Alex Claudio is a middle reliever (40) who, similar to the Poche example, is funky in a way that makes him a little better than that (40+), and the little gap in Claudio's FV versus the pick's expected FV can be explained by the time/proximity/risk component. Trades like this reinforce using the draft as a barometer for FVing pro prospects when they're age-appropriate to do so.

DURING THE FIRST DAY OF Kiley's first job in baseball—interning in baseball operations with the Yankees—one of the first things he saw was farm director Pat Roessler's dry erase board. They were introduced and Kiley asked what all the words on the board were. Roessler said they had just had meetings where the staff decided they needed to clearly define what makeup was, instead of everyone referring to slightly different things. All kinds of phrases like "work ethic," "competitiveness," and "aptitude" were on the board.

Near the end of that summer, Kiley was back in Roessler's office and he asked what came of that project, since there'd been a summer worth of player development meetings that he didn't attend, where he assumed this was hashed out.

"We scrapped it," Roessler said. "Nobody could agree on anything."

When Kiley worked for the Pirates, they also tried to work around the eyewash of just referring to makeup as "good" when it's really average, or liking a kid's personality and making it sound like that stands for other aspects of makeup. In draft meetings, instead of saying the word "makeup," the scouts would all say the word "buffalo." Then–scouting director Greg Smith's idea was that by changing the word you had to stop and think about it before just hand-waving all kinds of different qualities into the catchall of "good makeup."

It struck Kiley as an unusual, but a possibly successful idea. He was warned before his first meeting what that word meant, so he wouldn't be confused. He asked his boss, Pirates analytics head Dan Fox, what he thought of it, and Fox suggested Kiley sit through a day of draft meetings and then decide for himself.

During that day, Kiley heard the phrase "he's got good buffalo" said off-handedly with no supporting information or follow-up questions so many times that he lost track. Before the end of the first day of draft meetings, most of the front office people would roll their eyes every time "buffalo" was uttered by a scout.

Some teams, typically the most progressive ones, don't think makeup is important, likely because an analysis showed that the grades their scouts put on various aspects of makeup weren't predictive. We've been told that teams such as this think the instances when makeup predicts an outcome that scouting or analytics wouldn't predict are neutralized or even outweighed by times makeup grades would get you off of a player that you'd otherwise select.

It's hard enough to put a grade on makeup, and it's even more difficult to consider the context beyond the grade (for instance, different scales from each scout). It can be simpler to conclude that makeup is simply not a predictive number and analysis of this type is overrated. However, if you have lower-quality, less-motivated scouts that are constantly turning over, then there probably isn't anything to find, even deep in the makeup grades.

Makeup is broadly defined as the mental qualities of a player that influence his performance and development. For us, it's the factor you consider after coming to an FV decision for on-field purposes, to adjust things up or down. We break makeup into categories to separate similar qualities and avoid hand-waving over dozens of characteristics. You can use scouting grades/terms on them to characterize them in a standardized way:

- On-Field Makeup: competitiveness, aggressiveness, leadership, etc.—relating to how they handle tough situations on the field during a game
- Clubhouse Makeup: accountability, teamwork, work ethic, etc.—relating to how they handle themselves during practice, in the clubhouse, and in other team-related activities that aren't a game
- Off-Field Makeup: punctuality, dedication, responsibility, etc.—relating to how they conduct themselves on their own time, both in terms of staying out of trouble, but also staying on top of training when it isn't a team activity

Nick Swisher was known throughout his career as a good makeup guy, a guy that's good for the clubhouse. He was mostly on winning teams, but we've been told that his rah-rah-type demeanor really wore on teammates when he was playing on a losing team. Swisher had plus on-field and off-field makeup and plus-clubhouse makeup on good teams, but well below average on bad teams; call his clubhouse makeup average on balance.

Elijah Dukes was an intense competitor on the field, at least above average in that respect, and we haven't heard anything negative about his clubhouse makeup (though some negative stuff wouldn't shock us), but he's a stone-cold 20 in off-field makeup, with multiple arrests and truly terrible decision-making, including accusations of making teammates less dedicated to the team due to his influence.

A lot of weaker examples of various early-career hotshot prospects come to mind for the third category, of on-field makeup that lags behind the other two. When a much-ballyhooed first-round pick starting pitcher from a well-off family sails through the minors, makes the big leagues, and then has a start for a last-place team where his defense makes three errors in the first inning, you may see bad body language, showing up teammates, and the like. A 30-year-old veteran with plus on-field makeup may be just as pissed about the outcomes, but will wear it, knowing he will be the goat in due time.

While this construct makes it easier to categorize the disparate aspects considered, that doesn't mean this process is easy. For the clubs that value makeup and tend to have more continuity with more experienced scouts that have a robust track record, we think it makes sense to weigh it situationally.

Former Braves scouting director Brian Bridges gave it weight, and he has a similar idea to us: "Take the bad makeup guys out of your mix. Take the remaining guys, put them in tiers based on talent, and then rank them within the tier based on the makeup."

Once you've reached a certain threshold of talent, makeup is the intangible thing that often defines careers. We think if you had 100 percent perfect foreknowledge of pitcher health, the hit tool, and makeup, it would eliminate over 90 percent of busts from scouting. We haven't yet figured out the first two things, but we can get a pretty good idea on the third one if we've got the right people advising us. It can often sound, to the most objective thinkers, like revisionist history or cherry-picking stories from guys that worked out, but we think there's more to it than that.

Bridges instantly recalled the example of good makeup that came to mind back from when he was an area scout: Craig Kimbrel.

In 2008, Kimbrel was at Turner Field after having been drafted and agreed to terms as a third-round pick, to take in a Braves-Phillies matchup. Brad Lidge came into the game for the Phillies, arguably the best contemporary example for Kimbrel of his style of pitching: a high-octane fastball-dominant closer with a hellacious breaking ball.

Lidge strikes out the first two batters he faces while Kimbrel watches, sitting with Bridges and part-time scout (now area scout) Hugh Buchanan, known as Coach Buck. "I'm ready to go. I want to be better than him," Kimbrel said to the scouts, referring to Lidge. After the game, all three of them are in the service level walking out of the stadium and Bridges asked Kimbrel if he knows where Danville, Virginia (the Braves Appalachian League affiliate where Kimbrel's career would start) is: "Nope, but I have a map."

Bridges explains what he walked away from that game knowing about Kimbrel: "He was taking responsibility before he had signed his contract. He was motivated by just watching a star reliever, the kind of guy he wanted to be. Motivation, independence, he was driven, clearly he had the ability already. It wasn't surprising to see his career take off. You have to listen to the indicators."

It was more subtle with Alex Wood, a pitcher with a herky-jerky delivery whom the Braves picked in the second round out of the University of Georgia.

"You're not drawing that delivery up," Bridges said. "No delivery expert is picking that guy. When I met with the player, I said, 'Alex, why should I draft you? You've made improvements, but the delivery is still ehh.' And he said, 'Yes, sir, I hear that. I changed my arm angle myself, made the delivery adjustments myself.' It was clear from that and the rest of the conversation that he was a mature baseball mind. Going into the meeting, I didn't know what I had, but I liked the way the ball crossed the plate and the kid was more special than the pitcher. The makeup was there.

"J.J. Hoover was another classic case. In High-A, our farm director, Kurt Kemp [current Padres national crosschecker] was having J.J. make some adjustments. J.J. told him he didn't mind doing it, but can Kurt just do one at a time, because J.J. couldn't handle doing four or five at a time. Kurt slowed it down and J.J. made the big leagues a few years later. His good makeup was knowing when to speak up, knowing his limitations, but knowing he'd figure things out. Other guys on that team were just as good talent-wise and the on-field makeup was similar. There's so much anxiety and negative talk around failure.

"Mike Minor is another one. On-field, that guy will rip your head off. Off-field, he's a little misunderstood, soft spoken, not a rah-rah guy. He'll take full responsibility for himself and he competes. He won't be looking side to side with bad body language waiting for somebody to take him out when he's in a jam. Body language can tell you a lot.

"I don't know where Austin Riley's career will go. His mom told me at a game that he'll do whatever it takes to get to the big leagues. He'll catch, he'll do anything. It tells me what kind of kid he is. Moms don't lie. Dads can look at it a different way. I watched him. You can't ignore the things you don't want to hear as a scout. Instead of evaluations from the other side of the fence, you could get too close to the player and find reasons to talk yourself into it. We scout them so much, more than we should, we start seeing warts, picking at big leaguers."

There's a player Kiley reminds Bridges about, a high school player that Bridges liked for a draft they both worked on, but Bridges eventually got off of him. "I really liked the kid. The swing and miss bothered me, saw him hit well all summer, wasn't gonna back off him from a couple bad games in the spring. But eventually I gave in. You gotta listen to the people you trust and they all didn't see it. It looks like they were right."

We've both seen players where you can tell a guy has plus makeup just by watching him on the field in the scout seats and having no other information.

The body language, interaction with his teammates, how polished his game is, how good the internal clock is; it can be obvious pretty quickly. Bridges had one of those come to mind too: "[Astros 3B Alex] Bregman was easy to see. You'd miss on him as a shortstop because he isn't a runner, but I'm not betting against that guy. If you get him out, he's gonna grind you out the next time, get on base, and try to beat you again. It's fascinating."

"You can see it with Milwaukee. [Lorenzo] Cain, I remember him in JC. Doug Reynolds, the scout who signed him, would throw him BP when he wanted extra. Lorenzo would work camps. Whenever he mentioned it, Cain showed up. Moustakas is a winner, a grinder, a gamer. Yelich can't live without the game. They have these types of guys with the talent and the makeup, no wonder they're having success."

You can probably see some similarities here—maturity, assertiveness, confidence—but wonder if this is something you can predict. If makeup is the x-factor scouts believe it is, if it isn't predictable in some way, then it still doesn't really matter.

Well, sometimes it changes, or more often, the underlying issues are forced out when a new level of stress presents itself. "Phil Niekro told me about makeup changing at every level, that you've gotta get close to it. Him and his brother have over 40 years in the big leagues, but Phil says lots of guys come into the big league clubhouse and just couldn't get comfortable in their own skin to play at that level. Some have it within them, but maybe you have to tease it out."

Good luck solving this fickle mistress in less than a lifetime.

STAN MEEK IS CURRENTLY THE Marlins special assistant to the president of baseball operations, but he ran the drafts as amateur scouting director for the Fish from 2002 to 2017, landing Giancarlo Stanton, Christian Yelich, and José Fernández, among others.

"This is my oddest scouting story for sure," Meek told us. "I mean, drafting Stanton was an odd one too, because he didn't make any contact in high school, but this one was the oddest."

Meek lives in Norman, Oklahoma, near the campus of the University of Oklahoma, where he played baseball collegiately. In 2009, he was watching the 5A Oklahoma High School Football State Championship game on TV. He recalls a quarterback standing out, rushing a career-high 42 times for 125 yards in his last high school game, en route to the 10th state title for Carl

Albert High School. This wasn't anything new for the star player, who had set a career high with 40 carries two weeks prior in another playoff game. He also graduated as the leading passer in school history.

Meek filed it away when the commentators mentioned that the QB has a baseball scholarship to Oklahoma State. "He was a pretty good athlete and we had a new Oklahoma area guy that year. I moved our previous one to South Texas, so I passed [the QB's] name to the new area guy as a name to check in on in the spring. I hadn't heard of [the player] before that, he didn't play in any showcases.

"Early in March, our new area guy, Steve Taylor, calls me on a Sunday, telling me he's got a game for me tomorrow, getting his first look at [the QB]. I had no idea what I was doing that day, hadn't scheduled a game. Honestly, I was trying to catch a day at home; Mondays are usually pretty slow. It's only a 20-minute drive from my house to Carl Albert High School, so this was the next best thing."

For a higher-profile school playing a game on a Monday, just outside Oklahoma City, a place a lot of scouts live that cover this area, Meek remembers there was a surprisingly light scout attendance that day: zero other scouts. Meek and Taylor had the right game, getting their first in-person look at two-time All-Star and 2019 Gold Glover J.T. Realmuto.

"We walk up to the coach and he's like, 'You're here to see J.T.? Oh, it's a bad day for that. He's catching for us today. Sorry guys.'" The scheduled pitcher's arm was tender, the normal catcher was now pitching, and Realmuto moved from shortstop to catcher to take one for the team. Meek is pretty sure this was the only game Realmuto caught in his high school career.

The first hitter on the opposing team walks, then on the second pitch to the second batter, the runner tries to steal. "J.T. had no idea what to do. His feet were together, knees were out, it was a really bad setup. But his hands and arm and feet were crazy good. That first throw it was a 65 arm and threw the guy out."

This is when it's worth noting that the reason Taylor suggested this game for Meek to attend and for their first look at Realmuto is because they were facing Deer Creek High School. The opposing pitcher was a junior that Taylor had heard had a good arm, so he'd be a good one to see Realmuto face. The pitcher was future 44th overall pick in 2011, current Detroit Tigers pitcher Michael Fulmer. Deer Creek's best hitter was also a junior, named Brian Anderson. Anderson was drafted by the Marlins out of Arkansas in the third round three years later. He was the best player on the 2019 Marlins by

WAR and was the second best on the 2018 team as a rookie, behind only Realmuto.

In Realmuto's first at-bat, Meek recalls that he hit the second fastball he saw from Fulmer over the batter's eye, over 400 feet. "So now my head is spinning." In his next at-bat, Realmuto hits a grounder in the hole to shortstop and with a full swing, no jailbreak (no cheating out of the box that artificially juices the run time), he runs a 4.18; a hair better than a 60-grade run time. "Now I'm like, *'What in the world?'*"

"So we go over to the coach of the football team, Gary Rose, to ask about J.T. Gary has won eight state titles at this point and Steve [Taylor] grew up with him. He asks what we want to know and I say, 'Tell me who he is.' At this point, it's gotta be bad, right?" Not so fast, my friend. "Gary tells us he's sent guys to OU, Texas, and Arkansas and he's never had a kid as good as this one. And I'm thinking to myself, 'This can't all be true.'

"I ask Gary if he's ever timed him before, how fast is he? He says, 'We play all the inner-city schools and, if he turns the corner, no one catches him.' He goes on to say he's also the point guard on the basketball team and is one of the better athletes they've ever had at the school." Rose also told them that Realmuto's uncle is the Oklahoma State wrestling coach, two-time NCAA National Champion, four-time World Champion, and two-time Olympic gold medalist John Smith, whom Meek called, "The toughest guy you've ever seen." Realmuto wrestled until high school, until basketball, football, and baseball filled up his sporting dance card.

At this point, Meek is still waiting to find the wart with Realmuto. Things are going way too well. "We go talk to J.T. after the game and ask him if he'd consider catching. He tells us without hesitation: 'Yeah, whatever gets me to the big leagues.'"

Now you may be wondering how Stan handles the situation now. He's stumbled into a Disney movie in his backyard. He's thinking how does he make sure he gets this player? How does he make sure no one else gets him? How does he make sure no one else even knows about him? If Stan stumbled into him on a longshot and he lives nearby, there can't be many scouts that even have this guy on a list to maybe get around to if they have time.

"No one was there. I told Steve, 'You don't come back and I'm not coming back. It's March, no one will know we were here or even know he's caught. We'll call him back the day before the draft.'"

We're not sure we could hold back and not call or scout the kid for another three months, but that's what the Marlins did. They called the day before the draft and he told them he had a pre-draft workout for the Blue Jays in Fort Smith, Arkansas, and he "hit some line drives, nothing great," and casually mentioned that he ran a 6.5 in the 60, another at least plus run time. But the Jays hadn't had any discussions with Realmuto after the workout, so the Marlins were satisfied they didn't have any competition.

"So we're at the draft and I have no idea where to take the guy. We check in with him and no one has called him on draft day." In the third round, a scout tells Meek not to lose sight of Realmuto and Stan responds that no teams had called him yet, that it was still too early.

Stan's East Coast crosschecker Matt Haas weighed in with his take: "Stan, if you lose this guy, you're gonna jump off a building."

After the Marlins picked Realmuto in the third round, Meek heard Haas say into his phone, "Don't worry, it's not your problem." It was a rival scout calling Haas to tell him the Marlins were out of their mind and Realmuto was a terrible player. Meek recalls checking with friends around the game after the pick and hearing many teams didn't even have Realmuto turned in as a draftable player, because they didn't know about him. He only played summer legion ball instead of going to heavily scouted showcases.

There was still plenty of work to do for Realmuto in pro ball. "Tim Cossins [the Marlins catching coordinator] taught him to catch on a two-by-four to teach him balance." Meek recalls advice from a fellow scouting director who was also a minor league teammate and a former catcher, R.J. Harrison of the Rays. "I ask him what to do if I'm converting a guy to catching. He tells me to forget tools, he'd better have great makeup. The transition to catcher is really tough, it's a grind, it's the whole game."

Kiley had asked Meek if he had a story about scouting a player where makeup was key and this is the story he told. "It's like a movie, really. I knew nothing about him until we walked into the park that day. Anyone would do what I did if they saw what I saw. I was trying to catch a day at home and this is 20 minutes from my house. Seems a little too neat. He won a Gold Glove! Can you believe that? Steve and I still text about it."

SOMETIMES THINGS JUST FALL IN your lap, almost suspiciously easy. Other times, you go to a game and see almost the opposite of what you were expecting, then the work of reconciling the two begins.

In April 2012, Kiley was working for Keith Law at ESPN, covering mostly the draft, while between team jobs. He was in Alabama, staying with family, after driving through the night from a high-profile Florida-LSU game (eventual top 10 picks Kevin Gausman and Mike Zunino were the headliners), set to go to Tuscaloosa to see a Sunday Auburn-Alabama game. Law told Kiley that there was a high school doubleheader on Saturday in Tuscaloosa that he should see if he could squeeze it in.

The top quarterback recruit in the country, per ESPN and Rivals, was also a notable two-way baseball prospect as an outfielder and pitcher: Jameis Winston. His Birmingham-based high school had a doubleheader against a school in Tuscaloosa, so Kiley would have a chance to see Winston hit and play the outfield, then pitch in Game 2.

Winston was regarded as a football prospect first and foremost, and thus almost unsignable, despite looking like an early-round baseball talent as an underclassman. Winston had just been featured on ESPN's *Elite 11* documentary series with ESPN commentator Trent Dilfer peppering him with compliments during a one-on-one near the end of the 2011 elite quarterback camp.

"I don't have a lot to say to you," Dilfer said. "You're an incredible kid. You're funny, you're comfortable in your own skin, you're a leader, you're smart as a whip. You're one of the smartest kids I've ever been around; nobody learned faster… that's a gift, dude. Everybody is gonna talk about how gifted this is [touches Winston's arm] and how fast you are and I've seen your moves and how great you throw and you're tough and you pitch fast and that's great, it's awesome. This [points to his own head] is special. I mean, you are really smart."

While doing interviews at the Super Bowl in 2013, Dilfer doubled down, before Winston had even played a collegiate snap: "I know what's coming. I know the kid at Florida State, Jameis Winston, will be an absolute rock star. He'll be the first pick of the draft if the first pick goes to a team that wants to run the pistol, zone-read, have a passer. He's that kind of kid."

Winston's on-field football career has been a success, losing one game in two years as the starting QB for Florida State, winning a national championship, making the College Football Playoff the next year, and going first overall in the draft as Dilfer predicted, making $46 million through the 2019 season. He also pitched and DH'd at Florida State, but was never more than a fourth- or fifth-round baseball talent (as a righty relief pitcher who touched 95 mph) at best while in college, nowhere near good enough to try to entice him away from football.

Kiley hadn't seen Winston play baseball before but his exact skill level wasn't that important—he was notable for ESPN due to his football talent—so expectations were low and there were predictably only a few scouts there. They all left by the middle of Game 1, clearly just checking in to see if he'd changed at all, maybe to chat with his father, who was very visible, wearing Florida State gear head to toe and the loudest voice in a low-key setting.

Kiley wasn't blown away by Winston. He was told Winston was a plus runner and center-field fit, which he was the year before, but he'd clearly put on weight and was an average-at-best runner. But he couldn't get a good run time since Winston was going half speed most of the game, either due to lack of enthusiasm or waiting for a moment to raise his game amongst a field full of players that weren't Division I college quality.

At the end of Game 1, Kiley wasn't sure what to write. Winston was clearly physical and strong, but he didn't see batting practice and Winston didn't do much in the game. His body language seemed like he either didn't want to be there or wasn't fully engaged in the game and the tools didn't look anywhere close to where they needed to be to draw the kind of seven-figure baseball offers necessary to consider choosing it over football.

Kiley hung around to see Game 2 and see if Winston stood out on the mound, but it was also pretty generic there in terms of pro potential: middling command, 87–90 mph, fringy curveball. After watching that for two innings, Kiley was ready to head out, but he noticed Winston getting visibly frustrated on the mound and wanted to see where this was going. He put away the radar gun and stood behind the open fencing of the dugout of Winston's team, hoping to hear what was being said.

After the third inning ended, Winston came in silently and his teammates and coaches didn't say a word. It was surreal. A parent walked over to Kiley to ask what team he scouted for. Eventually, Kiley asked the parent how they understood this odd dugout silence. "Oh, the kids don't like Jameis, he thinks he's better than them. I mean he's more talented, but he thinks he's *better than them*, you know?" The parent opened up his stance to include other parents milling around within earshot and they all nodded, like this was a baseball team dominated by an unwanted sideshow.

The next inning, Kiley watched Winston intently on the mound, trying to figure out what was going on in Winston's head. After shaking off the catcher a few times, the catcher called time and came out to the mound to talk it over. Once he got within arm's distance of Winston, Winston shoved the catcher, almost knocking him down.

Kiley called Law and told him what happened, unsure how to proceed. Law advised to him to write what happened and put it at the end of the column, behind the other, more notable games for draft purposes, since Winston doesn't seem to be a factor for the draft, but is still notable enough to be mentioned due to his football exploits and baseball potential. Kiley wrote a couple hundred words about his football talent, uneven day in terms of tools and body language, along with a troubling and confusing shove.

Within hours of its publication, Winston's baseball agent reached out to Law, asking for a retraction. Law called Kiley to see what he wanted to do. Kiley told Law he stands behind it and it seemed like the Winston camp was trying to quash any negative press when there basically wasn't any at the time. Kiley knew he had put Law in an awkward position, so he told Law to tell Winston's camp that he had video of the incident.

Kiley didn't have the video, but he had his camera out the whole game and everyone there knew he did, since they were curious what the writer from ESPN was doing. Winston's camp would be much more scared of this video getting out than some words at the end of a baseball draft column behind a paywall in April. It didn't matter that the video didn't exist, because they couldn't take that chance and the idea was powerful enough that Law could use it to tell the agent to let it go.

Law responded to the agent, never heard back, and that was that. Then, a pattern of familiar behavior materialized, compiled by the *Tampa Bay Times*.

April 7, 2012: The aforementioned high school baseball game.

November 25, 2012: Winston engages in two BB gun incidents, with one causing $4,200 in damages to a Tallahassee apartment complex.

December 7, 2012: An FSU student reports being sexually assaulted by a man she later identified as Winston (then an FSU freshman). Winston maintained that the encounter was consensual.

July 2013: A Tallahassee Burger King accuses Winston of stealing soda, but the manager declines to pursue a criminal case against him.

April 30, 2014: Winston is suspended from FSU's baseball team after being cited for shoplifting crab legs from a Publix.

September 20, 2014: Winston, a redshirt sophomore, serves a one-game suspension in a prime-time football game against Clemson after making vulgar remarks on campus.

April 16, 2015: The accuser files a civil suit against Winston from their 2012 encounter. They agree in December 2016 to settle the suit.

January 25, 2016: FSU settles with the accuser, reportedly for $950,000, to drop her Title IX lawsuit.

March 13, 2016: An Uber driver alleges that Winston groped her in the drive-through of a Mexican restaurant in Scottsdale, Arizona. Winston, coming off his rookie season with the Bucs, denies the allegation, which becomes public through a BuzzFeed report in November 2017. The NFL begins investigating.

June 28, 2018: The NFL formally announced that it suspended Winston for three games. It concluded that he violated its conduct policy by "touching the [Uber] driver in an inappropriate and sexual manner without her consent."

When people tell you who they are, listen to them.

CHRIS COGHLAN SIMILARLY LEFT A strong impression on any scout that did the homework. That pesky bit of his on-field performance in his draft year is what got them off the scent.

Meek runs down Coghlan's profile coming off a strong Cape Cod League performance in 2005, where he led the league in batting average. "We'd all seen him on the Cape. This guy could hit. The question was if he could fit at third base. He played there at Ole Miss. Could he play some second base? Maybe outfield? Is there enough power for a corner outfield spot?

"I saw him on the Cape, then saw him early in the spring and he wasn't swinging the bat well after a few of our guys ran in there. The athleticism was okay. [He] never jumped out at you, but always hit. Dan Jennings [Marlins VP of player personnel, later GM and manager] and his son knew Coghlan, had some history with him, knew him personally, knew his story."

Meek learned that Coghlan lost his father in a car wreck in 2001 and had handled great adversity early in his life. He was drafted in the 18th round out of high school by Arizona in 2003 but opted to go to Ole Miss instead of signing.

"I got in there late to see him playing Tennessee. I hated sitting on relievers and it was later in the season and the one I needed didn't throw until Sunday—figures. So I got a whole weekend, three games to watch Coghlan. We had Coghlan in the fifth or sixth round at the time. It's a good lesson about scouting. We try to one-look guys, gotta get going to the next place and be efficient. The intangibles, instincts, how hard he played, feel for the game, it was all strong. He faced a few lefties in the series and handled himself well, stayed on them, it didn't bother him, he beat them up. He was competitive, great instincts on the bases, at the plate, great approach.

"Looking back, everything he did spoke to who he was intellectually as a player. He performed that weekend like he did on the Cape. Not a lot of scouts were there, they'd kinda moved on from him already. [He] had good makeup on him and he was trending up late when people weren't paying close attention."

Meek really moved Coghlan up the board after that weekend, drafting him 36th overall a little over a month later. "We took him good, some guys told us we took him a little too fast."

This isn't where the story ends. Coghlan had a swing flaw to correct, where makeup came into play. "He was a bit of a drifter on the front side. We needed to fix that. Jim Fleming was overseeing scouting and player development at the time. He said he thought he could fix the drift if Coghlan was a worker.... He was receptive, was strong spiritual kid, tough kid because of what he'd dealt with off the field. That was the one thing he needed to change and he did it pretty quickly, and off he went."

Coghlan reached the big leagues in 2009 and won Rookie of the Year—he even got a 10th place MVP vote. But then things were a little uneven the rest of the way. He was more of a role player for the next four years for the Marlins, then was non-tendered and caught on with the Cubs on a minor league deal. He had two more strong seasons for the Cubs before getting his last taste of the big leagues in 2017 and retiring in 2018. In the 30 picks after the Marlins took Coghlan, the only higher career WAR totals were Brett Anderson, Trevor Cahill, and Chris Tillman. The process and result were both top-notch.

Coghlan went viral in fall 2019 on baseball Twitter for a speech he gave to the Ole Miss baseball team about his career. The things that Meek found in researching Coghlan seem to still be present.

Okay I was just released by arguably the worst team in baseball... who's gonna take me? The Cubs call and... send me a minor league invite. I get there and they've got seven outfielders playing over me... this ain't looking good for me. I go to Triple-A... mind you I haven't started a season in Triple-A in five years, this is tough to swallow... Cubs roster isn't that good in 2014. I'm in Des Moines, Iowa... we're playing in the snow... I literally had to make a decision at that point... Am I gonna stay here complaining and sucking my thumb or am I just gonna go prove the whole world wrong?

At that moment is when things changed for me. Next thing you know, I'm in the big leagues… I'm still waiting for my turn to play, I'm only up there because another guy got injured… the whole time, this adopted mindset… "You better not play me, because if you play me, you ain't gonna take me out of the lineup. I ain't gonna let ya. You're gonna have to play me."

They finally give me a shot, bottom of the eighth… I go to pinch-hit for someone and they bring a lefty in… I remember thinking before I walked up there, "I'm gonna make you look good regardless." The guy throws me five or six sliders in a row. I haven't even swung the bat, it's 2-2. The first heater he throws me, I hit an opposite-field homer, we end up winning the game.

I was proud… but that was just the beginning. Bro, I told you you'd better not play me. From that point on, it wasn't long before I was the everyday leadoff hitter… That was the most proud year of my career. It wasn't the Rookie-of-the-Year, hitting-.320, breaking-some-records year. It was the you-suck, get-sent-down-to-Triple-A, we're-gonna-run-out-of-players-before-we-have-to-play-you… then-I-bang-my-way-into-the-lineup [year]. That was my favorite year. That was the most proud year I ever had, because of the adversity that I faced.

OTHER TIMES, THE DIFFERENCES IN the three categories of makeup are stark, like in the Elijah Dukes example. And sometimes it takes a while for them to come to light.

Reds VP of player personnel Chris Buckley has been essentially running or heavily advising both draft and international signings for the team since 2006 after being scouting director for the Blue Jays for years. He may have signed the most high-profile Cuban players of anyone in the 21st century. "I've had a lot of experience with Cuban players. Aroldis Chapman, Raisel Iglesias, José Israel Garcia, Vladimir Gutiérrez, Alfredo Rodriguez, and Yasmani Grandal and Yonder Alonso are both Cuban but came out of U. of Miami," he said.

"Agents and recruiters get high school kids in ninth grade. Scout teams are key for getting makeup, getting a glimpse of an asshole before you make a mistake. Sonny Gray's football team played in four state titles and he carried them there. That can't be 40 makeup, it's impossible. He competes his ass off on the mound and the football stuff makes you feel even better about it." Even with much more information, the signal can get murky: "Craig Biggio's psychological profiles weren't that strong, but how can you watch that guy play and question him?"

Buckley continued, "When you give Mark Teixeira $6 million out of Georgia Tech, there's a good chance he's had some money before. With Cuban players, they're coming from a communist country, they haven't had money, it's a different baseball culture, societal differences. They don't see high-level pitching except in the WBC. José Abreu is probably the one that's transitioned the best. The whole background really complicates the evaluation in a number of ways. They tend to not trust people and how can you blame them?"

Scouting the Cuban players' talent isn't always straightforward, either. "Puig was tough because his first time traveling was in Holland, then he defects. You know his showcase is gonna be great, 60 run, 80 raw, 80 arm, you're gonna like it. May see some things in the game you don't like, like running a 4.6 to first base, a right turn to the dugout, but there's no way you won't love his workout. You don't get to see into his head when it's just a workout, see the variance. When you get a meeting with him and his camp in an apartment, what's he gonna say in the meeting? 'I'm an axe murderer?'

"We saw [Raisel] Iglesias in Mexico and Haiti, lots with the Cuban national team. The front office can get you tons of video so you don't have to live and die with the open workout. Chapman [right field] and Iglesias [shortstop] both converted to the mound because they had huge arms and couldn't hit. Chapman was a late-inning guy on the junior and senior Cuban teams and I'm watching the video thinking, 'Man, this guy can do anything.' Both of them are 80 athletes.

"If you're domestic director and there's a weird situation, like Bobby Jenks flunked out of school in Idaho, you try to send people that can handle unique situations. You can't send a first-year guy to see Iglesias in Haiti or [Yoán] Moncada in Guatemala. What kind of workout can I set up at my academy in April and bring them in? Where can I find pitchers that aren't on our tight workload to pitch to guys to get a better look at a hitter? We brought pro pitchers in to pitch to [José Israel] Garcia, brought some to Panama in April to throw to [Yulieski] Gurriel. With a reliever in the draft, you chase him for three days, get a seven-pitch look, and put in a limited look report. You always want to avoid that situation, in any market."

We've both heard of multiple instances where Cuban players specifically are treated differently early in pro ball. It's common for teams to avoid sending them to cold-weather locales (the Midwest League specifically) to start their pro career, often when they haven't played a competitive game in almost two years due to the defection and workout process. Buckley had dealt with that and even with smaller instances: "It took [Vladimir] Gutierrez a while to get used to the new ball and to just be aggressive on the mound."

That brings us to Aroldis Chapman. "There's a car waiting for him outside the stadium, the day he's defecting. He's pitching in the WBC in San Diego, needs to pitch the best game of his life. When the Cuban national team travels, there's 100 scouts there, every time. Who pitches this way? What domestic pitcher has to deal with any of that?" Think back to the José Fernández story in the draft chapter; his background in Cuba and his defection were stressors that made his makeup obvious at an early stage, in a way domestic players would never be stressed.

"We had nine veteran scouts see [Chapman] at various times. Eighteen years was the least experience one of them had. They're all saying they've never seen anything like this, never seen this kind of athlete, velocity this easy. The closest comp was Brien Taylor."

Taylor, selected by the Yankees in 1991, is one of only three high school pitchers to ever be drafted No. 1 overall. His career was derailed by injuries before he could reach the big leagues, but he was the No. 1 prospect in the game by *Baseball America* a year later. He's still the player that many scouts point to as the best prospect they've ever seen to not become a star in the big leagues.

Now back to scouting Chapman: "We had two scouts at the game, [Chapman] argued with the umpire on some borderline pitches and then some people thought this guy has bad makeup. You've gotta consider the context he's in, the pressure." The Reds signed then-21-year-old Chapman to a six-year, $30.25 million deal in January 2010 after that WBC appearance in March 2009; he's made six All-Star teams.

This brings us to the incident most of you are thinking of now. This is how the AP described it:

> According to a police report, Chapman's girlfriend, 22-year-old Cristina Barnea, told police he pushed her, put his hands around her neck, and choked her during an argument. Chapman said there was an argument but that he was pushed down by Barnea's brother. Chapman

said he eventually got a handgun and fired eight shots into a wall and window while locked in his garage.... A prosecutor declined to charge Chapman due to conflicting accounts and insufficient evidence, which made a conviction unlikely.

The Dodgers were on the verge of trading for Chapman when this happened and walked away from the deal. The Yankees ultimately stepped in, securing Chapman for a return most felt was well below his pre-incident market value.

This brings us back to separating the three kinds of makeup. Clearly this incident, just this moment alone, speaks to very poor off-field makeup. But the other two components of makeup appear to be fine, maybe even above average from what we can gather. Chapman's off-field makeup, wanting though it appears to be, doesn't seem to have affected his on-field performance in the way you'd expect a lack of competitiveness or work ethic to. So while there is no dismissing or minimizing that moment, and the decisions that led to it, a signing scout signing off on Chapman's makeup at age 21 would technically be the "right call," allowing a GM to treat the talent as he sees it.

Writing that sentence churned our stomachs, but there have been plenty of Hall of Famers with good on-field and clubhouse makeup who were bad actors away from the field. If you're inclined to give the benefit of the doubt to players who have come from tough backgrounds, and thus might have had violence modeled in their family systems, where is that line? Those life experiences aren't an excuse for choices like this, even as they might help to explain their origins. If you had perfect makeup foreknowledge, but no special foreknowledge of on-field performance, you'd likely not draft or sign those future All-Stars and Hall of Famers based on their off-the-field actions, and missing on a couple of those guys is enough to get a scout fired. Makeup can put scouts in that impossible situation. You could be choosing between taking a principled stand and keeping your job, all based on a guess at what someone's future character holds. Sometimes, there is no easy answer.

THE ADVICE PHIL NIEKRO GAVE Brian Bridges, about makeup changing? That happens sometimes, or it can appear to, if you aren't paying close attention.

Javier Báez was the ninth overall pick in the 2011 Draft by the Chicago Cubs out of Arlington Country Day High School in Jacksonville, Florida. You probably know who he is if you're reading this. He's one of the best players in the game and does it with a flair and energy that's infectious. He's one of those players that's universally beloved. He was born in Puerto Rico, but moved to Jacksonville in 2004.

This was not the case earlier in his career. Arlington Country Day wasn't a part of the FHSAA, the governing body of Florida high school sports, so they couldn't play against high schools that were. This meant oddly scheduled barnstorming-type trips to play baseball academy teams and out-of-state opponents or in tournaments. We still haven't been able to track down a scout that was at the game, but we've heard a number of second-hand stories about a legendary game that ACD played in Puerto Rico in the spring of 2011.

The accounts all differ enough that it isn't clear exactly what happened, but that's the fun part of legends. The part that they agree on is that it was a boisterous crowd, due to Báez being the star player in the game and a native son, but also the opponent. Báez was having fun with the crowd, chirping and bickering back and forth throughout the game. Báez hit a pivotal home run late in the game to seal the win and the crowd explodes with emotion. Everyone seems to agree that Báez emphatically jumped on home plate to punctuate the homer, some people say he playfully threw up double middle fingers at one point when he ran around the bases. You can see how some scouts in attendance could perceive that as a playful, loose player having fun in the moment, if a bit juvenile, while other scouts would see this as a disqualifying set of antics. Whether it happened or not, scouts generally perceived Báez as though it did, since this story is well-known and oft-repeated, fair or not.

A couple years after he signed, Kiley was told something more concerning by a national crosschecker who had just come from Puerto Rico. He went in the winter to see a draft-eligible prospect workout indoors and Báez happened to be there at the time. The scout said he was immediately put off by Báez's demeanor and was legitimately scared when he heard how and what Báez was saying in a series of contentious phone calls while in the facility. The scout concluded by saying that he thought some of those qualities reminded him of things he had read recently about Aaron Hernandez, the NFL player convicted of murder.

Kiley had also recently scouted Báez late in the 2012 season and his hitting mechanics were wilder than anything he or any of the other scouts at the game had ever seen. The tip of his bat was pointing at the pitcher at release. Báez has 80 bat speed and can make something like this work better than anyone else, similar to Gary Sheffield's famous swing. But a pattern was developing from the high school home run trot story to the off-season scout account to his hitting mechanics, where Báez just seemed like a wild card to even a majority of professional evaluators that were somewhat removed from personally knowing him.

To those who knew Báez best and had done all of the homework, they were never worried. Tim Wilken was the scouting director for the Cubs that year: "His love for his sister was paramount. She was with him everywhere, at every stop in the minor leagues, in the big leagues she was at his first game, when he hit the homer. This probably made him more of a complete person. He didn't share it with me but I knew how diligent he was in taking care of her. There might have been some immaturity in there—actually I'm sure there was. It got erased over time."

In a 2015 *Chicago Tribune* article, Marc Gonzales and Colleen Mastony traced Báez's relationship with his sister:

> He plays with a glove embroidered with her name.
>
> Because every catch Chicago Cubs infielder Javier Báez makes, every hit and home run, is for his sister, Noely, who was 21 when she died in April from complications related to spina bifida.
>
> "Her dream was for Javy to make it to the pros," says their older brother, Gadiel, 24. "Javy's dream was to make it to the pros and give her everything she ever needed."
>
> From the time they were children, Noely watched her big brother Javier play baseball. No matter if he got a hit or struck out, she always cheered wildly.
>
> [...] When he was trying out for a local peewee baseball team in the mid-1990s, a coach stepped forward to show him how to hit.
>
> According to family lore, Javier—then just a 4-year-old—waved the coach away. I don't need help, the preschooler told the coach.
>
> Noely, the family's youngest, wasn't expected to live for more than a few hours after her birth. "The doctors said she wasn't going to make it for 24 hours. Two days later, they said she's not going to make it for a week," recalled Gadiel. But the baby survived and grew into a determined girl. "She was a warrior," recalled Gadiel. She refused to allow anyone to push her wheelchair and said she could get around by herself.

[...] When he was seven years old, their mother overheard him telling Noely: "If God would let me, I would switch legs with you, so you could walk."

In 2004, their father, Angel, a lawn worker, died after falling in the bathroom and hitting his head. Their mom, Nelly, kept the family afloat by selling cakes from their home and eventually decided to move the kids to Jacksonville, Florida, in search of better medical care for Noely.

[...] When the Cubs announced in the first round that they had selected Báez as the No. 9 pick, the crowd erupted with raucous cheers that seemed to shake the house. The deal would come with a $2.6 million signing bonus.

Báez, then an 18-year-old high school senior, turned to his sister and said: "You will never have to worry again."

Over the next few years, he kept his promise. He bought a new house for his mother and Noely and gave them a minivan, customized with a wheelchair ramp. The family traveled around the country to watch him play minor league ball.

In August 2014, he made his Major League debut against the Colorado Rockies in Denver. In the 12th inning, he hit a game-winning home run and, as he rounded the bases, he pointed to Noely and his family in the stands.

Those concerns clubs had from the beginning of this section seem pretty silly now, don't they?

The Cubs area scout for Báez was Tom Clark, the former head coach of Lake City Community College in north Florida, where he had also coached a couple dozen Puerto Rican players over the years, many getting their first experience of mainland baseball under his tutelage, including a few future big leaguers. "My mind was put to rest when Tommy did his evaluation and the work at Javy's place," Wilken said. "You hear a lot of stuff [about Báez]. It may or may not be true. When Tommy told me he thought the guy would be okay, that was good enough for me.

"I had made my mind up that if he got there, we'd take him, unless something unforeseen like [Gerrit] Cole or [Anthony] Rendon got to us, which was very unlikely."

Then we asked what Wilken would've done if Clark didn't sign off on Báez's makeup: "Certainly would've made me pause, would have to reevaluate for sure. The in-game skills were so good, he was so well-rounded, it would've been tough to swallow, because I was pretty locked in on him. It would've been a tough one."

What Wilken is hinting at here is he had already subconsciously signed off on the makeup because the on-field makeup—not the antics in Puerto Rico, but his feel for the game, how he played the game, how his teammates responded to him—was obvious.

Bridges saw the same thing: "People thought [Báez] was a turd or a knucklehead. He was darn competitive. He could've been an All-Star catcher. He never missed games, he was always there, always in the middle of the action. That stuff doesn't change, you could tell he was driven internally to be good."

When we were talking about Cuban players, Báez naturally came up as another example for Buckley of a bad habit some scouts have: "I just saw the Cubs big league team. [Báez is] a 70 makeup guy, some might say 80. People confuse immaturity with bad makeup. Some scouts don't want to like players. People did that to [Bryce] Harper too."

We've been told by multiple sources that the two teams picking behind the Nationals in 2010, the Pirates and Orioles, both would have taken Jameson Taillon, the eventual second overall pick (the third pick was Manny Machado), over Harper because they didn't like Harper's personality and makeup. And we heard some stories at the time, some from those two clubs, that made Harper sound like a schoolyard bully in some social settings.

You're liable to make some colossal mistakes if you get a lazy doing makeup homework, or if you don't value it at all.

WHEN HE WORKED FOR THE Yankees in Tampa, Kiley remembers a time when Johnny Damon was rehabbing an injury at the facility and playing in the GCL for a few days. He did the typical big leaguer things of buying the spread for the whole building and advised younger players that approached him.

Kiley was in the office and his boss stepped out to go listen when he was told Damon would be addressing the GCL club formally now that his last game was over. Kiley's boss came back looking annoyed, eventually spilling the beans on what happened. "Well it was great at first, some pretty typical big leaguer advice, then Johnny really sold it, had everybody lean in for the best advice he can give them, and he told them to 'get on the 40-man roster because then MLB can't suspend you for smoking weed.'"

WE HAVE TROUBLE BALANCING MAKEUP for our rankings because we don't get the level of access that teams get to these players. We have to trust what they tell us about in-home meetings and what they learn from scout teams. We can see on the field when the obvious, Bregman-like or Baez-like makeup guys are there and most players have average makeup, or close to it, but we're always going to miss guys because of this lack of information. We currently are higher than other publications on Twins prospect Royce Lewis, who had a bad 2019 regular season statistically, for this precise reason.

How should you, someone who works in baseball, or your favorite team, handle makeup as a part of decision-making? We've chosen to present it as a series of fables on the topic, because we both don't have a clear answer and we don't know if there even is a correct one.

CHAPTER 11

Everybody Wants a Job in Baseball (But Nobody Wants to Die)

Rod Fridley clamored to stay in the sun on what, for Phoenix, was a chilly, early-December Saturday morning, his advanced age no doubt intensifying his earthly discomfort. The sun seemed to rise skyward more slowly than usual, casting long shadows across the browning grass of a high school baseball field at the north end of the city.

Baseball fields are usually built facing the northeast so that, as most games begin in the evening, the sun is at a place in the westward sky where it can do the least amount of damage to spectators and players. At just before 8:00 AM, however, if you want to head down the third-base line and look at hitting and pitching mechanics like Rod Fridley is apt to do, your retinas are right in its crosshairs. It matters not for Fridley, whose eyelids sag down from his brow after decades of squinting into the glare, providing him with a sort of natural, Darwinian, ocular shade. His forehead wrinkled beneath a cap he probably bought during the Clinton administration, Fridley wears a permanent frown, the corners of his mouth having succumbed to gravity over time, his forearms scarred from years in the sun. This is the appearance of a baseball lifer, someone the game has chewed up and spit out several times over. Once near the top of the industry, Fridley now struggles to make ends meet.

GETTING A JOB IN BASEBALL is a goal for tens of thousands of young people in America and plenty of older ones too. The most common desire it to get a baseball operations internship or entry-level full-time job in the city/office of the Major League club, the first real step toward being a decision-maker in baseball ops.

Kiley was fortunate to get started right after *Moneyball* was published in 2003, when unpaid internships were still legal and widespread, so there was a small barrier to entry for the Yankees to give him his first chance working in baseball operations in their Tampa office while he was still in college. Kiley's first role with the Yankees was an unpaid spot created after he bothered a VP and his secretary enough that they pawned him off on other people in the office, until one said they could use some help.

What was supposed to be a couple days a week quickly became every day for the next two summers while he finished college. It didn't end in a full-time job or even an interview for a full-time job with the Yankees. He also didn't get a full-time job with an MLB club for over eight years, but the experience, knowledge, and connections from the summers with the Yankees are what allowed him to stay afloat in the industry as a writer (part-time, during the recession) in the interim. It was mostly luck that all six of his sub-director-level bosses over three summers with the Yankees became more prominent in the industry, including two future general managers, two agents, and two directors.

Luck and timing played a role for Eric too; they're almost always part of the equation. A brand-new Triple-A ballpark opened up in Allentown the same year he was finishing his freshman year of college, and it needed to be stocked with underpaid interns. He was the youngest of the inaugural bunch. He worked there for several years (while working other jobs), doing a variety of tasks around the stadium with declining effectiveness as he focused more and more on what was happening on the field. It was a lot of rubber-bottomed Sportline stopwatches which he anxiously picked apart, mini notebooks and pens left in the pockets of khaki pants that were ruined by the ink in the wash. Then came two seasons at Baseball Info Solutions (also, serendipitously close to his hometown) and various writing gigs, totaling eight years before baseball was his full-time job.

These days, every internship is paid and has a lengthy interview process, usually with hundreds of candidates if it's widely posted, like nearly all openings are, on FanGraphs or TeamWork Online. Summer internships of this type for current college students are rare and irregular, so the best options are usually even lower jobs (work in video for a short-season affiliate, do mindless work for a month or two if you can get into the main office) to raise your profile for the full-season baseball operations internship, which you can hopefully parlay into a full-time job after just one year. Many people with full-time jobs in baseball now had to intern full-time for multiple years; Kiley did a version of this sort of job for three years.

A NATIVE VIRGINIAN, ROD FRIDLEY has been around baseball for over four decades. Along that road, which has become increasingly rocky, he's been a player, coach, scout, and executive. His résumé reads like baseball's version of the Abraham-to-Jesus lineage passage of the Bible. The most successful stretch of that journey came with the Chicago White Sox in the late 1980s. "I was first brought on as an area scout," said Fridley in a bourbon-y drawl that sounds as though it aged in a barrel much farther south of the Mason-Dixon line than Virginia, "and on my own had to cover all of Virginia, West Virginia, Maryland, and Delaware."

Eventually, Fridley's area grew and changed to incorporate the talent-rich Southeast. This included Georgia, where Fridley would pluck future All-Star Mike Cameron out of, as Fridley puts it, "that awful football factory in LaGrange" in the late rounds of the 1991 MLB Draft. It was another feather in the cap of a successful talent evaluation regime in Chicago led by then–scouting director Al Goldis. Jack McDowell, Frank Thomas, Robin Ventura, Ray Durham, Alex Fernandez, Mike Cameron, Bob Wickman: all stars, all drafted while Goldis and his staff (including Fridley) were doing the picking. "I think, years later, Baseball America called our 1990 draft the Draft of the Decade," Fridley remembers. "We got an awful lot of big leaguers out of that draft. Six if I remember correctly."

More than 20 years later on this particular Saturday morning, Fridley isn't at Roadrunner Park in North Phoenix to look at any significant young player, no prospects of note who might be part of some historic draft class. The baseball this morning is bad. He's simply here to stay sharp just in case someone comes calling for work. That hasn't happened for some time now. Fridley has spent a good deal of what little money he has scampering about at various baseball networking havens like the Winter Meetings, or at Fall League games from Surprise to Mesa, as he tries to remind executives with hiring power that he exists. "I'm just tryin' to scratch together enough to get out there," Fridley said without specifying where "there" is, though it's wherever Social Security and his pension will take him, and no further.

Fridley's life has been choppy for a while now. No job, displaced by a fire in his home, seemingly little communication with a family that other people in baseball didn't know he had, even though they've known Fridley for years. He struggles to adjust to new technology and complete modern tasks that seem simple, almost intuitive to younger folks, like checking text messages and finding rosters online. This is the face and mind of someone the game has left behind.

THE PRACTICE OF LOWLY PAID (non-full-time salary, no benefits) internships that require an alternate source of income (usually well-off parents, since internship hours can be excessive) to facilitate the hands-on education, experience, networking opportunities, and leg up on a full-time job is problematic, because the deck is unfairly stacked against economically disadvantaged candidates. For this reason, front offices are overwhelmingly stocked with white males from more economically advantaged or baseball-playing backgrounds. The process favors candidates with industry connections and brand-name educations that read on paper as more promising and impressive than the average candidates if neither has any baseball experience. Those with the resources to intern multiple times and build a track record also rise above the average candidate with little to no experience.

In response to this, MLB has started a development initiative called the Diversity Fellowship Program under the guidance of Tyrone Books, the senior director of their Front Office and Field Staff Diversity Pipeline Program, who was also a scout and executive with the Braves, Indians, and Pirates. MLB maintains a database of recently graduated women and people of color to provide teams with diverse candidates and for spots within MLB itself. Over two-thirds of the 30 big league clubs have a diversity fellowship, though some have a similar program that runs outside of MLB's.

The aim is to proactively give candidates with less inherent advantages a chance to prove themselves so they have a better shot to earn a full-time job and diversify front offices. We both regularly hear from clubs that are hiring full-time positions and want the names of diverse potential candidates, especially women, for jobs in player development or entry-level scouting. Clubs are still having trouble sorting through all the résumés to find the best candidates, particularly those that fall outside the most common backgrounds.

Skills to Get Ahead

We're often asked what teams are looking for on a résumé and what college students or other young candidates should do to position themselves for a potential job. The short answer is to aim to have at least two of the following: programming, Spanish, and on-field experience, in that order. (Of course, having all three would be best, but you can also get in by just being truly elite at one.)

We aren't programming experts, but Kiley did learn SQL on the job while working for a few teams and it greatly increased the types of projects/departments he was able to work on, almost immediately. We're both good with spreadsheets, especially Kiley, who has used Microsoft Excel almost every day of his life since high school, and that's particularly valuable as that's what a lot of interns work in. We spoke with some R&D analysts for clubs and one piece of advice was both consistent and offered early on: learn Excel for manipulating data in a user-friendly way and learn SQL for pulling data out of a database. Going to the next level would include learning Python for web scraping, among other things, and R for advanced data manipulation and plotting.

We're told that's also the order in which you should prioritize learning each application, possibly flipping the last two for more technical roles. If there's a way for you to take classes, either via online bootcamp or in a college class, this skill will only get more important over the years. Learning some baseball-specific skills like understanding Statcast feeds, what each output means, and how to make metrics out of them are valuable, but with clubs you'll encounter lots of datasets that aren't publicly available, so a lot of this knowledge will be learned once you're employed.

We're assuming you're already fluent in baseball, by the way.

If your résumé has you in line for an area scout or coaching job, and you learn how to do—or at the very least intimately understand—things on the data side, it's akin to having an MBA and working in a more corporate job: you have the skills that decision-makers either have or value, in addition to helping you think/go about your job differently than some of your less autodidactic peers. If you get classified as "the coach/scout that knows SQL and understands data," teams will be knocking down your door to offer you a job after the last two off-seasons have seen a number of hitting coaches hired largely due to their tweets about how they use data at smaller college programs. This would be the number one recommendation we have and is also the top thing teams are telling us to advise job seekers to learn. An actual

MBA won't hurt you, but for the cost and opportunity cost, it likely won't change your path that much.

That's not to say social media is always a plus. It isn't, and there are several people who we've mentioned to teams as potential job candidates who are instantly rebuffed because teams have flagged their social media for any number of reasons (same goes for players). Some of them fall into the Justine Sacco column, sometimes team folks just don't want to be around insufferable assholes. The hang is important. We just spoke with a front-office staffer who asked for names for an internship that will take place in the clubhouse, interacting with players and coaches, and made sure to say, "This will be very personality-driven hire," because difficult people become outcasts in a clubhouse much more quickly than a front office. The taste for this varies team to team, the same way some teams are more apt to take players off the draft board for projected/current medical problems ("whacking him on the medical") than others.

FRIDLEY IS REGARDED BY SOME of those who know him (this qualifier is important) as one of, if not the best, scouts they've ever come across. The adjectives thrown around by some of Rod's peers are comically hyperbolic, especially for men who are paid to be abject realists. One of those peers is Dave Perkin, an author and former scout who has known Fridley since 2007. "Rod is the best scout I've ever come across. He's the most knowledgeable, the most thorough. He's the best in the business at breaking down pitching mechanics," says Perkin, who has a bombastic online presence. "I would stop him and ask what he was seeing. Arm action, hip and shoulder separation… Rod has a checklist of things he's looking for and he breaks down every one of them."

Even scouts with a more modern approach to the craft often come away from conversations with Fridley having learned something. In other instances, they hear stories he's told them several times, or have trouble parsing through Fridley's stream-of-consciousness tales, which often include countless, meandering details about people he's worked with throughout his years in the game. They have nothing to do with the thread of the story.

Fridley has some communication issues. His circuitous way of storytelling is endearing but inefficient and often confusing. Forty years of knowledge and experience forces itself out of his mouth like Coke from a shaken bottle and it often results in a verbal stream of consciousness that leaves the listener weary or, as Fridley calls it, "with a tin ear."

In a line of work where communication skills are just as important as one's ability to identify talent, executives don't want to sift through metric tons of verbal and written rubble to extract a few nuggets of gold. Even if Fridley is an excellent scout, he may not be able to delineate his observations in a way that is useful to someone willing to pay him. That could be impeding his ability to find work.

Another issue plaguing Fridley is his unabashed disdain for lots of people he's come across during his years in the game, and this also makes it tough to view him as a reliable narrator for some of his stories. Plenty of scouts, coaches, and analysts who have gone on to achieve resounding success can't escape Fridley's ire, and he's not afraid to say so, even to people he's only just met. He describes many of them as "perfectly nice guys" or "nice enough," before adding a "but" as he begins to rip their baseball acumen to shreds.

BEING FLUENT IN SPANISH IS an easy way to separate yourself for that first job. If you're going for an internship and someone in the office needs to pick up a Latin player from the airport to go to the team doctor, being able to translate eases the situation greatly. For on-field jobs or scouting, especially in the South Florida/Puerto Rico area, this is also key to communicating with a prospect/player, but also allows you the chance to get a leg up by learning more about the player in terms of makeup for your report or better understanding their point of view when coaching them. Like an MBA, this may not greatly change your profile once you have a track record and have been in the game for a decade, but being able to get those first jobs is the only way to get started and this increases your odds.

The last area would be on-field experience, which could entail throwing BP, hitting fungoes, lower-level coaching experience, or any familiarity/experience with using various on-field tech like TrackMan, Rapsodo, BlasMotion, K-Vest, Edgertronic cameras, etc. You can get the first part by volunteering to coach and simply getting reps on the field pitching in around more experienced coaches. You can go for the second part by either doing that work at a program that has some of this tech, like top college programs, or going to a training program that does, like Driveline Baseball (Kent, WA), Cressey Sports Performance (Jupiter, FL, and Hudson, MA), Texas Baseball Ranch (Montgomery, TX), and others.

The last major piece of experience is watching games critically, and writing scouting reports. There are full-time R&D employees who do this to better understand how the data they analyze is collected, and there are young, aspiring scouts who are seeing games to try to build their library. Everyone in baseball needs to understand this process to varying degrees, but if you're aiming to be a scout, this is the main skill you need to work on cultivating, because there's no good replacement for a robust mental scouting library. Context is important, and seeing many different levels and various qualities of baseball helps one understand it. Both of us noticed our scouting ability leveled up considerably when we started mixing amateur ball in with pro, lower-level minor league games in with upper. Chart pitchers, write reports, refine your process for a while before you even start having opinions on players. Eventually, you'll need to be able to compare any two players from a huge pool, and defend it with logic and reason. Writing reports is a key part of this, but it's rare for teams to have a template that their scouts must follow (the proliferation of scout note-taking on tablets may eventually change this) so it's fine to build your own thing slowly.

How to Get a Leg Up

If your strategy is to write cold emails to the entire front office, send them a résumé with no separating skills, no samples of work, and a promise that you'll do anything asked and work hard—these are the table stakes. Literally every single person of the hundreds of applications gunning for that opening are doing at least that much.

Put yourself in the shoes of the person tasked with whittling hundreds of résumés down to a couple dozen they have the capacity to follow up on. They'll pick out the people with the best education (any office job will have plenty of Ivy Leaguers and MBAs or JDs applying), those with the best experience (multiple year-long internships, maybe the director of operations for a college team), and those with the best work samples (usually work that's been published at places like FanGraphs, or is good enough to be). If you don't have one of those, or a very strong personal connection involved, it's going to be hard to even emerge through the first layer of eliminations. It may seem unfair, but how else can they tell that you're different than the hundreds of other people?

When Kiley worked for the Yankees, he was handed a pile of résumés to sort through for an entry-level video job and there were multiple lawyers from New York City that made over $500,000 pleading for any opportunity to leave their job and do something they loved for a team they loved. The position paid something like $30,000. When he asked for guidance, he was told to throw those out. He was told those guys don't really understand what they're signing up for, and if that's really what they want to do, they'll apply again or otherwise get in touch with someone to convince them otherwise. They were too overqualified to even get a call back.

When Kiley was talking to a scouting director in his eight-year odyssey to get a full-time job with a club, he was told that he wasn't quite ready for an area-scout job and then the next year the same guy told him he was overqualified. It was a great compliment since it was clear the director meant it, and he expounded on why he thought that, but it ultimately led to nothing more than a compliment, which was still frustrating.

At one point, most applicants think that their leg up can be that they will memorize the whole rule book. It's a good impulse, to think that you could grit your way into being an expert on something by reading the book like it's a college class (there are stories going around that this is how Brian Cashman began his ascent), but this also isn't realistic these days. Kiley was planning on doing this when he caught on with a team until he was told that countless emails are sent from MLB clarifying, expanding, and amending rules and they aren't compiled and bound in some handy way. This means that outside of employees enforcing the rules at MLB and the rules person (or couple of people) at each team, nobody really knows all the rules inside and out. Most of these people learn them from experience over the years, since the rules may read differently in legalese than when you learn of them because a team exposed a certain loophole.

Often even these team experts call MLB for clarifications on esoteric rules, and many of these rules experts for teams are initially hired away from MLB's Labor Relations Department (LRD). A number of assistant GMs and GMs (usually with Ivy League educations) have worked in New York City for MLB in the LRD, primarily focusing on arbitration and other economic studies in the league's and club's interests. Many people see getting a spot in the LRD as the shortest path to being a GM, as you enter a small, elite group, learn a unique skill set, start a strong relationship with the league office, and have the economic bona fides that more and more owners are looking for. Because baseball's rules and contracts are so specific to the sport, a law degree isn't necessary and, like an MBA, the cost and opportunity cost is too great to pursue one if all you want to do is work in a front office.

DESPITE THE SUCCESS OF THEIR amateur talent acquisition during Fridley's tenure, White Sox owner Jerry Reinsdorf mutually parted ways (though not on good terms) with then–general manager Larry Himes, Goldis, and the rest of the staff after the 1990 season. Goldis caught on with Milwaukee in '91 and left less than a year later after a spat with the team over the extent of his duties. All this left Fridley in limbo.

Himes, who had become the general manager of the Chicago Cubs, brought Goldis to the North Side, with Fridley in tow as a national crosschecker. After a disastrous 1994 season, Himes was fired and Goldis was canned a year later. Fridley was again left floating in baseball space before he latched on as an area scout with Cleveland. There were issues. Others in the org felt Fridley thought the area was beneath him after he had just come off a national job, and that he was stepping on others' toes in an effort to get back to one. Things came to a head during a verbal, in-office altercation during an amateur staff meeting in the penultimate year of Fridley's contract. He finished the final year on his deal and was not brought back.

Plotting a Path

Depending on what your career goals and timetable are, and despite the fact that everyone in baseball took a unique path, there are lanes to place yourself in to increase your odds at success.

If your goal is to be a GM (this is the most common dream), then you need to figure out what your separating skill will be (you don't have one right now) and go down the path to be an expert in that area. Increasingly, being an ace scout isn't a recipe to run a team, so that's not the smartest way to position yourself for a move up the ladder to GM. You can come up in scouting departments or player development, but be based in the office so you have a management point of view, are getting face time around those people, and are in those meetings. You may need to be a coach or scout as a first step, but know that your path needs to get you into the office sooner than later.

More commonly, GMs come from people who are office-lifer types, who come up as assistants in baseball operations (general contributors across departments), a step up to coordinator or assistant director (managing schedules and interns or entry-level employees, introduced to decision-making meetings), then becoming director of baseball operations (in charge of budgets, rules, running the office day-to-day, pitching in on hiring and higher-level decisions) then assistant GM, where your specialty (running the office, rules, overseeing a scouting or player dev department) is the flavor that your job takes, along with the thing that can headline your résumé for GM.

A sitting GM once described to us that he and his three AGMs are in charge of servicing the various departments (analytics, big league operations, international scouting, domestic scouting, pro scouting, player development). There's more departments than the four of them, so they're playing a zone coverage, constantly going between all the areas, making sure each department has what they need to succeed and, ideally, not needing further direction or correction.

Things get a little simpler if your goal is simply to be that director of baseball ops or the rules-focused, behind-the-scenes AGM, as you can focus on being good at your job, networking, and waiting for merit to dictate when the job comes along. GM is tougher because, like head football coaches or CEOs, you can get stagnant, age out, or lose the momentum you had, even though you're technically getting more qualified every day. Getting a job as someone in a GM's cabinet is more based on your relationship with them and how good you are at your job, while there's much more public résumé-building and political machinery behind GM jobs. Every team has three or more people qualified for a GM interview in some way, but the same dozen or so people across the league keep getting interviewed.

This advice also goes for coaches who want to get to the upper levels or big leagues, scouts that want to be the director of the department, or lower-level execs that want to be the farm director. If you want a decision-making role that's office-based, it's better to get into the office as early as possible, since you can always be fast-tracked there and play a hybrid role. Many assistant directors of amateur scouting were area scouts or regional crosscheckers. They take the assistant director job to play the role of national crosschecker, which also has an administrative element to get them trained to run a department one day. Keeping personal growth in mind is something you should do, but any good boss will also ask you what you want to do and put you in positions to succeed. In reality, this is rarer than you may think, as people tend to focus on themselves when put in positions of power.

The first job you get to set you on this course isn't that important, since getting in the door and starting the process of networking and building a track record is more important than having the perfect first step. The one area that's a little tricky in many organizations is video internships. For more progressive organizations, this could mean being at a minor league affiliate, organizing the video for coaches and players and also playing the part of junior analyst, using development tech like TrackMan, Rapsodo, and Blast Motion and making suggestions in the areas where you're given latitude to do so. This isn't a bad first step, as it gets you experience in a clubhouse, working with players and coaches on the development side, a chance to prove/improve your analysis chops, and experience working with widely-used analytics tech that you have to get a job to be around.

With less progressive clubs, this can be more of an eyewash position laden with menial daily tasks, no analysis element, no structure to allow you to shine, nor contribute in view of the front office, and there's no path to full-time employment unless the video coordinator is leaving their spot. Do well at this sort of job and you may not have learned skills that are transferable into an office or networked with the office types that can help you find your next spot. Paradoxically, succeeding at this job means you might be offered it again, then you're forced to take it due to lack of superior options and you're further pigeon-holed without adding diversity of skills, experience, or network to your résumé.

Knowing the level of structure around an affiliate video internship and the track record of previous interns getting full-time jobs in an area you're interested in is key to knowing if that makes sense for you. If it's more of a wheel-spinning type role, learning coding, publishing research, going to industry events, and working a part-time job to make ends meet is a much better use of your time.

Again, this applies to more traditional clubs. Milwaukee and Houston have made huge use of video and it might be a smart place to start with a team that thinks like them.

THE TERM "PITCHING DOCTOR" IS a particular favorite pejorative label Fridley likes to apply to coaches he thinks are ruining pitchers by altering their mechanics in inefficient or harmful ways. He often discusses new-wave coaches the way an old man might talk about how his young neighbors take care of their lawns. The only men for whom Fridley seems to have unblemished, professional respect are his former bosses, Al Goldis and Larry Himes. This is an issue in, again, an industry as socially inclusive as professional baseball.

"I've lost my sponsors," Fridley says of Himes and Goldis, the latter having been inducted into the Scouts Hall of Fame in 2009, both gone from the game. "I think that and some of it is a bit of age discrimination. Lotta the guys doing things now are young guys from Ivy League schools who have never set foot within a mile of a baseball field. I don't have that background, but they certainly don't have mine."

Dave Perkin echoed this, adding, "There's an increasing rate of 'numbers guys' doing baseball jobs and it's shutting out guys like Rod who have probably forgotten more about baseball than these guys will ever know."

Perkin continued, "Money is likely another factor. Rod's going to cost more with his experience and tenure than someone young will. Control is a big thing in baseball. People are hired to do what you want them to do. It's full of acolyte sycophants."

This is only partially correct. Yes, the background of front office personnel has shifted away from baseball and toward things like economics and math, and those sorts of people are less inclined to hire people like Fridley than past supervisors, who would only hire people like him. But the statistics vs. scout strawman narrative has existed for over a decade now, but most smart teams use a heavy dose of both evaluation methods. The idea that old-timey baseball men are an endangered species just because they're old is wrong. "Look around the stands right now," said one scouting source speaking with Eric while he was at the 2019 Area Code Games. "Do all these scouts look young to you?"

They did not.

"These are either the people who have been open-minded and willing to learn and change or they're lucky that they work for someone who doesn't care that they won't."

But part of what keeps front office people employed is their ability to execute their jobs cheaply, which means taking advantage of the hunger and energy level of young people willing to work long hours for very little, and in some cases reducing their staff. Fridley has spent fewer days behind a desk than most Americans, but is still a casualty of corporate raiders.

Whatever the reasons for Fridley's extreme difficulty finding employment, his struggle is ongoing. "It is my life and my love, a little bit," he said. "But I don't know why I keep doing this to myself."

Becoming a Scout

As we mentioned earlier, if you want to be a scout, the advice is pretty simple: go scout games. This allows you to both build your library, but also to network and get used to the grind and little details that come with the job. It's not really fair, but dressing a certain way (performance-material polo and pants), standing in certain places (down the open side for notable hitters at amateur games, behind home otherwise), having the right things in your bag (Accusplit stop watch, decent-looking notebook like a Moleskine), and how you chat with scouts are all indicators to them if you're the type to either help them or to recommend to their club or rival teams looking for scouts. Remember that you're surrounded by people who are observant and traffic in gossip for a living. Helping scouts is most often done as a "bird-dog scout," or a lightly-to-unpaid scout that lets the area scout know about games they aren't able to attend. This could be as simple as cheating off the radar guns and reporting velocities to the area scout, or a retired scout that sees second-tier players to stay busy.

As we mentioned above, writing reports is a key part of this process. The process of taking notes is a step up from just watching, as it obviously forces you to be critical the whole game. It's hard to fully explain, but writing a report that formally combines the notes with a full opinion and a projection for the player forces you to think even more critically about what you saw and then project years into the future and pass official judgment (with a Future Value, or something like it) that can later easily be proven to be right or wrong. This may be the most important aspect of the process for aspiring scouts, along with making sure that scouts are seeing these reports. It can be hard to do this without having seen a layer of players age from their teens into their physical primes, and that takes time.

Scouts and executives seeing these reports is key because you'll get feedback both on how good the reports are and how to fix the tics that give away that you're still a beginner, while also expanding and deepening your network for when a job comes along that fits you. This is tricky, because scouts don't start their day hoping to find an aspiring scout with nothing on their résumé and give a few hours to this kid. You have to be dogged but also not annoying.

Kiley found it served him well to not initiate conversation with any scouts when he started out, just go to games, stand around where the scouts stood, and wait for one to get curious and ask him why they've seen him four times this week. One scout said they saw Kiley more than their wife that week, so they had to know why he was following them. This is a bit of a long-term play, but it paid off because most of the scouts in Florida knew Kiley within a year or so and there wasn't a basket of cringe-worthy stories going around to make other scouts hesitant to talk to him. Stories were going around about many of the other aspiring scouts in the area; these awkward times are common, but the key is to not let them last too long.

PALO ALTO IS SPANISH FOR "tall stick," a phrase one could use to describe Chris Kusiolek. Like countless other lower-income families, Kusiolek's was pushed out of the Bay Area college town by astronomical cost-of-living increases brought about by the tech boom of the '80s and '90s. Two miles in one direction was Stanford University and the headquarters of several, world-altering tech giants. Two miles in the other were some of the most impoverished parts of the Bay Area. Gentrification squeezed the family like a boa constrictor and, with roots nearly half a century deep in Palo Alto, Kusiolek's family packed up and moved to Placerville, California, not long after his high school graduation. A shake up, an obstacle, another in a life that had already been full of them, the first move of what would soon become a half decade of transience as Chris pursued a life in baseball.

As is the case with most passions that follow us into adulthood, baseball or not, something ethereal about the game grabbed a hold of Kusiolek during his teens. He exhibits traits common among the most passionate seamheads. He grew up collecting things, had an interest in competitive card games, and remembers moments from his first trip to a Major League stadium with remarkable clarity. Things snowballed while Kusiolek was in his late teens, when he became engrossed with the Oakland Athletics during the early years of Bob Melvin's managerial tenure. Coco Crisp, Yoenis Céspedes, Josh Donaldson, three consecutive playoff appearances ending with losses in do-or-die games. "I greatly preferred the atmosphere of the Coliseum," Kusiolek recalls, contrasting it with his experiences at AT&T Park. "It was more intimate, fan friendly, it had a pulse."

But these sorts of anecdotes are where the overlap between Kusiolek and almost all of the baseball-watching universe ends. Both Chris and his journey are unique. Everyone carves their own path, but few have had to machete away as many vines as he has in pursuit of what, to many, is employment, but to him can be a source of comfort and refuge.

CHECKING IN WITH CONTACTS EVERY six months or so makes sense—maybe before and after the season—with an update on the role you have this year and then an update on what you're looking to land that off-season, with a few reports attached each time. If you're looking for more of an office or analyst role, having samples of work, whether it's some scouting reports or studies or analysis/articles, is key to include because the email update alone isn't very compelling in terms of a call to action.

We've both had contacts we stayed in touch with that we sent reports to or that followed us on Twitter and after a couple years, maybe they only responded to every other email, but they were engaged enough to have read these updates, so they felt like they knew us. Kiley got an interview for an area scout job in his early twenties and the team told him it was because he had a website with reports and video on it and none of the other candidates did, so he stood out and gave more comfort amongst other people with the same qualifications.

Another piece of advice popped up around this time: don't write a report online with video next to it and misdiagnose the video. That's the easiest way for someone to write you off for years or forever; it's one of the few ways to prove you don't really know what you're talking about. It's important to have opinions about the players you see, and to not write reports until you have one, but don't force an opinion or try to stuff a player into a box because of a preconceived notion that doesn't agree with the video you posted. Either change the report (because it's wrong, or too narrow) or don't include the video.

Standup comedians talk about not wanting to be "seen" by decision-makers until they're good, because they can bury you and never come back. Kiley has noticed the execs that he first talked to while in college are often the last to recognize what he's become, because they can't get the image of the pimply faced kid with no discernible skills out of their head. Don't be afraid to hone your five-minute comedy act in Tulsa until you're ready to be seen in Los Angeles. Or, said another way: retweets aren't all they're cracked up to be.

KUSIOLEK WAS DIAGNOSED AS BEING on the autistic spectrum at age seven. Specifically, he has Asperger's Syndrome, which impacts peoples' ability to deal with social situations, and identify verbal and physical cues that most people can decipher intuitively. For Chris, this manifests as heightened social anxiety. Later in his teens he would also be diagnosed with Tourette's Syndrome. "Baseball helps me diffuse whatever I'm feeling. I lose myself," he says, "and that's when I'm doing good work."

As his affection for the A's grew, Chris learned that the well of baseball from which he could draw in order to feel grounded and at ease was much deeper than even the two-team town in which he grew up. He started to engage in online baseball discussions during the early (less psychologically poisonous) days of Twitter and got lost in the marathon episodes of Baseball Prospectus' Up & In podcast, an auditory shooting star that has influenced many a millennial baseball writer the way The Clash and Frank Zappa influenced countless musicians who followed. Hosts Kevin Goldstein (Astros) and Jason Parks (Cubs, then the Diamondbacks) moved on to director-level roles with clubs.

It sparked Kusiolek's desire to branch out and begin seeing minor league games. A lot of them. "I had an '02 Volkswagen with 120,000 miles on it and drove it everywhere. From Placerville to Modesto, Stockton, San José, Fresno, Sacramento… I drove down to Arizona for AZL and instructs, drove all around Arizona. I put 50,000 miles on it in four or five months."

There's a lot of online chest-thumping about how many games writers in the prospecting realm attend, when going to games is the fun part, the reason you do the job. The other parts, like the driving, the note taking, the video editing, the diligent use of sunscreen and other matters of discipline and self care are where the work is, especially when long hours in California traffic are involved. Kusiolek outlasted the car.

"I was driving down the freeway in December and it had been smoking for two weeks before that. My uncle is good with cars and tried to figure out what was wrong with it but couldn't really pin it down. My dashboard starting smoking up to the point where I couldn't see anything, so I slowed down and leapt out on the freeway. Apparently it was electrical circuiting."

Undeterred by his lack of vehicle, Kusiolek found other ways to go to games. He'd come down to Arizona and stay in hotels, living off of some money provided by his mother, as well as some cash stashed away from child-support payments made by his father, whom Chris has only met a few times during the course of his life. He describes this as being "for the best" due to his father's volatile nature. "He was physically and emotionally abusive to my mother, often left my older sister unattended, would openly tell her he wished she were a boy, and he tried to break into our house several times."

Chris' mother herself has struggled with alcoholism and self-identity at various points of her life, though he cites her as "the driving force" behind his pursuit of a job in baseball. "She's a fantastic mom. She was getting up early to play catch with me, taking me to games, nurturing my passion."

IN ONE OF KILEY'S WEEKLY chats in September of 2019, he got this question (edited slightly for clarity):

Q: Hey Kiley, I am an accountant who is almost 30, knows SQL, Python, and some Spanish (but definitely not fluent), and has built a couple of small, but pretty neat baseball websites but otherwise have no relevant job history. How would be the best way of putting together a baseball résumé?

A: Do a project that is something close to what you'd do in a front office, make a résumé with some links/attachments and cold email it to people. Usually assistant director of baseball ops is about the level where their opinions matter, they have input into the interview/selection process and they aren't so swamped that they won't read the résumés (if they're interesting). Target people around that area with your emails; higher up people will, at most, just forward the email to people at that level.

You can see that this person is uniquely qualified to jump into the résumé pile. Being 30 and not 22 or 25 is less traditional, but having SQL, Python, some Spanish, and some baseball-specific work makes this person more qualified for one of the top-tier internships than 90 percent of applicants. Knowing just this, I'd assume this candidate gets multiple offers. If we're talking about a full-time job, that's a little tougher to predict because teams like having certainty and knowing the candidate, as firing is pretty rare from these jobs.

That's why the top-tier office internships are valuable (particularly now because they're paid), since you either get the full-time gig or now have the prerequisite everyone is looking for and some recommendations that can help it translate to other clubs. If you're looking for an R&D job, having that internship with a progressive club makes your experience all the more important, as just having a seal of approval and a vague idea of what a more advanced team is doing is a nice separator.

What Jobs Are There?

In research & development or analytics departments, the entry-level job (above the year-long internship) is baseball operations analyst. There's some variations there for the exact role, like developer or systems architect. There's the half-step up of being the most experienced at that tier, like senior analyst or coordinator of R&D where you're probably managing a few people. The director of R&D runs the department and could get a title of assistant GM if they have notable enough baseball and technical knowledge that the GM is worried another team could steal their top data person (and their knowledge). The salaries are a little better in this department since they have to compete with tech and financial firms, but, like all baseball jobs, there's a discount in here because there's a bottomless pit of people who want to work in baseball.

Interns are normally in the $12,000 to $25,000 area, without benefits. Analysts fit in the $45,000 to $60,000 area, while coordinators/senior analysts are in the $60,000 to $85,000 range. Directors can include the top analytics person in the organization and vary depending on how key that is to a team's success. These jobs start around $85,000 and we've heard of them going well into the six figures, probably topping around $250,000 for an assistant GM that also runs the department. We know of one club that recently was flipping the switch to bulk up their R&D staff and offered four years and well into the six figures annually to try to lure someone from a team with superior R&D. That offer was turned down and they hired a more technical person without club experience, we're told, for a good bit less money.

In the front office, the general tiers of jobs are similar to the analytics jobs in both function and salary, but maybe $5,000 to $10,000 lower in pay. Interns do more general tasks, with a lot of spreadsheets, airport runs, and double-checking documents before they're sent to the staff. Entry-level baseball ops assistants are doing similar things, but a notch higher, usually with some sort of specialty, internship experience, or connection with a department head that tends to push them more into one department doing a junior version of assistant director or coordinator work. These two similar titles tend to be in direct support of the director, either making schedule assignments for pro scouts, playing traffic cop in real-time for amateur scouts, managing player plans and schedules for the player development staff, etc. There's also some hands-on, director-type experience, like being the number two for department-wide meetings, taking a first pass at budgets, or going to games with the director as a mentorship-type program.

A director's duties vary a fair amount by department. We covered amateur scouting directors (the draft) in that chapter and international scouting directors in their chapter, along with director of baseball operations above. A farm director covers the entirety of the minor league system, managing and monitoring player, coach, and trainer progress; disciplining/mentoring these employees; managing budgets; helping run instructional league and spring training; and giving the best sense of the player to the front office staff at large.

A director of pro scouting is a bit of a hybrid role due to the nature of the players they cover. When it comes to covering lower-level players, it's similar to directing the other scouting departments, in terms of managing people, schedules, evaluations, budgets, and development of your staff.

ASPERGER'S IS AMONG THE AUTISTIC Spectrum Disorders classified by doctors as "high functioning," which means the symptoms are less severe than other ASDs and have no detrimental effects on intelligence. But the people who live with Asperger's often dislike change, something people who work in baseball are subject to constantly, and without any modicum of control over it. The people who hired you get fired and the new boss wants to bring their own people into the department, or an opportunity you can't pass up arises but you need to relocate your family if you take the job, or the very nature of your day-to-day work is altered by new equipment or procedure.

This is either not an issue for Chris or his drive to pursue baseball was simply enough to surmount it. In 2016, a few months shy of his 22nd birthday, Kusiolek came to Arizona for a six-week stretch. "I missed the first day of Padres and Rangers instructs, missed Adrian Morejón throw, but was there the rest of the time."

By this point people working in baseball in Arizona—coaches, scouts, players—began to recognize him because of his constant presence at the field. He got a lot of side-eye from xenophobic folks (baseball is full of them) puzzled by his mannerisms (Chris twirls his stopwatch between pitches like a bored lifeguard whips around their whistle as they pass the time watching competent swimmers, he often mutters to himself about what he's seeing on the field, and he has vocal and physical tics caused by his Tourette's) and put off by his Northern Californian aesthetic. Chris has a villainous, blond mustache and goatee, long hair that he wears up, and at this point in time was traversing the backfields in mesh shorts and a hoodie, no matter the temperature.

He kept plugging away, tweeting thoughts on players paired with video, and he made somewhat of a name for himself on the internet. People oblivious to—and unbiased by—his cognitive issues thought he was great.

After that extended run in Arizona, Chris went home for the holidays and was approached via Twitter by Michael Sherr, a man representing a training academy in the Dominican Republic. "He told me he liked my work, and after a week or two of dialogue he offered to fly me out to the DR. It came off as kinda sketchy at first but I said, 'Fuck it.' Thankfully I didn't wake up in a bathtub full of ice missing a kidney."

Chris flew from Sacramento to Los Angeles to Chicago to Punta Cana, then took a *guagua* (Dominican Spanish for bus) to San Pedro where he stayed at Astin Jacobo's academy in the northeast part of the city. He was there for a month. "I was out there moonlighting, following players and games at various places and giving my two cents, went to the IPL showcase my first week there. There are so many characters down there. There's a former Olympic track runner who was the athletic trainer at one of the academies, and he lives in an 8-by-6 shack. One team's director came to a complex for a workout that was supposed to be private. My interpreter was wearing a sweatshirt of his favorite team, was not affiliated with them in any way, but when the director saw another team's gear he blew a gasket. I rode around the streets on the back of a *motoconcho* dozens of times. Sometimes, if scouts were around and I'd say something positive about players, their trainer would hand me some cash. There was some in-fighting at the academy I was working for. Stuff like that.

"I always wanted to go the Dominican, not only for the cultural immersion but to understand where these guys come from. They live and breathe for baseball—it is the sport there. Unfortunately, part of the reason for that is due to the socioeconomic issues on the island. This is how you get off the island, or at least how you escape poverty."

AT THE UPPER LEVELS OF the minors and majors, the radar-based numbers and analytics they spawned make in-person scouting a smaller part of the puzzle, so analytics are a bigger part of the pie. When it comes to making recommendations about players for the big league team, you wade into getting thoughts from the big league coaching staff, possibly working with advance scouting, and going even deeper into the analytics for notes on possible adjustments or use cases for tomorrow night's game.

We cover this in some depth in the pro scouting–focused chapter, but transaction, roster, and contract rules also become key to understand how and when you can acquire certain players, much more often than they do in amateur settings. For this reason, pro scouting is a fusion between amateur scouting, analytics, and baseball operations. These days, it's a good place for the aspiring GM with a scouting interest or background to show a wide range of skills and work from the office, as running the amateur or international departments is done remotely and is more of a lone wolf or siloed department on a day-to-day basis.

We covered titles, roles, salary ranges, and context for what else goes into a negotiation for scouts within their chapters, but we'll include the top-line numbers here. There are exceptions to these on the high and low ends, but these figures represent the ranges that the vast majority of roles will pay.

Area scouts generally make $40,000 to $70,000, regional crosscheckers are around $70,000 to $90,000, national crosscheckers tend to range from $90,000 to $125,000, and amateur scouting directors usually make $150,000 to $350,000. On the international side, there are generally the same positions, but area scouts in the Caribbean make about half as much due to cost-of-living adjustments, while crosscheckers and above tend to be American-based. Coaches at affiliates tend to make $40,000 to $70,000 (again, much lower for DSL coaches), while their superiors, the roving coordinators, have a wide range, from about $80,000 to over $200,000 for the most sought-after.

Pro scouts generally make $50,000 to $100,000, with the top-tier pro scouts often called special assistant to the GM. They tend to make $100,000 to $300,000, depending on if this is just one of your better pro scouts that you don't want to lose to another club or maybe a former GM that's also an inner-circle advisor. Many people in the game think that after you've been fired as a GM the special assistant job is the best job in baseball, because it's always six figures, your opinion matters, and you get to set your schedule more than most. Kiley often says that the three best jobs in baseball are post-GM special assistant, TV commentator that's a former manager or GM (the money is great, hours aren't bad), or agent with multiple clients making eight figures per year (just interact with fellow millionaires, play golf, and count your money).

We referenced this in the draft chapter, but the salaries for top-tier decision-makers is something that doesn't get referenced much and strides are made to keep these figures secret. Both big league assistant coaches and vice presidents (and assistant GMs) make $150,000 to $500,000, managers make about $1 million to $5 million, and general managers on their first or second contract (usually three to four years per contract) make $1 million to $4 million. For a team president that functions as head of business operations with no baseball operations input, they tend to make $1 million to $3 million, while the head of baseball operations that either has the president title or is on their third contract tend to make $4 million to $10 million.

THE PADRES BEGAN POKING AROUND Chris. He first began meeting and talking to upper-level members of the org's scouting department late in 2016, since he spent so much time at their complex during instructional because "they had a fuck ton of talent."

By this point a small support group of scouts and media members, including A's and White Sox freelancer Kim Contreras and photographer, Baseball America contributor, and desert-baseball sherpa Bill Mitchell (who, as an aside, needs to write a book), began to coalesce around Chris, which helped enable him to trek across the Phoenix metro area, because he never replaced that Volkswagen. When he can't catch a ride, Kusiolek walks. The pedometer on his phone shows he averages nine miles per day. "It benefits me because I'm a very kinesthetic person in general; I like to walk regardless."

Chris and members of the Padres front office maintained a dialogue for a little over a year before they offered him an associate position, covering pro ball in the state of Arizona beginning in 2018. "It's nice to be with the organization, and be around individuals whom I call mentors and look toward for guidance. It's also nice to have a sense of accountability that I lacked before I was hired."

His report helped the Padres decide to acquire righty Ignacio Feliz from the Indians later that year, and his contract was renewed ahead of the 2019 and 2020 campaigns. "This is all I wanna do. I sacrificed my young adult years for this, it took everything. I've devoted my entire being to the game itself."

Do You Still Want That Job?

Now that you have a full view of what these jobs are, what they do, what they make, and what you have to do to get a job, we land on a key question:

Do you still want one of these jobs?

This may seem silly to some of you and we know when we were young go-getters we were single-minded in our pursuit of a baseball job that's just a single station ahead of where we were then, all in an effort to "make it." Kiley waited 10 years from when he threw himself into this pursuit to get a full-time job with a team and, while he's turned down plenty of those jobs recently, Eric hasn't had one and didn't have offers for a while. We've managed to find/make jobs that didn't exist until we had them and, luckily, we work well together and love working for FanGraphs, so we aren't in a rush to leave and just take whatever teams are offering. That said, there's reasonable scenarios years from now where a job that would tempt us could come along.

We have friends in the media and former media members who have been in this spot before and most of them have chosen to go to a club at some point, but there are some key things to ask yourself before you've been in the industry for 10 years and are wondering how you got here.

Once you've been around the game enough to see what it is that you're passionate about with specificity, as well as what you can do for years without it feeling like work, then you've done the key first step. After that, you can survey the landscape and see how your skill set and path matches with what you want your work life and lifestyle outside work to look like. We're both lucky to have full-time writing as an option to have a better work/life balance, while also staying in the industry and keeping our options open. We have lots of friends in the game that don't like the work/life balance in their role on the team side and could probably do well as a writer, but need a full-time gig to consider jumping and have no experience actually doing it before, so it isn't an option.

While this is happening, friends in the game who got in and paid their dues before or around the publishing of *Moneyball* are struck by the changing face of baseball and what skills are necessary. The Astros posted a job in October 2019 for a "Machine Learning–Computer Vision Analyst, Research & Development." We are in no way qualified for this job, but knew that it generally meant a highly specialized, highly paid job to take high-speed video and create software to automatically strip out TrackMan data from it. We're pretty sure no team has figured out how to do this yet (we know some do it by hand) and we were told a team could automate the process if they hired someone in this exact area. (We started writing this chapter before the Astros cheating scandal exploded, but this job posting reads a little differently after the fact. The job was posted only on TeamWork Online and not on FanGraphs, so the job listing is no longer online.)

The required education and experience is mostly words that we don't even understand and this person may well be paid more than every scout in the organization for a task of analyzing video of a type that didn't exist in baseball more than five years ago.

The Orioles, run by GM Mike Elias (a former Astros executive), posted a job for an "Economic Valuation Analyst," that called for a core responsibility of making economic models and listed these desired qualifications:
- Advanced degree in Economics, Finance, Mathematics, Operations Research, Statistics, or a related field. Applicants with a non-traditional educational background and experience in financial modeling will be considered as well.

- Fluency in probability theory and financial mathematics, including an in-depth understanding of financial instruments and of pricing their associated risks.
- Experience with relational database systems and knowledge of SQL.
- Experience with predictive modeling using tools such as R or Python.
- Passion for baseball and understanding of sabermetrics.

One front office staffer said these bullet points described a "unicorn." The realistic employee that the Orioles hire for this role isn't the point, it's that this is what the Orioles want, which has a lot in common with what the Astros want, and you could lump another half-dozen teams into that camp. This job was posted in September 2019, one month after the Orioles fired/didn't renew the contracts of 10 scouts and one front office member, with 25 total scouting and development employees let go in the first 18 months of Elias' tenure.

Maybe your skill set fits perfectly into this new vision of baseball and you're excited to see these sorts of jobs popping up. Regardless, it further encapsulates the changes in the game and the corporatization of what once was a little more human-focused.

CHAPTER 12

Is Data Swallowing Baseball?

"Data is the new oil. It's valuable, but if unrefined it cannot really be used."
—Data-driven consumer behavior expert (*gag*), Clive Humby

Technology began to creep up on scouting at least as early as World War II, when the radar gun was developed by Ben Midlock and John Barker for the purposes of measuring the speed of landing PBY aircraft. The guns then made their way to the police for reasons lead-footed readers are no doubt familiar with, but didn't end up in the hands of baseball people until the 1970s, when a light bulb appeared above the head of Pennsylvania native Dan Litwhiler, then the head coach at Michigan State.

After learning police were using them to measure the speed of cars, he approached the JUGS company, which to that point had mostly been in the pitching-machine business, to develop a radar gun as a teaching tool for baseball. Surely someone else eventually would have thought to use it not just for baseball but for evaluating players, but Litwhiler, a prolific tinkerer who cooked up several interesting baseball-related widgets throughout his life, is credited as the first, and the JUGS prototype he commissioned is currently immortalized under glass in Cooperstown.

Most scouts carry one now. It's a tool for them to more accurately measure pitch speeds than the days of yore, when the best we could do was race Bob Feller's heater against a motorcycle. At the field, that part of the scout's job was entirely subjective until this piece of technology came along and made evaluating that aspect of pitching more accurate.

Now, technology evolves exponentially and the way this interacts with people's jobs, across all industries, is becoming a problem for workers. Born a blacksmith? You probably died one. Now, technology evolves so fast that many of us will see our current occupations completed by machines during our lifetimes. Long-haul truckers are afraid of self-driving cars, beat writers are weary of algorithms that put together game stories based on play-by-play logs, and scouts glare at the growing number of robots that collect more information during a game than they can hope to.

It took about 20 years for another company, Applied Concepts, to develop an improved baseball radar gun, the Stalker Sport. The follow-up model had a more intuitive user interface, the next was smaller and lighter, the next had a wider range of measurable speed and was waterproof, the next had faster response times and could measure speeds at various systems of measure like kilometers per hour or knots if you wanted it to, and on and on until Stalker introduced a 2019 model that they claim also measures pitch spin rate.

The New Frontier

But baseball evaluation really began accelerating with PITCHf/x, a collaboration between MLB and a company called Sportvision that uses three tracking cameras and a central tracking system to calculate movement caused by the Magnus force (Google it if you're curious, we can't turn this into a chapter about physics), measuring velocity, movement, release point, pitch location, and spin. The system debuted during the 2006 MLB playoffs, and soon thereafter amateur analysts covering baseball on the internet got access to a treasure trove of data by way of nightly XML file dumps by MLB.

It told us much more about a given pitch than a radar gun could. Velocity and movement were the headliners, finally standardized to decimal points. This was light years better than the sometimes-reliable in-park radar readings on the big league scoreboard, and radar guns that would become useless when interference, lack of calibration, or bad angles would undermine an otherwise useful instrument.

The release point, flight path, and location where the ball crossed the plate were all able to be mapped in three dimensions with PITCHf/x, giving unprecedented detail to the core action of baseball. It was initially used to replace QuesTec (used 2001–08) as the system that graded (and was proven to improve) umpiring at the MLB level. It was also used, initially, to beef up MLB GameDay and give more detailed accounts (velocity, pitch, location) to fans via non-video means.

While MLB made this business decision to improve the fan experience marginally, amateur analysts on the internet saw something else: opportunity. In May 2007, Dan Fox of Baseball Prospectus (hired by the Pirates in 2008, currently their senior director of baseball informatics, and a former boss of Kiley's in 2011) issued this challenge:

> Now that we have these sorts of tools at our disposal, we can begin to ask and answer a variety of interesting questions. Which hitters tend to get bad calls? Which pitchers get the benefit of the doubt most often? On what counts is it more likely that pitchers or hitters will benefit? Which hitters swing at pitches out of the strike zone? What is each hitter's batting average when swinging at pitches in specific zones (the Ted Williams model)? How frequently do pitchers target specific zones against certain hitters? The list goes on and on from there—let's get started.

For Slate.com, Nate DiMeo called PITCHf/x "the stathead equivalent of a particle accelerator—a technical marvel that might just yield answers to the fundamental questions of the baseball universe."

What followed was a data gold rush and avalanche of studies by the most intellectually progressive clubs to find ways of identifying what aspects of player talent could be identified through these means and then acquired before other clubs caught on. Talent in this case also included those who were the best at analyzing the data. One of these was the Rays hiring of Josh Kalk within months of his February 2009 article at The Hardball Times called "The Injury Zone," where he used a neural network to see if PITCHf/x data could be used to predict pitcher injuries.

When Kalk left the Rays after his contract expired in fall 2017, some front office staffers joked that he was the most valuable free agent that off-season, in a class that included Yu Darvish and J.D. Martinez. Kalk joined the Twins as a senior analyst after leaving Bluefield State College, where he was a math professor during his entire Rays tenure.

While PITCHf/x gave analysts a look at more detailed aspects of a given pitch, TrackMan took things to a different level. Originally designed for golf, it was first used in affiliated MLB parks around 2010 and combined use of Doppler radar technology with a multi-camera array that tracked the location and movement of high-speed (the ball) and low-speed (players) objects on the field, respectively. While working for the Pirates in 2011, Kiley was the staffer assigned to come in on a Saturday while the team was on the road and let a TrackMan employee calibrate the system at PNC Park using tennis balls covered in baby powder.

And boy, did those systems need to be calibrated. While you can already see how the TrackMan concept would soon become a problem for the scouting industry, it wasn't as accurate at measuring some things out of the gate as teams needed it to be. For several years, over 10 percent of balls in play (usually pop-ups and balls hit into the outfield corners, among other outliers) weren't properly measured by TrackMan systems across MLB, and the number was 15–20 percent at certain ballparks.

What TrackMan offered was more detailed information about the full flight of the pitch in three dimensions as well as new information about how the ball was hit (exit velocity, launch angle, estimated flyball distance, etc.) that was only briefly available in a stripped-down version at the MLB level to MLB teams via an offshoot of PITCHf/x, called HITf/x.

TrackMan's ability to capture the pitched and hit baseball was combined with new technology to make Statcast, which debuted (and has only been used) at the MLB level in 2015. It's the public-facing, data geek arm of MLB's media package. The new elements allowed for the tracking of players, both on the bases and in the field, yet another step at tracking and measuring the various things on the field anyone may want to know about. Stripped-down XML files of Statcast data are publicly available from MLB, but it's very pared down, since seven terabytes of uncompressed data are generated, per game.

TrackMan was widely available for clubs to purchase and put in minor league parks. When Eric first saw a TrackMan unit during an outdoor presentation at the 2012 Saber Seminar in Boston, it was just a big black box with a single lens. He thought it looked like a combination of the black monolith and the vibrant, red, all-seeing eye of the HAL 9000 from *2001: A Space Odyssey*. He didn't realize, as far as player evaluation and scouts were concerned, it was almost exactly those things.

The Red Sox admitted during that Saber Seminar that they already had TrackMan units installed at Fenway Park and a few of their minor league sites, but it took five to seven years for units to be added to the vast majority of minor league ballparks. It was hard for teams to analyze TrackMan data beneath the big leagues at this time because they only had access to what was happening at their own units. Some of the stadiums lacked the structural integrity to hold a properly calibrated unit, creating more gaps in data. Kiley was involved in trades between clubs he worked for to fill these holes. Through data sharing, clubs would piece together stuff from every unit that had been installed at the level they had installed a unit, for the years they had one.

As an example (Kiley doesn't remember what the exact trades were anymore), if the Pirates had units at the MLB, Double-A, and Low-A levels, but the Braves had units at MLB, Triple-A and Double-A, the Pirates may trade games from their Low-A unit to the Braves for their 2011 Triple-A data. I'll give you my data from the February college tournament at our spring training ballpark if you give me your data from the junior college playoffs at your rookie-level affiliate. Clubs own the data from their minor league parks, but the data from the MLB parks was automatically shared, since MLB owns the units in MLB stadiums. This made hosting what appeared to be a money-losing college tournament at your Double-A park informationally lucrative if prospects were playing.

You could make swaps like this until you had a viable sample on the entire minors and some college prospects. It was common for clubs to have units installed at just a few affiliates because, at a per unit cost of about $25,000 per year, the whole organizational gamut of affiliates would cost about $150,000, and that was a big outlay, especially to clubs who weren't yet fully aware of the power of that data.

Analyzing the Data

When Kiley was at the 2008 Winter Meetings in Las Vegas, he was focused on getting as many interviews and making as many connections as possible in hopes of landing a job with a team. When Tampa Bay traded Edwin Jackson for Matt Joyce, he was a little surprised, as it looked like Jackson was about to turn the corner (he did the next season) after being a hyped young player, while Joyce was relatively anonymous, making his big league debut earlier that year after peaking as the Tigers seventh-ranked prospect in 2007.

Kiley ran into a friend that was in the Rays front office at the time and they asked Kiley what he thought of the trade, but he didn't know Joyce that well other than his high strikeout rates. "I think those will come down. His whiff rates with two strikes are much lower than his early-count whiff rates. He has contact ability, he just needs to adjust his early-count approach to be more selective."

This was years before TrackMan had come to baseball and Kiley had been reading scouting reports non-stop the last three summers while working for the Yankees. He'd never seen a scouting report mention that sort of detail, that could calm a worry so succinctly and objectively. This is the kind of extra layer of analysis this tech enables, even if the analysis is very baseball-y.

Because of Statcast, the average baseball fan is aware of the things that TrackMan units tell us at non-big league games, even if they're not aware that such data exists in the hands of teams. Much of the minor league and amateur data teams have to parse through looks like a lot of the stuff you'll find on FanGraphs and Baseball Savant (the website that MLB operates to house Statcast data). We break down the levels of analysis this way:

Levels of Modern Baseball Analysis		
Level	Hitting	Pitching
Level 1 Important Surface Stats	The Most Predictive Public Stats (BB%, K%, FB%, BABIP)	Peripherals (K%, BB%, GB%) ERA Predictors (FIP, xFIP)
Level 2 Surface Radar Tech	Define Raw Power (Max Exit Velo) Define Game Power (Avg EV, 95+ EV%)	Velocity, Spin Rate, Movement Usage Patterns, Release Point
Level 3 Radar-Derived Metrics	Plate Discipline Grade by Specific Skill Game Power w/Specific Definition (Barrels)	Whiff Rates By Pitch & Zone Metric-Informed Pitch Grades
Level 4 Predictive Metrics	Swing/Approach Change Candidates Optimize Swing/Approach to Strengths	Pitch Design to Improve Stuff Usage, Location, Sequence Optimization

For the minor leagues, the first level is easy to find online. Things like ERA and wins don't even qualify for the graphic because we don't consider them telling as far as prospects' futures are concerned. We have and post some of what's in the second level, as we get it directly from teams, who derive it from their private minor league TrackMan data.

Level 3 is where things are behind a curtain and the two of us only get glimpses of what clubs are doing with that kind of stuff because it's no longer raw data and is now proprietary. A team may tell us that Padres minor league RHP Luis Patino has the best stuff in the minor leagues per their metric-informed pitch grades, but they wouldn't even tell us the rest of their top 10, presumably all top prospects. Some teams go really deep into this process, but it sounds like at least 25 if not all 30 clubs have some version of it, internally.

The basics are pretty simple: do some regressions and find which pitch characteristics predict weak contact and whiffs, weight them based on those results, then score the pitches, regress them a bit based on results at higher levels of competition, calculate standard deviations, then scale the metrics in such a way that 50 is the average and the standard deviations are plus or minus 10 from the mean, and poof, you've got pitch grades.

This is more sophisticated than a scout seeing 10 sliders one night and calling it a 55-grade pitch because of mostly how it looks, but there's also some things that are missing when you totally ignore what the scouts say.

Ideally both grades agree, but scouts will pick up on things that the TrackMan unit can't measure. Various kinds of deception are the biggest example, but there are also smaller things, such as how the hitter responds to the pitch or the intended locations given by the catcher. There's also minute things like pitch-tipping, such as pitcher grunting when he throws a certain pitch, or makeup-related stuff like poise, coach interactions, and more.

The things that TrackMan picks up that a scout can't see are generally things scouts will speculate about but could never prove. When scouts said things like, "Those pitches look the same out of the hand," or "Guys were taking awkward swings tonight" more rigorous analysts would wonder if this was snake oil being sold to them, or just reporting what happened and making a narrative out of a couple poor swings. Now we can see that a fastball and breaking ball have exactly opposite spin direction, or the fastball and changeup have different release points, and more objectively define some elements of what leads to effective pitching.

A good way to keep from the pitch grades becoming a black box (i.e. you don't easily understand how the figure was computed) is to keep the components visible alongside the final answer. Maybe one presentation would call a curveball a 63 as an overall pitch with a 66 on characteristics (velocity, movement, spin, measurable deception) and 61 on outcomes (grading the quality of contact allowed, whiff rates) and 52 on command (locating in preferred zones).

Command is notoriously hard to quantify since the question of what is being measured (intended location is hard to know, not every pitch is best on the edge of the strike zone) is a moving target. Strike zones are different at each minor league level (bigger at the lower levels where umpires aren't as good) and of course vary ump to ump, so grading by called strikes is problematic too.

Maybe the pitch has a 20 percent swinging strike rate (MLB average is 11 percent) but is only being thrown 15 percent of the time. That would suggest a pitcher should maybe be throwing the pitch more often. But that ignores the possibility that the pitch might be that effective in part because it isn't thrown very often. Maybe a given pitch is thrown in the zone too often and is not getting as many whiffs as it should based on the quality of your scouts' visual look.

Maybe the whiff rate spikes when a pitch is thrown after another of the pitcher's offerings, like an old-school curveball just after a high fastball, or a slider off the plate just after a fastball paints the corner. This may be due to a concept called tunneling, throwing two pitches that follow the same path for much of the flight of the ball before diverging near the plate. Certain combinations work better than others (four-seam fastball up with curveball down, sinker with slider on opposite sides of the lower strike zone) but quantifying what the benefits are can also be tricky, and probably involves game-theory concepts.

Advanced analysts can use game theory to optimize how often each pitcher throws each pitch, in what locations and in which sequences. The smartest teams have a staff of player development analysts going through only this data to alert coaches and roving coordinators to areas for potential improvement and are looking for employees with a background in game theory. You can also imagine why an analyst in the office telling a coach what may work, or quantifying something too precisely without watching the game, can cause friction.

Early on, analysts laughed at the notion that fastballs had late hop or ride, as it's physically impossible for pitches to move like that. But now that we can measure vertical break, some fastballs with perfect backspin appear to rise since they fight gravity better and hit the mitt a few inches higher than your eyes would expect. "That fastball really gets on hitters," could mean there's some deception but often was seen objectively as not detailed enough to really mean anything. Now we can measure the extension a pitcher has, use that to calculate perceived velocity and see which pitchers have the most "unexpected" velocity given how fast their arm is throwing the ball vs. how fast it is when it crosses the plate.

An underrated development of advanced analysis using radar-based technology is that in many ways it's shown that scouts know what they're seeing—there has just been a communication barrier between them and in-office analysts who need numbers to explain it before they feel it's concrete.

Kiley helped define some metrics the Braves used on the hitting side on Level 3, a version of what MLB publicly calls "barrels," a ball hit at an elite combination of exit velocity and launch angle as to almost always be an extra-base hit, often a homer. It works out that the rate at which hitters do this is very predictable and stabilizes quickly. After about a month of games, whatever a hitter is doing is his actual talent level at the moment. Batting average takes almost two full seasons to stabilize like this, so you can evaluate what level a prospect should be at much more reliably, in-season, using these metrics.

Plate discipline metrics whose utility go well beyond walk and strikeout rate aren't that difficult to make. Once you define locations somewhat simply (example of four levels: middle of the strike zone, fringe strike zone, chase zone, wild zone) then label each hitter decision as take, swing, whiff, or contact, you can quickly see how a hitter approaches each at-bat. You can take the middle-of-the-strike-zone take percentage as a measure of passivity, the rate of swings on pitches outside the zone as bad swing decisions, and could also further refine or grade those by taking out some counts or scoring them based on how far in or out of the zone the pitch was.

These metrics can perfectly match the scouting reports, making decisions pretty easy. Kiley joined the Braves at the end of the 2015 season and the buzzy prospect, internally, was Ronald Acuña, whom you may have heard of. It may be hard to imagine, but in 2015, the media rankings of Acuña weren't bullish at all. The hotter name was another you probably know, Nationals CF Victor Robles. Both started in the GCL, then were promoted to a higher level, the Appalachian League for Acuña and the higher-level New York Penn League for Robles.

Both were teenage center-field prospects with precocious statistical performance and Baseball America ranked Robles second in the GCL and second in the NYPL league rankings while Acuña was 11th in the GCL and 14th in the Appy League. Acuña is seven months younger than Robles, but there was a clear separator if one were to look at the TrackMan data. Robles only had some of his balls in play captured that year, since not every stadium had units, but his exit velos were low by any measure, peaking at 104 mph. Acuña hit multiple balls 112 mph that season and his rate of hard-hit balls was above Major League averages (he hit 12 percent of his balls in play over 105 mph at a stabilized rate vs. a MLB average of 9 percent) while he was 17. As you may guess, exit velos map to physical strength, so even top prospects that play up the middle positions don't get close to Major League average power figures until the upper minors, if ever. Gleyber Torres is a year older than Acuña and was in Low-A and High-A in 2015, with a max exit velocity of 104 mph and three times as many measured balls in play.

Converting things like pitch selection and bat control to grades on the 20–80 scouting scale is useful to see alongside other grades as components of offensive production. This lets you see that certain archetypes you could recognize from a scouting perspective are present with a simple layer of analysis on top of the TrackMan data. A 4-A slugger that can't hack in the majors but wins homer titles in Triple-A will have big exit velos and game-power measurements, but just okay pitch selection and poor bat control. This means they hit only center-cut mistake pitches hard and still chase enough to not hit for high average, but a couple metrics could give you a similar idea of how this guy hits that a very seasoned scout could give you after a few games.

One goal is to look at data for this player and see if there's a path to making him a solid big leaguer, even in a lesser role. You can look at splits versus top-end pitchers of a certain type to get an idea of what the hitter may do, situationally, in the big leagues. A hitter need not have great bat control if the pitcher they're facing lives in the same part of the zone where their barrel does. Sometimes visual evaluations will tell you the player's current swing doesn't fully unlock the hitter's potential and underlying data supports that, showing that the hitter does an outsized portion of their damage in a small window of the hitting zone but little elsewhere.

This is the area where scouting and development are key. If your scout knows the player and his makeup, and knows he used to be more athletic and could be again, for whatever reason, then the potential is there to work with. A recent example of this is the case of Marlins 1B prospect Lewin Díaz. Díaz had a few promising years early in his career with the Twins, then the club asked him to drop some weight. He got too skinny, weak, and had a horrible 2018 season. Rebuilt in 2019, he looked better than he ever had and was traded to Miami. A multi-year statistical model would probably underrate Díaz because his 2018 season was so bad, but scouts who understood the context, who knew why he looked bad, would be able to tell you to toss that out for this particular player.

You could also have your hitting coordinator look at some video and advise on whether there's a larger swing change that can improve athleticism or a mechanical trade-off. Maybe there's more power to be unlocked through better sequencing of movements in the swing, possibly lowering the effort level in the swing will negate some power but increase plate coverage and bat control, maybe quieting the head movement will improve ball tracking and pitch selection, maybe the swing doesn't have enough loft. Maybe he's getting beat on pitches away and needs a second swing to punch a liner the opposite way or spoil/foul off that pitch to stay alive and get the pitch inside he can punish. These have all been issues that have been fixed before, so it's no wonder that an MLB-level hitter languishing on the bench or minors can pull a Max Muncy and break out when any of these could be the key.

For reference, here's a plot of what exit velos and launch angles tend to produce. The darkest areas are extra-base hits, while the areas at the top are almost definite outs. This is the chart that every team has looked at at some point and drawn on, chopping it into distinct groupings (weak grounders, pop ups, barrels) to help classify contact into buckets that make models more predictive.

Somewhere like Level 3.5 on the hitting side are metrics that predict what stats hitters should have, essentially by taking these predictive metrics,

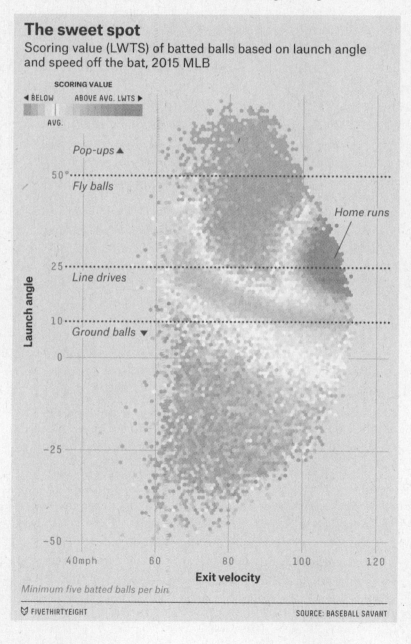

The sweet spot

Scoring value (LWTS) of batted balls based on launch angle and speed off the bat, 2015 MLB

SCORING VALUE

◄ BELOW   ABOVE AVG. LWTS ►

AVG.

Pop-ups ▲

50° Fly balls

Home runs

25 Line drives

10 Ground balls ▼

0

Launch angle

−25

−50

40mph   60   80   100   120

Exit velocity

Minimum five batted balls per bin

FIVETHIRTYEIGHT   SOURCE: BASEBALL SAVANT

based on pitch decisions and quality of contact. Most if not all teams have a version of this.

Level 4 is where only some teams are consistently going with confidence and getting results. When a playoff team has three key contributors and you didn't know any of their names at the beginning of the season, it's almost certainly due to Level 4 analysis. The work the Dodgers are doing with hitters, the Astros with pitchers, the Yankees with players from the discard pile—they are all elite organizations with elite analysis and elite development flexing their muscle. Sometimes it's a subtle swing change, sometimes it's big. One time it's something they knew they were going to do when they acquired the player, the other time it's a flyer and things just kinda work out.

Before the 2014 season, the Astros claimed Collin McHugh on waivers from the Rockies and the career -0.3 WAR pitcher posted 9.2 WAR over the next three seasons, a return of roughly $70 million for the team in that span. From an August 2014 Bloomberg profile of the club by Joshua Green:

> The Astros' analysts noticed that McHugh had a world-class curveball. Most curves spin at about 1,500 times per minute; McHugh's spins 2,000 times. The more spin, the more the ball moves during the pitch—and the more likely batters are to miss it. Houston snapped him up. "We identified him as someone whose surface statistics might not indicate his true value," says David Stearns, the team's 29-year-old assistant general manager.

Stearns is currently the GM of the Milwaukee Brewers and nowadays all 30 teams are trying to do things at this level of analysis, but very few were doing it in 2014. Taking a pitcher that throws a two-seamer and slider but has a high-spin four-seamer and curveball he should be throwing more often is something most internet analysts can diagnose and not even get much traffic doing so at this point.

Who's Got It

The teams that touched the TrackMan monolith first leapt way out in front of the others, and the effects of the evolutionary leap in talent evaluation reverberated for many years. The Astros, Dodgers, Yankees, Pirates, Red Sox, Rays, Cleveland, and Twins all seemed to be using data to target players in the pro and amateur arena early on, and there were probably more whose acquisitions (high-spin pitchers in the draft, for instance) were less overt than those clubs.

When TrackMan broke into the college ranks, the schools were also hesitant to pay for their own units until they knew the utility. We're told that a handful of schools (we believe Vanderbilt, Mississippi State, TCU, and UCLA) had their units sponsored by MLB clubs (we believe Houston and Tampa Bay). Those clubs exclusively got the data from regular season games in return for paying the majority of the cost while the college paid a smaller amount and got to also have this data and data from practices, scrimmages, and camps.

Exclusive deals are now no longer allowed, but colleges are aware of how useful the data can be and many have installed/own their own units. Here's the complete list as of the start of the 2019 college season:

Cincinnati, East Carolina, Georgia Tech, Duke, Florida State, North Carolina State, North Carolina, Notre Dame, Virginia, Virginia Tech, Wake Forest, Pittsburgh, Miami, Louisville, Virginia Commonwealth, Michigan State, Indiana, Iowa, Michigan, Penn State, Northwestern, Oklahoma State, Texas Christian, Texas, West Virginia, Campbell, Radford, Long Beach State, Cal State Fullerton, UC Santa Barbara, Cal Poly San Luis Obispo, Dallas Baptist, Missouri State, Cal Berkeley, Oregon, Southern California, Oregon State, UCLA, Arizona State, Georgia, Arkansas, Auburn, Clemson, LSU, Missouri, Ole Miss, Texas A&M, Kentucky, Vanderbilt, Ole Miss, Mississippi State, Coastal Carolina, and Appalachian State.

If you go catch a game at any of these schools you'll be able to see the unit hung behind home plate, typically up near the pressbox. They're all just big, black rectangles save for a few of them, like Arizona State's which is adorned with the school's pitchfork logo. Now that units are more widespread and colleges are paying to have them installed themselves, the data gets put into a bucket that teams pay the vendor to access. Everyone has access to the same pool of data and the gaps created by teams are all in how it's analyzed and dissected, rather than simply who has it and who does not.

There are even a couple high schools and tournament facilities that have units as well, like USA Baseball, most Cape Cod League stadiums, IMG Academy in Florida, LakePoint just outside of Atlanta, and JSerra High School in Southern California. Many of the key summer showcase events are held at these facilities, colleges, and minor league and Major League stadiums, so TrackMan units are recording most of the high-profile amateur action over the summer.

Well, at the pro level, anyway. Colleges need to opt into a data-sharing program where they give up what their unit captures in exchange for the other teams'. Not every school does this, but something like two-thirds of them do. Some athletic departments have huge budgets and think they need a unit, so they get one, but they don't have anyone on staff who knows what to do with the data. Or maybe they just want to use it for developmental purposes, the way other new forms of technology are largely being used around both pro and amateur baseball, which we detail a bit later in this chapter.

The same way unit access at the Division I level was once exclusive for some clubs during the early days of installation, so too was it at the junior college level until late in 2019. A few MLB teams had paid to install TrackMan units at various elite junior college programs, but MLB owners voted to end this disparity, and any future disparity on the international market, at the 2019 Winter Meetings. It was a cost-saving measure. A tech-driven, talent-evaluation arms race would be expensive, especially if it were to extend internationally. Rather than have 30 teams pay to install and maintain TrackMan units at various junior colleges, teams can now just share data collected by the current units and spread the cost of maintaining those units among all 30 clubs. Essentially, the owners voted to torpedo an edge for some clubs (the early movers in the JuCo and tournament/showcase space) so most of the league could gain data access for no additional cost. Only a few JuCo programs regularly have talent worthy of better understanding, and few JuCo facilities can support the technology installation, which is also a problem in DI ball.

For example, Long Beach State's unit sits on top of some wooden pallets and cinder blocks, and this seemed to impact the accuracy of readings during 2019 Area Codes. There's a correlation between fastball velocity and fastball spin. Usually, the harder the fastball the more it spins. During 2019 Area Codes, the pitch velocities, spin rates, and exit velocities were posted on the Blair Field jumbotron in real time, and the spin rates were often much higher than typical for pitchers throwing in the upper-80s and low-90s. TrackMan was kind enough to provide a graphic of Area Code spin rates and velocities that show many of the pitches at velocities identical to pro pitchers had more spin. This could be because of differences in the baseball used at ACG. In an email to FanGraphs and Driveline Baseball, a TrackMan employee noted the Area Code ball is tackier and has higher seams than what it's being compared to in this infographic, so that might be why the spin rates were higher than usual at the event.

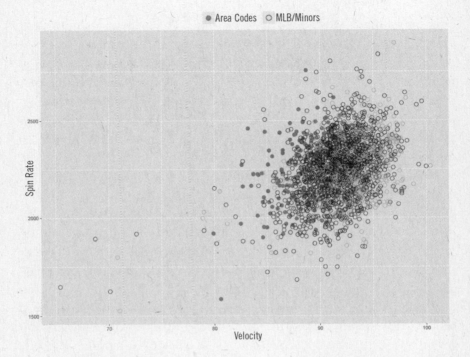

These are the sorts of things we and teams need to consider before they take any of this data at face value. There are other high school showcase events at which TrackMan units collect data, so an individual's output at any event can be crosschecked by the data they generate at others. Several of the prospects who suit up at Area Codes also play in the Perfect Game All American Classic at PETCO Park in San Diego, or at the Team USA baseball facility in Cary, North Carolina, or at PG National at Arizona's Chase Field, etc. This enables teams to "clean" the data by normalizing, or altogether deleting data from units like this. This is done with various specs from all across baseball, including big league stadiums. Pitch location data (some teams pay independent contractors like Dan Brooks of Brooks Baseball to make their pitch location data marginally better), spin rates, vertical movement, anything you can think of can be polished up and made more accurate, just based on the fact that these systems of measure are imperfect.

There are also some front office folks who think some of this vaiation is intentional, and that teams are trying to inflate the value of their prospects because they know opposing teams prioritize certain aspects of the data. For instance, a source indicated to us that one team employs six of the top eight upper-minors pitchers in terms of fastball vertical movement, which they consider to be fishy. This source tends to split up home and road data to see if the home units—which have an overwhelming influence on an individual's overall stat sample—may be miscalibrated, intentionally or not. Nearly 40 percent of the top few dozen lower-minors pitchers, again in terms of vertical movement, come from the Tampa-area pod of spring training complexes (Phillies, Blue Jays, Tigers, Yankees) who frequently play one another, a sign that one of the units in that area may be miscalibrated—or that several of those orgs target that type of trait (as we would). More on that in a bit.

These issues likely contributed to MLB's decision to consider Hawk-Eye as an alternative, first reported by Eno Sarris of The Athletic in May 2019, especially if MLB wants something it perceives as more accurate so they can implement an electronic strike zone at the big league level eventually. MLB piloted an electronic strike zone (if it's not eventually sponsored by AutoZone, someone's marketing director should be fired—into the sun with all marketing directors) using TrackMan during 2019 Arizona Fall League games at Salt River Fields in Scottsdale.

The extra split second between when an umpire would typically call a ball or strike and when the signal was relayed to their earpiece was initially jarring and disorienting, but added to some two-strike drama at others. It also created some amusing situations, as players who disagreed with strike calls had no vessel in which to pour their frustrations. Habitual glares at the umpire were met with shrugs.

Diamondbacks prospect Geraldo Perdomo flipped off the TrackMan unit and is probably No. 1 on its hitlist should it ever become self-aware. On October 15, Giants prospect Jacob Heyward became the first player in baseball history to be tossed for arguing balls and strikes in a game with an electronic zone. A source close to the Scottsdale Scorpions, Heyward's Fall League club, told Eric that Heyward was venting frustration toward the roboump, while home plate ump José Navas clearly thought otherwise. If/when you're reading this, we sympathize with your plight, robot.

Other tech became widespread soon after TrackMan hit its stride, saturating pro ball and the top of amateur baseball. Rapsodo is a relatively new pitch-tracking technology that debuted in a closed beta around 2015, and it blends the radar aspects of TrackMan with the optical tracking of other technologies. It calculates pitch trajectory using images of a pitch's spin rate and axis as it comes out of the pitcher's hand, rather than using the ball's flight path like TrackMan and PITCHf/x. Because of how close the first Rapsodo units needed to be set up to the catcher, it couldn't be used for in-game pitch measurement.

The original unit looked like a wedding DJ's speaker mounted on a tripod about six feet behind home plate, which created issues when space between the plate and backstop was tight, and because the units often broke if someone airmailed a pitch over the catcher's head and beaned the unit. The new model, which player dev people in baseball anticipated like it was the next Nintendo console, is about the size and shape of a monitor speaker that sits at the front of a concert stage. It sits on the ground about three quarters of the way from the pitching rubber to the plate, which again means it can't be used for in-game pitch measurement, and therefore has less overlap with scouting than TrackMan, unless teams have amateur pitchers in for private workouts. It's great for doing work in the bullpen and its cost, about $4,000 per unit, has made it the go-to player development tool for many colleges and big-budget high schools.

These technologies and their uncreative monikers are multiplying. YakkerTech (used by Catawba College and Old Dominion University) measures similar stuff, Blast Motion sensors fit over the knob of the bat like a condom and output visual swing plane for the hitter to see, K-Motion is a company that provides wearable vests that track hitters' kinematic sequences and body positions at various points of the swing, MoCap suits and systems can be used for similar purposes. Most of this is best-suited for player development rather than scouting, and their various uses are covered in *The MVP Machine*, Ben Lindbergh and Travis Sawchik's book on the subject. There are suddenly lots of ways to have immediate, detailed, semi-concrete answers to questions about how the body performs baseball movement we didn't even know to ask a decade ago.

Video Killed the Sinkerball Arm

One current frontier, a realm most teams are just starting to explore, if they are at all, is high-speed video. Edgertronic cameras shoot at nearly 2,000 frames per second (fps) at 1080p, and at higher speeds at lesser resolutions. They are now being used in scouting and player development by a growing number of teams, led first by the Houston Astros. For context, the footage from *Planet Earth* of breaching Great White Sharks exploding out of South African waters as they hunt seals, was shot at 1,000 fps.

With the ultra-slow-motion video recorded by an Edgertronic, teams can perform acute mechanical analysis and see pitch grips and releases, which they can then show to their players as a visual aid to help them make fine adjustments. Seam uniformity and spin axis influence pitch movement, and it's easier for coaches and players to see little inefficiencies and correct them; this process usually includes Rapsodo and is known as "pitch design." Some pitchers are just better at spinning the ball in an effectual way than others. You could argue we should be projecting more heavily on pitchers who currently don't spin the baseball well, in anticipation that this will eventually be corrected, but we're currently unsure how to handle that situation since our exposure to, and use of, high-speed video is in its infancy. In theory, this is the type of thing teams identify and target knowing they might be able to tweak prospects and improve them, and knowing the camera's frame rate enables teams to calculate spin rates and bat speed by hand at venues where there is no TrackMan unit.

The problem with Edgertronic cameras is they're incredibly expensive ($15,000 for the model that shoots at the above specs) and a pain in the ass to lug around and set up. The camera travels in a carry-on-sized case as if it's housing the protagonist's weapon in a horrible *Desperado* reboot. It's often connected to a laptop, a tablet/monitor, a battery pack that helps it last throughout batting practice and a game, and a little trigger remote that looks like the button you might use to call a nurse to your bedside. It can be cumbersome to set all that stuff up at a field in a remote area.

The folks who operate these cameras do not always appear engaged. They're surfing social media, prepping for their fantasy football draft, or playing Temple Run while the best high school players in the country take batting practice on the field in front of them, mindlessly triggering the camera to capture when they hear the crack of the bat, then watching in their periphery as the footage writes on the memory card until they're ready to capture again. No scout is rapt at attention for the entirety of their work day, the same as the rest of us, but this behavior is cold, drone-like, and heedless in a way that rubs many people the wrong way. It doesn't seem like these youngsters are eager to take notes in an effort to learn how to scout. Scouts dubious of the use of this technology readily admit that the slow-motion video, when projected on a giant screen in the draft room, is hypnotizing and almost always silences the room.

Sony makes a few model cameras that many teams are using as a cheaper, more portable alternative to Edgertronics, and it's what we're using at FanGraphs. They shoot at nearly 1,000 fps and, as the lens is about four inches across, they are small enough to be allowed into a big league stadium. We know the Diamondbacks, Marlins, Red Sox, Cubs, Giants, and Yankees are all using these cameras for various purposes.

Our first season with the Sony was illuminating, especially when viewed in concert with other data and transaction patterns. Our viewing of high-speed footage of hitters from either baseline shows that most hitters swing and miss due to location, not timing, and often swings and misses on fastballs come from pitches at the top of the strike zone or above. Relatedly, many of the pitchers who the intellectually progressive teams are acquiring—or the way they're changing them after they're acquired—prioritize vertical movement.

We know spin rate has a correlation with swinging strike rate, but focusing on it, alone, can be misleading, as there are other components impacting pitch effectiveness. The ball spins, pushing the air downward behind it, creating an equal and opposite upward force that causes it to move. So the movement of a fastball depends on the rate at which it is spinning. How much it moves *vertically* depends not only on the rate at which it's spinning but also the axis of the ball. Balls with truer backspin have more vertical movement than one at the same velo, with the same spin, but with sidespin. The best

SWINGING STRIKE %						
	1700-1900	1900-2100	2100-2300	2300-2500	>2500	ALL_SPIN
<86	6%	10%	5%			8%
86-88	4%	7%	7%	8%		7%
88-90	4%	6%	7%	8%	9%	7%
90-92	6%	7%	7%	9%	10%	8%
92-94	6%	8%	9%	10%	12%	9%
94-96	8%	9%	10%	12%	13%	11%
96-98	8%	10%	11%	13%	14%	12%
98-100		8%	13%	15%	15%	14%
>100			11%	17%	12%	13%
ALL_VELO	6%	7%	9%	11%	13%	10%
LAUNCH ANGLE (DEG)						
	1700-1900	1900-2100	2100-2300	2300-2500	>2500	ALL_SPIN
<86	24.3	23.8	25.4			24.7
86-88	15.7	24.1	24.4	30.2		24.8
88-90	17.6	22.2	26.1	27.2	23.1	25.1
90-92	15.1	21.5	25.4	26.6	24.0	24.5
92-94	14.1	21.1	23.8	26.6	27.9	24.3
94-96	15.0	20.1	23.0	25.3	27.2	24.0
96-98	13.2	18.9	22.1	24.6	25.1	23.3
98-100		17.3	19.0	21.6	23.8	21.0
>100			25.6	20.8	16.2	19.0
ALL_VELO	15.5	21.1	23.9	25.7	26.1	24.1

Table Credit: Driveline Baseball

examples have a handful of inches of vertical break more than average, but at 100 mph, a few unexpected inches is all the edge you need.

It's common sense that a fastball which moves vertically—sometimes called "life," "ride," or "rise"—would miss more bats than one moving horizontally because the barrel whips through the zone horizontally. Think about Roy Halladay's running fastball running right into Cody Ross' happy zone during the 2010 NLCS. This is an example of running fastballs having less margin for error in the strike zone than ones with rise.

The ball doesn't actually rise, it's subject to gravity, it just appears to rise because it's descending less quickly than the eye and brain think it should be due to the spin fighting gravity. This is part of why high-spin, rising fastballs are so effective at the top of the strike zone, because hitters who try to square up the baseball end up swinging underneath it. Toward the bottom of the zone, the hitter's bat path has more of a vertical plane most of the time, so the hitter is more likely to run into contact.

Arm slot and hand and finger position on release all influence the spin axis of the ball, and the high-speed cameras have helped us see who is good at doing this. TrackMan data can help too. Many of the pitchers who smart teams are acquiring have spin axes near 12:00 (on a clock), like Clayton Kershaw or MacKenzie Gore, which indicates perfect backspin and maximized vertical movement (for a given velocity and spin rate).

The fastballs of relievers recently acquired by Tampa Bay (Colin Poche, Emilio Pagán, Nick Anderson) are among the leaders in vertical movement; Justin Verlander and Gerrit Cole were altered to create more vertical movement on their fastballs after acquired by Houston; Josh Hader, despite his arm slot, has a hand position that enables vertical movement; Zac Gallen's 12:30 spin axis lets his fastball compete for whiffs in the zone, and on and on. The list of either good prospects or prospects who outperform expectations are littered with guys with several of these traits.

Targeting these traits alone creates a biodiversity problem among your pitchers. A lot of hitting is about anticipation, as you're about to learn, and if every arm thrown at you looks the same, you're probably going to be better at dealing with their stuff than you would if the other staff was full of a wide array of deliveries. The Brewers and Twins have mixed low slot arms (Devin Smeltzer, Alex Claudio, Sergio Romo) with vertical movement guys. The ability to identify or create pitchers with this trait currently has some orgs well out in front of others, in a way that seems like an unfair advantage in development to a casual fan.

Matching Up Planes

There's a lot of ideas to consider when a manager is setting a lineup for the game that night. Everyone in the front office (and most coaches) know that specific hitter vs. pitcher stats are useless: the samples are small but if they are big enough to mean something, it's across their entire career of different skill levels than what they are today. Some teams go really deep into this, but the basic idea is to take indicators about each hitter and pitcher to predict the strengths and weaknesses of a specific matchup.

One method is to replace those hitter vs. pitcher stats with a bigger sample of recent performance, lumping a bunch of similar hitters to the hitter in question vs. this pitcher, or maybe a bunch of pitchers similar to this pitcher in question to get an even bigger sample. How would you define similarity? That's up to both your opinion about what may matter, past performances, and how deep your interest and data can take you.

The most important concepts to consider in this situation are the plane of the pitcher's fastball to the plate and the plane of the hitter's swing through the zone. Imagine sitting in the dugout and watching a 6'8" pitcher (think Mark Hendrickson) with a short stride and high slot throw a sinker down in the zone. That's as steep as a pitch can get: the short stride keeps the pitcher tall on the mound, his height and release point stay on that trend, and throwing a ball that sinks and throwing it low will maximize that effect.

Now imagine the hitter being a power hitter who hits the ball in the air and has the bat speed to get away with having a bit of a longer path to the zone (think Ronald Acuña), designed to increase bat speed and scoop the ball into the air. The ball is steep coming down from the pitcher's hand, much steeper than average, and the hitter's swing path is also steep coming up at the ball, also much steeper than average. You can see why this is a good matchup, all else being equal, for the hitter. His timing is less important because, again, all else being equal, his swing path is "on plane" with the pitch for a longer time, giving him margin for error.

On the other hand, if the pitcher is at the other end of the spectrum, this gets very tricky for the hitter. Let's imagine Craig Kimbrel: short in stature, low arm slot, throws a "rising" four-seam fastball that's often thrown up in the zone. This is about as flat as a pitch can get, which means that Acuña will have a much smaller window where his swing will be on plane, so contact is much less likely (not even considering the much higher velocity Kimbrel has compared to Hendrickson). The type of hitter more geared for this pitch plane is a hitter with a flat swing that doesn't lift the ball much and will be on plane with this pitch for a while (think Albert Pujols).

You may say that the Kimbrel pitch plane (Koji Uehara did this same thing at about 88 mph if that's an easier mental image to compare to Hendrickson) seems superior since it would only have a good chance of consistently giving up hard contact to hitters than don't lift the ball. There's a second level to this simplistic way of thinking about the batter/hitter confrontation. If Acuña faces Kimbrel, the odds of contact are pretty low, relative to the sinker type of similar quality, but if Acuña hits the ball, he's probably going to lift it and the pitch is already up in the zone, so that increases the odds of a homer.

Obviously dialing this in for every hitter based on comparable hitters and pitchers can simplify and make the decision more objective, but it gets way more complicated. Velocity is a big aspect, as are pitch mix, locations, quality of pitches, sequencing, chase pitches, etc. Not every example is as clean as Kimbrel and Hendrickson, who are the most extreme examples. One of the most notable down-in-the-zone sinkerballers in the big leagues is 5'7" Marcus Stroman, and one of the most notable up-in-the-zone four-seamer pitchers is 6'4" Gerrit Cole, with the locations of their 2019 fastballs plotted below from the catcher's perspective. Very few decisions are single-issue and clean like above, but every game calls for hundreds of them.

Gerrit Cole Pitch % vs. All Batters
Season: 2019-03-29 to 2019-09-29
Pitches: FA | Count: All Counts | Total Pitches: 1802 | View: Catcher

3.2% 58	6.8% 123	7.3% 132	3.2% 58	0.3% 6
3.0% 54	10.4% 187	9.4% 170	5.8% 105	1.9% 35
2.2% 39	7.0% 126	12.7% 229	7.6% 137	2.1% 38
0.3% 6	2.2% 39	5.2% 93	3.9% 70	1.4% 26
0.1% 1	0.2% 4	0.9% 17	1.8% 33	0.9% 16

Marcus Stroman Pitch % vs. All Batters
Season: 2019-03-28 to 2019-09-27
Pitches: SI | Count: All Counts | Total Pitches: 1139 | View: Catcher

1.3% 15	1.1% 13	1.1% 12	0.1% 1	0.0% 0
4.1% 47	5.4% 61	3.9% 44	1.1% 13	0.2% 2
5.3% 60	10.1% 115	8.3% 95	2.6% 29	1.0% 11
3.8% 43	10.5% 119	11.5% 131	5.4% 62	2.1% 24
1.3% 15	4.6% 52	7.4% 84	5.1% 58	2.9% 33

You can see how a manager that had never used Microsoft Excel in 30 years of managing could be handed a binder full of this information to set his lineup and has information overload trying to balance all the factors. Or, he's wondering how the office came to its conclusions in the "recommended lineup" if they aren't intentionally summarizing research to make it more digestible.

About 10 years ago, Kiley asked a friend from a progressive team about how they gave their manager information to make decisions. Their manager was open-minded and liked to get all the information the front office would offer, but would make his own decisions and process the information mostly privately. Some managers that are open to this data like to process it in a more collaborative way, so that they can be sure everyone is on the same page.

When Kiley asked if there were ever any mistakes made by the manager, he was given a scenario. When facing the Red Sox, left-handed hitter J.D. Drew (one of Boston's best hitters) was coming to the plate late in the game and the team had a lefty reliever on the mound. The manager opted to take out the lefty reliever and instead bring in a righty reliever who was primarily a four-seam fastball, up-in-the-strike-zone type. The front office members sitting in the suite were confused how this was the matchup the manager preferred.

After the game, the GM asked the manager why he pulled out of the ideal lefty-on-lefty matchup. The manager said that the advance scouting report said Drew struggled with hard fastballs up in the zone, so he brought in the pitcher who excelled at Drew's weakness. The GM pointed out that the platoon advantage the lefty reliever offered outweighed the specific pitch and location advantage the righty offered.

The manager took the instruction and didn't make that mistake again, but pointed out to the GM that the fastball-heavy righty struck out Drew on three straight high fastballs, just as the manager intended. "So it wasn't that bad of a fuckup, huh?"

Machine Learning

"While peak knowledge may be closer than we think, the exploitation of raw information can continue infinitely, along with the damage it does to us and our ability to reckon with the world. In this way, information more closely resembles atomic power than oil—an effectively unlimited resource that still contains immense destructive power and that's even more explicitly connected to histories of violence."

—James Bridle, British author

The sheer amount of data and metadata generated by baseball's long schedule of games, each of them full of hundreds of measurable events, makes it ripe for data science. Some teams are making more frequent use of machine learning (a subset of artificial intelligence much better at recognizing patterns than we are) as a tool for advance scouting, and possibly during games. If you watch a particular team every day, you probably learn a lot about how certain pitchers sequence, how they set up their nastiest pitches. Fastball up, curveball down. Fastball away, changeup away. Cutter in, back foot curveball. But if we feed every pitch, from every situation, into Python or some other machine-learning software or neural network, it will be much better at predicting pitches in most situations than we are. And even if it's just a little bit better, or if the predictive model only has a high degree of certainty as to what's about to be thrown in some situations, that's meaningful over the course of a full season. After all, a gork, a ground ball with eyes, just one more dying quail a week….

In addition to there being myriad prospective applications for this type of machine learning, there are potential real-time applications for visual machine learning, which can draw conclusions by being shown images on video. Imagine being able to take video of a pitcher receiving a sign, getting a grip on the ball in his glove, and delivering home, then showing the video to a neural processing unit and telling the NPU what the resulting pitch was, and doing this over and over again until the NPU can identify little variations that hitters can watch to have a better idea of what pitch they're about to see. There's evidence teams are doing this, either to prepare for games or during them.

During the 2018 playoffs, a Houston Astros employee was caught filming the Red Sox dugout with, according to the original report on Metro Boston, a Huawei Mate 20 Pro phone. Recent Huawei phones have a Kirin 970 (or 980 or 990 depending on your model) chip and dual neural processing unit on board that can parse through and identify 2,000 images per minute. The phone is capable of being shown various food items and identifying what they are, as well as their volume and estimated calorie count, in real time. It's possible this type of NPU can be trained to parse through signs a base coach is giving, or little variations in pitcher movement so hitters know what's coming, though we have no idea what audio or visual means might be used to alert hitters in such a short span of time.

During the 2019 ALCS, Associated Press reporter Jake Seiner tweeted that during the prior spring training he spoke with big league catcher Erik Kratz about sign stealing and technology. Kratz, who has played for the Yankees, Astros, Brewers, Blue Jays, Phillies, Pirates, Royals, Rays, and Giants, told Seiner that "one of his former clubs placed cameras behind home plate to detect when opponents were tipping their pitches. After games, the team would use video editing software to overlay each delivery of the pitcher. If he was doing something differently on his breaking pitches, maybe moving an elbow in a funny fashion, the whole team would know what to watch for next time they matched up."

As we mentioned in an earlier chapter, in fall 2019 the Astros posted a job listing for a "Machine Learning–Computer Vision Analyst" in their R&D department. The listed duties included, "plan, design, and build new models, visualizations, and tools to support and collaborate with all facets of baseball operation: scouting, player development, player acquisition, video, and more." It asked applicants be proficient with scalable machine-learning frameworks like TensorFlow, PyTorch, and Caffe, as well as Python and R and other database-related and audiovisual skills.

There are rules against using tech and relaying signals to hitters, and it's possible further legislation will specifically target video and visual machine learning uses in advance scouting if MLB is aware it's going on. If the complete lack of broadcast shots of the signs catchers were putting down during the 2019 Yankees/Astros ALCS are any indication, they are. How badly this all offends one's senses depends on the tastes of the individual. There's something excessive and pornographic about it, something about the unintended consequences and selfish disregard for others that those who wield it seem to display.

When Performance Matters

In high school, stats mean nothing. In college, we can look at general indicators, and when taken in context (i.e. he's the only good hitter on his team and he gets pitched around a lot, he told our scout this frustrates him, etc.) can have some predictive value. For high school showcases with wood bats against good pitching, we can gather some information and from the couple good college summer leagues we can gather the most (in the amateur context). But, in general, amateur hitting stats mean nothing unless you have some scouting context and hopefully two of 1) strong competition, 2) a big sample, and 3) a wood bat.

At the professional level, stats are much more insightful. We wouldn't take much from short-season leagues (which are basically the same level of competition as the best amateur leagues, like the SEC or the Cape Cod League) but in full-season ball we can start to notice things.

Kiley was doing pro coverage of a Low-A club (following a minor league team for five to six days to write up all of their players) years ago for a team and thought he'd put a 45 bat on a prospect, from BP and recollections from the games. He then noticed when he went over his game notes there were a lot of positive comments and solid contact, thinking he might go as high as a 55 on the hit tool. Then he checked the prospect's stats for some context: the prospect went 12-for-15 in the games Kiley saw, but at that point near the end of the season, he'd hit .250 with poor peripherals. Kiley gave him a fringe prospect grade and he ultimately topped out at Triple-A.

As suggested in his report, Kiley thought his numbers would improve in the near future (they did) because he was told by development folks from this club that this hot streak wasn't a fluke, but the result of some adjustments and added comfort at the plate. Of the 12 hits, almost all of them were hard-hit line drives, more indicative of a skill to hit than if he had seen a bunch of bloopers and infield hits.

We mention that to tell you that in full-season minor leagues, the numbers are part of the hit-tool evaluation and they basically aren't or shouldn't be anywhere below that. When there's a generic little guy with a simple swing, you want to write him off after BP since there's no ceiling. When that guy squares a couple balls up and you look at his numbers and see that he's never hit under .300, then you start to investigate how real this is. You hedge because there aren't a lot of big league regulars that look like that little guy, but there's a bunch of bench guys and a big reason you're there as a scout is to find freely available bench guys.

If you're scouting a guy with big hitting tools and mediocre numbers but when you're watching him you see things that indicate he's better than the numbers and developing some feel, the numbers aren't very useful. If you're scouting a smaller guy that's short on tools but you see him squaring the ball up a lot, the numbers can help tell you how long of a track record he has of doing this in the games you didn't see. If he's only ever hit .300 in multiple years of pro ball, this makes it more likely he can keep doing this than if he just showed up to Low-A and you have no legitimate statistical history to look at.

Anything more than this sort of supplemental role for minor league stats is misguided. One analytics front office staffer told us that his pro scouts, ideally, would not even know the minor league hitter's batting average that they're writing up. His rationale is that he knows numbers and the scout knows scouting, so the other shouldn't let the thing they know less about inform their report. In the ideal world, both just write up their expertise, then their boss (who knows both) can make the determination with near-perfect information. In this world, Kiley (in a world where he didn't understand numbers from an office perspective) would probably put a 55 on that prospect's hit tool based on what his eyes told him and the office would adjust it down to a 45 or 50, rather than Kiley doing it on his own. The correct projection in hindsight was a 20 or 30 (shrug emoji).

One criticism of pro scouting is that when a scout walks into a Double-A, Triple-A, or big league park, they know their overall grade (FV or OFP) for every hitter is down to two options before they even watch any action. You can do so much background on players with their numbers, draft status, basic biographical info, and any buzz you know from where publications rank them, if the GM called him "untouchable" to the media, etc.

This also applies to basic scouting grades and fans. Very few tools for big league regulars are below average and you can use context clues to figure out the area of a specific tool grade (give or take a notch). As we reference above, specialization of pitching and advance scouting is helping to further eliminate overachievers, average hitting tools, and guess/mistake hitters. Beyond that, many tools (like hit and game power) can be defined completely by performance when we have multiple full seasons of similar MLB performance for players and no signs the player has "changed."

You can see how a GM with the mindset of a management consultant or hedge fund manager could see a pro scouting department with a dozen guys traveling all over the country for $1.5 million when you total up salary, benefits, and travel, and think it's ripe for cost cutting and automation/optimization. Scouts' fear after *Moneyball* came out in 2003 was that they'd be replaced by numbers/analysts. The opposite happened at that time, because scouting reports were more predictive than surface stats. Now that fear is well-founded because scouts are actively being replaced by growing numbers of teams, now that the tech and analysis have become much more advanced.

CHAPTER 13

Running a Modern Team

Owners place budget constraints on teams' operating costs, and they have to decide how to allocate those resources to collect information, and they also need to use that information to make decisions. Every team does this differently, and seismic shifts in organizational philosophy often occur when the top of a front office turns over due to regime change, though infrastructure (physical, technological, and ideological) takes time to install, and even longer to yield results.

In this chapter, we'll summarize what we consider the best practices of player evaluation and, to the best of our ability, describe where each team fits on the continuum of thought as it relates to the various aspects of baseball operations, breaking down the teams in each zone of a success/style matrix, as a broad way of showing where teams fall right now.

This is still an imperfect instrument as we're averaging clubs' positions across multiple departments—no team has every department in the same position on the matrix—so we use the comments below to illuminate the specifics of each situation.

Big League In-Game Approach and Roster Construction

In all sports, it's important to put your players in position to succeed. This is most obviously true and most often discussed as it relates to football (tailoring defensive schemes to fit personnel, rotating running backs depending on their competency, etc.) and basketball (floor spacing, defensive matchups, etc.) but it's moving to the forefront of how teams think about in-game management in baseball. The idea of platooning—a lefty hitter starts when a righty is on the mound and vice versa—is not new, but it's becoming more common for teams to start hitters whose swing paths do the most damage where the opposing starter likes to work with their stuff. Facing a sinkerballer? Start the hitter with the low-ball, lofted swing. Facing someone who works at the top of the zone? The hitter with the more compact, direct, flat-planed swing gets the start, all else being equal.

We also advocate teams making decisions that favor run scoring and run prevention depending on the game state. If your heavy-footed outfielder takes an at-bat late in the game and he's not likely to hit again, that player should come off the field in favor of a better defender. On the flip side, if you started a light-hitting, plus-defensive outfielder because you had a fly-ball pitcher on the mound that day, but you're down a run or two as you approach the latter half of the game, it's time to take an offensive approach. Versatility across your roster enables this type of dynamism so it can be enacted up and down the lineup.

We don't think it's prudent to have a pitching staff full of standard, pitch-design guys (those specs: rising fastball, cutter/slider, vertical curveball). It's fine if they're your core group, but you need to throw different looks at opposing hitters. Piggybacking pitchers who are drastically different—pitchers who, on their own couldn't last seven innings but, combined, work a great seven innings—is a viable once-a-week strategy without overtaxing your bullpen. Having a couple pitchers who present hitters with unique looks—side armers or some other form of deception—is ideal.

We're also in on shifting as long as the pitcher buys in. Teams are starting to shift in the minors so young arms are used to it, and the days of pitchers resisting are likely growing shorter because of this. We're reminded of a story from the early days of shifting when an All-Star pitcher told his manager he didn't want it happening during his starts. Eventually, the team's analysts gave the opposing hitters' spray charts to the pitcher and asked him to tell them where he wanted the fielders positioned. It was almost exactly where the analysts had recommended the fielders be positioned and it hasn't been an issue since. When with the Braves, Kiley was told about Ron Washington telling the staff members that he was skeptical about shifting, then charted outcomes and saw that it was a muthafuckin value-add.

This can also apply to team-building principles, with the concept of asymmetrical risk. From a player's perspective, a running back's holdout in football has this: save on wear and tear while sitting out games for which they're underpaid and approach the open market. The downside is still positive, with an even higher upside of a long-term deal and the only real risk is the iffy PR of a holdout, or the team stumbling into a player better than you in the games you skip.

In baseball, from the team's perspective, this applies to the depressed free agent market. A player like Mike Moustakas, a steady 2 WAR player without much risk, signing on a one-year deal for under $10 million is a great bargain. With a win costing basically $10 million on the open market, the team is paying for 1 WAR, expecting to get 2, with incentives included that only trigger if he's essentially a 3 WAR player. Clubs are increasingly being run in a way to limit risk and maximize flexibility and efficiency. When the outcome is solid, everyday hitters in free agency with a max downside of $10 million, why would the majority of clubs not just bootstrap a solid team with signings like this?

The soft free agent market for Moustakas (and Dallas Keuchel and other mid-tier talents) appears to be adjusting upward in the winter of 2019–2020, as Moustakas signed for four years, $64 million with Cincinnati after two straight one-year deals at lower salaries. Whether this is temporary or a longer-term correction isn't clear yet, but the market has shifted and now strategies will have to shift with them. It's our belief that the big group of GMs on the hot seat (far more than in recent years) and rising league revenues are serving to correct the overly soft free agent markets of the past few years.

Amateur Scouting

We like the idea of using a scouting report–informed draft model as the foundation of our team's board and then using the scouting staff to polish it, moving guys up and down based on makeup and other intel gathered by the scouts that would give better context to each player's standing. For example, if a draft model stuffs a player high on the board because of his age, but that player's body is mature, we'd round down on that player based on the visual evaluation of his frame, rather than dogmatically allowing the study to override what our eyes are telling us. Taking studies and using the logic gleaned from them is smarter than trying to overfit the past to explain the future, assuming everything will continue as it has and essentially turning off our reasoning ability.

In private workouts, we'd implement wearable tech or stuff that can't be used in games for whatever reason, like Blast Motion, Rapsodo, and K-Vests. This would only be for research purposes until we could determine which traits are meaningful.

Pro Scouting

Similar to how we'd approach the draft, the best teams use a mixed model that includes an underlying statistical engine impacted by their scouts' opinions. As we stated in the pro scouting chapter, org coverage in full-season ball and above coupled with dedicated complex-level coverage gives teams the best mix of opinion diversity and year-over-year player history for their scouts. We'd ask some scouts to take high-speed video if they're willing, as we think it would help with their visual evaluation and their ability to project on how a pitcher might be able to change and improve, but they'd only need to peek at the video as it renders on their camera, then ship it to the front office where video interns will sort and parse it more thoroughly.

This is also a great introduction to scouting for the interns, who would typically have seen baseball on TV only for most of their lives leading up to that point, and seeing pitch grips and swing mechanics in slow motion is a better teaching tool that trying to groom a scout in real time.

If we were dealing with a contending team, we'd be asking for a low-level prospect in every deal and dare them to say no to adding to a contending club because of a player who might be five years away from returning real value.

Tampa Bay is a model team in this area. They have aggressive, targeted coverage all the way down to the DSL. They have a loaded 40-man roster and loaded farm system that they have to aggressively stay on top of to make sure they aren't cornered into giving away assets in the fall just before the 40-man protection date for the Rule 5 Draft. Having a good process and regular transactions with other clubs also increases their edge via more chances to expose the gap between them and rival clubs.

Tampa Bay has the revenue disadvantage to justify eliminating some necessary elements of their process, but they instead invest more than other clubs that are more well off. We've also heard of times the Rays have passed on a good on-paper trade because of makeup; they have the R&D to hang with the most progressive clubs and still will allow makeup to carry the day when the information dictates it. Learning to make the most using the least is one reason why other clubs are plucking executives from Tampa Bay: Andrew Friedman with the Dodgers, Chaim Bloom with the Red Sox, and Matt Arnold with the Brewers are the most recent examples.

Model-Driven Contenders: PHI/CLE/MIL/MIN/TBR/HOU/LAD/NYY/ATL/ARI

Let's start with the **Houston Astros**, who, as we approached the deadline to turn in the manuscript for this book, were mired in multiple controversies that unveil how innovative they've been, and the collateral damage caused by singular focus on innovation without much regard for consequences.

There isn't a single organization in the history of baseball as good at developing pitchers as this current Houston group. In addition to the alterations they've made to name big leaguers, they have an incessant stream of exciting young arms moving up through their pipeline. It's a monochromatic approach to pitching: high-spin four seamers and vertical breaking balls, a slider/cutter that works away from same-sided hitters (often both), and, sometimes, a changeup that, on our high-speed cameras, typically all have the same grip/release. They know how to identify pitchers who aren't optimized by other orgs, acquire them, then change them through player dev that has been great at getting pitchers to buy in and make adjustments.

Their hitting stuff is not yet to that level, because hitting is just harder to understand since part of what makes good hitters is their cognition. There's less clear visual evidence of patterns throughout Houston's minor league hitting population, but they understand how to adjust hitters' attack angle to create lift.

Now we get to the cheating stuff. For years leading up to Ken Rosenthal and Evan Drellich's report on The Athletic about Houston's specific methodology, there had been rumors around baseball that the Astros were, in real time, stealing opponents' signs and relaying info to hitters via auditory means. Some rumors went as far as to mention the now infamous trash can banging. How the Astros parse mixed signs in real time is still not clear, but the org has shown interest in visual machine learning that could, in theory, diagnose complex signs in real time once you provide it with some initial feedback. Teams would have to constantly change signs to combat this as it would probably only take a few pitches for the AI to deduce what sequences of fingers mean.

Part of the reason former Astros players and employees were so chatty about what they learned during their time in Houston is because they were eventually fired, and were pissed about it. Houston shit-canned nearly all of their scouts in two waves, one in 2017, late in the summer of their 2017 World Series run, then almost all of the rest of them the following year. They still have some people who attend games, but most of their player evaluation is done by watching video in the office and by using data. During the 2019 GM Meetings, Eric asked general manager Jeff Luhnow about whether this approach was viable in the lower levels of the minors and in Latin America, and Luhnow said it was quickly becoming a viable approach in those markets.

The workload asked of the remaining scouts after that initial wave of departures was not reasonable, assuming the fundamental aspects of the job were not to change. One scout was asked to maintain his pro scouting coverage while adding an amateur area, even though he had no background on any of those players, nor amateur scouting. One was asked to cover what amounted to two or three areas worth of amateur coverage.

General manager Jeff Luhnow comes from the world of management consulting, where people parachute into a business or industry, learn about it quickly, and apply tactics to evaluate how their client might be able to alter their approach to produce better results. It appears Houston decided whatever benefit was derived from an army of scouts was not worth the cost when compared to what they could do in the office with video for less money with less staff, and that it was prudent to funnel that money to R&D to better understand tech and its application in player development.

It's worth noting that Luhnow worked for consulting giant McKinsey and the Astros have—and appear to still—pay McKinsey to consult about how to best run the team. When Luhnow came into the Cardinals front office, he did it with the posture of a consultant, there to learn what was being done and recommend best practices as an outsider. Quickly, Luhnow got the ear of the owner, gained power, and many characterized his next move as forcing out veteran GM Walt Jocketty, before getting a GM job of his own in Houston.

We know of a few instances where McKinsey recommended that Houston lay off personnel, usually replaced, in time, by a cheaper version, even after a playoff run that netted increased revenues—cutting costs just to cut costs. At least one executive left the organization and told friends it was primarily, but not completely, because McKinsey was influencing front office personnel decisions. Another source said the front office understood that Luhnow employed McKinsey to consult on front office staffing choices so he wouldn't be the only one held accountable for whatever decisions were made. That source described it as "detachment as a strategy."

But the way Houston did it, and when they did it, was cold. And because they were at the forefront of so much other cool stuff (high-speed video from which you can pull spin rates and bat speed, the player dev progress, etc.) that teams were curious about, and maybe interested in copying, the entire baseball-evaluating world felt threatened. Because the Astros had experienced success, they had some rope to work with and could try a scoutless model for a while to see how it went.

We could argue that their chances of rebooting a scouting department were slim because, at this point, no good scouts wanted to work for them, but let's be honest; all industries of glamour (TV, film, sports, whatever) leverage peoples' passion against their own well-being. We thought the lack of makeup work that would result from a scoutless model would eventually embarrass the org several times. They'd be vulnerable to accidentally acquiring many bad apples, but a former Astros evaluator told us they were eschewing makeup on later round draft picks which they didn't expect to generate big league value anyway, so they'd be fine cutting those players once they learned, first-hand, that they were bad guys. The club's acquisition of reliever Roberto Osuna was an indication bad off-field makeup was perhaps not a problem for the team, anyway.

When one scout was informed of the club's plans during one of the restructurings, he asked why the team was doing this now. He was told that the top of the front office was nervous that another team would do it first. "It" would be en masse firing/not renewing scouts. It was important to them that they get credit for being the first to do it. They weren't scared of the bad PR with fans, within the industry, or in the scouting community. And they weren't scared of the possible unintended consequences of thumbing their nose at baseball orthodoxy or changing their process in a notable way. Not all of that stuff is necessarily bad; it just may have been done for its own sake.

Whatever doomsday scenario might have occurred, at this time it seemed Luhnow's worst-case scenario was to become a Sam Hinkie–like nerd martyr, making six figures to speak in front of affluent college kids at sports analytics and current or aspiring CEOs at business conferences once Billy Beane's cachet wore off for that set. Luhnow has the Wharton degree to fit in. As one former Astros employee put it, Luhnow is "horny for efficiency for its own sake, often actively against the good of employees, morale, and the organization in the long-term."

Houston isn't the only team that cheats, they're not the only ones who've looked the other way and acquired a domestic abuser, they're not the only ones who employ a few loud, emotionally immature, misogynistic corporate-climber douchebags (most Houston employees are good folks) like disgraced former assistant GM Brandon Taubman is alleged to be, nor will they be the last team to move away from in-person scouting.

We've been told that manager A.J. Hinch grew so tired of Luhnow that he forbade him from entering the clubhouse for extended periods. Some of their decision-making has lacked social nuance and feel, they overestimated how public opinion would be driven by their on-field results, and now Luhnow and owner Jim Crane are eating crow, but only because public opinion has shifted. You don't have to wonder what the logical extreme of the McKinsey approach to baseball would be; we are seeing every aspect of it play out right now.

Hypothetically, if two orgs are exactly the same in every way except one of them is the Houston Astros and the other has a few dozen scouts, which one is going to be better? The advantageous knowledge will diffuse, other orgs will catch up. The other orgs will alter scouts' focus to areas the data doesn't occupy. Houston's model either assumes they'll perpetually be ahead of other orgs in some innovative way—which is unrealistically hubristic—or is ignoring this. In the meantime, they'll continue to be one of the more successful orgs in baseball.

If there are teams who can hold a candle to Houston's player dev it's the **Los Angeles Dodgers** and **New York Yankees**. The Dodgers have been especially good at making relevant swing changes (Max Muncy, Chris Taylor) while the Yankees have an unending stream of hard-throwing pitchers and seem to lose someone in the Rule 5 draft every year because they don't have enough room for them on the 40-man.

The Dodgers pursue volatile players in the draft, players who fall because of injury concern or because they have a lack of statistical track record or due to odd, unprecedented reasons. These are players who are perhaps undervalued for reasons that have nothing to do with talent. They typically do this in the second, third, or fourth round—Mitchell White, Mike Grove, Morgan Cooper (all injured), Brandon Lewis (one year of performance, extreme weight loss)—but Walker Buehler is a first-round version. They also take players with their dev competency in mind, meaning players who have physical ability but need a swing change.

We're unsure how a DOJ ruling might impact the org's otherwise excellent ops work. The Dodgers 2015 international class included nearly $100 million in expenditures when you count both the bonus amounts and tax paid for going over their pool amount. Many of the players were Cuban. The head of that international department, Bob Engle, and its coordinator, Patrick Guerrero, were in place before current president Andrew Friedman arrived, but they were fired a few weeks after most of that 2015 class signed. Those two were also dismissed under mysterious circumstances by the Seattle Mariners three years prior.

The Yankees employ more analysts than any other team in MLB, but many of them are hired with a consulting title and aren't listed on the official team roll, making it hard to know exactly how many they have. They have one of the better, more balanced approaches to amateur scouting, both international and pro, with both good communication between the departments and departments that run without a top-down heavy hand from the office that many progressive teams encourage.

Milwaukee Brewers GM David Stearns was once an assistant GM with Houston, and they're the most likely org to walk a similar path. They've already begun eliminating scouting positions. We expect that Milwaukee will learn from some of Houston's PR mistakes, though.

Milwaukee typically swims in the $1 to $2 million pool on July 2, seeking to spread some six-figure bonuses around rather than committing to just a few high-end players. The Brewers and **Minnesota Twins** are the two orgs most actively seeking pitchers with unique deliveries to throw at hitters after they've seen several innings of upper-90s gas.

The Twins and **Cleveland Indians** have a lot of the same organizational DNA, and both use a mixed scout/data model for pro coverage. The Twins seem attracted to measurable power in the draft, while the Indians are the best at executing a draft plan that includes multi-year consideration (if a college player had a good sophomore year but bad junior year, they seem to weight the sophomore year more heavily than other teams), which prioritizes very young high school players. Internationally, Cleveland has signed a lot of middle infielders with precocious contact skills, and this is true in the domestic draft, as well.

The **Tampa Bay Rays** and **Arizona Diamondbacks** also utilize a potent mix of old and new. Both pro scouting departments utilize org-based coverage (the Rays scouts crosscheck potential trade targets, lots of scouts see potential acquisitions) which is fairly traditional, but both have clear interest in some measurable traits, like vertical fastball movement, as evidenced by trades and draft picks both teams have made. Similar to Oakland, Tampa Bay takes a high-upside approach in the draft, but they often have a few supplemental and competitive balance picks, so their risk is somewhat mitigated because of volume. Both of these teams also utilize fairly progressive in-game management enabled by positional versatility.

The Rays and Dodgers are notable for shuttling players back and forth from Triple-A, and some of the players get annoyed at all the yo-yo-ing, similar to when a player gets claimed four times on waivers in a 12-month period via "churning." We know of one case where players literally popped champagne when one of these clubs traded them, because they would finally just be at one level for a while.

The **Atlanta Braves** have two years under the new Alex Anthopoulos regime and has moved in a more progressive direction after he spent a few years with the Dodgers between GM jobs with Toronto and the Braves. With sanctions about to loosen up in the international realm for Coppolella's indiscretions, we don't know much about how they'll approach that market, but it affected their approach to the draft. The Braves went under slot with almost all of their top picks in 2019, to then plow the savings into multiple mid-six-figure prep prospects after the 10th round. The lack of international prospects in the DSL and GCL meant getting more prospect-grade players overall, it was a high-volume approach to give the system an influx of mostly young prospects to balance a top-heavy system with Top 100 types at Triple-A and the big leagues. With this more progressive approach, Atlanta has staffed up their R&D department and has been taking that approach to team-building, focusing on long-term deals for core players, only trading second- and third-tier prospects, and making short-term deals in free agency.

The **Philadelphia Phillies** have been making moves in the progressive direction as well. Their player development group has had an influx of new blood (most notably hitting coordinator Jason Ochart from Driveline Baseball) and their new amateur scouting director Brian Barber came from the Yankees, whose process will surely be folded into what Philly was already doing in the draft. Their international department continues to get solid results, particularly in the medium- and low-figure signings, so they'll continue to use the more scouting-based, traditional approach that's been working for them. On the big league side, GM Matt Klentak is in the window where big league wins matter and has been acting as such, signing Bryce Harper and Andrew McCutchen and trading for J.T. Realmuto and Jean Segura. After a disappointing 2019 and the firing of manager Gabe Kapler, patience seems to be diminishing and competing with Atlanta and Washington is a must for 2020.

Something that's happening primarily in this quadrant is title inflation in player development. While this has been happening at the GM and AGM level for years across baseball as a way to keep talented executives in-house, and also justify higher salaries, it's now a way to keep top player development people on staff. It used to be that "pitching coordinator" was the top pitching person in the organization below the MLB pitching coach, but now there's a tier between them: director of pitching. This also applies to hitting.

The idea is if a team wants to poach a coordinator, they need a higher title to start the process, so a director title that doesn't run a department creates that opening. Interestingly, we were told about an in-demand pitching coordinator whose contract was expiring and he was offered a director of pitching position with another club. He asked that his new title be pitching coordinator, knowing that gave him an opening to get a raise if a new team wanted to poach him with a higher title while he was under contract. The offering team declined, insisting on a director of pitching title for that exact reason—he could only be poached for an MLB coaching gig while under contract, so the team had more security that he'd stick around.

Another interesting development in this area also appeared to be started by the Astros. Mike Elias, then Brandon Taubman, and likely soon a new person who fills the role of VP and AGM, were in charge of Houston's amateur scouting, international scouting, pro scouting, and player development—essentially running every department that isn't the big leagues. For Houston, the idea is that they have a unified process across these departments, so one person could run them and, in search of efficiency, if the process is heavily influenced by analysts and not scouts, then the departments are suddenly much more similar than they are for other clubs.

This colder, more corporate approach to staffing had spread across the league, with us hearing stories even about clubs we single out in this book for mostly doing things the right way. Due to baseball's anti-trust exemption, the teams can legally engage in non-competitive practices in regards to labor, the type of things that a number of companies in Silicon Valley have been accused of and sued about for years. When a club wants to interview a rival staffer for a job, they have to "ask permission," a formal process where the other club approves or turns down the request. It's generally understood in the industry that there is an objective criteria for doing so: a promotion in title.

Typically, if an employee is under contract but another club asks for permission for a promotion and the club turns it down, the employee gets the promotion with his current club, or a raise or a contract extension or some combination of those. We've been told of multiple instances where GMs will choose to not do any of these things, turn down permission for a promotion, give the employee nothing in return for limiting their career, and sometimes not even tell them permission was asked so they don't know they're in demand. We've also heard of a GM getting his owner to give a raise to one of his top lieutenants because of another team asking permission when in fact no team ever did that.

Some teams are known for giving vague titles ("special assistant" is a common job-title phrase for this) to important staffers specifically so they can claim almost any promotion to a rival club wouldn't be a promotion, helping to keep their intellectual property and talent in-house and with a lower salary. For some clubs, it's generally known that the only way to leave is when your contract is up, leaving staffers hoping there isn't a big lag between one job ending and the next one starting. They are generally pretty hush-hush, but clubs will complain to MLB and investigations are launched when GMs suspect another club is tampering, trying to poach one of their employees with back-channel conversations outside of the permission-giving structure.

Salaries of executives around the game are known on a need-to-know basis and the only staffer salaries that leak to the press are precedent-setting GM/president contracts that move the earnings ceiling of decision-makers north. It's often news when the public finds out, in the middle of a GM's contract, how many years are left on his deal. Sometimes extensions given to GMs aren't reported for months; this is possible when only two people (the GM and the owner) know the details of the negotiation.

This top-down paranoia can extend further down the ladder as well. One progressive club had multiple minor league coaches resign at the end of a recent season without other jobs lined up because they were tired of having everything they do dictated by player development analysts in the office that, in the coaches' view, were analyzing and optimizing everything to within an inch of its life and not communicating their motivations or analysis transparently. We've heard about instances with another club where they drafted a pitcher high in the draft in part because he changes arm slots effectively from pitch-to-pitch. The player development analysts flagged his wandering arm slot as a negative, directing coaches to correct it after his first few pro appearances. The amateur scouting staff luckily had good enough communication with the development staff to hear this was happening and to intervene to find a solution.

We like the idea of housing the amateur and pro departments under one roof, especially if you have hybridized scouts in some parts of the country. For instance, some teams are eliminating the Four Corners position on the amateur side because they think the amount of talent in that area can be covered by someone in a different area, but that scout could also cover complex-level ball during the summer and fall. The amateur/pro department demarcation makes chain of command in this situation more complicated, but if both departments worked together it wouldn't be.

But this has the function of depressing salaries since the day-to-day heads of the various departments aren't earning director-level pay (because the person above them is running the department) and it undercuts director autonomy and decision-making ability in a way that may harm front office culture. It's arguably a weakness of this Unitary Baseball Executive approach that your chief exec only has background in whatever department they came up through.

Street Smart: WSH/BOS/CHC/STL/OAK/SDP

This cluster of teams has had what we would consider success while generally utilizing methodology which, by today's standards, would be considered something between traditional and antiquated. That's not to say they ignore statistical analysis, and in fact some of these teams would have been further toward the right of this matrix about five years ago, before several teams shifted past them in that direction. Aside from San Diego (who we'd consider successful in a sense that we're optimistic about their future as a franchise despite their lack of big league performance to date) there's less to deduce about these clubs' pro scouting tendencies because most of them have been competitive for quite a while.

It's likely that the **Chicago Cubs** are one of the franchises who take a dynamic approach to pro scouting, allocating scouting resources and targeting players in ways that make sense given where they are on the competitive spectrum. It's rare for Eric to see Cubs personnel on the backfields of Arizona watching low-level players, but they've consistently acquired upper-level players, especially pitchers, on the 40-man fringe in an effort to bolster their MLB-ready depth.

Maintaining pitching depth seemed to be a focus in the Cubs draft room as, for several years, they took a lot of vanilla college pitching that, theoretically, should have moved through the system quickly and provided reasonable depth behind aging pitching on the 40-man. That hasn't happened, either because the amateur department wasn't picking the right guys or because the player dev side wasn't good at grooming pitchers. The team's pursuit of Driveline Baseball's Kyle Boddy, to whom the team offered a deal in the mid-six figures, is evidence of the latter. So are the improvements of some of the pitchers Chicago traded away, especially Alex Lange, who had a better pitch mix and was throwing harder a few months after the Cubs dealt him to Detroit.

Chicago's draft strategy seems to have shifted though, and they've ended up drafting some high-variance athletes in recent years, namely Arizona high school OF Brennen Davis. Player development on the hitting side has been better for the Cubs. Davis was a raw multi-sport athlete whose swing improved quickly in pro ball. Same goes for 2017 first rounder Nico Hoerner, whose attack angle was altered the summer after he signed. He's already in the big leagues. Chicago also tends to take an over-slot high school arm or two sometime during day two of the draft.

The fruits of the International Scouting Department's labor have mostly been shipped off via trade as Gleyber Torres, Eloy Jiménez, Jeimer Candelario, and Isaac Paredes were all top 100 prospects sent packing in deals. The Cubs do very well in Mexico, or at least they were doing well in Mexico during the previous era of bonus rules there. Mexican pro teams can sign players once they're 14 and, under prior rules, the team could take as much as 75 percent of the bonus teams paid to players while only the portion kept by the player counted against the team's bonus pool. It was a loophole teams like the Cubs and Dodgers exploited until MLB squashed those signing rules in 2018 and barred teams from signing Mexican players for a bit before rewriting the rules more equitably for the players.

In the draft, the **Washington Nationals** have a recent history of scooping up high-ceiling players who have fallen either due to injury or makeup concerns, overwhelmingly represented by agent Scott Boras. If you have the opportunity to get ceiling in the draft, even if that ceiling comes with extra risk, you should do it. The expected outcomes for players taken late in the first round (where Washington has spent most of the last decade picking due to their big league record) are already middling, so even if you only hit one out of every couple times you draft a player like that, it's worth it, and Washington has hit several times. The club hit it big on Jesús Luzardo, Lucas Giolito, and Anthony Rendon (who had a myriad of injury issues in college), while Matt Purke (injury) and Seth Romero (makeup) are the other side of the coin. Erick Fedde has had a median sort of outcome.

The team takes an old-school, eyeball scout approach to the draft, and one Nationals scout indicated to us that not only does the staff revel in the relative lack of analytics in the draft room, but also said they'd like it if the public-sector prospect content, specifically us and Baseball America, would disappear, because the scouts in their room hate having their reports compared to public consensus.

The Nats international program was left for dead after the 2009 Esmailyn Gonzalez scandal (which we discussed back in the second J2 chapter) and for years yielded absolutely nothing. The scorched earth fallout from that scandal resulted in then-GM Jim Bowden (who now writes for The Athletic) resigning amid FBI investigations for bonus skimming, while Washington fired most of their international staff, including former big leaguer José Rijo, their DR ops director at the time, and closed their complex, which Rijo owned and operated. It took years to recover from the damage, but recently Washington has done a fair job targeting players in the $1.5 to $2 million range, including young superstar Juan Soto, Top 100 prospect SS Luis Garcia, and converted pitcher Elvis Alvarado, who they traded for bullpen help during their 2019 World Series run.

Their farm system lacks depth, in part because the Nationals have been buyers for so long, and this is also why there's been little to be deduced about their pro scouting tastes. GM Mike Rizzo has a strong track record of signing big leaguers. Players under long-term contracts (Max Scherzer, Adam Eaton, Ryan Zimmerman) have played well, the team moved on from some players, like Jordan Zimmermann, at the right time and have patched holes with good veterans via trade and short-term deals (Suzuki, Gomes, Kendrick, A. Cabrera).

The **Boston Red Sox** were taking a similar approach under former GM Dave Dombrowski, shipping off prospects en masse to bolster the big league club, which had been Dombrowski's M.O. at each of his previous stops. It helped win the Sox a World Series in 2018. We expect the club to shift toward the right side of the matrix under new GM Chaim Bloom. While Bloom was with Tampa Bay, the Rays pioneered the use of the opener, used lots of situational, in-game matchups with their hitters and defenders, and they shuttled optioned pitchers to and from Triple-A frequently to keep big league arms fresh. We expect these types of things to take shape in Boston even though they were more of a necessity in Tampa due to the club's budget. Now that Bloom can loosen his payroll belt after leaving Tampa Bay, we may see more bombastic versions of this methodology, or we may see less, but probably not until the minor league cupboard, which was quite bare as we wrapped up this tome, has been restocked.

Whether the Rays' in-game style of personnel deployment comes to Boston will also depend on manager Alex Cora, who may end up in hot water over his alleged significant involvement in the Houston Astros' sign-stealing scandal. Cora was Houston's bench coach in 2017.

Boston's international scouting staff was already one of the splashier, more-successful groups in the game even before they added former Mets int'l director Chris Becerra to the fold. Becerra helmed a Mets department responsible for signing prospects who were either very projectable, or explosive and athletic—like Amed Rosario and Ronny Mauricio—which fits like a glove with what Boston had been doing—Rafael Devers, Daniel Diaz, Yoán Moncada, Daniel Flores, etc.—under previous int'l director Eddie Romero, who is now the team's executive VP and assistant GM.

Pitching-wise, the team has a lot of soft-tossing, Latin American pitchability arms in the system, but that's partially because some of the power arms, like Gregory Santos and Anderson Espinoza, were dealt away. There were a few dry international years due to Boston's 2016 bonus packaging schedule, which caused them to lose a handful of interesting prospects and be locked out of signing players for a year, and this contributed to the current state of their farm which, entering the 2019–2020 off-season, is ranked 30th in baseball based on our evaluation of their players and Craig Edwards' valuation of those evaluations.

Quite soon they'll be joined near the bottom of the farm system hierarchy by the **Oakland A's**, which have a top-heavy system of potential stars who will soon graduate and leave a shallow system barren at the upper levels, though much of this is due to pitcher injuries rather than poor scouting. The Moneyball days are long gone and what was once one of the more progressive orgs in baseball is now one of the more traditional, especially as it pertains to the draft. Perhaps because Oakland's payroll limitations prevent them from being able to afford star players in free agency, the A's have drafted high-risk/high-reward players with early picks, the most famous of which was Arizona Cardinals quarterback Kyler Murray. This is evidence of a tools-based approach to the draft but perhaps one driven by logic rather than a specific ideology.

The same is largely true of the A's international efforts. They seem to be targeting top-of-the-market J2 players to early deals now (like Robert Puason, after MLB disallowed his deal with Atlanta) and in the past few years have scooped up a lot of Cubans who hit the market after many teams have already committed bonuses elsewhere. Despite their financial limitations and stadium issues, Oakland is one of the more stable organizations in all of baseball, chugging along like a locomotive carrying 90-win season after 90-win season. The core of the front office—Billy Beane, David Forst, and Billy Owens—have all been around for a while. The scouting czar, Owens, was a two-sport athlete in college and is among the most charismatic individuals in baseball, which everyone in baseball knows because Owens' voice carries all throughout the scouting section and he loves to talk about old players. His name has been bandied about as a potential GM. We see Billy Beane out at the field once in a while (typically at instructs) but not often enough to think he drives player evaluation opinion in any way even though he's the face of the org.

Can't say the same about the **San Diego Padres**. You know what the general managers look like. You've seen the photos of them with a cell phone sewn to their temple on MLB Trade Rumors, scowling or grinning depending on whether or not they knew the photo was being taken. But there are about 6,000 players in pro ball and another 1,200 picked in every draft, so decision-makers, especially the busy GM, can't come close to seeing all of them.

Just how many players does a GM see over the course of the year? The number varies widely, depending on the GM, and at the high end of the range is however many players Padres GM A.J. Preller is seeing. Perhaps Preller's gaunt, olive face and steely eyes are simply easier to identify at the field than most other GMs, but he's the one most often seen by scouts, and it's not close.

Preller has a reputation as a shrewd, eccentric, baseball genius. Like many of his contemporaries, Preller has an Ivy League background, but he also has a tirelessness and bravado about him that old-school scouty types respect and find magnetic. That vibe is so intense that it cuts right through Preller's other observed and rumored idiosyncrasies, of which there are so many that it's likely not all of them are true.

Among them, he barely sleeps and is apt to call his employees at all hours, he has a photographic memory, he sometimes travels with a neck brace to wear on planes to help him sleep, he's an excellent break dancer and pickup basketball player, sometimes hooping as early as four in the morning. He's rumored to have among the most American Airlines miles of anyone in the country, after being based in Dallas for so many years when working for the Rangers. On consecutive days in 2017, the two of us saw Preller on opposite ends of the country (draft coverage in the Southeast, then an Extended game in Arizona) wearing the same thing he had the day before; mesh basketball shorts, a Team USA Baseball workout shirt and a bucket hat, accessorized with a giant, gas station beverage and a plastic grocery store bag that appeared to be filled with a second set of clothes.

It's an odd look for one of the 30 most powerful people in baseball and, some would argue, odd allocation of a GM's time. We saw him at a high school showcase days before getting the Padres GM job, then at a fall high school tournament a few months after, watching players he couldn't draft for at least eight months. We've spotted him on TV watching the SEC baseball tournament in the front row, hiding beneath the brim of a bucket hat. In the weeks before the draft, he'll sometimes hide in the press box to avoid being seen scouting a player he really likes.

Others sympathize with what they interpret as a desire to do all of this traveling in maximum comfort or to combat the heat, two perpetual scout goals. That Preller subjects himself to it in the name of finding players is part of why people respect him, even if they openly think he's odd. Preller is simultaneously unique and like everyone else in the game, tirelessly grinding and looking for an edge, often at the expense of his own well-being.

And there's so much Preller-related shit-shooting throughout baseball because he's given baseball a lot to talk about. Throughout the last decade, he's been at or near the center of several controversial transactions and has at least twice been suspended by MLB, placing him in select company among the few non-players upon whom MLB's ban hammer has fallen. He was suspended in 2010, when Preller was running the Rangers international scouting department, for improper negotiations with then-amateur free agent pitcher Rafael De Paula, who was serving a suspension for falsifying his age. De Paula would eventually sign with the Yankees and later be selected to participate in a Futures Game. He's played pro ball for a decade but never reached the majors. There are also wide-ranging and consistent complaints in the industry surrounding the Rangers methods in signing Jurickson Profar out of Curaçao in 2009, but it appears there was no discipline by MLB for this incident.

Then, throughout 2012, after Preller had been promoted to Rangers senior director of player personnel, MLB investigated the club's deal with amateur Dominican outfielder Jairo Beras as it investigated Beras' age. When he first registered as a prospect with MLB, Beras submitted paperwork indicating he was born December 25, 1995, making him eligible to sign on July 2, 2012. He used that age information to attend workouts and tournaments through early February 2012, but later that month he suddenly signed with the Rangers for $4.5 million (at the time the second-highest non-Cuban bonus ever), using a December 25, 1994, date of birth, making him 17 and eligible to sign immediately if correct.

Though age-related fraud has become less common in Latin American free agency, there have been several instances of players falsifying their age and/or identity. They almost always say they're younger than they really are because scouts and teams perceive younger individuals to have more physical and technical growth ahead and thus prefer younger players. But in 2012, with a new, unbreachable $2.9 million spending cap per team about to be enforced by a new CBA in July, it suddenly became advantageous for Beras to be older, which he in fact was, and sign before restrictions were put on team spending during the next signing period, when Beras would likely get a bonus less than half of what he got from Texas.

The Rangers had become aware of and interested in Beras as a prospect long before he was eligible to sign, likely during Preller's tenure as international director. They liked the player (teenage Beras' tools were almost indistinguishable from those of teenage Aaron Judge; both were the size of NBA wing players, had huge power, arm strength, and concerning strikeout issues) and had money to spend. For the Rangers, moving on Beras before the international signing calendar turned over to the new year meant retaining their entire $2.9 million 2012–13 international pool to pursue other players later in the year, and acting immediately meant minimizing risk that other teams smitten with Beras would outbid them once they learned his true age, even if it meant paying a premium bonus to convince the player and his trainer.

It was a mutually beneficial agreement that would undoubtedly raise alarm somewhere in the league office because of Beras' DOB change but, viewed a certain way, all the Rangers did was sign an appropriately aged player. The "shoot first" style of doing so, in this case, had a sympathetic, strategic-supporting argument.

The deal was put in limbo as MLB investigated. They determined Beras had falsified his age during registration and was older than he first said and suspended him for a year, but they did not seek to confirm his actual date of birth. Many cases of identity fraud among international prospects results in the deal being void, but Beras only faked his age, not his identity, so MLB allowed the deal, and levied no punishment on Texas nor Preller, who was the public-facing member of the Rangers staff throughout media coverage of this incident.

Beras' strikeout issues, amplified by a lack of plate discipline, proved too severe for him to overcome, and after parts of five years in the minors as an outfielder, he moved to the mound, where he's become a raw-for-his-age, 25-year-old, Double-A reliever who throws in the upper-90s with little command or breaking ball consistency.

Reaction from individuals around baseball was mixed. People from teams that liked and had planned to pursue Beras, many of them unaware of his misrepresentation until it was too late, were perturbed. Others appreciated the Rangers' hustle, thought it clever and well-executed, a rare instance in which a team worked to learn relevant information that most others did not, and reasoned that the team got a player it liked, the player got a much bigger bonus than he otherwise would have because of how proactive Texas was about pursuing him.

What seems to be agreed upon by international sources about Preller and his tenure in Texas is that the Rangers international department was aggressive and thorough in a way very few teams were then and still very few are now. Old-school scouting types universally like Preller's mentality in terms of scouting players, but broadly question how far Preller seems to be willing to go, landing in controversial situations of some sort almost every year he's been operating in Latin America. There are all kinds of small grievances and minor gripes that are certainly at least partly sour grapes that come due to Preller's success in signing players, making money, and continuing to stay relevant in high-profile jobs.

These stories were rehashed when Preller was hired to be San Diego's GM two years later, and while his approximately five-year tenure (as of publication) hasn't been without incident nor questionable transactions, it's also very promising. After an ill-fated, possibly owner-mandated push to compete early during his incumbency, the Padres engaged in a proper rebuild and Preller led an effort that would quickly and emphatically build the game's best farm system. Then that farm system began to bear big league fruit in the form of Fernando Tatís Jr., Chris Paddack, and others, while potential Hall of Famer Manny Machado was courted via free agency.

So deep was San Diego's farm system that, even after the graduations of Tatís, Paddack, Josh Naylor, Luis Urías, and more, their collection of minor league talent remained among the best in baseball, falling just one spot on our 2019 end-of-year farm system rankings. For context, Toronto ranked eighth in our preseason estimation, then fell into the bottom third of farm systems when Vladimir Guerrero Jr. and Bo Bichette lost rookie eligibility and were no longer considered prospects.

But, of course, there have been some incidents. Sources tell us that MLB handed down a fine for an incident in late 2015 when Preller and some of the Padres international staff had an illegal workout with a group of players, headlined by the top prospect in the 2016 class, Venezuelan SS Kevin Maitán. The workout was in Curaçao (a common place to bring Venezuelan players to avoid the various complications of Venezuela) while MLB rules at the time were such that players of Maitán's age couldn't have a private workout for an MLB club outside of their home country.

Multiple teams—the White Sox, Marlins, and Red Sox—accused the Preller-helmed Padres of withholding complete medical information during trade negotiations in 2016, according to an ESPN report by Buster Olney.

Righty Colin Rea, who the Marlins acquired from San Diego as part of a seven-player trade centered around Andrew Cashner and prospects, walked off the mound with an elbow injury just 3.1 innings into the first start of his Marlins career. Miami felt hoodwinked, and eventually the teams agreed Rea, who hasn't thrown a big league inning since the injury, would be returned to San Diego for the prospect he was, in essence, traded for to balance that swap. And so the Padres sent 23-year-old A-ball pitcher Luis Castillo back to Miami.

Later, Castillo would again be traded by Miami, develop one of baseball's best changeups, and become an upper-echelon Major League starter. Had the Padres been up front about Rea's injury at the time of the trade, perhaps the deal never gets done in the first place. Or perhaps, in an alternate reality, Luis Castillo is currently a Padre.

Later that summer, Preller would be suspended for 30 days without pay after MLB investigated a Red Sox complaint that Drew Pomeranz, who they acquired in July from San Diego for then–top 100 prospect Anderson Espinoza, also had medical issues the Padres had failed to disclose (though there are also industry rumors the Red Sox kept pertinent health information from San Diego during a previous trade). After an investigation, MLB determined that the Padres were keeping two sets of medical records. One was a thorough file for internal use while the other, which omitted minor treatments and ailments that didn't require a stint on the Injured List, was stored in the central, shared injury database used by all teams as part of MLB protocol. The Padres had made it so other teams thought some of their prospects were healthier than they actually were.

Major League Baseball was furious. Sources have told us that MLB ordered the Padres to either fire Preller or pay a multi-million-dollar fine.

Again, this prompted vocal reaction from people in baseball. Now Preller had engaged in active deception that might harm the livelihoods of others in the game who were making decisions based on bad information. And it involved medical intel. The collection and use of medical information by teams remains one of the more difficult areas for MLB to control, and so it's one of baseball's many nooks and crannies in which individuals are policed only by their own morality. Teams work medical angles in all kinds of ways, mostly in amateur scouting, where they seek to decide who's injured enough to move off a draft board, or who might flunk a physical and be leveraged into taking less money, an ugly maneuver teams have incentive to execute because of the hard slotting in amateur markets and asymmetrical participation in pre-draft medical disclosure by prospects, driven by their agents/advisors.

Unlike the Marlins deal, there was no rejiggering of the components. The Red Sox retained Pomeranz, who contributed to their 2018 title run, and the Padres retained Espinoza, who pitched in San Diego's system for the rest of the summer of 2016 before his next several seasons were sidetracked by multiple Tommy John surgeries. Sources indicate there's still some bad blood between the teams over this transaction, as Espinoza has also been injured for so long, it could be suggested that Boston also knew something that wasn't shared. At this point, public and industry sentiment turned strongly against Preller, with many pointing out that Braves GM John Coppolella was banned from baseball as part of the punishment for his first suspension while Preller seemed to have nine lives.

The White Sox informal grievance likely stems from the now-infamous James Shields–Fernando Tatís Jr. trade. Up to that point, Shields had been an excellent, mid-rotation, workhorse starter that was signed to prop in the ill-fated playoff run when Preller joined the Padres. He made at least 33 starts in nine consecutive seasons, thrice led baseball in games started, and only Justin

Verlander and Félix Hernández pitched more innings from 2006 to 2016. If feats of strength are your thing, Shields threw a whopping 11 complete games during his 2009 All-Star season in Tampa Bay, a franchise he helped carry to first-time relevance. Only 16 pitchers threw more than 11 complete games, combined, during the following decade, and one was Shields.

All seemed right with Shields when 2016 began. He had made 10 good starts for the Padres before getting shelled while pitching on extended rest, on May 31, 2016. His velocity was down in that start, the fastball sitting more 88–91 rather than 90–94 as it had his previous outing. It was the worst start of his career. Four days later, he was traded to Chicago for Tatís Jr. and righty Erik Johnson.

Tatís, on the other hand, hadn't even played an official pro game for the White Sox. He had only signed the previous summer and, as is almost always the case for recent Latin American signees, Tatís was working out with other youngsters and rehabbers at the White Sox spring training facility in Arizona, playing in scrimmages against other teams' greener prospects, waiting for rookie-level ball to start later in June. The Padres amateur reports on Tatís were on par with the industry mean. He was an instinctive, heady player— typical of the spawn of former big leaguers—but not physically exceptional in an obvious way, the type of player who typically gets a $500,000–$750,000 bonus.

But in the 11 months that passed between when Tatís signed and when he was traded, he transformed. He had gotten taller, his shoulders broadened, and became round with muscle at their ends. His raw power got louder, he'd become faster.

An overwhelming majority of teams did not have comprehensive instructional league and extended spring training scouting coverage at this time, but San Diego had something close to it, and so they had Tatís scouting reports from his amateur days, from the fall of 2015, and then again from 2016 Extended Spring leading up to the trade. During that time, Tatís generated no statistics of any kind, but even if those reports weren't lucid, psychic visions of Tatís' superstar future, they likely showed significant growth over a short period of time, enough to pique interest in him as a player and get decision-makers in to see him while negotiating with Chicago.

Preller has publicly aimed praise toward his pro staff for this trade, namely pro scouting director Pete DeYoung and pro scout Jim Elliott, who is now with Detroit. Preller's dogged presence at the field meant he, too, had an in-person history of looks at Tatís dating back to the kid's days as an amateur, which likely helped close the book on this trade.

Many teams are apprehensive about acquiring talent with so little pro experience via trade, and some teams largely ignored the lowest levels of the minors and allocated little scouting resources there. Until recent years, many GMs wouldn't let almost any player below Low-A stand in the way of a trade, in part because they didn't know much about those players. Even if they pan out, most prospects at that level are going to take nearly five years to ascend the minors and grab hold of a big league role, and many GMs don't have the job security necessary to wait, even if they have the stomach for the risk. Preller, meanwhile, has been known to prowl the backfields himself, "looking for treats," as one scout put it.

Does this behavior set a valuable tone throughout the talent-evaluating part of the organization? We think so. Is it also a bit of an ethical high-wire act that has the potential to destabilize a burgeoning franchise? Maybe, but there has been no reported malfeasance since Preller returned from his 2016 suspension and anecdotal reports make it appear that he's mellowed in terms of testing the limits of MLB's discipline.

The Padres are transitioning from "aggressive rebuilders" to "postseason hopefuls" pretty quickly. They're closing the gap between themselves and the juggernaut Dodgers the way someone with the right combination of items and weapons makes a hard charge from the back of the pack in Mario Kart. It's just that the rest of baseball may have little tolerance for Preller's history of banana peels and green shells.

The Padres international scouting staff is consistently cited by rival executives as among the best in baseball, which is especially noteworthy because in 2014 the department director, Chris Kemp, leapt right from an area gig with Texas to his current role. The position players San Diego has signed during Kemp's tenure have no real trend, other than being good at baseball. There's a mix of good-framed projection guys (Reginald Preciado, Yeison Santana), skills-first players (Tucupita Marcano, Jeisson Rosario), unpolished, tooled-up goons (Jordy Barley, Gabriel Arias), and makeup-driven profiles (Tirso Ornelas), while the club clearly has a taste for crafty, pitchability arms.

The same is true for the amateur department, which has drafted several quick-moving college arms who were among the fastest to the big leagues in their draft class. The thirst for pitchability extends to the high school side, both in high-profile names (MacKenzie Gore) and late-round sleepers (Joey

Cantillo). Paired with these relatively stable sorts of prospects, especially the college versions, have been lots of risky picks of various stripes. Players coming off of injury (Mason Thompson, Reggie Lawson, Cal Quantrill) or who had little track record against quality competition (Mason House, Logan Driscoll, Josh Mears) have been selected early in drafts.

Momentum Seeking: NYM/CIN/CHW/MIA/COL/KCR/DET

Both our sources in baseball and the recent hirings by the **Cincinnati Reds** and the **New York Mets** suggest they're each rapidly moving toward the methodologically progressive end of the spectrum, but it takes time to install that infrastructure. Cincinnati has been especially proactive on the player development end of things, hiring hitting coach Turner Ward away from the Dodgers and bringing in one of Driveline Baseball's founders, Kyle Boddy, to coach pitchers. We expect how the Reds approach amateur scouting may change now that Chris Buckley, the former scouting director, has changed roles, though we're not sure exactly how yet. Buckley also has a hand in the team's international operations and their splashiest signings have almost exclusively come out of Cuba (Aroldis Chapman, Raisel Iglesias).

The Mets pro scouting department had ignored the lowest levels of the minors for several years but there are recent rumors that's going to change, which will be significant if they end up having to rebuild. Prior to current GM Brodie Van Wagenen's arrival, the club acquired a lot of mid-minor relievers when they made sellers trades and the org is paying for it now. Since his arrival they've played catch-up by adding in-office analysts but have also made buyers trades in which they took on albatross contracts and traded away prospects who were relatively close to contributing, action that mirrors what happened early on during Preller's tenure in San Diego, which fell short and required a full reset. This could be because Mets ownership, which is notoriously meddlesome, hired Van Wagenen on the condition that he take a short-term approach, or hired him because he convinced them he could do so without mortgaging the team's long-term competitiveness.

Van Wagenen's former role as an agent with CAA created what some in baseball felt was a conflict of interest, even though Van Wagenen divested his clients when he took the job. Later, the Mets made a deal with Yahoo! Sports, in which Yahoo! paid for an elevated level of access (though this deal died before ever going into effect), and the Mets hired TV analyst Jessica Mendoza to advise the club while she was a member of ESPN's *Sunday Night Baseball* broadcast, also a potential conflict of interest.

The Mets first draft under Van Wagenen was pretty crafty. The club selected some flashy high schoolers early, paid one (Matt Allan, a high school pitcher) an over-slot bonus, and then drafted a lot of high-priority seniors with their next several picks to make the pool math work. There are teams who think this strategy lacks risk mitigation but it's how the Braves built their current club.

The **Chicago White Sox** rebuild hasn't quite materialized in on-field success even though most of the players they picked up via trade (Yoán Moncada, Lucas Giolito, Dylan Cease, etc.) are pretty good. Those players haven't fallen short of expectations so much as they just haven't reached what we perceived their ceilings to be based on their physical talent. Perhaps this is a player development issue, but finally some Sox minor leaguers began showing clear improvement in 2019 while in prior years, especially on the pitching side, many of them were getting hurt or regressing. A slight tweak to the swing of Cuban CF Luis Robert, one of the few international players for whom Jerry Reinsdorf has ever opened up his checkbook, led to an incredible season that put him on the precipice of the big leagues. He may be that elite player the org really needs.

On the amateur side, the Sox have taken a lot of burly college hitters early in the draft, players who offer no defensive value and who need to rake to profile at their respective positions.

Like Chicago, the **Detroit Tigers** have begun to show progress on the player dev side, especially with pitching. Our use of high-speed video indicates players the Tigers have acquired via trade have altered their repertoires in such a way that shows the Tigers have a growing understanding of pitch design, and GM Al Avila confirmed this to Eric during the 2019 GM Meetings in Phoenix. The Tigers are building pitching labs in Detroit and at their spring training complex in Florida.

Detroit's scouting department has also increased their use of technology. We've seen Tiger personnel operating Edgertronic cameras at amateur games. They seem focused on polished, performing hitters both in the amateur and pro realm.

The opposite seems to be true of the **Miami Marlins**, who appear very attracted to premium tools even when they come with considerable risk. The trades they made in 2019, sending Zac Gallen to Arizona for strikeout-prone SS Jazz Chisholm and trading relief ace Nick Anderson to Tampa Bay for free-swinging OF Jesús Sánchez, are indications of that. This is true on the amateur side as well. Miami has used early picks on toolsy high schoolers, though they shifted a bit in 2019 in their first draft under new scouting director—and another former Yankees scout—D.J. Svihlik.

Most of the Marlins current brass comes from New York, brought in by part-owner Derek Jeter. Gary Denbo is directing player development, an area where the Yankees were quite successful while he was there. Denbo has a little bit of a Dick Cheney vibe, influencing many aspects of the organization that seem to be outside the scope of his title.

People in baseball, unprompted, often mention how overtly religious both the **Kansas City Royals** and **Colorado Rockies** are. Baseball is full of faithful individuals, but it's not typically something thought to be part of any org's core except for these two. The Rockies are notoriously difficult for scouts to deal with, which confuses scouts because they think teams have incentive for others to like their prospects. But getting schedules for extended spring and instructional league games from Colorado is tough, the rosters passed out to other orgs' scouts are often out of date or just wrong, and sometimes multiple players are wearing the same number on their jersey, with no name on the back, making it impossible to tell who is who.

The Rockies recent track record of scouting amateur hitters is very strong. You know about the guys on the big league roster (Arenado, Story, McMahon, Hampson, Tapia, etc.) but the system remains flush with more. The same is not true on the pitching side, where it's been a lot of college relievers and pitchability types who haven't panned out.

Kansas City also spent most of their many early 2018 draft picks on college performers, which was surprising to many in the industry who connected them to toolsy high schoolers with at least some of those picks. That draft felt like many San Antonio Spurs drafts: all the picks were good value and should make up a huge chunk of KC's next big league rotation. They've had trouble developing hitters, though. Most of the toolsy high school hitters the Royals have selected—and this is true for some of the Dominican players as well—have severe strikeout issues. Even Nick Pratto, who we viewed as a polished, fairly safe high school hitter, has struggled.

Fine-Tuning the Formula: SEA/LAA/TOR/BAL/TEX/PIT/SFG

Maybe no team has altered its approach to scouting and development as quickly and relevantly as the **Seattle Mariners**, who had a pro scouting overhaul two seasons ago and a player dev shift in 2019. The Mariners don't have a "type" of player, per se, though they do seem to like college arms who throw strikes in the draft.

Seattle parted ways with former international director Tim Kissner, which was a somewhat puzzling move considering that other teams had significant interest in the players he was signing, many of whom were traded away during the early days of Jerry Dipoto's very active tenure as GM. Other than the Juan Then boomerang (Seattle traded teenage Then to the Yankees for a 26-year-old reliever who isn't with the club anymore, then reacquired him for Edwin Encarnacion; it wasn't a great look), the deals Dipoto has made during the rebuild have been strong, and most of the players he and Seattle's staff have acquired look like they're going to be good big leaguers quickly, a few might be stars. Several pitchers in the minor league system improved throughout 2019, again due to coherent pitch design and velocity development, which should give Seattle the depth they need to withstand the injuries that plague every big league staff during the course of the next several seasons.

The **Los Angeles Angels** have also had a somewhat recent strategic shift in amateur scouting, beginning when they hired department director Matt Swanson away from the Cardinals. Under Swanson, the Angels began taking what appears to be a hybrid-model/tool-hunting approach. They've taken high-upside athletes early in drafts, and many of them have skewed young for their class (a trait model-driven teams target).

The Angels pro scouting efforts rarely have a chance to shine in a typical way because the club has been patching holes around Mike Trout in perpetuity, never really undergoing a rebuild under current pro director Nate Horowitz. The few times when the Angels have moved a big league piece for a prospect, or when they've acquired a prospect to balance a trade, they've hit. Luis Rengifo and Patrick Sandoval are going to be big league role players, Ty Buttrey is a late-inning reliever. The scouting of Shohei Otani also fell under the Angels pro scouting umbrella, and they nailed that. Mostly, the Angels have done work on the 40-man fringe, on waivers, trying to make marginal improvements to the big league roster without giving up prospect assets. This has been particularly important because pitching injuries have severely hindered their ability to compete with Houston in the division. The Angels have also targeted scrapheap minor leaguers, guys who formerly received a big bonus or were real prospects for one reason or another, but fell by the wayside. This hasn't quite yielded anything yet, but conceptually, the idea that a change of scenery can be beneficial for a player, especially when there are drastic team-to-team differences in player dev, is sound.

Angels player development has also undergone significant changes recently, including multiple hires from non-traditional backgrounds. Obviously player development can't reasonably be evaluated until after several years, but the scouting side of the industry has been dismayed by the cookie-cutter nature of swing implementation, especially at the lower levels of the minors. It's a lot of hitters swinging like Josh Donaldson, there are a lot of moving mechanical parts, and not all of them are athletically suited to do so. Players appear to be thinking through the checkpoints of their swings and focus on this stuff has slowed their development as baseball players. To their credit, Angels dev staff has backed off some hitters for whom this type of swing was not working (former top 100 talent Jahmai Jones has undergone several swing changes during his time in the minors) and the swing has worked for a bunch of players in the system, but we're skeptical of its universal prudence.

You see a lot of the same types of swings in **Toronto Blue Jays** minor leaguers, which makes sense given that Josh Donaldson and José Bautista had their peak years with this sort of cut. On the pitching side, it appears Toronto has improved their understanding of how pitch mixes work together, but they haven't yet learned how to fundamentally alter their pitchers' stuff the way Houston and other successful clubs have. Toronto has taken a proactive approach to paying their minor leaguers more, giving players a 50 percent raise entering 2019. That earned Toronto some brownie points they'd lost with public opinion after team president Mark Shapiro made several pragmatic comments regarding things like years of player control and the marginal value of wins, appearing to value those over actual wins.

Many of the best big league teams have good players who get squeezed out of regular playing time or off the 40-man, and the Jays have been most proactive about scooping up those players and seeing what they can do with regular big league at-bats. Players like Randal Grichuk, Bill McKinney, Teoscar Hernández, and Derek Fisher were acquired seemingly in an effort to make a patchwork quilt of average players to surround franchise cornerstones Bo Bichette and Vlad Guerrero Jr. Because those players had big league time, we know they had high-end, measurable physical ability before acquisition (Sprint Speed, big max exit velos), so this may also be a focus area, both in the club's amateur and pro scouting.

The **Texas Rangers** have a similar scouting approach, and their backfields are filled with premium athletes and giant frames. They're traditional from a player dev standpoint in a sense that they still play games during instructional league while many teams have abandoned that in favor of work in a class and weight room. But this org is shifting on the dev side. It explored a partnership with Driveline Baseball that fell through, then hired Matt Blood from Team USA to run dev, then reassigned him to an R&D role several months later, then just lost him to Baltimore, where he's heading up dev. Many of the club's pitching prospects have gotten hurt, though the rash of injuries was so severe that some of it is just due to bad luck rather than dev problems, but so pervasive were the injuries that some of it also probably had something to do with dev. Their deloading program was constantly in flux and months of inactivity during the season appears to be a bad idea for young pitchers.

The Baltimore Orioles, **San Francisco Giants**, and **Pittsburgh Pirates** are starting from scratch with new general managers—the Orioles hired Mike Elias, who had his hand in several aspects of Houston's operation before he defected, the Giants poached GM Scott Harris from the Cubs to work under president Farhan Zaidi (who was hired the previous off-season), and the Pirates hired former Red Sox GM Ben Cherington—and as we stated before, it's going to take time to install infrastructure on par with other top teams.

For years, Baltimore was inept at developing pitching and put zero resources in Latin America. Because of how the Latin American market works, it's going to take a couple of years for the Orioles to get a foothold on top talent since several of the top 2020s and 2021s are already locked up. They've already had big staff turnover, which is typical of any regime change, but it's unclear how closely they'll adhere to Houston's organizational architecture considering the Astros PR problems. They can't realistically 86 their in-person scouts the way Houston has until they have a flow of video and data that enables it, and that would take some time if they're even inclined to do it. It seems like the general direction will end up in a front office and scouting structure similar to Houston's.

The Pirates have progressive elements—analytics under Dan Fox's guidance are particularly strong—and they nailed many early draft picks, but under former GM Neal Huntington there were some player dev shortcomings exacerbated by 30-grade ownership and bottom-tier financial resources. Cherington has his work cut out for him with middle-tier player personnel and a big league clubhouse that devolved into literal fights: one player needed surgery on his pitching hand after a clubhouse fight (Kyle Crick), another has multiple DUIs and was accused of sexual assault before being released (Jung-Ho Kang), while arguably their best player's career appears to be over after more than 20 charges of sexual crimes (Felipe Vázquez). Cherington was said to want a GM job that wasn't like Boston—short-term focus, big payroll, high-stress, outcome-oriented—where he could focus on leading and forming a process and Pittsburgh is a nice fit for that desire, though the resources will always be limited with this ownership group.

Now that the Giants are helmed by Farhan Zaidi, formerly of the Dodgers and before that Oakland, we expect the Giants to follow framework similar to LA. Zaidi spent his first year on the job throwing 4A types against the wall to see which of them might stick and become either a tradeable asset or long-term piece. Their international department has signed three hitters with top-of-the-scale bat speed in consecutive years (Alexander Canario, Marco Luciano, Luis Matos). The int'l director, Joe Salermo, is a holdover from the previous regime, but the backfields are flush with exciting players from Latin America, so we doubt he goes anywhere. San Francisco's spring training facilities are being renovated, which means they have an opportunity to build structures that optimize the use of technology rather than what most teams have had to do, which is install tech after the fact.

On Overall Organizational Operation

The concept of market inefficiency was introduced to most of the baseball-watching public around the time *Moneyball* was first published. At that time, objective thought was the market inefficiency, not any of the specific statistics the Moneyball A's were chasing. Once everyone embraced that at some basic level, being the most progressive/corporate approach was the next market inefficiency. This has been the case for the previous decade or so, culminating in the last several postseasons—teams leaning heavily on bullpens, and they had stopped bunting and stealing bases—led almost entirely by clubs the industry would describe as "smart" teams.

Now, the tech and data that made those teams smart is accessible to everyone—TrackMan, Edgertonic, Driveline, etc.—and corporatization as a market inefficiency has also passed. The next one, to us, is being a good person, treating employees well to attract the best candidates, and having multiple decision-makers who are open-minded and adapt to solve problems as they arise. Some teams have figured this out as it pertains to player dev, but haven't considered it a core trait in other areas. The low-hanging tech/analyst fruit has been picked. Being the best at deciphering data is still an edge, but implementing the information on the field is the low-hanging fruit that no team has fully figured out in every department across the board. Very few organizations have top-tier R&D and top-tier implementation across multiple departments; it's less than five.

An analyst (who works for a non-Astros team) told us, "In 10 years, scouts won't exist, or at least not in any way that's recognizable to us today." In a way, we see what they're saying. If every major college game and high school showcase has Statcast-level metrics, Edgertronic video, and various advanced tech sensors, the value of scouts is concentrated more in administrative, paperwork type areas than it is today. There is value in precisely knowing how hard the ball is hit rather than reading a scout's report saying, "He hit the ball hard this weekend."

But if you'd read this whole book and think that, in this tech-saturated future, there isn't value to zigging when people are zagging, then you haven't been paying much attention. There's anti-corporatization, pro-scouting teams zigging now and one of them won the last World Series. There will always be room for every spot on the spectrum, if done effectively, and arguably most so when it appears that approach has been invalidated.

In a way, you could say that elite executives may be the market inefficiency going forward. If we're advocating for valuing scouts and scouting, less callous treatment of employees, and a nimble, reflective approach that emphasizes continued improvement, analyzing data from a perspective that truly, *truly* considers all of the available information, then all of this needs to be driven by a handful of decision-makers at the top. Houston's approach of consolidating power into a few people has merit, even with a more traditional approach, particularly if the people are well-rounded.

Think of it like the old-school NFL coach who can connect to players but also play the CEO role of running the organization and take an innovator's posture of drawing up creative plays. The Ringer's NFL writer Kevin Clark broke down Ravens head coach John Harbaugh in this context in a podcast in November 2019:

> Instead of complaining that Lamar Jackson can't do this, this, or this, they are celebrating Lamar Jackson. That scheme is amazing… they saw that he had the potential to be good, they did everything they could to surround him with talent, they went all-in on scheme, they promoted a guy, Greg Roman, to offensive coordinator that had some experience with running quarterbacks… we're gonna make this a Lamar Jackson franchise.

[...]They understood exactly what it took to make him a franchise quarterback. If you gave Lamar Jackson to 28 head coaches, they would fail. There's four, maybe five coaches who would do what John Harbaugh is doing.

[...]Harbaugh was a special teams coach... most head coaches were offensive coordinator or defensive coordinator. Special teams coaches are in charge of kicking, punting, punt return, kick return, all this stuff. What ends up happening with those guys, I've heard coaches say this before, special teams coaches are the great inefficiency. Those are the guys that only get to deal with the scraps... 80 percent of roster decisions are made without special teams in mind... You have to adapt every single week... You're running a fire drill every single play, there's so many moving parts. The ability to adapt like that every single week and get your brain in that mold is really important when you're a head coach, because you're always running a fire drill when you're a head coach because so many different things are happening. I've heard special teams coaches are the underrated part of the coaching pool and no one ever hires them, because of the way their brains have to be shaped.

[...]The guys now who are relevant, the old guys: Bill Belichick, Andy Reid, and John Harbaugh. All three of them are obsessed with new information... When you pair football smarts... with new, urgent ideas like analytics, that's where the actual magic happens.

If there are only a handful of NFL head coaches who could maximize Lamar Jackson, it stands to reason that only a small cross-section of GMs can really elevate a baseball team. We've indicated who we think those people may be and they have pretty varied backgrounds, while most of the recent GM hirings seem to be pretty homogenous. There aren't a lot of special teams–coach types running baseball teams right now, but, to us, that seems like as good of a strategy as any for an owner to have.

An article from Sheil Kapadia for The Athletic went into more detail on ways Harbaugh is merging old-school gut feels and personal connections with new-school analytics in unique and successful ways:

One thing Harbaugh has taken a close look at is how he can best give the Ravens an edge with his in-game decision-making. For years, he's had a staffer in the booth communicating win probabilities to him during games. First, it was Matt Weiss, who has since become the running backs coach. This season, it's football analyst (that's his official title) Daniel Stern, a 25-year-old behavioral economics major who grew up in Baltimore, got his degree from Yale, and is in his fourth season with the Ravens.

During the week, Stern, Harbaugh, and other members of the Ravens coaching staff come up with a plan for how they want to approach each game from a strategic perspective. They decide on a set of rules that will give them the best chance to win, and Stern reminds Harbaugh of those rules on the headset during the game.

[…]Before Jackson's third-down run, the field-goal unit was on alert. They were told to go out on the field for the kick if Jackson didn't get the first down. But now Harbaugh wasn't sure if that would be the right decision. Stern sits next to Roman in the booth during games and views the TV feed so he can fill Harbaugh in on exact distances in situations like this one. He reminded Harbaugh that according to the rules they decided on during the week, this was a go and that they could use a timeout if necessary. Harbaugh then started talking to Roman. He wanted to know what the play call was going to be—again, this was something that had been mapped out during the week. Roman told him it was going to be another run with Jackson.

In that moment, Harbaugh had to weigh the win probability numbers with how the Ravens were playing offensively and how much he liked Roman's call against the Seahawks' defense.

"We were doing okay, there was some looseness going on, I wasn't feeling great about how things were going," Roman recalls. "We weren't dominating the game. I could have gone either way with it. It made sense either way. But I liked the play we had for it. We were prepared for the situation."

Harbaugh heard what he needed to from Roman and Stern and saw Jackson coming to the sideline as Justin Tucker lined up for the kick.

"Harbs saw him as he was running off the field," says Stern. "And Harbs takes his headset off. I knew as soon as he took his headset off that we were going because I've talked to Lamar about it before, and Lamar always wants to go. He's obviously extremely confident. Our offense has been awesome all year—especially in short-yardage situations. So when he went to Lamar there, I knew that was the direction we were gonna go. He put his headset back on. He's like, 'Alright we're calling timeout.' He goes down there, he calls timeout, and then we went for it, which I was obviously really happy about."

At this point in the story, there's a video showing Harbaugh casually asking Jackson as he's coming off the field, "Do you want to go for that?" and before he can finish the sentence, Jackson sounds like he's leading a chant for the whole stadium, but doesn't have a microphone, so he's gotta yell it: "HELL YEAH, COACH, LET'S GO FOR IT!" Jackson looks back at his teammates on the sideline and technically asks a question but is telling them what's going to happen: "Do you want to go for it? Let's go!"

Harbaugh called timeout with just five seconds on the play clock. Roman found QB Power on his call sheet, and Jackson worked his magic for an eight-yard touchdown.

In the introduction, the Drew Lugbauer story wasn't about the drafting of a franchise-altering talent, it was about a process being improved. There's a guy with a Yale economics degree prominently involved in this Ravens story, but that doesn't mean the humanity of anyone involved was neutered; he was a positive addition to the process.

Harbaugh's most notable adjustments in 2019 include being much more aggressive on fourth down—a nod to the most progressive, analytics-heavy approach to the game—and running single-wing and option concepts that happen to specifically fit his personnel, the style of offense run at the dawn of football—something so traditional that no teams have tried it in decades.

In the case of John Harbaugh and Lamar Jackson, unpredictable success was found and it was specifically because they fully embraced both extremes of the spectrum in the moments that called for them.

What these progressive, "move fast and break things" corporate teams are presenting to ownership is about cutting costs and automating various aspects of baseball ops, seemingly because they can't be quantified. Cut the amount of scouts, get young ones that are cheaper, cut travel expenses, cut meetings, cut scout teams, deemphasize makeup since it's vague and defined differently person to person. That means you'll get worse scouts and worse inputs for your model, but that degradation of information can't be completely quantified, so it's not a part of the PowerPoint shown to ownership. Cost cutting is very easy to quantify.

An analyst for a club with a diminished amateur scouting staff told us about a few players that they would've paid mid-six figures for, but they didn't know this until they got TrackMan data from the GCL when the pitchers debuted. With fewer scouts covering double- and triple-sized areas, the under-the-radar, late-rising $125,000 prep prospect with poor grades that will sign is the guy they never know about on draft day. It's lost value that varies each year, an unintended consequence since the team believes they won't miss on any players, but the reality is they can't have a good scout for more than one season, if at all, with how they treat them.

The result is after all the savings that are easy to calculate and amount to maybe a million or so, they miss out on a couple prospects they never knew about whose collective worth is...a couple million. The difference is now they have done real damage to the value of the team's brand in the industry and probably harmed morale of those still with the team. Does that seem like a sustainable competitive advantage?

These teams' research may say that scouts don't matter or are unreliable (some of them suck, it's true, same as any job), but there's a good shot these teams have never had many good scouts around for very long. That one extra prospect helps you win baseball games, which, unless we missed something, is still what we're trying to do here, right?

What's happening in baseball generally, and most harshly to scouting departments right now, is not surprisingly reminiscent of how McKinsey and Bain strip mine companies for parts and make big money in a short period of time. But your scouts—and mid- and low-level employees—do a worse job if they think you don't care about them, and by severing arms of the org, teams are proving they don't. You aren't selling this company for parts, collecting a fat check, and leaving town. You're trying to improve a company that's going to exist for a long time, which means burning bridges isn't quite the shrewd strategy it's been sold as.

Acknowledgments

Eric:

I was nominated for a local theater award as a high school senior, and I wrote an acceptance speech for the ceremony and everything. I didn't win, and quickly became grateful for it as each subsequent winner recited heartfelt thanks for kith and kin through welling eyes, while my speech was sarcastic (I made fun of the local conservative radio host who announced my category) and trite (I thanked people like Steve McNair). I'll do my best to avoid that here.

Thanks to my parents, Glen and Patty, and brother, Scotty, who not only tolerated my obsession with sports, but actively supported me even though they didn't share it. Instead, my early sports education came at the hands of my maternal grandfather, Bob, who taught me how to play cards, read a box score, pour a beer, and told me countless stories about old Celtics and Notre Dame teams he loved. All of my grandparents are incredible people who played indelible roles in my upbringing, and I should call more often. My extended family is also lovely, but too large (Catholic, Irish, you get it) to list entirely without this turning into Chapter 5 of Genesis. I have to single out my eldest cousin, Phillip, who is wise from experience and folly, my wartime consigliere.

To my teachers, and educators in general, who I think our culture underappreciates, thank you. Mine often taught me more than their job description required. I learned much from Janet Hassler (confidence), Joe Abraham (charisma), Eric Murray (process), Eric Snyder (introspection), Joe Galm (humility), James Angeline (balance), and, most significantly, Paula Semmel (I can't pick just one thing). Frank Molchan, who ran the Wiffle ball and adult basketball league at my local playground, was also an educator. I either played ball or worked at the North Catty Playground for a decade (I was paid cash under the table to keep score starting around 13), made several of my most important friendships there (LaBar, Alex, Dom, Shark, Scott, I love you guys), and fucked up my shoulder by throwing Wiffle balls as hard as humanly possible three hours a day.

My prospect-writing ancestors, Jim Callis, Kevin Goldstein, Jason Parks, and especially Keith Law, continue to offer me professional and, more often, personal advice even though ~~I'm clearly better at this than they ever have been~~ they're at least as busy as I am and have families to care for on top of it. You really don't know what this very specific job has in store for you until you have it, and each of them has steered me in the right direction several times, and given me the best chance of staying sane. There are countless scouts who can't be named here, as well as my friends in Arizona, especially Bill Mitchell and Kim Contreras, who have helped as well.

And finally Jillian, who emboldened me, stoked my curiosity, fought and scrapped with me to start a life far from any kind of support system, and shared with me the work and stress caused by our mutual ambitions until they diverged, thank you. I love you.

Kiley:

Firstly, thanks to my parents, Steve and Denise, for encouraging me to follow my passion as a profession and for supporting me through the toughest times. I'm only here because of your help.

To my sisters, Gentry and Jenna, thank you for support through the ups and downs of my personal and professional life. To Lennie, you were there for me daily during the toughest parts of writing this. Here's to being there for each other's next chapters.

Thank you to Clarissa Young of Triumph Books, who first approached us about the book and championed the project throughout.

To my various friends around baseball, I can't and won't name all of you, since I'll invariably leave someone out and many of you helped with off-the-record direction of how to shape these chapters. So many of you directly helped with the book, my life direction in general, or were bosses that (indirectly) told me I couldn't do something, maybe the most helpful thing of all.

And finally, thanks from both of us to Jesse Jordan for his invaluable help in guiding us through the process of writing our first book.

Sources

Chapter 1

https://www.nytimes.com/2019/10/18/sports/baseball/minor-league-changes.html

https://www.nytimes.com/2019/11/16/sports/baseball/mlb-minor-league-proposal.html

https://www.washingtonpost.com/world/national-security/trump-administration-cancels-mlb-deal-with-cuba/2019/04/08/99c7d9be-5a2f-11e9-842d-7d3ed7eb3957_story.html

https://www.milb.com/milb/news/astros-headed-to-buies-creek-in-2017/c-209072660

http://m.mlb.com/glossary/transactions/rule-4-draft

https://www.espn.com/mlb/story/_/id/28283499/mlb-union-agree-opioid-testing-marijuana-removed-drug-abuse

https://blogs.fangraphs.com/mlb-outlaws-amateur-trackman-data-exclusivity/

https://d1baseball.com/news/mlb-draft-headed-to-omaha-in-2020/

Chapter 2

https://www.espn.com/mlb/story/_/id/26866071/anarchy-ingenuity-lot-gain-how-one-team-blow-mlb-draft

Chapters 3 & 4

https://www.ocregister.com/2015/08/10/brazil-has-more-than-200-million-residents-and-is-near-other-baseball-powers-so-why-isnt-it-a-major-pipeline-for-mlb/

http://www.espn.com/espnradio/play/_/id/4500135

https://blogs.fangraphs.com/we-analyzed-the-value-of-international-signing-bonus-money/

https://www.lamag.com/longform/escape-from-cuba-yasiel-puigs-untold-journey-to-the-dodgers/

https://www.espn.com/mlb/insider/story/_/id/14502075/hyun-soo-kim-byung-ho-park-profiles-thoughts-pacific-rim-talent-more-notes-mlb

http://www.jadesas.or.jp/en/aboutnikkei/

https://www.nytimes.com/2009/03/02/sports/baseball/02bowden.html
http://arizona.diamondbacks.mlb.com/ari/team/exec_bios/watson_dejon.jsp

Chapter 5
https://www.mlbtraderumors.com/2019/11/brewers-josh-hader-super-two-cutoff-
  arbitration.html

Chapter 6
https://nypost.com/2017/11/25/shohei-ohtanis-unique-recruitment-includes-a-30-
  team-written-quiz/
https://blogs.fangraphs.com/swing-changers-the-shift-to-emphasizing-big-tools-
  and-player-dev/
https://ncaaorg.s3.amazonaws.com/compliance/recruiting/calendar/2019-
  20D1REC_MBARecruitingCalendar.pdf

Chapter 7 & 8
https://streamable.com/s0euy
https://baseballsavant.mlb.com/
https://library.fangraphs.com/misc/war/
https://blogs.fangraphs.com/eight-lessons-from-my-long-weekend-as-an-impostor-
  scout/
https://blogs.fangraphs.com/qa-adrian-gonzalez/

Chapter 9
https://baseballsavant.mlb.com/

Chapter 10
https://blogs.fangraphs.com/the-new-fangraphs-scouting-primer/
https://blogs.fangraphs.com/scouting-explained-the-20-80-scouting-scale/
https://blogs.fangraphs.com/an-update-on-how-to-value-draft-picks/
https://blogs.fangraphs.com/an-update-to-prospect-valuation/
https://blogs.fangraphs.com/putting-a-dollar-value-on-prospects-outside-the-
  top-100/
https://www.youtube.com/watch?v=jqXEpHMDVi8
https://www.al.com/sports/2013/02/espn_nfl_analyst_trent_dilfer.html
https://www.tampabay.com/blogs/bucs/2018/06/21/timeline-of-investigations-
  suspensions-and-allegations-involving-jameis-winston/
https://twitter.com/OleMissBSB/status/1191547221583552514
https://www.espn.com/mlb/story/_/id/14317320/aroldis-chapman-fired-gun-
  accused-choking-girlfriend-domestic-violence-incident
https://www.espn.com/mlb/story/_/id/14620135/aroldis-chapman-not-face-
  charges-domestic-dispute
https://www.chicagotribune.com/sports/cubs/ct-javier-baez-sister-met-20151001-
  story.html

Chapter 11

https://blogs.fangraphs.com/kiley-mcdaniel-chat-9-18-19/

https://blogs.fangraphs.com/instagraphs/job-posting-orioles-economic-and-scouting-analyst-positions/

Chapter 12

https://slate.com/culture/2007/08/pitch-f-x-the-new-technology-that-will-change-baseball-analysis-forever.html

https://www.baseballprospectus.com/news/article/6269/schrodingers-bat-batter-versus-pitcher-gameday-style/

https://tht.fangraphs.com/the-injury-zone/

https://fivethirtyeight.com/features/the-new-science-of-hitting/

https://www.bloomberg.com/news/articles/2014-08-28/extreme-moneyball-houston-astros-jeff-luhnow-lets-data-reign

https://twitter.com/mlbpipeline/status/1175450239584677893?lang=en

https://theathletic.com/975903/2019/05/14/sarris-mlb-moving-from-trackman-to-hawk-eye-tracking-system/

https://www.drivelinebaseball.com/2019/01/deeper-dive-fastball-spin-rate/

Chapter 13

https://theathletic.com/1396091/2019/11/22/analytical-edge-how-john-harbaugh-and-ravens-have-gained-an-advantage-with-fourth-down-aggressiveness/?source=shared-article

https://www.theringer.com/2019/11/7/20953119/the-2019-sports-mega-pod-with-kevin-clark-and-kevin-oconnor-dave-chang-show

https://theathletic.com/1363451/2019/11/12/the-astros-stole-signs-electronically-in-2017-part-of-a-much-broader-issue-for-major-league-baseball/

https://www.espn.com/mlb/story/_/id/27752301/what-cincinnati-reds-hiring-kyle-boddy-means-changing-game-baseball